# Fourth Regiment Ohio Volunteer Infantry

IN THE

WAR FOR THE UNION.

THE LAST REGIMENTAL COLORS OF THE 4TH OVI

# HISTORY

OF THE

## THREE MONTHS' AND THREE YEARS' SERVICE

FROM APRIL 16TH, 1861, TO JUNE 22D, 1864,

OF THE

# FOURTH REGIMENT OHIO

# VOLUNTEER INFANTRY

IN THE

## WAR FOR THE UNION.

---

By WM. KEPLER, Ph.D.,

*Private of Company C, Commander Berea Post, G. A. R., Act. Frest. Baldwin University, Secretary of N. O. Conference of the Methodist Episcopal Church.*

---

CLEVELAND, O.:
LEADER PRINTING COMPANY, 146 SUPERIOR STREET.
1886.

Originally published in 1886.
Copyright © 2023 by Commonwealth Book Company, Inc.

All rights reserved. No part of this book may be reproduced in any form or by any means without the prior written consent of the publisher, excepting brief quotes used in reviews.
Printed in the United States of America.

ISBN: 978-1-948986-57-1

☙

COVER IMAGE: View of Romney, Hampshire County, Virginia. Original pencil and ink wash sketch by Alfred Rudolph Waud, circa 1862, detailing the 4th OVI camp and the road to Winchester.
*Courtesy Library of Congress.*

## DEDICATED
#### TO THE
## Comrades and loved ones of the "old Fourth Ohio,"
#### Whether still fighting life's battles or gathered on the Eternal Camping Grounds.

# FOURTH O. V. I. ASSOCIATION.

CANTON, O., December 1, 1882.

*Dear Sir:*

At the last Re-union of the 4th O. V. I., a Committee was appointed to arrange for the preparation and publication of a History of the Regiment. By arrangement with the Committee, Professor WILLIAM KEPLER, of Baldwin University, Ohio, late of Company "C," Fourth Ohio Volunteer Infantry, will write such a history. He has in his possession considerable material for the work, but desires the assistance of every member of the regiment who can in any way aid him. Will you send him copies of any official papers you may have, and write out and send him anything in the way of personal experience, or incidents of camp life, that you think will be of interest?

The History will, so far as possible, contain an account of the organization of each company, with a complete roster of all officers and men; a detailed statement of the different campaigns, marches and battles; official reports of the Commanding Officers, showing the part taken by the regiment in the different battles and skirmishes, with lists of the killed, wounded, etc., and other information that will be invaluable to every member of the "Old Fourth."

All material should be sent direct to Professor William Kepler, Baldwin University, Berea, Ohio, and letters of inquiry may be addressed to A. M. Anderson, Delaware, Ohio, or to George F. Laird, the Secretary of the Fourth Ohio Volunteer Infantry Association, at Canton, Ohio.

JAMES H. GODMAN,
GEORGE F. LAIRD, (K)
A. M. ANDERSON, (C)
*Committee.*

The following were added:

| | |
|---|---|
| I. UNDERWOOD, (A) | CHARLES COLLIER, (G) |
| PHILIP ROBERTSON, (B) | H. WILSON, (H) |
| O. E. LEWIS, (D) | WILLIAM M. CAMP, (I) |
| C. W. MCCLURE, (E) | A. TILTON, (O) and |
| L. S. ENSIGN, (F) | WILLIAM KEPLER, (C) |

*Chairman.*

COMRADES:
After much hesitation and many misgivings, the request of the "4th O. V. I. Association" was complied with, additional material gathered, and most of the work written in short-hand by April 1st, 1883; corrected and re-written with Caligraph by August 1st, 1883; then came two years of patient waiting for comrades to send in promised incidents, etc., most of which is still *promised*. Knowing that *many* other regimental histories had *not* paid for their printing, a number of comrades at the Reunion in Kenton, August 6th, 1885, gave assurance for a sufficient sum to print and bind, yet by some misunderstanding the list did *not* reach the author for three months. We are indebted to Comrades Patterson, Ustick, Keiser, Krug, Collier, Lewis and McPherson for information; to Lt. Jeffries in regard to Company E; to Lt. Anderson for invaluable assistance and encouragement; to Capt. Olmstead for figures in regard to Camp Pendleton; to Adjutant Wallace for dates, details and Rosters; to Capt. Laird for much information and assistance; to President Garrett and Genl. Pass. Agt. Lord of the Baltimore and Ohio for six electrotype plates, and passes to Baltimore and Harrisonburg; to B. F. Horner, Genl. Pass. Agt. Nickle Plate, for information and favors; to Wm. Swinton, the "American Napier," for privilege of using his maps as published in his "Campaigns of the Army of the Potomac;" to the publishers for their courteous treatment and excellent work.

Captain Laird's scrap-book up to battle of Fredericksburg, the author's diary—with pen and watch in hand—written on the spot, giving time, words, incidents, occurrences and locations, together with memory's tablet, form the basis of the history; there is and has been no attempt to relate all, but to make an octavo of no more than three hundred pages, which accounts for the brief statements in regard to the spring campaign of 1864. Two trips were made to Washington to gain access to the regimental records, but neither times were the records seen because it was "against orders."

Mention of other commands is frequently made, yet they are necessarily kept in the background, because we are not writing *their* history. In order to be truthful many undesirable slang phrases have been recorded, and reflections preserved. An honest effort has been made to reproduce the sayings and doings of the boys of the Fourth, and since so little was furnished the author by others, much is from necessity given from his standpoint. The obituary of Captain McMillen was furnished by Lt. Jeffries; of Captain Wallace by Captain Laird; that of Surgeon Morrison was taken from the Delaware *Gazette*. The writer knew nothing of the life Dr. McAbee previous to enlistment until the time the items were printed. Most of the work has been carried forward midst many cares and responsibilities, and it is a matter of rejoicing that the last pages of our labor of love are now ready for comrades, whose memories, may they be ever cherished by a grateful country.

Yours, in Fraternity, Charity and Loyalty,

WM. KEPLER.

CLEVELAND, OHIO, April 12th, 1886.

# CONTENTS.

## CHAPTER I.
The Fourth Ohio—Where Raised—Age and Character of its Men, With the Questions They Had Settled and Determinations Made Before the "Overt Act" on Fort Sumpter—Intense Indignation—Call for Troops by Lincoln—By Dennison—Enlistment—Organization of Companies—Election of Officers—Drilling—Settlement of Business Affairs—Good-bye—Off for Columbus—First Arrest and First Forced March—Mode of Designation of Officers.    13–18

## CHAPTER II.
The Fourth Organized for Three Months—Names of Field and Staff—Place and Organization of Companies—Off for Camp Dennison—Soaking Wet Before Midnight—Wading Mud and Putting up Board Tents at Early Morn.    18–25

## CHAPTER III.
Mustered into United States Service for Three Months—Tents Finished—Drill—Calls—Fooling With the Guard—Re-enlist for Three Years—Home on Furlough.    25–29

## CHAPTER IV.
Off for Western Virginia—Grafton—Clarksburg—To Camp Elk Creek—To "Camp Starvation"—Rain—To Buckhannon—Fourth of July—Grand Review—Camp and Fun at Middle Fork Bridge—First Glimpse of Rebels—Reconnaisance—A Night's Terrible Experience in Rain and Darkness—Battle of Rich Mountain—To Beverly—Guard Several Hundred Rebels—Through Huttonville to Top of Cheat Mountain and Return.    29–35

## CHAPTER V.
First Man Killed—McClellan Leaves Us—Whither the Fourth? To Laurel Hill—Phillipi—Webster—By Rail to Oakland—In Thunderstorm—To New Creek—Scattered as Railroad Guard—March to Fort Pendleton—Work on Fort—"Johnnies Too Many for Us at Petersburg"—Being Reinforced, Drive Them From the Town—Death of Colonel Andrews.    35–44

CHAPTER VI.

Rapid March to New Creek—The Next Day to Mechanicsburg Gap—Skirmish—The Charge Into Romney—First "Romney Race"—List of Wounded—Confederate Lying and Boasting—Return to the Monotony of Fort Pendleton—Snow on Mountains. 44-49

CHAPTER VII.

Colonel Mason Assumes Command of the Regiment—Across the Country to New Creek—Toward Romney—In Sight of the Town—Shelling Cemetery Hill—The Charge Into Town—Rebels Stampede—Second Romney Race—Locate Camp at Western Entrance of Town—Foraging—Rout at Blue's Gap—"Stonewall" Jackson Proposes to "Scoop" Us—Hilarious Times of Company E at Fort Pendleton. 49-56

CHAPTER VIII.

Evacuate Romney—Joined by General Lander at Springfield—In Snow—Rains Abundant—From Dunning's to Mason's Artillery Brigade—Death of Lander—To Paw-Paw—To Back Creek—General Shields Commands Division—To Martinsburg and Winchester—In Line of Battle with General Banks—Scattered to Harper's Ferry, Winchester and Berryville as Provost Guard—Fourth Ohio Times—Mason in Charge of Artillery at Battle of Winchester—With Advance to Cedar Creek, Edinburg, Mt. Jackson, Rood's Hill and New Market. 56-65

CHAPTER IX.

"On to Richmond"—Join McDowell at Falmouth—Disobey Orders to Camp in Plowed Field—Return, Route-Step, Via Catlett's, Manassas and Thoroughfare—The Charge into Front Royal—Forward to Help Fremont bag Jackson—To the Rescue at Port Republic—Our Rapid Retreat, Fearing Longstreet Might bag Us—Surgeon McAbee Enters Enemy's Lines to Care for Wounded—By a "Happenstance" go to Bristol by Rail. 65-71

CHAPTER X.

By Rail to Alexandria—Steam Down the Chesapeake, Pass the Wrecks of Congress and Cumberland, up the James—Cover Retreat of Grand Army of the Potomac—First Severe Skirmish—Line Advanced—Second Skirmish—Reviews—Monotony—Intense Heat—Stagnant Water—Much Sickness. 71-75

## CHAPTER XI.

Form Rear-guard of Army Down the Peninsula—Yorktown—Big Bethel—Newport News—On the Cahawba to Acquia Creek—On Long Island to Alexandria—Hurry to the Rescue of General Pope—Criticisms of Comrades—Battle of Chantilly and Rainstorm—All-Night March of Three Miles—To Rockville—Relieved—Rendezvous at Fort Gaines.     75-80

## CHAPTER XII.

Statements of Colonel Mason and Surgeon McAbee as to Cause of the Prostration of Nearly Seven-eighths of the Men in the Regiment—Rejoin Corps at Harper's Ferry—With Raid to Leesburg—To Halltown—As Provost.     80-86

## CHAPTER XIII.

With Army "On to Richmond"—Foraging—Puckering Persimmons—In Line of Battle to Gregory's Gap—As Skirmishers into Snicker's Gap—Mason Returns—Grand Review—Snowstorm—McClellan Relieved by Burnside—Hard March—Many Overcome in the Pineries by Heat—In Camp Near Falmouth—The Long-roll Calls to Arms.     86—91

## CHAPTER XIV.

Preparations for Winter Quarters—Forward Against Fredericksburg—Over Pontoons to Rear of City—Send Out Skirmishers—Anticipate a Forlorn Hope—Advance as Skirmishers to the Slaughter—Establish Line in Front of Marye Heights—Witness Horrible Scenes—Relieved—Wounded Taken into the City—Bivouac at the River—Return to Old Camp—Partial List of Casualties.     91-102

## CHAPTER XV.

Grand Review—Forward—A Flank Movement Under torrents—"Burnside Stuck in the Mud"—Mason Leaves Us—Causes of "French Furloughs"—"Fighting Joe Hooker" Relieves Burnside and Reorganizes the Army—Blue Trefoil Adopted—Furloughs and Leaves Granted—Camp Life, Sensations and Amusements—Snider, Brooks, and Finally Carroll, in Command of Brigade, and Carpenter of Regiment—Grand Review by Lincoln.     102-108

## CHAPTER XVI.

"On to Richmond" Via Chancellorsville—On Picket at United States Ford—Cross River—In Advance Over Confederate Works—Bivouac at Whitehouse—Forward to Support of Hancock's Division—Return to Bivouac—Assist in Bringing Order out of Chaos—Bloody Charge on Sunday Morning—On the Skirmish Line for Several Days—Bring Up the Rear—Return to Old Camp. 108–117

### CHAPTER XVII.

Move into Camp in the Grove—Hancock in Command of the Corps—Prof. Lowe's Last Aeronautism—Leave Camp as Rear-Guard—With the Advance Over Bull Run Battle-field—The "Monkeying About" at Edward's Ferry—Northward Through Frederick City—Meade Relieves Hooker—Comrades' Determinations Against the Invader—Hancock's Statement to Carroll in Regard to Our Position. 117–126

### CHAPTER XVIII.

Forward to Cemetery Ridge—Companies Sent Forward on Picket—Relieved by G and I, Which Are Made to Suffer Severely—Go with 14th Indiana and 7th West Va. to Rescue of Howard—Capture Many and Repulse the Rest of Hoke's "Louisiana Tigers"—The Racket at Culp's Hill—The Terrible Onset of July 3d—Partial List of Killed and Wounded. 126–134

### CHAPTER XIX.

Confederate Retreat—The Pursuit—To Frederick City Past Dangling Spy—Bivouac at Crampton's Gap—To Keedysville—In Line of Battle at Jones' Cross Roads; Reconnaisance Toward Hagerstown and Skirmish at Funkstown—Lee's Escape—To Harper's Ferry—Down Pleasant Valley—To Uppperville, Through Manassas Gap—Meade and the Forager—The Attack of Black Ants—To Kelley's Ford and Elk Run. 134–140

### CHAPTER XX.

To Alexandria—On Board Steamer Atlantic to New York City—To Jamaica Plains—Grand Times in New York and Brooklyn—Return by Boat to Alexandria—Rapid March to Rejoin Corps in Command of General Warren—Foraging and Squirrel Hunting of the Boys Provokes Gibbon's Ire—Vote for Governor—Battle of Auburn—Of Bristoe—To Centerville—Return to Greenwich. 140–147

### CHAPTER XXI.

Getting Ready for Winter Quarters—To Kelley's Ford—Through Wilderness—Battles of Robertson's Tavern, and Mine Run—March to the Left—Skirmishing—Serious Preparation for a Forlorn Hope—Warren's Sensible Decision to Sacrifice His Commission Rather Than His Men—Return to Camp and Winter Quarters. 147–152

## CHAPTER XXII.

Camp Located at Cole's Hill—Log Huts—Lively Times—7th West Va. Re-enlists—Diversion in Favor of a Movement on the Peninsula—Wading Morton's Ford—Battle; Carroll on His Own Account Charges the Enemy—Captain Stroub's Account, and Resume of Good Work—List of Casualties.   152–159

## CHAPTER XXIII.

Marsonian Literary Society Organized—Marsonian Literary Casket Printed—Brigade Chapel Built—Lectures, Schools, Debates—Decided Improvement in Morals—Gathering of the Elite at Corps Headquarters February 22—Music ad Nauseam—Hancock and Grant With Us—Grand Reviews—Reorganization and Consolidation—Eight Regiments in the Brigade—Preparations for Our Last Campaign—The Black and Crimson Sand-storm.   159–163

## CHAPTER XXIV.

Leave Our Last Camp and Winter Quarters—Cross Rapidan at Ely's Ford—Wagon-guard to Chancellorsville—On the Double-quick to Join in the Grand Charge at Wilderness—Enemy is Driven—We Are Nearly Captured—Fall Back—Rally—Join to Repel and Make Successful Counter-charge in the Evening—Move Toward the Right—List of Casualties—Beyond Todd's Tavern—Vigorous Skirmishing—Artillery and Musketry—We are on Reserve—Across the Po River—The Volley Into Our Bivouac at Night—Vigorous Artillery and Musketry in the Morning—Toward the Left and Join in Charge at Laurel Hill—Sad Havoc Made in Our Ranks in Five Minutes—Join in Grand and Successful Charge of Spottsylvania—Reconnaisance—Carroll Wounded.   163–175

## CHAPTER XXV.

Battle of the Ny—Grand Early Morning Charge and Repulse—To Massaponax Church—Guinea Station—Bowling Green—Cross Mattapony—Skirmish—Join Reconnaisance—Reach North Anna—Artillery Duel—Skirmish—Volunteer Inspectors of Bridge Wounded—Cross River—Severe Skirmishing—Toward Left Flank—Cross Pamunky—In Line of Battle on Huntley's Farm—Severe Skirmishing Daily and Advance in Force Beyond the Totopotomoy—Forward at Night Toward Left—Grand Charge at Cold Harbor—Repel Charge—Serious Work—Narrow Escapes—Smythe's Farewell Order—Good-by to Comrades—Homeward—Discharged at Columbus, O., June 22d, 1864.   175–186

Place and Date of Skirmishes and Battles in which part or all of the Fourth was Engaged.   186–187

## CHAPTER XXVI.

Experiences in Rebel Prisons  188-189
Memoirs: Colonels Andrews and Cantwell—Surgeons McAbee and Morrison—Chaplain Warner—Captains Wallace and McMillen.  189-199
Chronological Record Giving Daily Doings, Incidents, Times and Distances Marched, Etc.  199-217
Correspondence Regarding Failure to Recognize Our Work at Gettysburg—Howard Criticised by A. A. A. Genl. Reid, of Carroll's Staff, now of Chicago—Gibbon's Letter to Carroll—Captain Huntington's Tribute to Carroll and His Men—Howard's Communication to the Editor of the Chronicle and Letter of Thanks to Carroll.  217-221
Muster-Roll of Three Months' Men and Rosters of Three Years' Service.  221-287

———:o:———

## ILLUSTRATIONS.

| | |
|---|---|
| Frontispiece—Old Flag and Standard | 1 |
| Cranberry Grade—Going Eastward | 30 |
| National Bridge—Near Cumberland | 37 |
| Colonel Lorin Andrews | 42 |
| Along the Potomac—Near Sir John's Run | 58 |
| Harper's Ferry, Looking East | 62 |
| Surgeon H. M. McAbee | 69 |
| Map of the Peninsula | 72 |
| Map of Pope's Campaign | 78 |
| Jefferson's Rock | 84 |
| Colonel James H. Godman | 95 |
| Map of Fredericksburg | 98 |
| Map of Chancellorsville | 109 |
| Map of Gettysburg—First and Third Day | 125 |
| Map of Gettysburg—Second Day | 130 |
| Harper's Ferry, Looking West | 136 |
| Surgeon Morrison | 146 |
| Map of the Wilderness | 164 |
| Map of Spottsylvania | 170 |
| Map of North Anna | 176 |
| Map of Cold Harbor | 179 |
| Map of Country Around Richmond | 182 |
| Captain James Wallace | 196 |

# CHAPTER I.

THE GREAT UPRISING IN THE NORTHERN STATES—
ENLISTMENTS FOR THREE MONTHS—EXPERIENCES
AT CAMP JACKSON, COLUMBUS.

The Fourth Ohio Volunteer Infantry, in the War for the Union, made up of companies raised in the Northern Central part of the State of Ohio, in the counties of Wayne, Stark, Knox, Delaware, Marion and Hardin, and mostly from the cities of Wooster, Canton, Mount Vernon, Delaware, Marion and Kenton, within one week after President Lincoln had issued his Proclamation calling for seventy-five thousand men to serve for three months, was composed principally of young men from prominent families and comfortable homes of farmers, merchants, mechanics, and the various professions, and who had also had more than ordinary facilities for education and improvement.

These young men had also been brought up in the very midst of the heated discussions of the day concerning slavery, the "Missouri Compromise," the "Dred Scott Decision," and the "Struggles of Bleeding Kansas;" had questioned the wisdom and object of "John Brown's Raid" on Harper's Ferry; had just passed through the most exciting Presidential campaign known in the annals of the Nation; had criticised the course of the out-going as well as observed the men and purposes of the in-coming administration; had witnessed the secession from the Union of one Southern State after another; hoping, too, that these States, seeing their error, would yet retrace their steps, but fearing also that they might commit some overt act which would plunge the Nation into a civil war that might cause it to be counted among the things of the past.

In the home, in the social circle, in workshops and in college halls, they had debated and settled for themselves some of the gravest questions of their times; settled that no State had a right to secede, and that the General Government could, ought and must coerce any and every State that seceded, and that the Union must and shall be preserved.

It was because of such conclusions and determinations, and not on account of the excitement of the hour, that this thousand, with other thousands of America's youth, without asking a word about the pay or bounty, sprang to arms when the first gun that fired upon Fort Sumter sounded the reveille that reverberated from every hilltop throughout the land which our forefathers had wrenched from the tyrant's grasp.

On Sunday, April 14, 1861, there flashed over the telegraph wires the news, "Fort Sumter is taken!" The terrible suspense of the three past months was now broken; there was unparalleled excitement; the usual quiet of a Sabbath gone; unnoticed were the peals of the evening bells that called together the worshipers. The leader of the services was constrained to earnestly pray, "O God, save my country!" but how could he preach when the church was empty and the streets thronged? Yet the preacher began his sermon, forgot the text, to speak burning words for his country to a constantly increasing audience that was seeking wisdom, guidance and comfort in the Holy Place, where God had promised to hear and answer.

Let us not forget that the scene in one city found its counterpart in every other.

The last patriot had not yet lain down to rest when the first blush of early dawn came and found families bestirring themselves, and anxious ones hurrying down street to learn the latest news. Men sat down to the prepared meal, but could not eat; went to their shops, but could not work; entered their offices, but could do no business. In offices, in shops, in hotels and on the streets there gathered groups, hearing and discussing the news, expressing opinions, commenting upon the situation, and, for the first time in their lives, applied to their countrymen with whom they had sympathized, worked and voted, the odious terms of "traitors," "rebels," "secessionists," "nigger-drivers" and "fire-eaters."

Before noon hundreds had left the early plow and their country homes, hastened to the city, where all business was now forgotten, and joined the gathered throng that worried through the streets. The press was issuing "extras" each recurring hour. In the wildest excitement the day passed, and another night and another morning came with renewed excitement, flying reports, canards, misgivings and queries. What is to be done? what will be done? has the Ship of State been wrecked upon the secession-rock? were questions, asked and that morning forever answered, when, in the early papers, the tens and hundreds of thousands of patriots read the call of Abraham Lincoln for seventy-five thousand volunteers to serve for three months. The call met a quick and hearty response, and stamped joy and confidence upon countenances that thus far had worn expressions of the deepest anxiety. There was no longer any question in regard to the attitude of the President, which now gave the fullest assurance to the most fearful that he was the man for the occasion. No one dared to express sympathy for the secession cause, for already there had been reported the fact that, for so doing, one man had been hung and another shot down in his tracks, and that even in Delaware a preacher came near serving a like fate.

This day came Governor Dennison's call for thirteen thousand volunteers. Before ten hours had passed great crowds gathered in the most spacious halls of the cities, and most of the companies of the Fourth Ohio began enlisting, while stirring speeches were made by prominent men, some of whom either headed the list or added their own name to the rapidly lengthening roll of volunteers.

Officers were nominated and elected by those who had enlisted, and the authorities of the State apprised of the action. In most of the above-named cities and counties a second company was organized before or as soon as the first company had its full quota of one hundred enlisted men. Evening after evening the people were called together by fife and drum to help fill the quota of companies already organized, and listen to the flow of eloquence of some who had already enlisted, as well as of others who were very willing that their neighbors should enlist, and, indeed, that their neighbors' sons should at once go forth to do and dare in so just a cause, and "return, very probably, in a few weeks or months at least, all covered with glory, for it is only a breakfast job."

The mighty tide of loyalty and patriotism swept each speaker beyond all political affiliations and party lines; some even were torn from the moorings of a lifelong faith. One such especially comes to mind, who, gyrating about the platform and with arms sawing the air, proclaimed with mighty voice that he "had never believed there was a hell; but, if there is none, there ought to be one for the traitors, who, because they can no longer rule, are determined to destroy the grandest government upon the face of the earth."

There came several rainy days. Rain or shine, each company met in its own hall, where the men were assigned their places, in front or rear rank, according to looks and size, beginning with the tallest man as No. 1. They marched and countermarched, each doing his utmost to perform the difficult task of "keeping step" to the tap of the drum, or the command "right"—"left." The "Phunney Phellows," and there were not a few of them, soon travestied the commands into "hay-foot"—"straw-foot," and for a brief time afforded considerable merriment.

After having mastered the "keeping step," and each man knew without doubt his number and place in the ranks, the company was marched through the streets, where the dextrous maneuverings excited the admiration of friends, and the mighty strides of the short-legged fellow that brought up the rear gave occasion for roars of laughter. There was but little drilling, since many were men of affairs, which they must settle as rapidly as possible in order to be ready to go to the front without a moment's delay.

There was not much time to make calls upon friends and visit relatives, and those we vowed and pledged should become relatives when we, as "bold soldier boys, returned home from the wars," for by the beginning of another week an order came from Columbus to report there for duty.

The hour for leaving had been set—an hour that tried men's souls—when fathers, mothers, sisters, brothers and lovers bade "Good-bye" to loved ones, then instantly obeyed the command "Fall in; forward, march!" moved through the main street, following the beautiful flag presented by wives and sweethearts, marched to the tap of the drum, and greeted on all sides by waving kerchiefs and flags, the ready hat high in air, and words of cheer of the gathered thousands, until the depot was reached, seats and standing room all taken in the passenger cars, "three cheers and a tiger" given, and the iron horse hurried the happy hundreds, that cheered to the echo the waving of the solitary handkerchief from the log hut or the glorious flag floating from a lovely mansion, as well as the greetings of the hundreds and the thousands in the towns, until the Capital was reached. Never was there a gayer set of men. "Hurrah! who wouldn't be a soldier?"

Columbus was reached and the march immediately made to Camp Jackson. Up to this time there was and could not have been much restraint or discipline; but now there was a new order of things, fully realized by the men just as soon as they reached the camp and entered the cordon of men dressed in uniforms. Quite a number of these stood about a cloth tent called a guard house; others walked to a fro in a path, or beat, with old muskets at a shoulder. There was also a multitude, dressed in citizens' clothing, either lounging about on the grass under large oak trees, or pitching quoits, or running and wrestling. It was a huge picnic of not "privileged characters," surrounded by guards, each of whom seemed to do his utmost to excel his neighbor in yelling "Corporal of the guard!"

Many of our boys, immediately upon breaking ranks also broke for woods and fields, thus crossing guard lines without permission, which caused the most vociferous uproar, all along the line, of "Corporal of the guard!"

The following, related by one of the boys, was the experience of quite a number: "As soon as we broke ranks at Camp Jackson I started for the woods, when one of the guards yelled 'Halt!' I looked at him, and walked faster, and was just crossing his little path when he brought down his old musket, shoved his bayonet at me, and thundered, 'Halt! Corporal of the Guard, number seven.' I stopped, asked, 'What do you want?' He said nary a word. I started on. 'Halt! Cawporal of the Guard, number seven!' he yelled with all his might, and was going to shove his old iron into my side, and says, 'Halt! halt!' just as a fellow came up and excitedly asked, 'What's the matter?' 'Cawpral, this fellow crossed my beat,' said the guard. 'Come with me to the guard-house,' says the Corporal to me. 'Guard-house, thunder! I 'avn't done nothin';' and I was madder'n a wet hen as I said it. 'Yes you have,' muttered the guard, 'you crossed my beat without permission from an officer.' I begged off—promised I wouldn't do so again—would ask permission of an officer; but 'twas of no use. I got madder. 'Crossed your beat? Didn't know you had a beat. Didn't know I had to ask an officer,' I growled, as I started off with the Corporal, who marched me to the guard-house. It was my first forced march, my first and last arrest. My Lieutenant had me released immediately, and with a dozen more, and permission of an officer, I crossed the fellow's beat."

We noticed things on the arms and shoulders of the guards, and soon learned that they were called chevrons and shoulder-straps, by which one was enabled to distinguish the distinguished. That things on the shoulders were worn by commissioned, and those on the sleeves by the non-commissioned officers, we had already found out, and now learned that a Colonel wore a silver embroidered spread-eagle, a Lieutenant Colonel a silver embroidered leaf, a Major a block, a Captain two silver bars, and a First Lieutenant only one; a Sergeant Major had two cloth bars above his elbows, a First Sergeant three, and if there were only two stripes, then, no mistake, it's a Corporal—look out for him.

On account of the camp already being uncomfortably full of citizen soldiers, wearing garments of every conceivable cut and color, most of our companies were quartered in different public buildings located in the city of Columbus.

# CHAPTER II.

## ORGANIZATION OF THE FOURTH OHIO VOLUNTEER INFANTRY TO SERVE FOR THE PERIOD OF THREE MONTHS—OFF FOR CAMP DENNISON.

The Fourth Ohio Volunteer Infantry was organized at Columbus, O., on the 26th of April, 1861, to serve for three months. The following were appointed on the field and staff:

Lorin Andrews, Captain of Company A, to be Colonel.

James Cantwell, Captain of Company G, to be Lieutenant Colonel.

James H. Godman, Captain of Company H, to be Major.

Henry H. McAbee was appointed Surgeon, May 2d, 1861.

J. Y. Cantwell was made Assistant Surgeon, May 1st, 1861.

Bradford R. Durfee, First Lieutenant of Company K, Adjutant.

I. Underwood, First Lieutenant of Company A, Quartermaster.

Addison S. McClure, Sergeant in Company E, Sergeant Major.

COMPANY A was raised at Mount Vernon, Knox county, O., on the 16th of April, and was first known as the "Knox County Guards," of which Lorin Andrews was Captain, I. Underwood First Lieutenant, and Leonard W. Carpenter Second Lieutenant. At the time of the organization of the Regiment, James C. Irvine was elected Captain, Carpenter First Lieutenant, and F. A. Coates Second Lieutenant.

Israel Underwood, afterward Quartermaster of the Regiment, was the first man to enlist in Company A, and having done more than any one else to raise the number to twenty-four in twelve hours, was entitled to a Captain's commission. Lorin Andrews had several months previous offered his services to his friend, Governor Dennison, and had now just returned from another visit to him at Columbus, where he was offered a Colonel's commission in case he raised a company of volunteers. Underwood learning these facts, and esteeming his friend Andrews better than himself, at once generously offered, urged and persuaded him to accept the company and thus ensure the commission. After considerable hesitation and persuasion Andrews accepted the command of the company in which he had enlisted as a private, and reported it for duty on the 21st.

COMPANY B. In the meantime Henry B. Banning was actively engaged in raising a company of one hundred and thirteen men in the city and county, called "Union Guards," afterwards Company B, of which he became Captain, W. C. Cooper First Lieutenant, and George Rogers Second Lieutenant. On the 21st both companies, followed by thousands, marched down High street and took the cars for Columbus, and with Company A, was quartered in Camp Jackson.

COMPANY C, or "Delaware Guards," was organized on the evening of the 16th of April in the overflowing Templar Hall at Delaware, its officers elected, and its services immediately tendered to the Governor. James M. Crawford was made Captain, and has the high honor of receiving the first Captain's commission signed by the Governor, bearing date of April 16, 1861. Eugene Powell was elected First Lieutenant, Byron Dolbear Second Lieutenant, and William Hills Third. John S. Jones was afterwards elected First Lieutenant, to fill the place made vacant by the resignation of Powell. The company was assigned the left flank, and adopted the Zouave drill.

COMPANY I, or "Olentangy Guards," was organized on the 18th of April at Delaware, with Eugene Powell as Captain, N. W. Scott First Lieutenant, and William Constant Second Lieutenant.

A beautiful flag was presented to each of the Delaware companies by the ladies of the city. On the 23d they marched through crowded streets to the depot and boarded the eleven o'clock train, remained at Camp Jackson several hours, and then marched to the Insane Asylum, where they were quartered for several days.

Companies D and G were raised in the city of Kenton and neighboring villages, and were each presented with a beautiful flag by the ladies of Kenton.

COMPANY G. On the evening of the 16th, a large gathering at the Court House in Kenton listened to speeches, and adopted patriotic resolutions. The next evening, at another meeting, a committee was appointed, which provided blank lists. In a short time one hundred and twenty-five enrolled themselves, and at once organized by electing James Cantwell, a Mexican veteran, as Captain, James S. Robinson First Lieutenant, and Peter Grubb Second Lieutenant. In a few days the company left for Columbus, and was quartered in the City Armory.

COMPANY D. The first company having some thirty-five more men than its quota, and others being anxious to enlist, another was immediately formed, of which George Weaver was elected Captain, Gordon A. Stewart First Lieutenant, and D. R. Timmons Second Lieutenant.

The Captain moved his headquarters to Patterson, in the northern part of Hardin county, and on the 21st took the cars at Forest with his men, and was for several days, until tents were furnished, quartered with Company G at the Armory, when both companies were sent to Camp Jackson.

COMPANY E was organized as the "Given Guards," at Wooster, Wayne county, on the evening of the 16th of April, 1861. Previous to this Jacob Shultz, Reason B. Spink and Leander H. Scoby had headed a list, and induced some fifty others to volunteer. Judge Given presided at the rousing gathering in the Court House in the evening, when the quota was filled, and James McMillan, Secretary of the meeting and an officer in the Mexican War, was elected Captain, J. Shultz First Lieutenant, and Reason B. Spink Second Lieutenant. On the Sabbath, Rev. Lorenzo Warner, future Chaplain of the regiment, honored the volunteers with a special sermon. On the 22d, after a grand dinner at the Arcadome, and speeches by citizens and soldiers, the latter departed amid the enthusiasm of ten thousand patriots, reached Columbus at night, quartered in the Capitol, and took meals at the Galt House until they could be accommodated at Camp Jackson.

COMPANY F had been known at Canton, Stark county, as the "Canton Zouaves," numbering about forty active members, dressed in Zouave uniform, equipped with muskets and knapsacks, well drilled in "Hardee's Manual of Arms" and "McClellan's Bayonet Exercises." In early winter they had determined to offer their services at the first call for troops. While the Captain, James Wallace, was absent at Columbus to secure their acceptance, First Lieutenant Percy S. Sowers and Second Lieutenant George F. Laird proceeded to fill out the quota. After Dr. L. M. Whiting, the oldest physician of the city, had examined the men, and rejected those who were disqualified on account of age, stature or disease, the company was reorganized, the old officers re-elected, and drilling vigorously continued. After reaching Columbus, the men were quartered in an upper room on the marble floor of the Capitol and lunched at St. Paul's for two days, after which they enjoyed the hospitalities of Dr. Lord and wife at the Blind Asylum. At the organization of the regiment the company was assigned to the right flank.

Companies H and K were organized at Marion. The Court of Common Pleas was in session when the news of the fall of Sumter came. General Godman was trying a civil case, had the Court adjourn, and at once enlisted a company of volunteers and tendered its services to the Governor.

COMPANY H at first elected James H. Godman as Captain, and upon his appointment as Major promoted E. B. Olmstead to the Captaincy, William Stroub to be First Lieutenant, and elected Sergeant John R. Pritchard as Second Lieutenant.

COMPANY K elected Albert H. Brown as Captain, M. J. Lafever First Lieutenant, and William H. Garrett Second Lieutenant.

The very windy and dusty Saturday, the 27th, was spent in seeing the sights in city and camp, reading the news, and getting on the *qui vive*, because of some very sensational rumors of going to the front. Sunday was spent in church-going, lounging about in the shade, or writing letters. On Monday many friends from home visited the boys.

During the day, at Camp Jackson, Adjutant General Carrington, in full uniform, with tall feathered cockade and spread-eagle epaulets bobbing about, by an address, endeavored to bring our patriotism to a white heat.

The next day there was a greater sensation, when two deserters of some other regiment were, with shaved heads, marched through camp. This seemed to reflect upon our patriotism, although intended as punishment, which to our minds was very slight, as hair would soon grow out, and we had conceived the idea that all deserters would lose not only their hair but also their heads.

On the first of May many troops left camp, which made us anxious to go somewhere, too, and we were gratified at the order to be ready to move. The next morning the regiment was formed in line for the first time, marched to the depot, took passenger cars at 10 o'clock, and we were soon on our way southward, greeted on all sides by the acclamations of the people and waving flags, while the sun, rapidly hastening westward, disappeared, and as darkness had already come on reached Camp Dennison, in a beautiful valley on the Little Miami River and Railroad, situated twenty miles north of Cincinnati. We were at once marched to the foot and on the north side of a high knoll, where was a board fence. Cord-wood was soon blazing; boards were inclined against the fence to shield us from the storm whose approach from the southwest was heralded by the lightning's glare. By midnight the sleepers were roused by the hum of voices and a driving rain, which began to pour through the cracks and knot-holes in the boards of the improvised roofs, into eyes, ears and necks. Some, not at once realizing the situation, sprang up, thudded their heads against the boards above, producing uproarious laughter, which was increased by many mirth-provoking remarks that followed, such as "Lie quiet!" "Here, you are pulling off my cover!" "Great Cæsar, get over, the water is running under me!" "Hoo, it's run into my ear!" "Shut up!" "Quit your music!" "Keep quiet!" "Want to go home!"

'Twas only a shower, and under wet blankets, quilts, and what not, balmy sleep soon hushed all into quiet. Morning came, and such a morning! Cloudy, misty, and chilly. Mud was soon more than ankle deep. Around burning cord-wood stood the men, turning now a roasting side to the chilly winds, and the cold side to the scorching fire, asking, "What are we going to do?" "Put up cantonments," answered one, in terms of the Army Regulations. Soon it was settled that board tents were to be put up at once in a plowed field on the west side of the railroad, and some twenty rods from it.

Orders were given for each mess to put up its own tent. There were about eight messes to a company, formed on the principle of "birds of a feather flock together." Carpenters and tools were in great demand. There was no more singing in plaintive tones "I want to go home," or the ringing question "Where is the enemy?"

Officers and men carried heavy boards some fifty rods, through mud and water ankle-deep. All day long there was the confusion of voices, rasping saws, and whacking hammers. At night more than half of the tents were up, and in many of them were board floors. Many of the buildings had no floor at any time on account of an order forbidding it, since floors were considered unhealthy.

The arrangement of the barracks and position of companies on parade were from north to south, in the following order: A, F, D, I, C, H, E, K, G, B.

# CHAPTER III.

SWORN INTO THE UNITED STATES SERVICE FOR THREE MONTHS—TENTS FINISHED—LIFE IN CAMP DENNISON—DRILLS—UNIFORMS AND ARMS RECEIVED.

The next day, Saturday, May 4th, the regiment was mustered into the United States Service for the period of three months from date of enlistment. But very few were rejected. At the close of the day some eighty tents had been put up, four to five deep, in lines parallel with the railroad track. Each company had two files of four or five tents facing on a street at right angles to the railroad and color line. Each company had thus a row of tents on each side of its street. The door of each tent was at the right hand of the gable end of the left row, and on the left hand of the right row of tents, bringing door opposite door; in front of the door was a long table; to the left or right of it were two tiers of bunks, where the men sat, reclined or slept day or night. At first the officers took up their quarters with the men. On account of a brook passing near to the rear of the regiment, the Field and Staff occupied board-tents on the immediate right of it, toward the town of Milford, which was distant about two miles.

The 5th and 6th of May were dull, dreary, rainy days, with very meager fare, spent in story-telling, eating, sleeping, getting acquainted, letter-writing and the study of the tactics.

The 7th, clear and beautiful, gave opportunity to vary a life already monotonous by squad-drill, when drill-master showed his skill. His words of command were at first rather feeble—possibly fearing to give offence—or lacked that necessary qualification, self-confidence. Both commanders and commanded soon surmounted many difficulties, made great advancement, and, in a few weeks, some claimed that we were indeed the best drilled regiment in the army—equal to Ellsworth Zouaves—and that we, too, might make a journey to Washington and astonish the natives. Why, of course, we were able to parry the thrust of any rebel; to punch him anywhere about his harness; hold him dangling on the point of a bayonet. Until the muskets came we not only obeyed the "Forward, march," "Eyes right," "Dress up," "Out in the center," "Out a little more," "There now," "Right wheel," "Left wheel," and many other orders—even improvised some which ought to have been given in the "Tactics"—but we learned what we ofttimes found so very desirable: the "How to lie down very close to the ground when the enemy fired at us," or we thought he was going to; also how to hold that position at all hazards while loading and firing.

Visiting friends expressed their profound admiration; General Officers gave flattering compliments; newspaper correspondents voiced the feelings of many by the "Why is not the Fourth sent to the front?"

The monotony of camp was further relieved by our giving heed to the "Calls" of the bugle, such as "Adjutant's Call," "Sergeant's Call," the "Quinine, quinine, come get your pills; come get your pills, quinine," of the "Doctor's Call;" and "Reveille," followed by the calling of the Roll, as well as "Retreat," "Tattoo" and "Taps;" the latter ofttimes followed by the order, "Lights out!" Aside from drill there were the daily diversions of "Mounting Guard" in the morning, "Dress Parade" toward evening, and occasional inspections, especially on Sunday morning.

At the guard-house the frequent "Fall in, Guards," when some of "ye mighty men, men of renown," were passing by, was often a trial of patience; but to be thus called out at night was always most provoking. For some time the "Grand Rounds" put the guard 'twixt hope and fear; in hope, to be able soon to see the marvel itself; and fear, that he may have forgotten the "countersign" when "Advance" called for it, and thus relegate himself to twenty-four hours in the guard-house to develop his memory. The novelty soon gave way to business, and the Guard became more than a match for the fooling about of the "Grand Rounds," as Major De Villiers found out when he was trying this game, and was hit under the chin with the butt of a musket in the hands of one of the boys and laid on his back in a twinkle. Springing to his feet, and laughing heartily, he exclaimed: "Goot soldier! goot soldier! Vas goot—did right." Such escapades, with such results, he knew would inspire the soldier with confidence and the further determination to do his duty in times of danger, come who or what may.

The heat of May 9th was very oppressive. Twenty-one men were now in the hospital, sick. On the 10th the regiment was ordered into line, and remarkable developments were anticipated. Possibly we would at once go to the relief of Washington. An order—Special Order No. 1—was read. In silence and disgust the men returned to their quarters. "What was the order about?" was asked, and was met with the sarcastic reply, "Oh, somebody has stoned the telegraph wires. Somebody musn't stone the wires any more or somebody will get hurt."

On the 14th the regiment was equipped with a lot of old muskets, some of which were made in the year 1828.

The rainy days of the 12th and 13th gave the officers an opportunity to make out the Muster-in Rolls, in accordance with Special Order No. 2. The height of the men and color of the hair could easily be determined, but in regard to complexion, age and the color of the eyes, there might be some mistake and difference of opinion.

On the 17th we had a glimpse of Major Anderson, of Fort Sumter fame, as he passed, standing on the rear end of the car. On the 22d the regiment was formed in line, marched to our Colonel's quarters, and listened to stirring speeches made by General Cox, Colonel Andrews and others, urging the men to re-enlist for three years. The great majority at once determined to re-enlist. Furloughs and free transportation were promised those who re-enlisted.

Little else was done than the work of reorganizing until Thursday, June 6th, when those who had re-enlisted were mustered into the United States Service "for three years or during the war." Most of the men were under the impression that the three years' term of service would date from time of first enlistment. Such seems to have been the intention, as the regiment was never mustered out of the three months' service. The men who had re-enlisted now went home on furlough for six days, wearing their new uniforms, which had just been furnished and were becoming a necessity, as the citizen garments were in rags and tatters. The new were soon not much better; the pantaloons, especially, were shoddy, and many of them began to go to pieces on the first wearing.

On the 12th the furloughed men returned. On the 17th General McClellan inspected the nine hundred and seventy-six men present for duty. On the 20th orders were received to cook two days' rations of beef. It was evident that we would now leave the dusty, filthy quarters, the wretched monotony of camp life, and go to the front. In the afternoon we received our arms and ammunition. The flanking companies, C and F, were furnished with Enfield rifles, and the rest of the regiment with Springfield muskets, caliber 69, and, by way of ammunition, buck and ball.

The companies were now assigned the following positions: F, A, D, I, H, E, K, G, B, C, giving F the right and C the left flank.

## CHAPTER IV.

OFF FOR WESTERN VIRGINIA, GRAFTON, CLARKSBURG, BUCKHANNON, RICH MOUNTAIN, HUTTONVILLE, TOP OF CHEAT MOUNTAIN—RETURN TO BEVERLY—FIRST MAN, COOPER, OF BAND, KILLED BY BUSHWHACKERS.

The Regiment left Camp Dennison on board box-cars, at 5 P.M. Friday, June 21st; passed through Xenia, and Columbus—where coffee and bread were had for breakfast—then on through Zanesville, and reached Bellaire at 5 P.M. on the 22d. We quartered in machine shops; bathed in the Ohio, which was crossed the next forenoon, and at 2:30 P.M., on board box-cars, moved rapidly through a beautiful country, with here and there the Stars and Stripes floating in the breeze. Mountains came in sight, and soon little could be seen but high hills, while we glided along the muddy Monongahela, then away from it, among higher spurs, until, at dark, Grafton was reached. The train backed to Fetterman, where, in the cars or on Old Dominion's "sacred soil," we slept until morning; then awoke to find a high mountain on the one side and a rapid stream, the Tygart Valley River, on the other.

In the morning, Monday, June 24th, we began to look about, and found many acquaintances in the Sixteenth Ohio, who told us of the "Phillipi Races," rebels arrested, scouting expeditions, and that the enemy was massing his forces some thirty miles east, and no doubt there would be music in the air, and we would have a chance to smell powder in a few days. Some went on guard, others were engaged in target practice, and many in roaming about. There seemed to be no danger near, as the people were mostly loyal. It was hardly credible that we were now one hundred miles from the Ohio River, and had yet to see the first rebel this day.

The 24th of June, being St. John's Day, Colonel Andrews and Surgeon McAbee made addresses to the Masonic Fraternity of Grafton, and a number of others who had gathered there from different parts of West Virginia; encouraged them to be loyal, and thus insure protection from the Government, which would not infringe upon, but rather jealously guarantee them their rights as citizens and as a State. The speeches and greetings were productive of excellent results. At eleven in the evening, after four hours had been spent in getting a car back upon the track, the Regiment was taken to Clarksburg, the birthplace and early home of the afterwards famous "Stonewall Jackson."

On the 26th we drew horses, wagons, camp and garrison equipage. We now belonged to the "Army of Occupation," under the command of General McClellan, and were brigaded with the Ninth Ohio, under command of Colonel McCook.

As we awoke the next morning, Thursday, June 27th, breastworks around the crest of a high hill, constructed by our forces, were the first fortifications we had as yet seen. On account of hills, mountains, and gullies, there could not be found a spot large enough for regimental drill, so that the time not spent in marching gave opportunity for rest and sight-seeing.

On the 28th we marched to Camp Elk Creek, a distance of ten miles, and tented on the gentle slope of a hill covered by low and stunted oaks. During the rain and mud of the 29th we waited for provisions and reinforcements.

The 30th was the Sabbath. "The better the day the better the deed," as usual. We marched this time six miles, until we reached Camp Ewing, or "Camp Starvation," with its scarcity of provisions, in a region of few houses—possibly one to every three miles. Fresh beef was on hand in the afternoon, which, having been spitted over fires built only of brush and top rails—rare or well done—satisfied the hungry. In the afternoon Captain Wallace took his Company on a scouting expedition, Indian file, through woods, rain, and mud; over hills, rivulets, and precipices, stumbling over roots, sticks, and stones, in pitchy darkness, some fourteen miles, in quest of prowling rebels.

July 1st Captain Crawford advanced several miles with Company C, and stood guard during the night, while the Regiment remained in camp and let it rain. On the 2d the entire force

CRANBERRY GRADE.

advanced rapidly for fifteen miles, and found itself in the cosy town of Buckhannon, nestled among the hills and mountains. After having rested one day, we must celebrate the glorious Fourth, whilst we yet had a Fourth. Loomis' and Howe's batteries fired a National salute at noon that sent the echoes bounding and rebounding, far and wide, to the delight of the boys and astonishment of the hundreds that had come from their mountain fastnesses, on horses or rickety carts, to see the old flag again and hear the cannon roar. The lasses, straight as a measuring-rod, with forms in relief, as they were in dimities clad, fine subjects for painter or sculptor, and in striking contrast to the daughters of men the boys had been accustomed to see. Still greater delight awaited the loyal ones, as they beheld McClellan review his "Grand Army of Occupation," as it moved by regiments over high grass, dewberry vines and briers, along river and wash-outs, as best it could. "Lordy!" says one, "I didn't know there was so many folkses in the world," and possibly expressed the appreciation of most of the ladies that witnessed the grand display which had such an excellent effect upon the men, inspiring them with confidence that their commander knew how to handle his troops, be they few or many.

More than a week previous the commanding General had issued a proclamation to the people, saying: "Your houses, families, and property, and all your rights will be religiously respected; we are the enemies of none but armed rebels, and those voluntarily giving aid." To the soldiers he had issued the following: "You are to support the Government of your country, and to protect the liberties and lives of your brethren threatened by a rebellious foe. Take nothing, destroy nothing, unless you are ordered to do so by your general officers."

Because the people had, at the ballot box, rejected the proposition to secede, General Lee sent troops among them to burn their railroad bridges and seize their mountain passes, whic "were the gates to the Northwest." The "rupture of the railroad would be worth an army" to the Confederates, in the language of Lee. For such purposes was Garnett at Laurel Hill Pass, with three thousand men; Colonel Scott at Beverly, with one thousand, and Colonels Heck and Pegram at Rich Mountain Pass, with thirteen hundred. General Morris, of Indiana, was to menace Garnett, while we were to cut off his retreat and capture Pegram.

We had spent four days in resting and awaiting events and reinforcements. At dress-parade on the evening of the 6th of July we received orders to march, and in an hour were in camp two miles distant. The next morning we followed the Ninth Ohio twelve miles to Middle Fork Bridge, "Camp John's," or "Dead Man's Camp," stacked arms by companies, in lines parallel to the river, on the farther side and to the right of the bridge. Here we were unable to see twenty rods in any direction on account of the woods around us and the hill in front. Within a few rods, in some tall ferns near the river, was in a few moments found the body of a member of the Third Ohio, killed by the Confederates the day previous, and after whom our camp was named, he being the first victim of the enemy we had as yet seen.

There were many rumors afloat of an enemy near at hand, an approaching battle, and overpowering forces. Some acted as if they expected to see a rebel behind every rock, bush and tree, but in a few hours cooled down to a disposition only to shoot when the enemy made his appearance. About 4 P.M., a squad of our cavalry rushed into camp, and there was a call to "fall in," just as a prominent officer was bathing. Having heard the order, it is said that he rushed out of the water, grasped his fine uniform, hugged it to his dripping body, ran through the bushes toward his company, shouting "Where's my sword; where's my sword?" He needed no sword, as the rebels were yet five miles away.

Soon there was the usual bathing, and much fun, because the clear, crystal stream strongly refracted the rays of light and the depth of six to ten feet appeared to be not more than four to six, so that one after another, as he leaped in, found to his chagrin that the water was over his head, and it seemed as though he would never touch bottom. Some went on picket, others on a scouting expedition, the remainder kept themselves near the guns. Details were mostly made by companies instead of a certain number from each company.

On Tuesday morning, July 9th, we broke camp at four o'clock, made a continuous march of thirteen miles, and about noon came in sight of a squad of the enemy's pickets, with gun-barrels glimmering in the sunlight, going up the mountain on the double-quick toward their Fort; it was afterward learned that they reported "Roaring Run Flats are alive with men." The bridge having been destroyed our column halted, went into camp, but soon crossed the stream, advanced some distance, and put up tents. Many will remember at this juncture the altercation between General Lander, of McClellan's staff, and Colonel McCook, because McCook's Germans determined to forage their dinner, as sheep and hogs were quite abundant.

On Wednesday, July 10th, with the Ninth Ohio in advance and Loomis' Battery in our rear, a reconnaisance was made in force to within two hundred yards of the breast-works; shots were exchanged, and soon several wounded were taken back. But little could be seen on account of the dense underbrush of oak and laurel. We returned to camp toward evening.

The next morning, July 11th, Generals Rosecrans and Lander, with the Eighth, Tenth and Thirteenth Indiana, Nineteenth Ohio and Burdsall's Cavalry, moved to the south and east of the Fort, through rain and underbrush, over gullies, reached the rebel rear, attacked several hundred of them on Hart's farm, on the top of the mountain, two miles distant from us. We had also left camp at an early hour during a pouring rain, formed in line and took up our position a little in advance of that occupied throughout the previous day, and could hear, about noon, while we were guarding roads and blind paths and watching the movements of the enemy, the firing of cannon and volleys of musketry, which sounded like an approaching tornado. About three o'clock, just as the firing had ceased, Lieutenant Poe, of the Topographical Engineers, had succeeded in finding a battery position overlooking the Confederate works. A squad of men from our Regiment, by request, volunteered to act as pioneers, and proceeded to cut a road through the thick undergrowth and dense laurel to the position that had been selected. Supported by four companies of the left flank they cut their way to the place, and were greeted with several rounds of shrapnel, about an hour before dark, that cut the leaves and limbs some twenty feet above their heads.

Most of the troops remained all night guarding the road and position, and held themselves in readiness to pounce upon the enemy early in the morning. They had the longest night, seemingly, of their lives, and a terrible experience. All night long did the rain come down in torrents, while the men, with teeth chattering and bodies shivering with cold, waited, and watched and waited for the morning. Early in the morning did the axmen, who had been relieved and those who had been left to guard the tents, bestir themselves, cooked beef and made hot coffee which they took to the most grateful set of mortals they had ever seen. Soon a white flag was seen floating over the breastworks. Rosecrans had moved into them and captured 63 men, 4 cannon, 204 tents, 29 wagons, 75 horses and a lot of camp-equipage. Colonel Scott had come with his force from Beverly, but seeing Rosecrans' men, returned, pell-mell, and hastened to a distance of thirty-two miles before he rested his Confederate comrades.

We immediately went back to camp on the double-quick, struck tents, packed knapsacks and were in a very brief time marching at quick pace through the rebel works; saw the dead just as they were being buried, passed over the battle-field, left four companies in command of Colonel Cantwell to take charge of the prisoners, the left wing of the regiment reaching Beverly at noon, and were in a position to cut off the retreat of any forces coming in on the Laurel Hill road. Soon our four companies had eight hundred more prisoners to guard, for Pegram's force, which had taken to the mountains, now surrendered and reached the town in gray uniforms and citizens' dress, many having large dirks and pistols in their belts.

Most of them, realizing their situation, manifested excellent sense. A few were disposed to be saucy, saying we had the better of them because they could not see us in the darkness and bushes, and if they had only been able to have met us in open field the result would have been different. Our boys treated them kindly, which was not only appreciated but acknowledged by Confederate officers and men.

On the 13th we made an early march to Huttonville, twelve miles, and found no enemy. On Sunday, the 14th of July, soon after sunrise, we were up the mountain climbing; halted near noon at "Traveler's Repose," took dinner near the top of Cheat Mountain, and for an hour viewed the magnificent scenery. It was intended to push forward over the Alleghanies to the valley beyond, but General Scott objected because it would take us too far from our base of supplies. Lee, anticipating such a movement, was getting ready to overwhelm us. All were in the best possible spirits. We had marched up hill for thirteen miles, yet no one was tired, everybody jubilant. With pure water, bracing air, grand scenery, a whipped, captured or fleeing enemy, a short campaign pointing to great results, a young, active and fine appearing General, a manly, noble, intelligent Colonel in whom all had the utmost confidence, we felt ready to meet all Secessia. "We have met the enemy and they are ours," except those that ran.

The Cavalry returned from their advance into the next valley and reported no enemy this side of the Alleghanies. Enjoying the fine scenery of Rich Mountain and the Valley, we reached camp at dark, having found it more tiresome to come down the mountain than to ascend.

In the Valley we found the sun's rays intense, the nights cold and damp, the men threatened with fevers and bowel difficulties, and we were glad to return to Beverly the next morning, there to remain until the 23d, to await developments. On this march all were surprised to see a mowing machine that had been manufactured at Canton, and the Canton boys far more so on their return to see two of their townsmen, Messrs. Lahm and Aultman. Such visits of friends were always highly appreciated, and were an answer to the oft-repeated song, "Do they miss me home?"

## CHAPTER V.

FROM BEVERLY TO LAUREL HILL, PHILLIPI, WEBSTER—ON RAILROAD TO OAKLAND AND NEW CREEK—SCATTERED AS RAILROAD GUARD—TO FORT PENDLETON—BUILD FORT—SKIRMISH AT PETERSBURG, NEAR LAND OF CANAAN.

While at Beverly rations became scarce, as well as tobacco, paper and envelopes; flour was issued, and "slap-jacks" supersede "hard-tack." Coffee and sugar are exchanged with citizens for cakes, pies and bread.

The first man of the Regiment killed was a Mr. Cooper, of the Band, shot down by a bushwhacker on the 18th, when but a short distance from the camp.

McClellan at this time left us for Washington. On Tuesday, July 23d, thirty days after crossing the Ohio, we marched nineteen miles and camped at the western entrance to Laurel Hill Pass. Nineteen miles more brought us through Phillipi to camp six miles from Webster, where we took the cars on the afternoon of the next day, Thursday, July 25th. "Where are we going?" "To Washington?" "To guard railroad bridges?" No one seemed to know where.

To our train were hitched two "mighty camel-backs;" puffing and snorting, they hurry us by Grafton, up a ravine for many miles, puff, snort and bellow more and more, while the wheels whine and grind, and the hills and vales reverberate the strange echoes. To the left the deep gorge grows deeper, and the slate and sandstone is piled higher on the right. Tunnelton is reached, and for some time all is darkness; cinders shower upon us, the smoke stifles, the boys lie on their faces or climb down from the top of the box-cars. Now all is light, and grander scenes await us. What bracing air! Why not stop awhile and enjoy the running brooks, dashing waters, shadowy vales and

NATIONAL BRIDGE.

mountains green? Is it because we are wanted to head off Confederate hosts in other mountain fastnesses, or are we to hurry on to the rescue of the National Capital, for it has not been a week since the Bull Run disaster. Soon our engines are making for a mighty overhanging cliff, and it seemed as if they were about plunging into the very bowels of the Alleghanies; they turn and creep along the massive wall on the right, and we gaze up the dizzy heights, then with bated breath down the fearful chasm right beneath us, over five hundred feet upon the chocolate-colored waters of the Cheat River, that dash themselves against huge rocks that once had crowned the domes of either side, and gnawed loose by the tooth of time had thundered down the mountain side, plunged into the angry waters and furnished hiding-places for the teeming millions, and certain footing for the angler. We leave Buckthorn Wall and bridge behind. Rowlesburg lies just before us, down in the valley, and beyond the outlines of mighty gorges and towering heights lose themselves against the heaven's blue and the far off silvery waters disappear in the shadows of the setting sun.

The river is gone, but to the right and down below us are white clouds that hang over farms that extend for miles over hills and into valleys, with millions of acres of forest in the distance, crowning hill and mountain, affording a most inspiring scene. Night is fast coming on; we hasten into dark shadows and again into welcome light; the echo of jostling cars and coughing engines becomes more distinct; we watch the weird shadows cast on rock and trees by the engines' flames and curling smoke; we listen to hollow rumblings as we pass over bridges, peer into the deep dark gorges, and watch the outlines against the sky. There is a halt and sleepers are aroused; the cars are needed. Soldiers may rest, but for loyal engineers and firemen there is little rest now. The Nation can be thankful for the energy and loyalty of the officers of the Baltimore & Ohio Railroad, especially to Mr. G. W. Garrett, who had held the honored trust of President since 1859.

After a night's needed rest we found ourselves much refreshed on the morning of July 27th, at Oakland, in a charming region surrounded by undulating hills and mountains near at hand. The elevation is over two thousand feet, giving us bracing air, cool summer days and cooler nights—just the place to recuperate failing health and strength. It is evident that it is not to be for us a resort, for we have orders to be ready to march after dinner. It is two o'clock; we are in line, and stand for nearly two hours in a pouring rain, while the lightnings flash and the thunders roll. A tree was struck near by, stunning one of the men. At night we camped in a cemetery, although many took shelter in a hotel. The next morning on board of the cars, we passed through a country with scenery and grandeur enough to inspire the most phlegmatic, and reached New Creek, now called Keyser, at 2 P.M. Company C went to Piedmont, I to Sheets' Mills and Burlington, K to Rocky Point, and H on a scout to Cabin Run, Frankford, Old Gum Spring Pike to B. & O. R. R., thence to New Creek. We were in sight of Knobly, formerly Cresap Range, and a region surveyed by Washington in 1750 for Lord Fairfax.

On the morning of the 7th of August, when wagons, horses and men were no longer scattered for a hundred miles along the railroad, the Regiment started over the mountains and camped at Stone House, whence forty-nine mountain peaks were visible. Another march of fourteen miles brought us at noonday on Thursday, August 8th, to the Pendleton Farm to relieve the Eighth Ohio Volunteers.

The boys could not make themselves at first believe that we were only fourteen miles from Oakland, or that there was a squad of rebels within fifty miles of us. They were satisfied that we were near the backbone of the Alleghanies. Why build a Fort here, even though the Northwestern Pike did cross the Potomac at this point? since no rebels would think of marching through "such a forsaken country" as this seemed to be, where the "laurel was as thick as hair on a dog," and infested with bears and wildcats. "How in creation did the Government ever find out that God had such a country?" asked one as we stacked arms. "This isn't God's country," replied another. But we soon learned that the "glades" which were near at hand, furnished us the best beef we had ever tasted, and that the enemy relished it, too, as was shown by his raids on the cattle ranches.

On account of frequent rains but little work was done until the 14th of August, when by order of General McClellan and command of Colonel Andrews, and direction, plans and engineering of Captain Olmstead, digging trenches, throwing up breast-works and felling trees toward the river to form an abatis, was begun in dead earnest and carried forward with vigor until completion. Some sixteen thousand days' labor were performed on Fort Pendleton.

The Fort was begun by the Confederates, and was 368 feet above the North Branch Potomac River; it had seven sides; the fortifications had a perimeter of 5,089 feet; the Pendleton mansion was about one-half mile to the south and west, and a church —where some half-dozen comrades were buried—was the same distance toward the north and east; Tabbs' log hut and the covered bridge were distant about one and one-half miles; east, north and northwest was a forest of great oaks and pines; in fact the entire region of country for many miles in all directions was covered with oak and pine, but mostly oak in every stage of growth, with here and there a log hut in a small clearing overgrown with briers. The regiment camped in and near the Fort; in every direction save toward the Pendleton mansion there was quite an abrupt slope; directly north there was a cannon-way for a distance of 950 yards; toward the northeast there extended a covered way for 1,100 yards; near to and west of the bridge was a covered stockade, with a covered way leading northwest, then west to southwest until it reached the main covered way, 214 feet above the river, where it was joined by another covered way that led west and north to a battery position. The magazine was at the southwest side of the Fort. The position might truly have been considered impregnable save from the direction of the Pendleton house.

Soon an oven was built, excellent bread was baked that strongly contrasted with the miserable stuff called pies and cakes, the latter "with the shortening in lengthwise," brought into camp by the natives. Blackberries were very abundant, yet there was but little time to gather them or to catch the trout and bass. There was an order in vogue for several weeks "not to shoot at anything at any time but rebels," so that deer could not be killed nor the bear fired at that one day came in sight of a picket-post, nor even the wild-cat dispatched that once made regimental-guard dubious and night hideous.

Although we had excellent water and pure air, some of the men, from overwork and exposure, were prostrated with fevers and rheumatism, but were well cared for in the hospital in Pendleton's large house of many conveniences. The health of our Colonel had begun to fail and he returned home, leaving the Regiment in command of Colonel Cantwell. Much hard work was done. Picket and cattle-guard went two to seven miles. No enemy disturbed us. One day—a dull, lazy day—a squad of horsemen was seen taking observations of our position from a point in an open field across the river. There were but few men in camp and the commanding officer could not be found, so Sergeant Lester, who had charge of the cannon, fired a shot that went over the heads of the riders, and plowed the ground, scattering the dirt on the hillside several rods beyond them and in full view of every man in the fort. There was instant commotion among the horsemen, who brought down their opera-glasses, vehemently spurred their horses and charged down the hill, and were soon out of sight along the river, and acted strangely as they came straggling into camp, and wondered why we should fire at our own men. They had been rightly served, since those in camp ought to have been informed of the intended inspection.

The Fort had been completed, and camp life was becoming very monotonous and guard duty extremely irksome, when Howe's Battery and one company of cavalry joined us on the 29th of August. Citizens came in and reported that a number of rebels were conscripting union men, and raiding, some thirty miles south of us. About this time Company A, in command of Captain Carpenter, was quartered at Greenland, and assisted in protecting the people and organizing a company of home guards, that was afterward known as Company I of the Seventh West Virginia Volunteers.

On the 6th of September came the report that the enemy was conscripting, ravishing, destroying and killing near Petersburg. Captain Brown left at once with Company K, and was joined at Greenland by Company A and the Home Guards. The entire force now moved forward, and on the 8th, when within three miles of Petersburg, while marching up a long slope through a dense forest, and without any warning, received the fire of a squad of rebel horsemen; no one was hurt; the fire was returned and the Major commanding the squad fatally wounded and his horse captured; skirmishers were now deployed and our force moved cautiously forward until it came in sight of the town of Petersburg, where near a church a considerable body of cavalry and infantry was getting ready for action. An escaping negro having informed our men that the rebels numbered over five hundred, it was concluded that we should fall back and await reinforcements. It was evident that retreat must be made immediately to a hill a mile to our rear, or we would be cut off by the superior numbers of the enemy. Captain Brown at once ordered his men to fall back to the crest of the mountain, where the forest began. The Home Guards, without regard to order, made rapid strides for the position, formed in line at the very place where they had been directed, exciting the admiration of the rest of the command, which followed in good order at a double-quick. Hardly were our forces in position at the bend of the road in the woods on the side of the mountain when the enemy moved rapidly after—across the valley, up the slope—and was warmly received as soon as he came in range; several saddles were emptied; he made no further demonstration, and night coming on we returned to Greenland to await orders and reinforcements. Companies F and G, fourteen men from Company C, and Ringgold's Cavalry, in command of Major Godman, joined the forces at Greenland on the 11th, and at noon on Thursday the 12th the entire force came in sight of Petersburg, unobserved. A detail from F and C, all in command of Captain Wallace, moved forward as skirmishers, closely followed by the remainder of our forces, and soon closed in from different points upon an unsuspecting lot of rebels quartered in and about a church. Companies A and K endeavored to get to the right and rear of the church, while G and the remainder of F moved to the left, and the Home Guards, cavalry and artillery pressed forward. A shot from our cannon, which made the church door open and the rebels fly, was evidently the first intimation they had of our presence; a general fusilade was now begun; the enemy, rapidly retreating through the town, failed in his attempts to make a stand until the river was crossed, when he halted for a moment, returned our fire, and sent a round of shrapnel, which cut the bushes quite near our men, and started the Major's horse into a lively prance, to the amusement of the boys and enjoyment of the rider, who was quite certain that some of the missiles had wounded "Charley" and made him caper. The Home Guards pushed across the river, hoping to avenge themselves on the dastardly cowards who had during the past several weeks so atrociously wronged them but were now fleeing for life. The cavalry followed for several miles and captured wagons and horses.

Dinner was just ready at the tavern and "old rye" on tap, and considerable of both was soon secured. "Boys, that whisky is poison," said Major Godman. "We know it is," was the instant reply. Every nook and corner of the town having been thoroughly searched for "Secesh" and "Secesh goods," the expedition started for camp with corn, wagons, horses, contrabands and several prisoners. The latter reported that their commander, as soon as the first shot had been fired, rushed out of the church, exclaiming, "They have got a cannon! Somebody will get hurt!" and soon left town and river behind. We had two wounded: J. C. McKenzie, of Company A, and a citizen who had gone along to see the fun. It was certain that several of the enemy had been killed and wounded. Some two miles from town on the homeward journey, while the boys were sampling the blackberries, some one spied under the brier-tangle two curious looking objects, which proved, on close inspection, to be kegs half-filled with stout and aged apple-jack, which was also sampled, and a requisition for a number of canteens full of the wonder immediately made. In spite of this "ready relief" every man reached Greenland before dark, and camp at five the next evening, some in high "spirits," with wondrous stories of "the battle of Petersburg."

On the 8th two men started a rumor and said that a large force of rebels was cutting its way across the mountains in order to attack us in the rear. There was considerable stir in camp. Captain Banning, with Companies B and E, went ten miles from camp to Blackwater and Horseshoe, but found no enemy. After helping themselves to blackberries and forage they returned, and had the satisfaction of seeing the men who had created the sensation for the fun of it lodged in the guard house, which made an end of publishing canards.

COLONEL LORIN ANDREWS.

## DEATH OF COLONEL ANDREWS AT HIS HOME IN GAMBIER, OHIO.

On Thursday, September 29th, the flag upon the tall staff on the highest point of the Fort was at half-mast, in honor of our now much lamented Colonel Lorin Andrews. He had been for some time prostrated with fever, and had died at his home on the day previous, surrounded by his family and other loved ones. They felt his loss hardly more keenly than did his men, who had from the first respected, then honored and loved him. He was what this world so seldom sees, an ideal man, affectionate, self-sacrificing, noble, pure, honorable, upright, faithful, intelligent and God-fearing. Our loss was great, but it was to Education, Church, State and Country a greater loss. He lacked naught that makes men heroes, and could have shone in the councils of the Nation, and honored its highest positions.

He had infused into the regiment a spirit of self-respect and desire for excellence that comes from diligence, application and self-denial, and brings about solid worth to one, whether he is citizen or soldier. His strictness of discipline never in the least manifested any disposition to tyrannize. In all his efforts, it is but just in this connection to say, that he was most heartily seconded by all his subordinates. With him were buried many and great possibilities. His memory is ever precious.

## CHAPTER VI.

EXPEDITION TO ROMNEY, VIRGINIA, IN COMMAND OF LIEUTENANT COLONEL CANTWELL—OUR MARCH TO NEW CREEK—ARE JOINED BY THE EIGHTH OHIO AND TWO WEST VIRGINIA COMPANIES—SKIRMISH IN MECHANICSBURG GAP—BATTLE OF ROMNEY—RETURN TO PENDLETON, MARYLAND.

Past successes and a desire to do more for the country than to dig trenches where no enemy would ever be likely to come, found all willing to start out in the rain at three in the morning on Sunday, September 22d, and move rapidly forward over the mountain range, seldom halting, until New Creek (Keyser) was reached at 5 P.M., where, after the thirty-two mile march, we were heartily greeted by the Eighth Ohio, our future brigade comrades. The next morning, Monday, September 23d, five hundred of the Eighth Ohio in command of Colonel Parke, Captain Dayton's company of the First West Virginia, and Captain Hagan's company of the Third West Virginia, joined our regiment, and made our force about one thousand strong. Ringgold's Cavalry in command of Captain Keyes, led the advance, the entire force being in charge of the brave, cool and collected Lieutenant Colonel Cantwell of our regiment; marched southeast, passed Knobly range, crossed Cabin and Patterson Creeks, took dinner near Sheets' Mill, resumed the march in one hour, drove in the Confederate pickets two miles from Mechanicsburg Gap, where the pike passes through the transverse fissure of the Mill Creek Range, having marched fourteen miles; skirmishers were advanced more rapidly from our regiment, but night came on before we could force our way through the Gap, which was guarded by four companies of rebel cavalry.

Soon after dark the first platoon of company C was sent forward to the left of the Gap, in the hazy moonlight, deployed up the mountain side, and was at once fired upon, as it moved through tall grass and clover, by some of our own men stationed behind some buildings; the platoon fell back under cover, formed in line, emerged from behind a stone building, started four abreast to join the column, when from across a garden fence came two shots, followed by a volley from an entire company of the Eighth Ohio, some three rods distant; the platoon once more made for the rear of the stone house, now in quick time. Fortunately no one was hurt, and no one to blame. They were a mad, yet jolly set; mad because our own men, when they had been told again and again that friends were advancing, were determined to keep up their firing; laughing at the tall running and prodigious leaping over stone wall and picket fence. One vowed that he had "bounced a rod;" another had "burst his pants;" another, striking his knee against a stone, felt for his leg, being certain that it had been shot off; another vowed that he had leaped at one bound a fence three feet high. Afterward the men returned to their company, one by one, as best they could.

Early the next morning, Tuesday, September 24th, five of the rebel cavalry came up the road within a few rods of Company C, the advance, who cocked their rifles, took aim, but a voice rang out "Don't shoot, they are our men!" Angry men, who knew it was the enemy, obeyed orders, and the horsemen taking the hint, wheeled and were off at breakneck speed. The boys determined, if another such chance presented itself, to be deaf and not able to hear orders.

At an early hour the Eighth Ohio and Ringgold Cavalry, in command of Colonel Parke, attacked Hanging Rock Pass, three miles to the west of us, drove the enemy, and returned by midnight.

In the forenoon Companies A and I, a few volunteers from other companies of the Fourth, and Dayton's Company of Virginians, skirmished along the side and top of the mountain, on both sides of the Gap, while our regiment followed Sergeant Reynolds and his cannon through the Gap; the remaining forces that had not gone with Parke were in supporting distance, and also kept a lookout for any attack in our rear. Several shots were exchanged along the sides of the Gap. The skirmishers soon came in sight of Romney, and for a short time watched the maneuverings of the enemy, when the entire force fell back to Mechanicsburg at the entrance of the Gap, where another night was passed. Our rations were giving out, and rapid work must now be done or a retreat made without having accomplished our object.

Early, therefore, on Wednesday, September 25th, the Fourth advanced, followed by the entire command. In a few moments shots were fired from the top of the mountain on the left, and Willie Breyfogle, the youngest man in the regiment—save, possibly, O. Lewis—was severely wounded in the left foot. A volley was fired at the ledges from whence the smoke proceeded. Sergeant Anderson, with a platoon of Company C, moved rapidly up the slope and flanked the enemy, who gave us now no further trouble until the force had advanced to the eastern entrance. We then followed the road to the left some sixty rods, with bluffs of the South Branch of the Potomac immediately on the right for several rods about one hundred and fifty feet high. Back of this bluff, and nearer the town, the enemy was getting into position on Cemetery Hill. Our column continued to advance, and had now the very steep, precipitous bluff to the left and the river on the right, giving no opportunity for cover and little chance for action, as the rebels were behind earthworks. In a few moments they let drive at us; our column halted and returned the fire; many stray shots continued to come into our midst, when came the order "Forward!" It was forward, on the double-quick, the infantry and artillery over the bridge and the cavalry through the river, then both onward up the slope toward the town. Away went the Confederates, too, and were soon out of hearing or sight, our cavalry after them through and beyond town toward Church Hill and Winchester. Before nine o'clock most of our forces were in or near the town. At about eleven the cavalry observed the gathering of forces from the direction of Winchester, Frenchburg, Church Hill and Hanging Rock Pass, with a disposition to mass at Cemetery Hill, whence they could make us great trouble by firing into our flank in case we returned by the same route we came, and we might easily be cut off by a force which now outnumbered us two to one; a force that had also seven companies of cavalry composed of men brought up in this very region of mountains paths that led directly to our rear, and of which we had no knowledge.

## ATTACK UPON ROMNEY.     47

The object of the expedition—to find out the disposition and strength of the enemy, "scrape his acquaintance," and to try the mettle of our men—being now fully accomplished, and our provisions having given out, the order was given to retreat. Several union men were released, other loyal citizens encouraged by our boldness and the manifest cowardice of the enemy who so soon left his works when he had a larrger force. A flag was captured by Company B, the press and other material of the "*Intelligencer*," which had given aid and comfort to the rebels, were confiscated. Shortly before noon our entire force right-about-faced, recrossed the bridge and nearly all had re-entered the Gap, when a squad of horsemen opened fire from Cemetery Hill upon our rear, which immediately halted and returned a well-directed fire. The gunners, too, did royal service. Many of the enemy reeled from their horses, while most of them dashed hurriedly out of sight, and their firing ceased. Our column now moved through the Gap, and was ascending a rise of ground and had mostly passed around a strip of woods, when the enemy opened upon our rear with cannon, their shot coming far short, but near at hand their cavalry sent their balls into our midst, doing some execution. In a few moments our men were behind the woods and out of range, but not until there was another attack, which so raised the ire of Captain Weaver, that with eyes snapping, and squirting the tobacco juice, he called out in imperative tones: "Hardin County heroes, about face and kill four hundred of the —— —— of ——." After this the rebels followed us at a safe distance, not getting near enough to be fired at, yet serving the good purpose of keeping our men from straggling.

No one of the regiment was killed during the expedition; the following were wounded:

B Company—J. M. Cline, William O. Van Voorhes and Henry Graff.
C Company—John Parks and William D. Breyfogle.
D Company—John Brum.
E Company—John F. Barrett and W. C. Cline.
F Company—W. Ferguson.
G Company—F. Beck, W. Noel and J. M. Nichols.
I Company—W. C. Howard.

There is no report of the "Storming of Romney" from the standpoint of the Unionists in the "Records of the Rebellion," but the Confederates occupy fourteen pages explanatory and recommendatory of themselves as having gained a remarkable victory; how they drove us out of town, scooped up prisoners, killed and wounded between seventy and eighty of us and made us run all the way to New Creek, and would have captured our entire force had not night set in so soon. They further state that we were in the town until eleven o'clock; that they followed close upon our heels with seven companies of cavalry, several regiments of infantry and cannon, who fired into each other by mistake several times and into us often, harassing us until within two miles of New Creek, when night prevented further pursuit. Now, darkness on the 25th of September closes in at about half-past six o'clock, which would make our alleged stampede at the rate of two and one-half miles per hour. Why did not their cavalry charge upon us again and again on the very farms where many of them had been brought up, and force us to battle? they knew every acre of ground, cross-road and by-path. This was certainly the biggest set of liars and cowards we met during our term of service. "Stonewall Jackson" some months afterward reported them to the Confederate authorities at Richmond as "demoralized," and dispensed with the services of many because he could place no confidence in them; so some of them were sent to Tennessee.

On the morning of the 26th we boarded the cars, reached Oakland toward night and immediately started for Fort Pendleton, the latter half of the march being through mud, rain and intense darkness until we entered our now very desirable quarters at midnight, footsore and weary. Three days of chilly rain followed. Many of the men were soon prostrated with rheumatism, camp-fever and other maladies. Snow began to make its appearance on the tops of the rugged mountains east and south of the camp. The usual round of duties—picket, regimental and cattle guard—were resumed and camp-life became more monotonous and debilitating than ever.

## CHAPTER VII.

COLONEL MASON ASSUMES COMMAND OF REGIMENT—SECOND "ROMNEY RACE"— CAMP KELLEY AT ROMNEY —EXPEDITION TO BLUE'S GAP, JANUARY 7TH, 1862.

John S. Mason, of Ohio, graduate of West Point, Second Lieutenant Third Artillery July 1st, 1847; First Lieutenant September 7th, 1850; Regimental Quartermaster June 27th, 1854, to June 1st, 1858; then Captain Eleventh United States Regular Infantry and appointed Colonel of the Fourth Ohio Volunteer Infantry October 3d, 1861, took command of our regiment on the 16th of October, and immediately made his presence felt by his General Order No 1, which was the quintessence of Army Regulations, and at once convinced officers and men that our new commander was "business."

On the 22d of October, General Kelley, commanding, received the following order: "Proceed with your command to Romney, and assume command of the Department of Harper's Ferry and Cumberland until the arrival of Brigadier General Lander. Winfield Scott." This seems to have been the last order General Scott issued.

The Fourth did its part in complying with this order, by leaving camp at six in the morning, and marching over the mountains, twenty-eight miles, to near New Creek, on Friday, October 25th, where it was joined by other troops the next morning, and at six marched at the head of the column, in the following order: Ringgold Cavalry, Captain Keyes; Fourth Ohio, in command of Colonel Mason; Seventh West Virginia and one company each of the Third and Fourth West Virginia Infantry; Eighth Ohio, two guns of the Fourth Ohio Battery, Sergeant Nixon's six-pounder and McGee's Cavalry. At noon the column halted at Patterson Creek for half an hour, took dinner, then moved rapidly forward, the left-flank company of the Fourth Ohio being sent in advance as skirmishers. Some two miles from Mechanicsburg Gap Pass, and before proceeding more than half a mile, they were fired upon by rebel artillery to which our battery at once replied and drove the enemy. The entire force now moved forward, entered the Gap, passed through, followed the road some distance to the left, and was fired at as soon as the advance companies came in sight and range of Cemetery Hill, where could be seen artillery, mounted and dismounted cavalry, behind the entrenchments. An artillery duel now began and was continued for an hour, when the order "Forward, double-quick!" was given, and the entire column quickly obeyed, charged under flying shell and whizzing bullet along the road, over the bridge—the cavalry through the river—then onward both charged up the slope toward the town, while the Confederates limbered their guns, and the infantry, many of whom flung their muskets, together with the cavalry made for the hills in quick time. Our cavalry, supported by the infantry, moved rapidly through and to the east of the town, captured their guns, wagon-train and a number of prisoners, as well as stores in town. Thus ended "Romney Race No. 2." "If the buggers would only stop and fight," ejaculated a disgusted private. Soon after this Stonewall Jackson preferred charges against the commander of the Confederate forces, who was ordered to report at Richmond, and his command was sent to Tennessee. Our loss, all told of the entire command, was one killed and twenty wounded. In the regiment, J. Meredith and J. Sines of Company F, S. Black of G, and H. Meily of K, were wounded.

General Kelley reported to General Scott as follows: "The officers and men of my command all displayed great coolness and courage under fire. It seems almost a miracle that our loss should be so small, considering that we had to advance across a causeway and over a bridge in the face of the enemy's entrenchments." In a few days came from Washington the following: "Your late movement upon, and signal victory at Romney, do you great honor in the opinion of the President and General Scott."

It is quite certain that to Colonel Mason, seconded most heartily by all his officers and men, belonged considerable of the above praise, as they were in the advance. Colonel Cantwell, who had resigned several days before the expedition, and accompanied the boys on this charge, now returned home. The wagons at once brought up the camp equipage, and the camp was located at the western entrance of the town, and soon camp life with its drills once more went forward. Captain Brown acted as Provost Marshal and his company as Provost Guards. The camp was named "Keyes," in honor of the Captain of the Ringgold Cavalry, who had twice displayed dash, daring and courage. How the boys used to cheer the Ringgolds as they sailed into the Johnnies. In a few days Sibley tents, five to a company, took the place of the old wall-tents. Eighteen men could sleep in one of these at a time, by lying "spoon-fashion." The officers continued to occupy wall-tents.

Within a week there were quartered at Romney the Fourth, Fifth, Seventh and Eighth Ohio, First West Virginia, Fourteenth Indiana, Daum's and Howe's Batteries, Ringgold and Washington Cavalry. Out of this number six to eight hundred went on picket daily, from two to six miles, the greater part of them toward Winchester, whence an attack was expected under Jackson, who was at this time busy collecting a large force, with which he intended to crush us at one blow.

Company I was soon detailed to act as Provost Guard. October 29th forty-four recruits joined the regiment. On the 5th of November the Ringgold Cavalry, Kelley Lancers and fifty-two of Company C, went to Blue's Gap and drove out some three hundred militia. Within a month a number of men were sick; sixty-two in the hospital in the town, and seventy-eight absent, sick. Of these a number died. Our Regimental Surgeon, H. H. McAbee, was appointed Medical Director of the Department, with over five hundred sick in his care. Cold weather had set in about the first of December, and several inches of snow was upon the ground in the valleys during the latter part of the month, and it was several feet deep on the mountains. Frequently pickets were not relieved during an entire night, and then there was the long march home, considerable part of the way through deep snows. This, added to other hardships, caused much sickness. There was also frequent battalion drill. Whisky with quinine was issued every other day, with the intention of overcoming any malarious troubles that might have been contracted; but many of the men refused to accept these rations, and threw them on the ground or gave them to some "thirsty" comrade, so that the practice was in a few days discontinued. The soldiers were not the drunken offscourings of the earth as some of the stay-at-homes, who were more nice than wise, had claimed. Most of our men were of the country's best citizens.

There were frequent foraging expeditions which supplied horses and mules with hay, oats and corn, and occasionally some extras for the tables of such as obtained enough money for their services to enable them to buy. Once, indeed, a certain foraging expedition did not return, but were compelled to turn over their wagons and mules to some Secesh Home Guards and report at Richmond. Lieutenant J. S. Jones, with a squad of men, went in pursuit, found where the wagons had tipped their hay and fodder, also the blind-paths along which they were afterward taken. This path the squad followed until it was lost on the top of the mountain under two feet of snow. On the return horsemen could be seen half a mile away, charging from the hillside and rapidly disappearing. This expedition found, as did also one under Captain Crawford on the 1st, and Captain Carpenter on the 3d of December, that blind roads and paths were numerous in these mountain regions and all leading directly to Romney, or into some road that ran direct to the town, so that it is passing strange that the rebels did not make us more trouble.

On the 15th of December S. S. Carroll was appointed Colonel of the Eighth Ohio.

On the 5th of January, 1862, Colonel Dunning of the Fifth Ohio, received orders from General Kelley at Cumberland to make an expedition to Hanging Rock Pass, or Blue's Gap, fifteen miles southeast of Romney, in the Short Mountain, on the road to Winchester, in order to divert the attention of Jackson, who was at this time making a raid upon Hancock and other points upon the Baltimore & Ohio Railroad.

In compliance with orders, six companies were taken from each of the following regiments: Fourth, Fifth, Seventh and Eighth Ohio, Fourteenth Indiana, First West Virginia, one Section of Baker's Parrott guns, Daum's Battery, the Ringgold, Washington, and three companies of the First West Virginia Cavalry, the entire force not exceeding two thousand men. At a little past midnight the troops left their blankets and comfortable quarters, made a forced march through pitch darkness and several inches of snow and ice, with the wind at a gale, over Big, Stony and Briery Mountains. On the latter, at break of day, the Ringgolds captured one prisoner at the outer picket-post and soon came in sight of the bridge over the Great Cacapon, which the retreating enemy tried to burn, but was prevented by the sure work of the Parrott guns and the charge of the Fifth, Fourth and Eighth Ohio, on the double-quick, down the hill, over the bridge toward the breast-works, after the Confederates who were rapidly vanishing toward the farther end of Blue's Gap. Some had just begun breakfast, others were waking out of sleep. All were seized with consternation. Rallying as best they could, they began firing upon our advance. The Fifth rushed up the steep sides of the mile-long pass on the left, while Colonel Carroll charged into the Gap at the head of the Eighth, and Colonel Mason with the Fourth scaled the right, the rest of the troops moving up as a support.

The rebels got their cannon into position, but could not get sufficient elevation to reach the flankers, who were close upon them, causing them to flee to safe hiding places in the mountains, and but few were overtaken. Two guns, caissons, ten horses, ammunition wagons, and valuable papers which disclosed Jackson's movements, were captured. Our troops right-about-faced, recrossed the bridge, took breakfast and moved homeward. Fire was set to rebel Colonel Blue's house, barn and mill, and most of the houses within eight miles of the Gap, because they had harbored a set of guerillas that waylaid union men and soldiers. The Confederacy complained of this act "of vandalism" perpetrated on cowardly guerillas.

Fourteen hours from the time of starting, most of our men were once more in their quarters, weary and footsore with the hardest march which they had yet made. The men were more than ever pleased with their new Colonels, Mason and Carroll. "Now there is no discount on Mason, I tell ye;" "he is just the man;" "didn't he go for 'em?" "and Carroll is lightning, too," "no discount on him either," with other like compliments, could be heard from enthusiastic men, who had again met the enemy only to see him run. He had over one thousand men, the choice of position, and could have made our victory dear-bought; he had thirteen killed, a larger number wounded; we had not a man touched. The expedition had the effect of compelling Jackson to fall back toward Winchester, thereby saving to us railroad bridges and towns. It soon became evident that he was determined to punish us for our audacity, that Romney must be retaken and the rebel spirit in and about it fostered by a glorious victory; accordingly, a force of sixteen thousand men, twenty-four pieces of artillery, one a thirty-two pounder, moved against us and endeavored to get between us and the railroad. At this juncture General Lander took command, with orders from McClellan at Washington to evacute Romney and get nearer to our base of supplies, and not hazard any force in a position that was by both armies considered a trap for a less number than twenty thousand men, on account of the many roads that must be guarded and the facility with which supplies could be cut off by a far inferior force.

Company E remained at Fort Pendleton from October 24th until January 15th. Some of the men were quartered in the Pendleton house, others at the Fort in charge of the cannon, and the remainder in Old Tabb's log cabin, where, when the snow was three to ten feet deep and covered with a thick hard crust, a Christmas dinner was had by officers and men, of honey, turkey, venison, oysters and apple-jack. Some wild deer were shot within half a mile of the Fort. Venison was obtained from hunters in exchange for sugar and coffee. Night was ofttimes made hideous by the wails of a catamount. A bear that had come up to the Fort during the night, eluded capture although eagerly pursued for fourteen miles. "Mountain Dew" could readily be had at twenty-five cents a gallon. The singing school at Bush's was especially popular because of the excellent music and the attendance of nearly a dozen girls who had come a distance of three to six miles on foot and must be escorted home ere the early dawn. The occasional "stag dance" and theatrical performance in the old church were considered as never-to-be-forgotten innovations that helped to drive dull care away. In the play of "Romeo and Juliet" all went well until Romeo was shot at with a musket while he was climbing into the balcony, (over the pulpit) the "buck and ball" making a wreck of the wall. Such startling applause was of sufficient effect to arouse the guard at the Fort, who, thinking the pickets had been attacked hurried to their support. Actors and audience, hearing the advance of the guard, instantly put out the two candles and vanished into the darkness, save poor "Romeo," who was caught and put into the guard-house for giving a false alarm. In spite of these hilarious times the officers and men frequently requested to be sent to the regiment. On the 15th of January the two twelve-pounder cannon were spiked, the magazine blown up, the supplies that could not be removed were destroyed, the march made to Oakland, and for several days quarters were taken in the hotel, and on the 22d the regiment was joined at Camp Kelley.

## CHAPTER VIII.

ROMNEY EVACUATED — GENERAL LANDER JOINS HIS TROOPS AT SPRINGFIELD—EXPEDITION TOWARD WINCHESTER—DEATH OF LANDER—PAW PAW TUNNEL—SHIELDS IN COMMAND—FOURTH AND EIGHTH AS ARTILLERY BRIGADE — TO BACK CREEK—MARTINSBURG, WINCHESTER—"CUT UP" TO MAKE PROVOST GUARDS AT HARPER'S FERRY, BERRYVILLE—"FOURTH OHIO TIMES"—ADVANCE OF ARMY TO CEDAR CREEK, WOODSTOCK, EDINBURG, MT. JACKSON, ROOD'S HILL, NEW MARKET.

The evacuation of Romney began on Thursday, January 9th, and at eleven at night of the 10th, our regiment brought up the rear, marching toward Springfield and Patterson Creek. The night was still, stars shone dimly, weather quite cold, the mud but little frozen, making progress slow and difficult. Occasionally rockets could be seen toward the east, leaving their colored fiery lines high in air. At five in the morning there was a halt near Springfield; fires were built to broil the beef and boil the coffee, but most of the men were so fatigued and sleepy that they snuggled together in squads and slept. Jackson, with twelve thousand men, was only six miles distant, with other thousands in supporting distance. General Lander had just joined us and inspected our position, and concluded in his usual style, "Let him come, we'll whip him like hell." We were not to hazard a battle with our small force, and therefore soon moved toward old dilapidated Frankfort, reaching it at noon, and Patterson Creek Station just at dark, wet to the skin. The entire march had been made along the roadside, through fields, over fences and swollen streams, rain over head and mud under foot. We had just escaped a fair chance of being captured or compelled to fight a much larger force than our own; on the other hand Jackson was too far from his base of supplies, and in danger of being intercepted and bagged by forces in the vicinity of Harper's Ferry, and he therefore hastened back to Winchester, and Romney was in a short time reoccupied by Union forces.

Our camp "Kelley" was by nature a beautiful spot, where Washington had encamped in his early days. During the greater part of our month's stay it rained or snowed, the mud was deep, picket and scouting duties very heavy, clothing old, ragged and filthy; blankets too scarce for comfort, so that many took sick, and some of our best boys died in the hospital at Cumberland. Generous friends in Ohio furnished those in the hospital and some of the most needy in the regiment, through a Mr. A. E. Strickle, 134 blankets, 588 pairs of socks, 24 sheets, 3 bedticks, 100 pairs of mittens, 276 pairs of drawers, 24 pillow cases and 24 towels.

The Fourth, Fifth and Eighth Ohio and Thirty-ninth Illinois, composed the Second Brigade, commanded by Colonel Dunning. Company inspections were frequent, and on the 17th General Lander inspected the Division.

During the first week in February troops were daily passing us toward the East, and on the 9th we were very glad to exchange our camp in the mud for a better one at Paw Paw Tunnel, which we reached by rail on the morning of the 10th. Here snow, rain and sunshine continued to alternate. The success of the Eighth Ohio and Seventh West Virginia made us wish that we had enjoyed the sport with them. The surrender of Fort Donelson set the camp wild with excitement, as well as did the exploits in Kentucky and the Burnside expedition. All were in the best possible spirits, having confidence in their commanders. Papers, letters and boxes came from home; new clothing and the free application of soap, blacking and brush brought us to the requirements of the Regulations. The Division had 482 officers, 11,367 men, and 26 pieces of artillery.

Saturday, February 22d, was ushered in by booming cannon, and closed with a grand review by General Lander, who constituted himself the orator of the day by making a "well-seasoned" (with oaths) speech to each regiment. The pallor of his cheeks, tone of voice, and glassy eyeballs, showed that disease was making very rapid progress. Himself feared that the worst might soon come, as was evident from his earnest and frequent request to be relieved from duty for awhile, and the fact that although being terribly profane he was now much given to reading his Bible and praying. The worst did come. On Saturday March 1st, the troops—with several days' rations—ourselves among the number, had proceeded under his direction as far as Sideling Mountain, distant eleven miles, the beginning of an expedition against Winchester. A cold night was passed, and with the morning came great flakes of snow which adhered to everything and soon melted. In every direction the whack of the ax was heard as the men put up shelter. It was provoking to be ordered back, but murmuring soon ceased when it was learned that "Lander is dead." Eyes were filled with tears as we silently returned to our old quarters in the raw, cold night. We had first known him at Rich Mountain, as the noble, brave, daring and fearless Lander. A great and noble man had fallen. The next day the troops were in line and his remains were conveyed to the train. In a few days President Lincoln and his Cabinet, Senators, and many others, with tearful eyes bade adieu to one from whom much had been expected.

Colonel Kimball succeeded to the command until General Shields could arrive. The Fourth and Eighth Ohio, with the batteries, constituted the Artillery Brigade, in command of Colonel Mason.

At 3 P.M. Friday, March 7th, we again boarded the cars and moved eastward, taking in the inspiring influences of high cliffs and pine-covered mountains until dark, and in the morning found ourselves opposite Hancock, three miles from the Pennsylvania line, with scraggy Round Top in full view toward the north, having just crossed the great Cacapon and Sir John's Run, named after General Braddock's Quartermaster. About a mile to the south were the famous Berkeley Springs, where the Fairfaxs, Washingtons, and others of Colonial days, sought health in drinking the waters, shooting the deer, and baiting the trout and bass. We remained here the greater part of the day awaiting orders; before the middle of the afternoon we were again onward; North Mountain soon greeted us, and before night we were at its foot; crossed Back Creek on a wire bridge and went into camp for the night. At early dawn, north of us about a mile could be seen old Fort Frederick, which was famous in 1755. The trains could proceed no further, since the bridge

ALONG THE POTOMAC.

had not yet been rebuilt; leaving the baggage behind we marched for ten miles over a mud road, then six more on a hard pike to Martinsburg, on the 9th, where we remained a few days awaiting the arrival of additional troops. The country was more like a plain, with high ridges in the distance, and the houses looked different from those in the mountains.

We were now in General Banks' department; he was moving on Jackson at Winchester, whither we proceeded on the 10th, and on the morning of the 11th formed in line of battle, and thus marched in rear of Banks' force, that now moved to the attack by brigades. It was a magnificent sight. The enemy had gone—Winchester was ours without a battle. On the west of the town we camped. Our brigade was now composed of the Fourth, Eighth and Sixty-seventh Ohio, Fourteenth Indiana and Seventh West Virginia, commanded by Colonel Kimball; with the exception of the Sixty-seventh Ohio these regiments marched and fought together, under different commanders, sharing the same vicissitudes, fortunes, hardships and glories until they were each mustered out of service, in June, 1864.

On Friday, March 14th, came the provoking order that broke the regiment into scouting parties and provost guards, serving a like fate with the Seventh West Virginia. Companies F and C went to Harper's Ferry, in charge of Captain Crawford as provost marshal; A, D, H and K went to Berryville, and B and I were provost guards at Winchester; E and G were scattered along the Winchester and Potomac Railroad, in charge of Major Weaver. Colonel Mason had charge of the artillery of Shields' division, with headquarters at Winchester, and aided materially in the battle of the 23d, directing the batteries personally. He had also made a reconnaisance at 9 A.M. General Kimball says in his report: "To Colonel John S. Mason and his adjutant, Lieutenant Green, I am deeply indebted for valuable assistance rendered."

The boys at Berryville must have had an excellent time. On Sabbath Dr. Warner preached in the Methodist church. Captain Olmstead edited, and Sergeant Ustick and W. T. Hutchinson published, the first number of the *Fourth Ohio Times*, on the 21st, having the motto: "Equal Justice to All." It was of quarto size, and spicy. The following is one of the four poetic effusions "How Goes the Day?" by Lieutenant Straub:

They're falling back, the rebel pack,
   They falter and they fly;
While after them the loyal men
   Of Union onward hie.
The lines of fate, drawn not by hate,
   But Justice and The Right,
Are circling close the traitor host
   Who've darkened Truth and Light.

Potomac, famed, whose shores are stained
   By fratricidal strife,
Is rid at last of lawless mass
   That shook the vengeful knife.
The hero, dead, now rests his head
   In peace on Vernon's clay;
For valiant sons and loyal guns
   Have driven foes away.

All o'er the land the Union band
   Is claiming back its own;
Kentucky's free, and Tennessee
   To her first love has flown;
Missouri's ours, while fortune lowers
   On traitors everywhere—
Our starry flag towers o'er the rag
   Of treason in the air.

Brave boys, let's on—'tis only dawn
   Of glory-dazzling day;
Up, stripes and stars—down, stars and bars,
   On, onward leads the way.
We'll show the world ne'er can be furled
   Our banner, or be trailed
By mortal foes or civil throes;
   Though by dark powers assailed.

Also, from the same pen:

## TO KING JEFF.

You're played out, Jeff, you've fizzled;
   Secession's proved a bore;
The cloud that long but drizzled
   Commences now to pour.
Your unstable throne is tottering,
   Your dazzling crown has paled;
You'd better be "a-pottering,"
   For your wicked schemes have failed.

From Captain Stewart's pen the following is taken:

> Then were changes, dark and sudden,
>   Like the swoop of stormy skies;
> Broken households, tender partings
>   Sad with love's delicious sighs.
>
> May the strong arm of our Union,
>   And its true and holy cause,
> Bring the erring back to Justice
>   And restore its broken laws.
>
> Then will summers come as lovely
>   And as peaceful as before,
> To the village in the valley
>   Of the flowing Shenandoah.

The first page begins with an original poem by Captain Stewart, entitled "Battletown," a name sometimes applied to Berryville. From this poem the above extract is taken. This is followed by the latest news, "Our Chair," an editorial on the secesh sentiments of the publisher of *Clark Journal*, who had the year previous occupied the office, and said, "Pennsylvania may be as well adapted to slavery as Maryland, but not being there, there is no slave order or civilization." The last article is a description of the people and things of the country. On second page is the "Salutatory," followed by "Our Marches Since March First," then a poem, "Our Thoughts Turn Homeward," with a card of thanks to the ladies for the "nice meals donated." The page closes with "An Imprudent Stamp Act: The imprudent soldier carries postage stamps in his pocket-book; the prudent soldier never does, for he knows that he can always borrow of the one that has them." Page three has a statement concerning "Battletown," that General Morgan, the "prince of cock-fighting," had lived and died near here, was buried in Winchester, and that Washington's office was still standing near town. "Explanation" follows, and is a defense of our conduct at Blue's Gap. In the second column are the poems, "How Goes the Day?" and "To King Jeff." The last column states that "at the fight near Bloomery Gap a Dutch Secesh Colonel, Sencendiver, called to his men: "Poys, te enemy's comin'—take care of yourselves. I'se got te rheumatis—I starts now;" and away he went, never halting until he got to Winchester. The fourth page has "Later from Jackson's Army," "Berryville," and a grumble that the regiment is fated to act as provost guards.

On the afternoons of the 22d and 23d firing was heard in the direction of Winchester, where the remainder of Shields' Division was watching Jackson, Banks having removed his forces toward Harper's Ferry. On the morning of the 24th six companies, having marched during the night, joined the two at Winchester, and now in command of Colonel Mason after having helped to bury the dead slain in the battle of the 23d took the advance on the morning of the 25th, marched beyond Cedar Run toward Woodstock, following Jackson's whipped army. Ten men were now detailed from each regiment of the division to constitute the Pioneer Corps, and were commanded by Captain Olmstead.

On Thursday morning, March 28th, the Fourth and Eighth Ohio and one company of the First West Virginia, started in the fog to made a reconnaisance toward Woodstock, by the way of Barb's Tannery. Banks' forces were kept on the front for several days; there was considerable picket firing, and an occasional artillery duel.

On Monday evening, the 31st, the Fourth took the advance toward Woodstock several miles, went on picket until the next morning, then again led the advance on the pike, supported by a company of cavalry, Clarke's Battery and the remainder of the division. Progress was slow, on account of the burnt bridges and occasional skirmishes with Ashby's cavalry and three guns. Woodstock was reached at noon and Edenburg about 4 o'clock, and camp entered near a high bridge over Stony Creek, where coffee, bacon and tack, in a beautiful country, with blooming fruit trees and a fleeing enemy, were greatly enjoyed. The artillery firing as we entered camp, and the slight skirmish and artillery practice of the next day, added zest.

In this camp we now had two weeks of rest and comfort. The slight fall of snow reminded us of the winter of snow, mud and discontent just passed. The artillery practice of the 15th was witnessed by many of the boys as they stood near and back of the guns, and imagined they could see the missiles flying through the air, making the Johnnies play "hide and seek."

On the 16th Colonel Godman, with three hundred of the Fourth, joined an expedition led by Colonel Carroll; started at four in the evening, marched all night through mud and water

HARPER'S FERRY—LOOKING EAST.

for twenty-three miles, and came in sight of Mount Jackson just as the rebels had fled; while the remainder of the regiment, the left flank, having started at midnight and led the advance, also came in sight of the town about the same time, drove in the enemy's picket, followed rapidly, coming into close quarters with his rear guard at eight o'clock. The skirmisher on the extreme left, seeing a man to the left of an orchard some two hundred yards distant looking through a field-glass, observing our forces, raised the sight on his rifle and fired; down upon his horse squatted the observer, whirled his steed, plied spurs vehemently, "lit out, lickety cut," for his comrades at the road, who had just unlimbered a gun; but before they could load the order was given to limber up, which was hurried by a volley from our entire skirmish line; an immediate charge by our cavalry, who secured several prisoners but failed to capture the gun.

The skirmishers were hurried forward rapidly, and soon smoke was emerging from a bridge, when Lieutenant Jones, Aide de Camp on Shields' Staff, with an orderly, rode forward at a gallop, captured two prisoners on the bridge, and extinguished the flames by the time the skirmishers arrived. This daring was highly complimented by the General. In a few moments Mount Jackson was entered, just as the rebel rear was leaving the town. The entire division was now formed in line of battle, with our brigade occupying the center; the skirmishers in the meantime continued to advance, and had a lively brush at Rood's Hill, the artillery also joining in giving the enemy a parting salute. Camp was soon entered at New Market, and occupied until the 25th, when a march of six miles toward Harrisonburg was made; on the 26th the forces remained in camp; on the 27th another advance of ten miles, to Camp Cave, was made, and on the 28th Wier's Cave was explored by some five hundred, accompanied by the band, which played several tunes while the boys were examining the monster "icicles," as they called the stalactites.

News of the fall of New Orleans reached us. On the 30th we were mustered for pay; there were over eight hundred present for duty, who the next day drew four months' pay. On the 4th of May, there was inspection of arms. Late in the evening of the 6th the camp of the regiment was changed to the foot of the Massanuten Mountains, one mile east of town, near to a large bridge, where it remained about one week.

The nights were cool, the health of the troops excellent; wheat was about knee high. Here a "good Union (?) man," harangued such as would listen, and sang, "From Maine to the Rio Grande Treason Must Go Down." The boys suspected him of being a "Secesh spy," and endeavored to swear him in, which so hurt his feelings that he suddenly left camp. Some are certain that we saw the same "chap" after the battle of Gettysburg, hanging by his neck, near Frederick City.

Here, too, some less than a thousand hounds scampering over the forest-covered mountain slope, made night hideous with their ye'lep, ye'lep, mixing their "infernal music" with the delightful dreams of the sweet soldier, wooed and won by snoring sleep.

## CHAPTER IX.

TO FREDERICKSBURG AND RETURN — FRONT ROYAL SKIRMISH — PORT REPUBLIC — FRONT ROYAL — LURAY — BRISTOE STATION — READY TO GO TO PENINSULA.

On Monday, May 12th, tents were turned over into the care of the Quartermaster, and wagons toward the rear; everything that belonged to a soldier must be carried. Men with huge packs upon their backs accosted each other with, "Good morning, mule!" "Bring along your howitzers;" "There is still room on top for a howitzer." Nor had the deep shadows over bridge and meadows shortened much when, all in the best spirits, started through Brook's Gap, over the Massanuten Mountains, "on to Richmond," down the South Fork Valley, with its magnificent scenery, stony roads, fields of wild onions and garlic, passing through Luray, camped, after having marched sixteen miles. The next morning we were in the advance, marched nineteen miles, and were again onward at five on the morning of the 14th, and after six more miles reached Front Royal, just as the railroad whistle was heard for the first time since we left Winchester, and answered by lusty cheers. It had begun to rain in the night, and now it came in torrents, nor did the sun again appear until the 16th, after we had started out once more during a heavy shower, the clouds parting as we reached Chester Gap.

We leave Manassas Gap at 6:30 A.M., pass Gaines' Cross Roads, march seventeen miles, and camp; then push forward the next morning to Warrenton, eleven miles. On Monday, the 19th of May, we reached Catlett's Station, remain in camp during the 20th, with scarcity of food, and an opportunity to see Duryea's men, in full regimentals, sleek and clean, fight a sham battle, while we in rags and tatters are onward for sixteen more miles on the 21st, and fifteen on the 22d; two days of heat through pine barrens, nothing stopping us but the Rappahannock River at Falmouth, a thunderstorm, and the mercy of General King, who ordered us to camp in a plowed field, where after the storm our beds would be soft enough in mud nearly a foot deep. King might go where he pleased, we "went to grass" and camped on it, and as usual took only the top rails to make coffee. King wanted us to move our quarters to the plowed field, and replace the top rails. We did neither; again did he send orders, by a headquarter understrapper, with no better result; then he sent a lot of guards to arrest us. The brigade was just as ready to pitch into King and his "gingerbread," "band-box fellows," under such circumstances, as into the Johnnies. The boys stayed "in clover," and King kept himself, aide and guard in comfortable quarters at a mansion fair.

Matters were not mended the next day, when it was learned that McDowell, in whose Department we now were, had given orders that the men should carry their knapsacks, blankets, five days' rations and forty rounds of ammunition. This produced general discontent, and serious threats on the part of some officers that they would resign if the order was enforced, and some of the men vowed that they would not obey. There were some things our brigade would not do for any man. This was one of them. Yet the men who stood for their own rights could ever be depended upon to contend to the death for the rights of their country.

Colonel Carroll was at this time commander of the Fourth Brigade of our Division, and the left flank, while our brigade, the First, was on the right flank, with our regiment, as it had been from the first, on the right of the brigade.

On the 21st we were reviewed by Lincoln and Stanton and other notables. It was intended that we should accompany McDowell, with his thirty thousand men and one hundred guns, on his march south for fifty miles, and join the right wing of McClellan's army before Richmond, which could be done in three days, since there were only twelve thousand Confederates to interfere with the project. Our division rested, bathed, fished, washed, explored the regions round about, and returned in the evening to learn that rations were to be cooked and the men ready to march early in the morning, in the onward to——Shenandoah Valley once more, after Jackson, who had driven Banks up the valley, and Geary and Duryea had fallen back to "protect Washington," and themselves.

It was no great surprise to men or officers. Kimball's prediction made the evening before we started "on to Richmond," and concurred in by other officers, "that in two weeks General Banks will be driven up the valley, and the work of a whole winter and a whole spring will have to be done over again," had come to pass. Washington was now again nearly frightened out of its wits, the militia called out, and McClellan forgotten.

The Valley business demanded haste, and we were off early on the morning of the 25th, and by way of Catlett's, Turkey Run, Manassas, Hay Market, Thoroughfare Gap, Rectortown, Manassas Gap, a distance of one hundred miles, came in sight of Front Royal at 10:30 on Friday, the 30th of May; Company C having been sent forward as skirmishers, saw the enemy fleeing, and smoke rising as of buildings on fire; hastened forward on the double-quick, followed closely by the entire force, entered the town, removed two carloads of burning muskets from other cars and depot buildings; many of the loaded muskets becoming heated, kept up a dangerous fusilade and drove the men from the cars and a burning building.

In the meantime part of the Eighth Ohio came in on another side, assisted in capturing over one hundred prisoners, mostly the sick and stragglers; Ainsworth's Cavalry, supported by some of our regiment and others, dashed after the retreating foe, saved the bridge one mile north of the town, and released many more of Banks' men.

Three locomotives, ten cars, a large amount of muskets and equipments were saved. Companies B and C were detailed as provost-guards, and took charge of the town and prisoners.

The next day McDowell arrived with a number of his troops on the cars, a day after "Shields' light-horse cavalry had made the one hundred miles on foot." Canonading was heard toward the west; Fremont with his usual rapidity of movement had fallen upon Jackson. It had rained in torrents. Our division must again rush forward, this time to intercept the enemy by way of the Strasburg road. For some reason, Shields having taken the wrong road, was permitted to continue up the Luray Valley. On the 2d of June, the men having stood in the rain for a long time, lay down at night without supper, and moved hurriedly forward the next morning, the 3d, until 10 o'clock, without breakfast. Torrents of rain and swollen streams prevented marching on the 4th, as well as the order that Shields should protect his rear and at the same time head off Jackson, while McDowell, Banks and the militia protected Washington. The humble private could see through and into such a state of affairs and wondered what "nincompoop" was in command of the United States Army. Rain did not keep Fremont from pounding away at Jackson, as we could hear his cannon. Rations were becoming very scarce; fresh pork, mutton and flour-paste cakes—"slap-jacks"—made us a very unhealthy diet. On the 5th, Shields was reported to have issued a cranky and uncalled-for order, to the officers, that "if any of them did not wish to go with him, they should resign and leave, and he would fill their places with better men." Columbia Bridge was reached at night, but we were ordered to return at once to Luray, on account of a probable flank attack by Longstreet from the direction of Culpepper Court House.

On the afternoon of the 6th, Companies B and C marched to a ferry near the town of Massanuten, destroyed several flat-boats used some days previous by the Confederates. One of the boys tried to buy something of a woman to eat, especially bread and honey. "Honey? I'll put daylight through you!" hissed the "Seceshess," as she attemped to snatch his gun. Morning came; her sheep, calves and "porkers" were missing, and forty-five beehives had yielded their contents. "You'ns 'ell ketch it, when the Kurnel, my husband, gits hold of you'ns with his ridgement!" she screeched at the backs of the men as they started for camp with their forage of honey and fresh meat.

On the 8th of June all baggage was stored in Luray, and Columbia bridge was reached at 5 P.M., but the command (First and Second Brigades) hurried on until late at night, and started early the next morning up the valley on a forced march for some twelve miles, when it met Generals Shields and Carroll with the remnant of the Third and Fourth Brigades; cheer after cheer went up from these poor comrades, who had to contend against ten times their number at Port Republic, and were compelled to fall back after they had again and again hurled back superior numbers, and even now kept at bay the large force that was follow-

SURGEON H.M. McABEE.

ing them; these halted when they heard the cheering and saw Companies C and F of the Fourth coming toward them as skirmishers, supported by a heavy force. We were now only some two miles from Port Republic, where had this morning of the 9th occurred one of the most fiercely contested and important battles of the war. Jackson's whole army was near at hand, driven by Fremont; Carroll having been forced back by superior numbers was not able to burn the bridge, which was a very unfortunate circumstance for us. Could he have done so there might have been excellent chances of bagging Jackson's entire force. McDowell might have given his men more to do than to make excursions through the country on the cars, following up our division as it moved on foot, had it not been for stringent orders from the Secretary of War to make no movement that would throw his forces out of the position of defending the National Capital; thus, now, as in other instances, did the "shakiness" of politicians and others at Washington interfere with success in the field. McDowell could not move beyond Front Royal for fear that some one might move between himself and and the Capital; therefore our division must move away from its base of supplies against a greatly superior force. Shields had instructions to keep his men well in hand and permit no part of his force to be advanced beyond the immediate support of any other part. This was a very difficult order to obey, since Jackson's retreat is to be cut off, and the very probable attack on the flank by a force from the direction of Culpepper must also be guarded against; the order was not, and very likely could not have been obeyed, under such circumstances. Generals Carroll and Tyler, after they saw a large number of reinforcements rushing across the bridge and advancing against our two brigades that had stood their ground so bravely, ordered and conducted a retreat in an orderly manner, and their men were in their places, marching in good order when we met them, although the enemy was close upon their heels.

The four brigades now marched back to near Shenandoah Furnace, a distance of some eighteen miles. Surgeon McAbee entered the enemy's lines under flag of truce to obtain permission to care for our wounded and bury our dead, but was refused because Jackson had already planned a movement, which he intended in accordance with instructions from General Lee to keep "secret from friend and foe;" he did keep it until a very short time before he fell upon McClellan's flank and forced him back to Harrison's Landing.

Our division reached Luray on the 15th, rested the next day and explored Luray Cave, received two months' pay the follow-day; a number of men were without shoes, and had actually worn their feet until they left the blood in their tracks; we were beginning to be a ragged set, when on the 18th the new clothing that was issued put upon us again the appearance of decency, if not of comfort. On the 20th the Regiment, by some streak of good luck, was put on board a train and started for Manassas, but it was hardly out of sight when an orderly who had been detained a short time by the breaking of his saddle girth, brought instructions for the entire division to move on foot. The regiment went into camp for a week at Bristoe Station, where on the 22d the band received its new instruments, purchased by voluntary contributions of officers and men. The remainder of the division arrived on the 24th.

## CHAPTER X.

FROM BRISTOE STATION BY RAIL TO ALEXANDRIA—BY BOAT DOWN CHESAPEAKE BAY, UP THE JAMES RIVER —HARRISON'S LANDING—SKIRMISH—"THE GLORIOUS FOURTH"—SKIRMISH—CAMP LIFE—DIGGING TRENCHES MORNING AND EVENING—TRANSFERRED FROM THE SIXTH TO THE SECOND CORPS—GRAND REVIEW.

At Bristoe we learned that McClellan was getting the worst of it near Richmond, whither Jackson had rapidly moved after his escape at Port Republic, and fallen upon the right flank of our army. On the morning of the 29th of June came the order to "Pack up." Our destination was immediately guessed; there was manifest entire satisfaction in getting out of the command of McDowell, in whom the men had but little confidence, into that of "Little Mac," in whom they will soon be compelled to have less. The cars could not carry the men fast enough, as whooping and cheering they faced the eastern breeze, and the Capitol soon appeared in sight, and we were at last going into Richmond with the Grand Army of the Potomac.

The morning of the 30th found us aboard of the South America, with the loss of Captain McMillan, of Company E, who who had lost his balance while on the dock, and disappeared in the darkness and watery deep. Before 8 o'clock Fort Washington and Mount Vernon were passed, the band sending forth its plaintive tones, which, with the historical associations of this sacred spot, put everybody into a quiet for some time, in spite of the bracing air. Chesapeake Bay was reached before night, Fortress Monroe was passed at daybreak the next morning, then the wrecks of the Congress and Cumberland; before night Jamestown was found to have no attractions for us, and that at City Point there was neither point nor city, but the

"Grand Army of the Potomac" came into view, with its "everybody help myself" sort of condition; for it was not possible to discern any appearance of organization.

We remained on board until about one o'clock the next day, awaited orders on shore until four, and then waded through the mud for some four miles to a point near Herring Creek and Charles City road, drew up in line of battle, and thus made the best we could of a rainy night, on the soft beds that soon soaked us to the buff. The entire region was a vast mud-hole; wagons and cannons were in to the hubs; some mules failed to reach bottom; drivers were swearing, officers "cussing," mules braying; at places horses, mules, wagons, caissons, cannons, everything, was huddled together; nobody seemed to know where himself or anybody else was, or where "Little Mac" had gone; gaunt, lean, tired, hungry, muddy men, were inquiring in plaintive tones for regiment, brigade, division, and even for their corps. "The whole army is lost," said some of the "original thinkers." We had changed by the right-flank and the left-flank so often that we could not even tell anyone where to find the James River. Midnight came and no sleep, on account of the moist beds, the braying, cussing, whooping and halloing; straggling men were telling their sad stories; some of our boys became provoked at their version of affairs, but soon all were satisfied that the Army of the Potomac had done some hard fighting and could have gone into Richmond if we had kept Jackson in the Valley. The men that were asking for their regiments did not seem demoralized; they were as ready for the fray as ever; none were more indignant than they when it was reported that McClellan was on board of a gunboat considering the policy of surrendering his forces. They condemned in unmeasured terms any such proposition, and had sooner died fighting than surrender; it was no fault of these men that in this swampy country, wading through mud, water and underbrush some had lost their commands.

We were now in Kimball's Brigade, Second Division (W. F. Smith's), Sixth Army Corps (Franklin's). We had nearly three thousand officers and men in the brigade present for duty.

On the next day, July 3d, at 11 o'clock, we crossed Herring Creek; the skirmishers soon discovered the enemy beyond a small swamp at the intersection of the road on which we

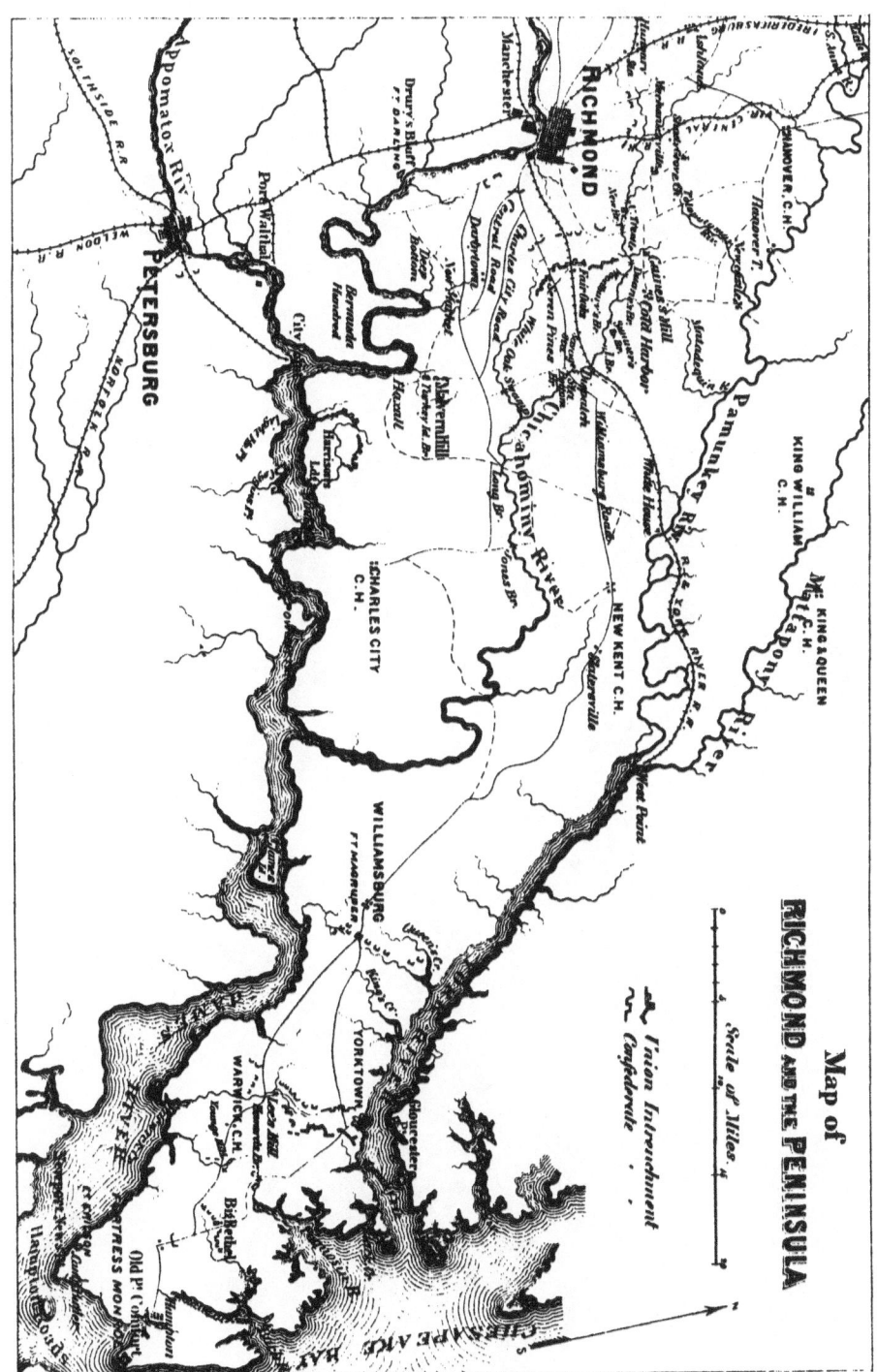

marched and the Charles City Road. General Kimball, commanding the brigade, having gone to the front was fired at by sharpshooters. The brigade was immediately ordered forward to take the guns. The Fourth marched in line of battle on the right of the road, the Fourteenth Indiana on the left and the other regiments were held in reserve. Soon after the entire brigade had moved rapidly forward to take the guns, General Ferry having command of the division, ordered a halt just as the enemy fell back nearly half a mile. The brigade soon moved forward; the Fourth on the right of the road, the Seventh West Virginia and the Fourteenth Indiana on the left, with the Eighth Ohio supporting Tidball's Battery. The Fourth soon reached a strip of woods and underbrush some twenty rods wide, waded through water at places nearly knee deep, and was shelled most vigorously as soon as we reached the edge of the woods and were in full view of the enemy, loading their guns a short distance beyond us and across a ravine. We were at once ordered to halt and lie down; at first the shell only cut the leaves and limbs of saplings, but soon they struck a few feet in front and flung the dirt over us. At this juncture Tidball's Battery opened vigorously upon the enemy, just as we reluctantly obeyed an order to fall back, while the two regiments on our left across the road moved forward on the double-quick but not soon enough to capture the guns that had been silenced. Several prisoners were captured. This position was maintained. G. Witlinger of the band was killed; William Kepler of Company C, J. McKnight of D, and C. Erline, J. Hardy, A. Kightlinger, J. F. Mummea and J. Studdebaker of K, were wounded.

Early on the morning of the 4th the rebel pickets were quite demonstrative; their fire was vigorously returned by our pickets, who were in charge of Lieutenant Laird; the brigade was again in line ready for action; the picket line was advanced and a position taken that gave us the advantage over the enemy. At noon the booming cannon made us at first suspect a general engagement, but it was soon learned that it was the firing of the national salute. We heard no orations nor the reading of the Declaration. The men were engaged in making their quarters as comfortable as pine boughs for shade and bed could make them. Boats with provisions and clothing, sutlers with luxuries and paymasters with greenbacks, were soon on hand; our baggage was brought to camp and soon the army showed but little indication of the hardships through which it had passed. The heat shortly became excessive. On the 8th there was a grand review, when men swung their hats and cheered to the echo. The boys concluded that "army headquarters" must be a mighty affair, if one could judge from the grand display of orderlies and aides that rode tantrum after the General.

The boys spent evening after evening in songs and mirth in the shelter-tents, surrounded by pine boughs that were from four to ten feet high. The rations were mostly corned beef, beans and hard-tack; coffee was rather scarce, and the water very filthy. There was almost daily inspection and policing of the company quarters; guard duty, except picket guard, was light; at times the thermometer rose to one hundred degrees in the shade. Squads were at work on fortifications from daylight until nine in the morning, and from four until dark in the evening. The workers were divided into reliefs, each relief working twenty minutes, and then resting on account of the excessive heat.

On the 16th of July we moved camp to join Sumner's Corps, and lay in the hot sun without any shelter for eight mortal hours. No one knew why. Neither the Chaplain nor Surgeon had ordered it. Such treatment would sicken a dog. On the 22d there was a grand review by Sumner, at which our regiment made a slender appearance, three hundred and six having been reported unfit for duty. Our designation now was: First Brigade, Second Division, Second Army Corps, Army of the Potomac.

On the night of the 31st the enemy shelled our shipping with forty-three guns, sending consternation among sutlers, contrabands and adventurers, but their batteries were at once silenced by the gunboats. Some men slept so soundly that they did not hear the terrific uproar nor see the magnificent display of fireworks.

On the 10th of August we marched to Malvern Hill and were held in reserve until the next day, when all the troops returned to camp, McClellan having received positive orders from the President to report his army at Washington, because of our unhealthy locality.

The Brigade (Kimball's) now numbered 103 officers and 2,217 men, present for duty.

## CHAPTER XI.

THE MARCH DOWN THE PENINSULA — ON THE STEAMER CAHAWBA TO ACQUIA CREEK—ON THE LONG ISLAND TO ALEXANDRIA—MARCH TO CENTERVILLE—COVERING RETREAT OF POPE'S ARMY — ORDERED TO FORT GAINES TO RECRUIT STRENGTH.

On Saturday, August 15th, all of the regiment, who were not able to march were ordered to go on board of the transports; although they left camp before noon, and in an hour reached the wharf, they lay there until nearly midnight before the last of them went on board the boat. The troops had gone and rebel cavalry traversed the camps to and fro in search of booty, and were so busy that they did not offer to molest our sick, of whom there were over five hundred ready to take ship for Alexandria.

The remainder of the regiment started with the brigade on the afternoon of the 16th, forming the rear guard of the army, and marched five miles; was on picket at night, and enjoyed the luxury of roasted ears of green corn for breakfast; all were glad that they were not compelled to go on board "the lousy boats," on account of sickness, although the marl-dust with which we were covered was nearly as bad; we soon passed Charles City, which consisted of one Southern mansion, a country tavern, one law office, and some half a dozen low, dilapidated, 16x20 wood colored shanties in the background; we took our dinner of corn in the bounds of the corporation—that is, on the Tyler farm—the birthplace and home of a President of the United States, who had died in Richmond in the beginning of this year, a Secessionist and traitor. We crossed the Chickahominy on a pontoon bridge a quarter of a mile long, then over a narrow causeway, with swamp on either side, and went into camp at about 2 o'clock the next morning; on the afternoon of the 19th we passed through the old capital of Virginia (where Patrick

Henry made his famous speech), the curious and antiquated town of Williamsburg, and the entrenchments that had recently been thrown up, noticing the bullet-marks on trees, extending from the roots to the very tops, but most abundant at the height of six to twelve feet; nine miles more brought us to within two miles of Yorktown, where for more than a mile the river was literally filled with men that were bathing and diving for oysters; it was a grand time for the boys and worth more than a month of hospital endurance. Yorktown could hardly be seen, when we marched by it the next morning, on account of the high fortifications, which had not, it seems, been taken into consideration by McClellan when he ventilated his plans before Lincoln; quite a number of huge shells were lying about, that had doubtless been fired from the gunboats; one of the boys grasped one of these monsters, thinking he could easily lift it, but found, to his astonishment, that he could not even turn it on end although he might have won a bet of five dollars by so doing; the "thing looked so bilious" that no one else tried it. The old lines of Cornwallis were eagerly looked for, and it was a satisfaction to learn that our boys were pretty well posted concerning the facts of his surrender, although it was sometimes manifest that in the estimation of some officers, brains and acquirements did not amount to much, or that themselves had it all, and that probably wisdom would die with them; our brigade had none such; if it had had, the boys would soon have stung them out by their sarcasm; for the most bitter sarcasm mortal ever heard was uttered occasionally, without fear or favor, by men in the ranks of Western regiments; officers dared not punish such offenders of propriety, because such offense was never given except when well deserved, and because the boys stood like brothers by any comrade that "acted white;" woe to the man that put on airs, blessed the officer or private that "behaved himself like a white man."

The evening of the 18th found us in camp near Big Bethel, weary and dusty; on the afternoon of the next day we found ourselves at Newport News, where apples, peaches and melons were in abundance, with but little money in camp; this was so because some men spent everything freely as soon as they got it, others had to pay debts, while others sent nearly every cent to widowed mother or needy brother or sister, saddened that they could do no more than hand over to loved ones the pittance of a few "greenbacks" given to a private, for the greatest risks that are ever taken and the severest hardships that can be endured. About this time a private received about five dollars in gold per month. For two days it was rainy, misty and disaagreeable. Several of the boys had a new experience, that of bathing in the ocean brine whilst a rising tide was making off with their clothing, which had been left on the sandy beach, near the water's edge.

On the 25th we were transported to the Cahawba by the Canonicus; raising anchor early the next morning, we passed the new Ironsides, a school of porpoises, disembarked by Acquia Creek at noon on the 27th, went into camp for a short time, heard heavy firing toward the west, and at evening went aboard the Long Island, where we were so crowded that there was hardly standing, much less lying-down room; having reached Alexandria at 11 o'clock the next day, and lounged about the dock for two hours, we went into camp some two miles from the town; the next day, the 29th, heavy firing was frequently heard toward Manassas; at five in the evening we moved forward about eight miles, and found ourselves at early dawn of the 30th near Chain Bridge, but a short distance from our sick that had been sent by boat from Harrison's Landing; about noon we were furnished extra ammunition, and at 2 o'clock were hurried toward Fairfax, which we reached before dark, and a halt made late at night near Centerville; fully one-third of the men had fallen out of the ranks because of weariness and sickness, but most of them came up before the command moved forward the next day; it was almost impossible to keep in the ranks whilst one had to march in quick time around numerous ambulances, wagons and buggies, running counter of men rushing frantically to the rear, announcing, some that "we whipped 'em," others that "it's another Bull Run." About all we could make out was, that by the way we were hurried up our services were needed at the front, and very likely, too, Pope's gasconade proclamation to his troops had had all the gas knocked out of it.

The morning of the 31st was misty and cloudy; after breakfast we were moved to the heights of Centerville, from which we could see our men coming from the direction of Bull Run; many as they passed us asked why we had not come sooner, since they had with inferior numbers contended with the same force that had beaten McClellan; men of both armies looked for their friends and acquaintances; matters as well as men were freely discussed. Porter and King were severely censured by their own men; remarks like the following were frequent: "Lee and Jackson pull together, our generals don't;" "McClellan wanted Pope to get whipped;" "He thinks he is bigger than Lincoln;" "Our generals are a jealous, incompetent set;" "Banks is a good man, but no general;" "Pope is no coward;" "They ought to give us better generals." The dissatisfaction was almost universal.

A great battle had been fought; Sigel's and McDowell's corps, of Pope's Army of Virginia; Hooker's and Kearney's Divisions Third Corps, and Reynolds' Division of the First Corps, Army of the Potomac, and Reno's Ninth Corps, had driven Jackson from a strong position behind a railroad embankment, when Longstreet opened from the left flank a destructive fire of musketry and artillery, enfilading the victorious troops, compelling them to fall back to a new position, which they held until dark, when they began to fall back to our rear, because their provisions had given out. Jackson attempted to cut off the retreat by falling upon our forces at Fairfax. To Franklin's and Sumner's Corps had been assigned the double duty of resisting a front and flank attack, until all who had been engaged the day previous had started for Washington, whither all the troops had now been ordered by General Halleck; we were just preparing to bring up the rear, when firing was heard to the north of Fairfax, just as a severe rainstorm burst over us and checked hostilities, while night put an end to farther demonstrations; it was Jackson's attack at Chantilly; had it been earlier in the day, our corps would no doubt have come upon his right flank, with good chances of gaining a great victory.

Our brigade was the rear-guard until we reached Fairfax, where we learned the sad news that Generals Stevens and Kearney had been killed the evening previous at Chantilly; the latter especially was well known, and had the unbounded confidence of all who knew him.

Now came the experience that always tried a soldier's patience until many had no more patience left to try; it was the slow marching in the dead hour of the night, moving a few steps at a

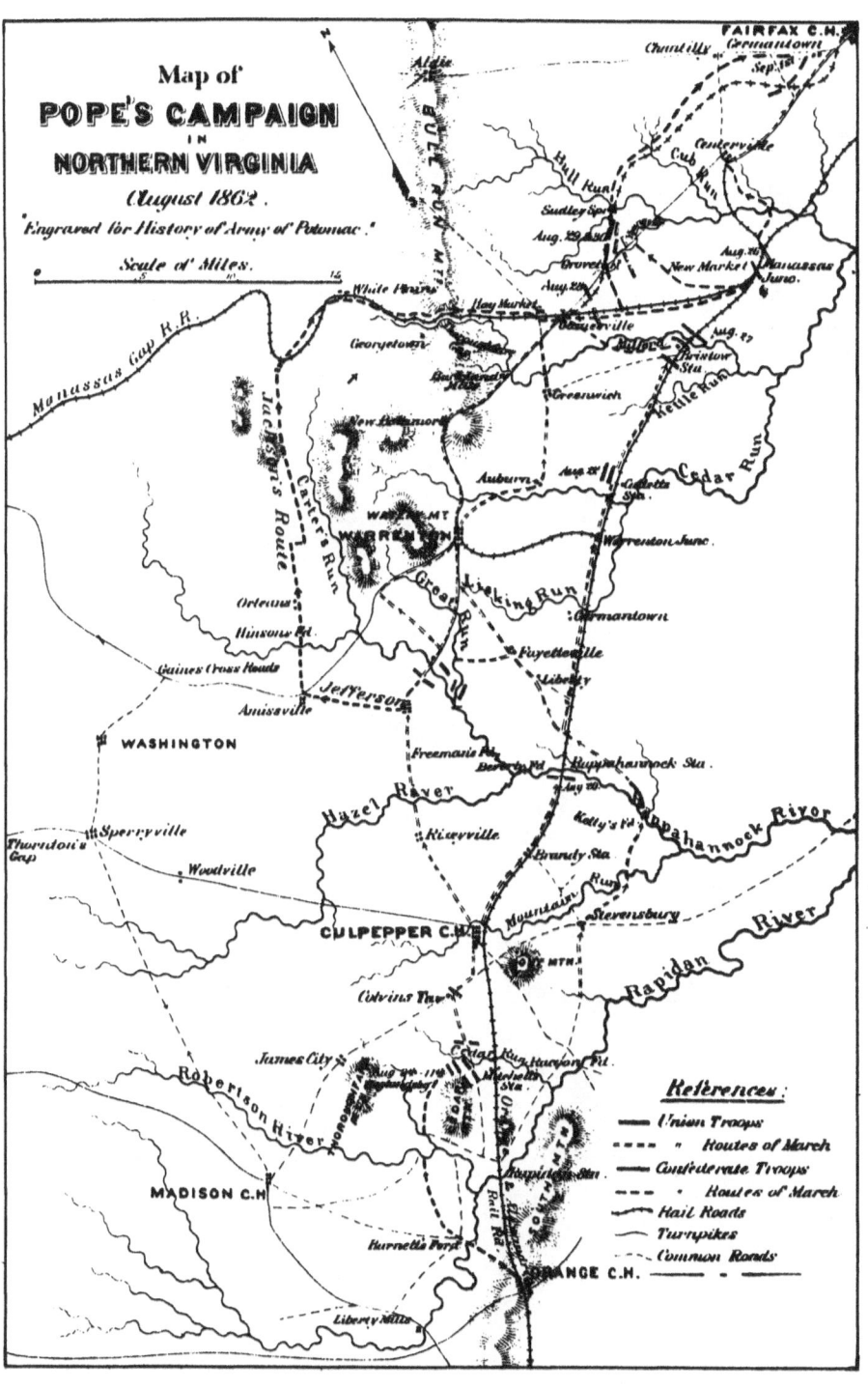

time, then halting a few moments, then onward a few steps more, then standing with knapsack getting heavier and eyelids becoming more and more unmanageable, marching while asleep, butting against the load on the back of the man in front; or possibly some weary arm drops the gunbarrel on the head of a comrade, which starts a torrent of epithets from the mouth of the sufferer, waking up everybody within range, some of them just in time to find that they are standing or wading in water over shoe-top deep; occasionally one lies down only to bounce up again, and before he has time to settle back there comes another halt, and he thinks it is of no use to squat this time as they will start in a minute; he stands awhile with gun at a shoulder-shift, until it gets most wretched heavy, he then brings it to an "order," leans upon it, and tries hard for a long time to keep awake, and from blessing somebody, steps to the roadside, bends his weary joints to lie down, when he hears the command, "Forward!" Frequently soldiers become so weary of such marching that they will, either alone or with some trusty comrade, nestle down for the night, and take the risk of being captured or of having to make a forced march in the morning to overtake the regiment. Rapid and continued marches were rather exhilarating, if not too long continued; slow and broken gaits were exhausting, but the fits and starts—no gait at all—could hardly be endured by the most pious. We marched all night, and at breakfast at 9 o'clock on the 3d of September, we were yet in sight of Fairfax, having gone about three miles in twelve hours, and were wet to the skin, and blinded most of the time by burning baggage. At five in the afternoon we made a forced march to Falls Church. On the 5th we marched with the corps beyond Rockville, Md., where the One Hundred and Thirty-second Pennsylvania took our place in the brigade, and our regiment, in compliance with orders from McClellan, marched with its handful of men to near Fort Gaines, in the District of Columbia, to recruit its strength.

## CHAPTER XII.

CAMP OHIO—STATEMENT OF REGIMENTAL SURGEON Mc-ABEE, AS TO THE CAUSE OF SICKNESS AND DEATHS IN THE REGIMENT—REJOIN THE SECOND CORPS AT HARPER'S FERRY—MARCH TO LEESBURG—PROVOST GUARD—GETTING READY TO FOLLOW LEE.

It is at this point due the many comrades who had far sooner laid down their lives on the bloody field than to be sent to any hospital, and there waste to death with loathsome disease, as well as to those who in part recovered, that the following from the pens of Colonel Mason and Surgeon McAbee, is placed on permanent record:

"Decimated as we have been, without having been slaughtered in battle, it is due the public as well as the men who have campaigned it through two summers and one winter in the mountains, that the facts as to our condition should be published. When the regiment disembarked at Harrison's Landing, Virginia, with only their haversacks, ammunition and arms, to help cover the left front of the retiring Army of the Potomac during the first night, to skirmish all the next day the regiment numbered over eight hundred men, present for duty. But a fortnight had hardly passed until more than five hundred of that number were put *hors du combat* by that scourge of the Peninsula which has cost us more by far than the audacity of Davis, the cool, quiet planning of Lee, or the far-reaching flank movements of Jackson.

When called in from the front, attached to Sumner's Corps and ordered into camp along with the rest of the reserves, it happened that our camp was located upon a low, flat, sandy triangle, of the most recent diluvia or drift, which was washed on the south and east by a little stream into which the filth of more than a city was daily emptied, and which was held at bay by the rising tide twice in twenty-four hours; and skirted on three sides by a wood where an army stepped aside every day "to corner their feet," and where lay in putrescent death, horses, mules and horned cattle.

The only water sources in such a soil were a little below the surface, or if lower down, they were filled by direct and easy percolation through a very open sieve, which let the surface drainage through, with all its stains of filth, to be dipped up and drank by thirsty men, as poison, for water.

## CAUSES OF MUCH SICKNESS, STATED.          81

Soon a diarrhœa of the meanest kind attacked vigorously the right wing of the regiment, and swept across it to the left, cutting down men by platoons. In three or four days after its approach but one medical officer was left fit for duty, and he had the snug little task of prescribing for from three to five hundred men daily. From the Colonel down every shoulder-strap and chevron bowed to the hateful thing, until literally every man was victimized."

---

SURGEON'S OFFICE, FOURTH REGIMENT O. V. I.,
CAMP NEAR NEWPORT NEWS, VA., August 24th, 1862.

SIR:—I have the honor to represent the following facts connected with the sanitary condition of the regiment which you command, viz:

1st. Of ten companies numbering nine hundred and nine enlisted men, there are not to exceeding three hundred in good physical condition, present for duty.

2d. During the three months ending June 30th the regiment reported a daily average of seven hundred and forty enlisted men present for duty.

3d. The marked depression of the strength of the regiment is due to the prevalence of a prostrating diarrhœa, which attacked alike the officers and men of the command, on or about the 10th of July, and while occupying a camp near Harrison's Landing, Va.

4th. During the continuance of this endemic there occurred more than six hundred cases (without being associated with a single death from whatever cause), and although its violence has now materially abated, its victims are still haunted with leanness, great muscular prostration, and remarkably feeble digestion.

In view of the foregoing facts, it becomes my duty to recommend and to urge, so far as may be warranted, that the regiment be allowed to remain in camp for a period of not less than thirty days, as being necessary to restore to their accustomed vigor and efficiency the men who since June, 1861, have been constantly engaged in the most active campaigning both summer and winter.

The regiment having been recruited in Central Ohio, it is suggested that their early recuperation will be facilitated by locating their encampment not materially south of Washington City.

Very respectfully,
Your obedient servant,
(Signed)                                    H. M. McABEE,
                                    *Surgeon Fourth O. V. I.*

To Colonel JOHN S. MASON.
*Commanding Fourth Ohio V. I.*

The above communication was endorsed as follows:

Respectfully referred to the commanding General for such action as may be deemed necessary.

This regiment has, until its arrival on the James river in July, been quite as efficient, and probably has seen as constant service since its organization in June, 1861, as any regiment in the field. I only hope that some step may be taken that it may again, at the earliest possible moment, be able to take the field in a condition to render efficient service, with its full strength and vigor, which it is not now able to do, and consequently must necessarily bear the reproach of being classed amongst the poorest of the service—a position which it has not deserved, nor is it one it desires to attain.

(Signed)              JOHN S. MASON,
*Colonel Fourth Regiment O. V. I.*

This communication brought the order from McClellan to go into camp near Fort Gaines; on the 19th of September he sent an order for the regiment to report for duty; this brought a statement from our Surgeon that there were only 185 men fit for duty, and that in his judgment it was a "serious question whether the majority of those ordered to duty are in great danger of early and permanent disability, by being taken into the field before they are permanently restored." That the sequela which is so much to be dreaded, in case the men are now overtaxed and exposed, is typhoid fever, which, when superadded to such a condition, will in a large number of cases result in death, or at least in a complete wreck of health."

The following are additional extracts from Surgeon McAbee's reports:

September 20th. "Of the 635 men belonging to your regiment, but 135 are fit for duty."

November 8th. "There are of the regiment in this camp (Camp Ohio) 140 invalids; there are at Harper's Ferry 350 non-effective men; there are in the field ready for duty but 120; the remainder, almost 200, are scattered in hospitals."

November 23d. "There are in this camp 387 enlisted men, the Chaplain and one Lieutenant."

Camp Ohio was placed in charge of Dr. McAbee, who did all in his power for the welfare of those under his care; three days of each week he devoted to the examination of such as were probably entitled to furloughs or discharges. At first this camp was only intended for the Fourth, but soon many other Ohio men were sent here for treatment. This arrangement ceased about the middle of March, 1863.

From the 8th of September until the 28th, there were two camps near Fort Gaines, the one the hospital, and the other the regimental camp. It was especially desirable to be a member of the regimental camp, where one could eat all the fruit he wished, bathe when he pleased, and stroll to the city whenever he took the notion. On the 14th and 15th heavy firing was heard west of us. On the 28th the able-bodied took the cars near the Capital. Among these were a large number who were hardly able to march two miles, but were determined to try it, rather than remain longer inactive in a monotonous camp; one such, Charles Gray, a noble, intelligent and much beloved comrade of Company C, fainted soon after the cars were in motion, fell out and sustained injuries that eventually proved fatal. Harper's Ferry, and our place with the old brigade on Bolivar Heights, was reached on the morning of the 29th. It seemed necessary for a large part of the army to remain here to prevent a raid into the north.

At early dawn on the 1st of October came the order to be ready to march immediately. General Kimball at the head of his brigade, with Frank's Battery (G) First New York, ten-pounder Parrott guns, and one squadron of the First United States Cavalry, crossed the Shenandoah, marched between the river and Loudon Heights, then up Pleasant Valley, through Waterford, where the Star Spangled Banner was flung to the breeze by several ladies as we approached. Milk, cider, cakes, pies and apples were furnished free. At Lovetsville there were like demonstrations, but at Hillsboro this was reversed, as a woman of some forty summers urged a little three-year-old to curse "Lincoln's hirelings."

The cavalry reached Leesburg before dark; captured several prisoners. The infantry camped some two miles from the town. We started early the next morning to return, halted near Hillsboro at three, moved again at ten, and reached camp at three on the morning of the 3d, having made the distance of fifty-two miles in less hours, through an intolerable heat that caused many to fall out by the way.

On the 4th, we accompanied the Corps on a reconnaisance to Halltown and beyond, and returned on the 6th, having had a little picket skirmishing.

On the 12th camp was changed. From 16th to 19th we were on picket, and thoroughly drenched. Entire regiments went on picket instead of having the picket force composed of a small detail from each company of several regiments.

From the 8th to the 20th quite a number of the regiment enlisted in the United States Regular Artillery.

Ham was 25 cents per pound, cheese 30, eggs 35 per dozen, a can of fruit one dollar, and potatoes two dollars per bushel.

Several of the companies were on provost guard for several days. One day while the provost were enjoying their wormy hardtack and salty pork they spied a neatly dressed woman tripping down street. Many were the demonstrations and numerous the expressions of admiration, and tossing of kisses, and "Oh honey," "Darling," "Tulip," "Rose," were heard, and a score were gazing after her. She turned, and horrors, phew! a face as black as midnight, teeth like toe-nails, "eyes like peeled onions," and a "grin like an alligator," the ugliest visage the boys had ever seen; she stared at them for some time—charmed, fastened to the spot by what she had heard—but could hear no more, and with a kind of scare-me-again expression she moved on, followed by prolonged applause on the veranda of the hotel, and the chorus "Oh the girl, the pretty little girl I left behind me."

One day some lovers of sport filled six large wine bottles with water, corked them neatly, took them just before dark to several officers in command of a battery, and sold to them the entire lot at one dollar a bottle. From some bushes in a ravine that leads into the Shenandoah gorge they watched the proceedings; in less than an hour seven chums were on hand, the corks drawn, the wine sampled, and night made hideous with the uproarious laughter that followed; explanations were in order, and duly made; again and again they wished that they had only asked the men that sold them where they belonged. They never found out.

Our camp was delightful for situation. From an eminence near at hand one could get a view of the town, with its principle street leading up a steep hill, and ancient houses, one above the other on the brow of the hill, with the third story and roof on a level with the pavement; yonder are the chimneys of the old arsenal, and the low engine-house where Old John Brown defended himself; in the river are abutments of the Baltimore & Ohio Railroad bridge; scattered about are the pontoons; right up against and under overhanging ledges of Maryland Heights is the railroad, and within range of a six-pounder are the Loudon Heights; between them, in this transverse valley of the Blue Ridge, thirteen hundred feet deep, the waters of the Potomac and Shenandoah rush together over mighty boulders, in a head-

JEFFERSON ROCK.

long race for the ocean; up the Potomac are the now historic Falling Waters, South Mountain and Antietam; on yonder heights Miles might have kept the entire force of Jackson at bay, and insured the utter rout of Lee before he reached Antietam, instead of showing a white flag and surrendering eleven thousand men that were eager to honor their country with the sacrifice of their lives, if need be.

Many of the boys clambered upon Jefferson's Rock, stood upon the same spot where Thomas Jefferson once stood, and viewed the same grand scenery which he said was worth a journey over the Atlantic to behold; near at hand, but down in a deep gorge, the Shenandoah leaps, rushes and foams against the massive abutments of the Blue Ridge, and over huge granite boulders that had thundered down the mountain side ages agone. All this magnificent scenery did not satisfy; it would do well enough in times of peace, when one with loved friend, in stately drawing-room and not box cars, could take his time along the entire route. We had been here long enough; Lee had been granted abundant time to gather the entire harvest in the very productive Virginia Valley; rains would soon fall and then he would get nearer to a safe base of supplies. The soldiers as well as the government were getting out of sorts with McClellan. Some said he would move just as soon as the rains began to pour. Our camp was getting very filthy; many were sick, not sick enough to go to the hospital, nor well enough to march; officers and men, since the Leesburg forced march, did a "rushing business," night and day, until the diarrhœa had threatened to turn them inside out, so that when the order came to be ready to march, every soul was glad save those that were so reduced that they were not able to carry a gun nor endure the cartridge-box or belt buckled over the stomach; because of this a large number of sad boys were left behind; some fifty could not be moved, and over two hundred were taken to Camp Ohio.

# CHAPTER XIII.

LEAVE HARPER'S FERRY — SNOW STORM — McCLELLAN RELIEVED — BURNSIDE ASSUMES COMMAND — MEN OVERCOME BY THE HEAT — CAMP AT FALMOUTH — SUMNER'S THREAT TO BOMBARD FREDERICKSBURG.

At four on the morning of the 30th of October came the order to be ready to march, followed by the consequent hurry and bustle that attends the taking down of tents, cooking three days' rations, cleaning guns, filling cartridge-boxes with ammunition, packing the wagons, going to the doctor's call to find out who is well enough to march and who is sick enough to go to the hospital, where he is likely to get sicker. At five in the afternoon we crossed the Shenandoah, were soon rounding the Loudon Heights, moving up Pleasant Valley, and went into camp several miles from Hillsboro, tired out with the fearful load of bulging knapsack, bursting haversack, sixty rounds of ammunition, heavy gun, woolen blanket, rubber blanket and shelter tent, with possibly the additional articles of canteen and frying-pan. We laid down to sleep as soon as the guns were stacked, having satisfied our hunger by an occasional raid into the haversack whilst on the march, taking out a morsel of cooked beef, or a piece of hardtack with a pinch of sugar, in case the latter had not already mixed itself through everything. True, a cup of strong coffee would have tasted so good; most of us would be willing to testify that there was nothing that gave such tone, strength and vitality to a weary, sleepy, "done gone" soldier, as a black quart cup full of foaming hot coffee, and it also added to the variety; coffee, tack and meat for breakfast; tack, coffee and meat for dinner; meat, coffee and tack for supper, varied occasionally by scorched beans, or rice, or even spring chicken, and possibly roast pig, as opportunities for foraging did abound. Such an opportunity presented itself this night, for just as we had taken a good nap a sleepy lieutenant came with an order for a goodly number to go on picket. "Where? How far?" was asked. "Oh, not far," came in a tone of pity from the noble Dolbear, that showed the feeling he had for his weary comrades. It was but a short distance: some twenty rods away, at a crossroad, where troops and trains were passing all night; where crowing roosters, quacking ducks and noisy geese had their necks wrung, and carcasses plucked and roasted; where shoulder-straps and chevrons counted themselves in with the boys, so that when morning came the nasty-smelling, new haversacks (now "called de groats") were heavier than ever, and the belt buckles had to be let out a notch or two. These little episodes made marching desirable.

The next morning we moved several miles further up the valley, taking time to club the persimmons, picking up the solid as eagerly as the mushy ones; some were so nice about it that they would not even touch the "nasty, smashed things;" soon there was as much expatiating as in an ordinary town council; the solid things puckered and double-and-twisted the lips, cheeks and tongue, so that it was difficult to talk or swallow; some remarked that "they would so pucker their 'innerts' that they could not keep goose and duck from spoiling;" others concluded that a peck of persimmons ought by all means be sent to the convalescents at Camp Ohio, as "they would just do the business better than quinine or blue-mass pills."

At ten the next morning, November 1st, the march was resumed, and enlivened by the firing at the front; shortly after noon some Confederates were seen in Gregory's Gap, and the order was at once given to form in line of battle; Lieutenant Colonel Godman, in command, led us rapidly forward until we were even with the skirmishers; in an orchard some excellent apples slackened the pace for a short time; presently the Gap was reached, but not a sign of the enemy remained, but eastward on hills and plain was the magnificent spectacle of over one hundred thousand men, with their camp fires and thousands of white, canvas-covered wagons; night came on, when in the mild breeze groups of men from jutting cliff and huge rock gazed upon the inspiring scene, in the meantime arguing concerning the merits of commanders, maneuvers and campaigns, or having a social chat.

The next day was occupied in easy marching and the Fourth deploying as skirmishers into Snicker's Gap; several squads of the left flank, clambering over rocks, found their way far enough through the Gap to enable them to see that quite a force of Confederates were in the Shenandoah Valley. Captain Jones went over into the valley, where he came in short range of the cavalry, and not returning until late at night it was thought for some time that the daring man had been captured. General McClellan came along at evening, as we were going into camp near the town of Snickersville, and was most heartily cheered by men who had in the weeks gone by done considerable growling at his expense; General French, our division commander, had the implicit confidence of all.

On the 3d the army marched in several parallel columns, halted frequently, and went into camp between Ashby's Gap and Upperville, where most of it remained, having most delightful weather until the 6th, when by a rapid march Rectortown was made by noon, where Colonel Mason, on his return to the regiment, received a most hearty greeting from officers and men; the afternoon was spent in marching over rough, stony roads to Piedmont, where we went on picket, and returned the next morning to the brigade in a heavy snow storm; in the afternoon some of us went on picket on the farm where the Confederate General Ashby had been raised, by his uncle; on the morning of the 8th the pickets were hurried back to their regiment, and then all rushed forward toward Salem, through melting snow, going into camp several miles southeast of the town, from which we moved at nine the next morning, going into camp in the afternoon, where wood and good water was abundant. The next day, the 10th, McClellan, in reviewing the troops, was greeted with tremendous cheers all along the line, but before night it became generally known that he had been superseded by General Burnside, which was condemned on all sides as a most ungracious act; complaints were bitter and criticisms severe, but when it was learned that the President had made the change at his own option, and although the confidence of the men in McClellan was great, in Abraham Lincoln's honesty and judgment it was unbounded; they believed he had had good and sufficient cause to warrant the change, even at this time, so that before the day had passed criticisms ceased and general confidence prevailed, save the criticism that somebody was permitting Lee to escape.

The regiment now had one hundred and ninety-six officers and men for duty. It was now known that Longstreet was ahead of us, and Jackson over in the valley, and that the army had been divided into three Grand Divisions, and that General Halleck had been consulting with Burnside for two days, each giving color to the rumor that we were to have a general engagement very soon; the weather was exceeding fine during our eight days' sojourn at Warrentown, but the 15th doomed us to a long tramp through dust, and close, sultry pine forests, when many overpowered by the heat dropped out of the ranks; yet the next day, with its rain in the forenoon, and our slipping, sliding and dodging around the wagons, as wagon-guards, for fifteen miles, capped the climax; for the greater part of the way there was no place to squat down to rest save on the damp mould of the pine forests, where in a few moments wood ticks were in one's shoes, climbing up the legs, crawling down the neck, or lancing a hole in one's scalp, soon pushing their pincers and head through the skin, so that the more one tried to pull the vermin off it only stuck the faster, until off came a part of the body, leaving the head to fester and itch most intolerably for a day or two.

On to Richmond, this time sure, for have we not ten days' rations and one hundred and twenty thousand men, against seventy thousand under Lee? On the afternoon of the 17th our corps reached Falmouth and the troops were as anxious as was Sumner to cross over to Fredericksburg and take the battery and a few hundred men that were guarding the city. But nay, Burnside would not have it so; he had been so intent on getting to Falmouth, that he seemed to forget for a few days to keep himself posted as to the whereabouts of Lee, and evidently thought that his entire force might be on hand to scoop any force that might have been thrown over; it was certain that Burnside foresaw no contingencies, or could not easily change a plan, or consider details and adapt himself to them; he had given orders not to cross, and the orders must not be changed, if for no other reason than to give Sumner and his men to understand that "orders is orders," and that Burnside commanded the Grand Army; already did we begin to lose confidence in our new

Commander in Chief. We remained in camp about two miles from Falmouth. The next day several muleteers, mules and wagons were captured near Banks' Ford, and the brigade was hurried out, only to return in a short time, as the Fourteenth Indiana had accomplished all that was desired. For two days the roll was called every hour. On the 18th Franklin's Grand Division camped a few miles northeast of us, and the next day Hooker settled down about the same distance to the northwest. Soon the Confederate pickets became more numerous, and many of them were busy throwing up earthworks on the Heights back of the city; considerable part of Longstreet's Corps had arrived, and about the 25th, the day the pontoons came to hand, Jackson took his position below the city, so that we had Lee's entire army, huge earthworks and a river between us and Richmond; to all appearances we were farther from that coveted city than ever, and the dissatisfaction in the ranks increased. On the morning of the 21st Sumner demanded the surrender of the city, because from the houses along the river our men were constantly being fired at. The authorities having promised that the city should no longer be used for any warlike purposes, it was spared a bombardment.

# CHAPTER XIV.

### BATTLE OF FREDERICKSBURG.

On the 8th of December the Twenty-fifth and Twenty-eighth New Jersey regiments were assigned to our brigade. Preparations were soon made to go into winter quarters, making the fatigue duty very fatiguing, in the endeavor to hack down and cut up with blunt, serrated and edgeless axes, large pine trees with which to build log huts.

On the fine morning of December 9th came the order to be ready with three days' rations in the haversack. The people of the North kept constantly complaining, "Why don't the Army of the Potomac move?" and the Confederates had their earthworks and cannon ready for us and we had our huts pretty well under way, which gave three very plausible reasons that we ought to move against the enemy. On the 10th there was inspection, and the old song "Be ready to march at a moment's notice," was changed to be ready to march at three in the morning. Morning came with its booming guns sounding reveille; we took our position at about 7 o'clock, between the Phillips House and the river, on the Stafford Heights; a heavy, impenetrable fog had closed down upon the city and both armies; the guns ceased firing, and for a short time all was quiet, when there came the peculiar crack of rifles and wounded men were carried back; the Mississippi Riflemen, from stone walls and houses, had been firing upon the men that were putting down pontoon bridges; orderlies were soon seen galloping from headquarters and General Hunt, Chief of Artillery, along the river with instructions to fire fifty rounds from every gun; from ten until eleven one hundred and forty-seven guns, varying in caliber from a ten-pounder Parrott to four-and-a-half-inch siege-guns sent destruction into the town; the spectacle was most appalling, although nothing but fire, stifling smoke and the sun's red disk could be seen; the city was shrouded in the cloudy, sulphurous gloom, and silent as the grave; not a single response came from the enemy; the mists cleared away, and many houses in the city were on fire; another attempt was made to put down the pontoons, but failed, until the Seventh Michigan crossed in several pontoon boats and drove the enemy through the city. Toward night we were marched near to the Lacey House, and held ourselves in readiness to cross at any moment; many of the men were at the bank, taking observations, as the sun was setting back of the fortifications on Marye's Heights, when there was a puff of smoke that hid its glory, and a frightful whirring noise was heard overhead, probably made by a piece of railroad iron, fired at us to test the range of gun, or as a matter of experiment with such unusual missiles; we were at once marched to the rear under cover.

All slept soundly until four the next morning, when after a hasty breakfast we crossed the river on the pontoon bridge, and immediately, the Fourth being in advance, deployed as skirmishers, up the streets, past the smouldering embers of burning buildings, furniture and dead Confederates; no enemy could be seen, until the outskirts of the city were reached; the people had forsaken their homes, with the exception of a very few; some taking with them all their goods, others leaving pretty much everything in their houses; orders were given to protect the property, and not as much as might naturally be expected was carried away; there were a number of homes that indicated taste and refinement; in Lieutenant Maury's house were entire boxes of maps, charts and books presented to him by the French government; there was but little indication of damage done by the bombardment save the burning of buildings. A few people that remained said that most of their neighbors were back of Lee's forces, in tents and huts, expecting soon to return.

The fog had raised sufficient for operations, and several squads were detailed from the Fourth and sent out in command of Captain Jones to determine the "where" and "how many" of the pickets on the edge of the city; the details moved out on two different streets and were immediately fired upon on Hanover street, and Watson McCullough, of Company C, was wounded, causing a halt, and a sharp engagement until the squad on Princess Ann street took possession of a log house, flanked the rebel pickets, and caused them to fall back; advancing still further they noticed the depot and machine shops, and made for them one by one, under a shower of bullets coming from a new source, a railroad cut, yet no one was hit; here a number of arms were captured and the pickets routed out of the cut; William Kepler, of Company C, happening to be the first man to reach the depot, captured an eighteen by thirty-two inch flag—the stars and bars—which he still has in his possession; the squad now crossed the bridge over a canal, a stream about four feet deep and twelve wide, moved to the right oblique to the house that was the furthest out of any, went up stairs where they obtained a full view of the battle-field of the morrow; looking out the west window, they saw near at hand the pickets taking good aim, and firing on our men near Hanover street; the window was opened and a volley sent into the flank of a number of "graybacks" lying in a ditch, when there was a lively climbing and rushing to the rear by fifty or more Confederates, who did not stop until they were under the protection of their comrades, behind the stone wall, by the telegraph road at the foot of the hill.

After this flank movement there was but little firing back of the city during the day. Before leaving the house a noise was heard in an outhouse; the squad marched to the door with guns at an aim; the door was tried, but found locked; Lieutenant Byron Evans, with drawn revolver, demanded a surrender; in a moment the door was burst open with a stick of cord wood, when, lo! scores of chickens fluttered in every direction; the next morning drumsticks and wish-bones, which had been picked whilst the situation was being discussed, were scattered about a large building.

Franklin, it was understood, had crossed his division below town, and was supported by part of Hooker's Corps. It was concluded that they were to turn the position of the enemy, and that Sumner's Division was to move forward to help in the grand rout, when Jackson's flank had been turned by a coup de main, for it was certain, they thought, that he could never carry the works back of the city by storm, for it was evident that the enemy had complete range, and could concentrate the fire of all his guns to one point, and mow us down. All were pretty well agreed that Lee had us just where it suited him best, and that was the reason he did not reply to our guns the previous day; "he wants us back of the town where he can give it to us," says one; "all creation can't drive the Johnnies out of those breastworks," said another. These men knew as well as any general could know, the entire ground, for they had looked at it for some ten hours the previous day; they knew that troops could cross only at two places over the canal; that there was a rise of ground that must be crossed, and could be swept by a large number of guns; that beyond this was a ravine with the longest slope toward the enemy where his muskets and rifles, fired from a stone wall and breast works, would likely bring down the few that were spared by the cannon; and that if Marye's Heights are taken, there are more guns and troops in earthworks, further back; some of them thought our forces had better go around by the fords up the river.

Nine o'clock of December 13th had come, and with it the order to fall into line; General Franklin was already hard at it on our left; the orders were overheard, "Three regiments are to be deployed as skirmishers, followed by divisions, two hundred yards apart; "do you hear that boys?" says one; "there is going to be some terrible hot work," says another; the men looked downcast; they were willing to do their whole duty, but were perfectly satisfied that it would be a useless waste of lives unless a continuous bridge spanned the length of the drain ditch, and several divisions moved rapidly against the enemy with fixed bayonets.

Colonel Mason was to take command of and advance the line of skirmishers, composed of the following regiments: Fourth Ohio, in command of Lieutenant Colonel Godman, to move on Princess Ann street, as the left flank; the First Delaware, as center, in charge of Major Smyth, was to follow, and the Eighth Ohio, as right flank, commanded by Lieutenant Colonel Sawyer, was to move out on Hanover street; Captains Jones and Grubb, of the Fourth, had been detailed to act as guides, the former of the First Delaware, the latter of the Eighth Ohio. This force was on the first street east of the drain ditch, and parallel with the river; on the next street north—Caroline street—General Kimball was waiting, in command of the Seventh Virginia, Fourteenth Indiana, Twenty-fourth and 28th New Jersey regi-

COLONEL JAMES H. GODMAN.

ments, which were to follow and support the skirmishers; all the streets were filled with infantry and artillery. We had been in readiness for over two hours; the pickets had been called in and were in line; Franklin's and Jackson's booming cannon had been heard during all this time, contending with each other on our left; on our front, Longstreet, as well as we, had remained quiet all morning, probably awaiting developments.

Colonel Mason, commanding the skirmishers, near noon gave the order to advance. Colonel Godman now commands: "Attention! Shoulder arms. Forward—file right—March!" Our regiment, now numbering nineteen officers and ninety-eight enlisted men, moves in the advance, rapidly out Princess Ann street, to the rear of the town, crosses the canal bridge and we are just in the very act of climbing up an embankment two to three feet high, and can plainly see the rebels upon redoubts on Marye Heights move rapidly to and fro, while Godman riding coolly at our head, gives the order: "Deploy as skirmishers! By the left flank!" when there is a puff of smoke on the Heights and two men fall; immediately several more cannon belch forth fire and smoke and sixteen more fall; Peter Akum and Captain Wallace have received mortal injuries, and Godman is wounded in the thigh. The wounded are immediately laid back of the embankment or helped to the house a few rods to our right and soon cared for by Surgeon Morrison.

Hundreds who had watched our advance and had seen the batteries open on us, and the men falling right and left, thought we had been annihilated. Shot and shell are still hurled over, to right, left and front of us, while the line in command of Major Carpenter and Captain Stewart, with the right flank of the regiment at the street and the left flank extending to the right until we join with the First Delaware; we continue on the run up the slope over the rise of ground, down the further slope, under a continued storm of missiles, which does now but little damage to our thin line; we cross a ravine, with its mud and fence, then up the Marye Heights slope, a triple line of rebel skirmishers rapidly vanishing behind a stone wall from which there now comes volley after volley from some half a dozen lines of rebels; again one after another of our boys fall; human nature cannot endure facing such a storm of bullets and not reply; we have reached the crest of the slope and open a vigorous fire.

We hug the ground for some time, hoping reinforcements would soon come to help us drive the enemy from the stone wall; General Kimball's other four regiments now come over the hill behind us on the run, closing the gaps that are made in their ranks by the storm of missiles; they reach us, drop down by our side, and open fire. General Kimball having been wounded in the thigh as soon as the plain was reached, left the command of the brigade to Colonel Mason, and the skirmishers in charge of Lieutenant Colonel Sawyer of the Eighth Ohio.

Nearly an hour has passed by since the ordeal began, when the Second Brigade of our division forms at the canal and comes charging midst a terrific hurling of shot and shell; crosses the ravine, comes up the slope, drops down at the crest and joins the general fusilade against the stone wall. In like manner at intervals of less than half an hour comes brigade after brigade, doing just the same things, rush over the plain for one-third of a mile, over dead, wounded and dying, closing up the gaps, while the showers of lead and iron leave the field more difficult to cross because of the increased number of mangled remains that must not be trampled into the earth; French's Third and last brigade is followed by Zook's, Meagher's and Caldwell's Brigades of Hancock's Division; at about four o'clock comes Howard's Division, Owens' men first, then Hall's just as we were relieved by two regiments of Sully's Brigade, and soon the other two regiments tried the ordeal, followed to the first slope by Hazzard's Rhode Island battery, which being terribly handled by the concentrated fire was soon relieved by Franks' New York battery. At this juncture Humphrey's Division, just at the time when most of our regiment are able to get back as far as the buildings, goes forward as if determined by running toward the Heights and cheering vociferously they could strike consternation into the rebels that were safely cuddled down behind the stone wall, where nothing had as yet molested them or made them afraid.

We had thus seen thousands of men come over the slope and get down at the crest with us before the Heights and there remain, while on the hill and slope behind and among us the sight is horrible and heart-rending; hundreds of the bleeding and mangled are dragging themselves from the dead and dying, are trampled upon by the thousands, many of whom in the excitement hardly knew whither they were going save to the certain slaughter. Wounded men fall upon wounded; the dead upon the mangled; the baptism of fire adds more wounds and brings even death to helpless ones; as we look back the field seems covered with mortals in agony; some motionless, others are dragging themselves toward the rear; occasionally the shell or cannon ball that comes into their midst, sends arms, hands, legs and clothing into the air; on the front line there is no safety, for here men fall; our colors for a moment are down, for our noble color-bearer George B. Torrence, (after whom the G. A. R. Post at Delaware is named,) falls, having his head blown from his body, leaving his blood and brains upon comrades and the flag. It is a baptism of fire and blood. Blood is everywhere. Overhead is a pandemonium of shrieking missiles. Comrade is separated from comrade by the thousands that have come to the crest and there huddled together, so that several of our boys fall, no one knows when or how. Some were so separated that they did not see a soul they knew, as they were lost in the mass until they returned to the rear in the evening.

By about 4 o'clock our ammunition was gone and all had been used that could be found upon the helpless and dead; the entire brigade was ordered to fall back into the town, form in line where we had formed in the morning, get ammunition and await orders.

When we reached the house at the outskirts a wounded comrade called to the writer, "Company C, take me along;" again and again did others use the same words, and beg most piteously and in imploring tones, "Take ME along;" a solid shot fired at Hazzard's Battery plunged through the house; returning comrades heard the imploring voices, were asked to take hold of doors, boards or window-blinds, place a wounded man upon each and take him to the rear; Aide de Camp Lester, with orders from Mason, came to hand at this juncture and ordered that every man be removed as soon as possible, as the house would probably be shelled; not a man refused to do his utmost, and soon every wounded man was removed to the rear and placed in charge of surgeons. It was none too soon, for shot and shell came with a vengeance before the last man was carried away; one of the shells plowed through the bed from which Chaplain Warner's son, "Tommy," had just been removed.

We shall never forget how a comrade asked to relieve us, took hold of the improvised stretcher in our place, nearly reached the bridge, when a solid shot took him and the wounded comrade through their bodies, neither ever knowing what had befallen him. At this juncture, just as Humphrey's men were going forward, a plucky little fellow of some sixteen summers came from the front, swinging the stub of his right arm, from which by shreds dangled his hand and the spurting blood describing a circle he shouted at the top of his voice, "Hurrah! Hurrah for the Union!" and his watch-word was vociferously echoed by the line that was just passing as the little fellow sank to the earth.

The carnage would certainly soon end for the sun was getting low and nothing had been accomplished. Men were getting angered at the useless slaughter. Says one: "Great gods, if only one of those shells would take Burnside on the head!" Surely there was reason for complaint, when men are sent in to be whipped by detail. It was certain, too, that our men would obey orders even though it is a forlorn hope.

"Six times," says Lee, "did the enemy, notwithstanding the havoc caused by our batteries, press to within one hundred yards of the foot of the hill, here encountering the deadly fire of our infantry." Some of our men were within twenty-five paces of the stone wall and not a single line went nearer the enemy than did the skirmish line at noon. Before us, behind the stone wall, were massed four brigades: Cobb's, Kershaw's, Cook's and Ransom's. Says Ransom: "Another line was formed by the enemy, he all the while keeping up a brisk fire with his sharpshooters—few lingered under cover of fences and houses, and annoyed us with a scattering and well-directed fire."

Night came on; our thin ranks were very much thinned; we had gone into the fight with nineteen officers and ninety-eight enlisted men; we lost one officer killed and four wounded, two mortally; six men killed, thirty-four wounded. During the entire night could be heard the moaning, groaning, and shrieks of our wounded; many of the poor fellows were brought in under cover of darkness; the lower rooms of houses in the

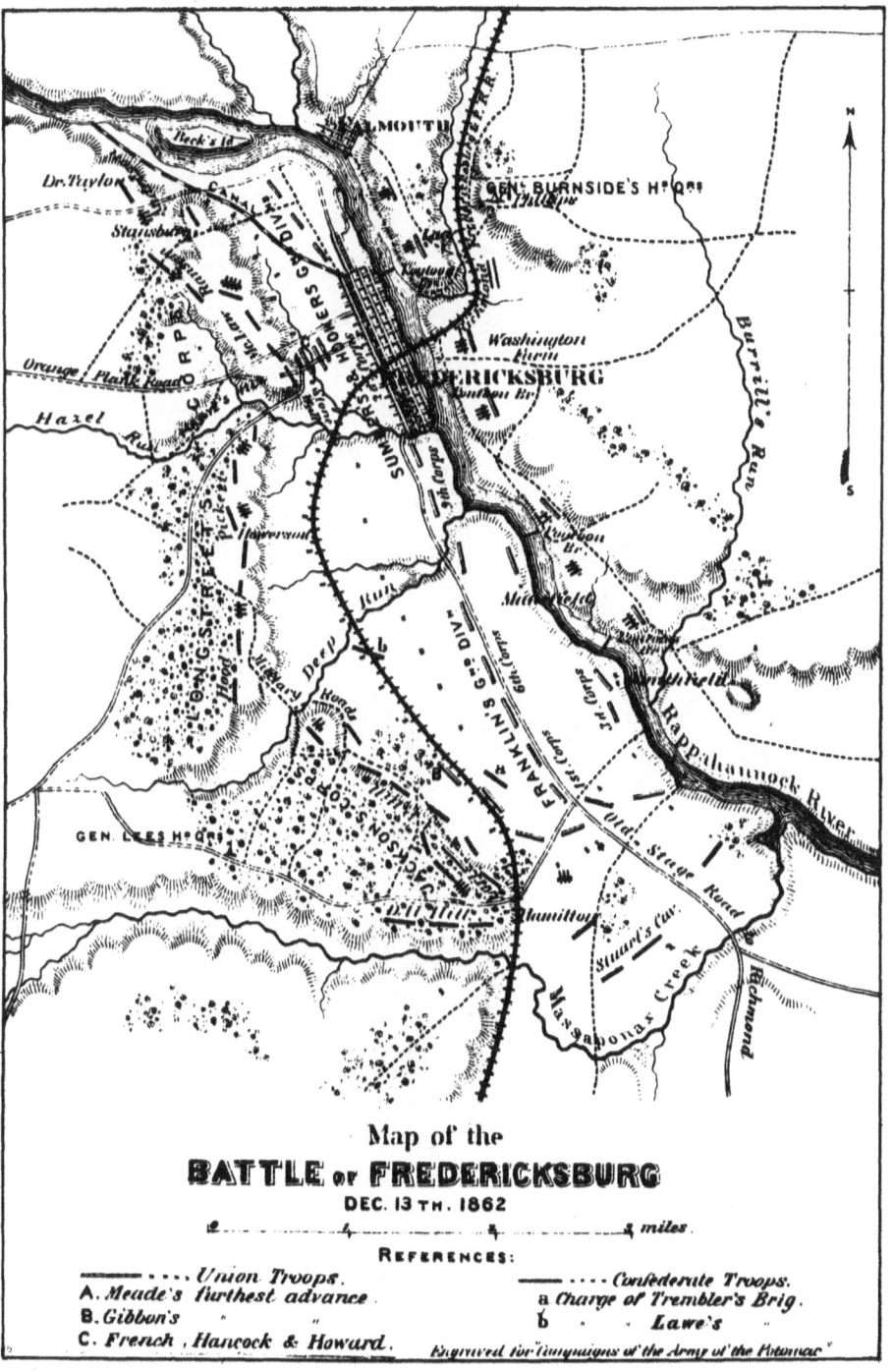

town were filled with the wounded; surgeons were exhausted with their tasks; masses of blood were upon floors; legs and arms lying in heaps.

The next morning we were again in line. The Ninth Corps was in readiness. Burnside threatened to lead his old corps and take the Heights at the point of the bayonet. General Sumner persuaded him to do no such thing. Had he placed dozens of bridges over the canal on the night of the 12th and then ordered his men to attack with empty guns and fixed bayonets he would doubtless have driven the enemy at the first onset.

Burnside, in his report, says: "For the failure of the attack I am responsible, as the gallantry, courage and endurance shown by the men was never exceeded, and they would have carried the points had it been possible." General Couch says: "General Kimball's brigade was in front, and by its subsequent conduct showed itself worthy to lead."

On the morning of the 14th there was a skirmish, but nothing transpired save the caring for the wounded and sending them north as fast as possible. In the evening the heavens were lit up by the aurora. The mail was distributed; many letters were for fallen comrades: missives of love never read, never answered. Morning came again and with it the order to make out reports of losses and the part taken in the action. Colonel Mason commanded the division and Colonel Sawyer the brigade. We had our quarters along the south side of the river. The roll is called; instead of the familiar "Here," came the answer, "Killed," "Wounded," and caused a breathless hush as of death. Oh, the horrors of war!

On the 15th nothing special transpired. At night we recrossed the river and returned to our old quarters on Claiborne Run, and slept in a driving rain.

On the forenoon of the 16th there was regimental inspection, and in the afternoon the brigade was drawn up in line of battle in the rear of the camp in expectation of an attack from the direction of Banks' Ford, where a fatigue party had been fired into as it was going after wood.

On the 17th some of the men, having assisted in the burial of our dead, brought back word how our fallen comrades had been stripped of their clothing; making it the more difficult to identify them. In camp there was an irrepressible gloom, so much so that comrades wept as they talked of their beloved brothers who had so uselessly laid down their lives. Some of the log huts that had been begun had not a man return to occupy them; every hut had less men to finish it. On the 22d, when the huts were all ready, there were only twenty-eight men present for duty subject to detail. Surgeon Morrison was with us and was kept busy. Dr. McAbee was still at Camp Ohio with the convalescents. The baggage for officers and men now began to be brought to camp. Lieutenant Dickerson was Quartermaster of the regiment and Lieutenant Underwood of the brigade. On the 24th we were reviewed by General Sumner, and in the evening, it being Christmas Eve, camp was once more lively for the first time since the battle. Major Carpenter was in command of the regiment, and Mason, now a Brigadier General, commanded the brigade.

On the 29th, 30th and 31st, we were ready, with three days' rations and sixty rounds of ammunition, to march at any moment. Burnside had determined to retrieve his misfortunes by an attempt to flank Lee's position. The cavalry had moved down the river to be followed by the infantry, when President Lincoln sent him word that no movement should be made before he had been notified. The forces returned to camp and Burnside went, after some hesitation, to Washington, and there learned that he had been preceded by some of his general officers with complaints of lack of confidence on the part of officers and men in their General in Chief.

On the 14th the officers of the regiment at a called meeting passed suitable resolutions in respect to their fallen comrades, and also for Lieutenant Lippett, who had died at his home a few days previous.

The following is a list of killed and wounded as taken from the Roster:

Company A—J. B. Woolverton, wounded.

Company B—Lieutenant George Brophy, C. Bergan and O. L. Stoughton, wounded.

Company C—George Torrence and George Ropp, killed; T. C. Warner, wounded; Watson McCullough, died of wounds.

Company D—J. G. Baily, H. Heater, F. Herbert and M. McCan, wounded.

Company E—Lieutenant Brighton and D. Hummer, killed; A. Dice, wounded.

Company F—L. D. Hane, killed; Captain Wallace and F. Sell, died of wounds; F. B. Hane and S. P. Sylvester, wounded.

Company G—F. Brant, killed; F. Beck, D. Griner, G. Jones, A. W. Jamison and J. S. Philbrick, wounded.

Company H—J. B. Walker, killed; J. B. Kearfoot, died of wounds; Capt. Pritchard, N. Durfee and T. C. Likens, wounded.

Company I—Captain Ferguson, P. Akum and T. Plant, died of wounds.

Company K—T. McCullough, wounded.

## CHAPTER XV.

"BURNSIDE STUCK IN THE MUD"—IS RELIEVED AT HIS OWN REQUEST—HOOKER TAKES COMMAND AND REORGANIZES THE ARMY—WINTER QUARTERS OF 1862-3—FURLOUGHS GRANTED—PREPARATIONS FOR THE CHANCELLORSVILLE CAMPAIGN.

Very few returned to us from the hospitals, so that we were but little more than a corporal's guard when Burnside reviewed his newly shod and clothed troops on the 17th of January.

After a vigorous division drill by General French, Division Commander, we were dismissed with the exhortation to "be ready to march at a moment's notice." Some of us were engaged in constructing corduroy roads, over which Hooker's and Franklin's Grand Divisions were beginning to pass, with pontoons, ammunition trains and artillery. Most of the troops were in high glee, whilst confidence in the commanding general was rapidly being restored, for "he is going to make the right move this time, flank Lee's position and make him get out of his breastworks." We had taken the shelter-tents from the huts, where they had served as roofs, packed our knapsacks, while the winds were getting chilly, the clouds growing denser, and night came with its pitchy darkness and mist, then rain followed by torrents, that continued with but little intermission for several days, in spite of which a hunchbacked-looking mass of humanity waded and staggered on toward the upper fords, until the evening of the 21st found the "Grand Army stuck in the mud;" and such mud, like "Burgundy pitch and plaster," the more one tried to pull out of it, it only stuck the faster. Desperation again seized the "now-or-never" Burnside, who in defiance of the elements determined to put down his pontoons by hitching not only team to team, but also men by the scores to his boats; horses, mules, men and boats were simply stuck; it was far easier to pull than to walk; men in stocking feet made lunges for their disappearing boots; night came again, the troops squatted down into the mud; those that had not left camp spent the night wet and shivering on their soaked bunks. Early on the morning of the 23d the troops were straggling and struggling back to camp; roads were blockaded, wagons upturned; wagons, guns and caissons were in to the hubs; whips were cracking, mules whinnering, teamsters cursing; after several days all was again quiet on the Rhappahannock, and the sun once more beamed upon men and things that had settled down in camp. Burnside again made a trip to headquarters, now to request of the President that his order to dismiss Hooker and others, and to relieve Franklin and certain others, should be immediately seconded or his own resignation accepted.

At the close of January General Mason was granted "leave of absence, on account of ill health," and Colonel Snyder, of the Seventh West Virginia, was in command of the brigade. Many untoward circumstances conspired to bring about a gloomy state of affairs. Many of our comrades had been "slaughtered;" the "peace party" in the North seemed to aid the enemy by their large majorities; our mails came loaded with their documents, and doings; the idea of freeing the slaves was obnoxious to many; the heavy fatigue and picket duties, with the seemingly useless regimental guard, the exchange of coffee, tobacco, ideas and feelings with the "Johnnies" on the picket lines, the resignation of officers, and the refusal to grant "leave of absence" to officers and furloughs to enlisted men, whilst they were being granted in Lee's army, helped in the general discontent. Many men conceived the idea that an officer—who had enlisted under the same conditions as an enlisted man, and even as such, but had in some cases by mere fortune, fortuitous happenings, through friends or otherwise, been given authority to put on shoulderstrap, and too often permitted himself to lord it over his betters, it was strenuously held—had no more moral right to resign than a private. That all had enlisted as privates, and that promotion did not set aside the original contract to "serve for three years or during the war;" again, there could be no move made within three months, and many were already at home and the authorities did nothing to bring them back, and since friends at home were so many of them threatened by their neighbors that called us "hirelings," asked us by all means to come home, and that when there were so many that did absent themselves without leave, more could, and no one would be punished, and all could soon return in case they were needed, and there would be a saving to the government, and everybody would fight better after he had seen the loved ones at home, were among the many plausible things that men set before themselves, and some, many, (but few in our brigade) in the army, took "French furloughs," and thus swelled the number of absentees on detached duty, sick, with and without leave, from the Army of the Potomac, to nearly three thousand officers and about eighty-two thousand enlisted men, when General Hooker took command on the 25th day of February. He at once ordered companies and regiments to send him the descriptive list and whereabouts of every officer and private; this he followed with an order for every able-bodied man to return to his command immediately or be treated as a deserter; he at the same time granted leave and furloughs for two weeks at the rate of two men from each company. This was fair dealing, and appreciated by the men, who were now willing to swear by "Joe" Hooker, and fight with him, after all had returned to their commands. In a few weeks hundreds of men, cleanly dressed, could be seen coming into camp, ofttimes amid the most vociferous cheering by those who had borne the brunt of battle, and endured the hardships of camp-life duties in winter. The entire army was reorganized; the cavalry was made efficient; huts were built for the pickets; these had no longer to stand, as ofttimes before, for an hour, even in several instances for two hours at Corps Headquarters, in the cold, awaiting orders or for some disgruntled officer to head the column, if he was sober enough to do so; incompetent and disloyal officers were removed. Corps badges were adopted; to our division, the Third, was assigned the blue treefoil. After this, for a year, we wore the blue treefoil on our caps, but at the reorganization, in 1864, we changed to the white treefoil.

In March the mud began to dry up, when drills and reviews were more frequent; camp wore a more cheerful aspect, as men were almost daily going home, whilst many were returning with greetings and numerous tokens from the friends left behind us nearly two years agone. We were constantly assured by the returning ones that most of the people were as loyal as ever, and as much determined as at first that the rebellion must go down. Men told us that they were anxious to return as soon as the two weeks were up, and showed by their willingness to do duty that furloughed men enjoyed their huts and put up with the monotony of camp life with more patience than ever.

As to the style of the huts, "deponent is at a loss to give it; some huts reminded one of pictures of heathen temples, others of a Yankee woodshed; some of an Indian wigwam, many not unlike the Dutch cow-barn; others of a woodchuck's hole; but the Hottentot style seemed to predominate." Before the month of April all the forests with the exception of a few trees had been cut away, and the camp surroundings were cheerless enough to give the most vivacious soldier the blues; the chimneys of red clay and cross-sticks, bordered by the dirty brown shelter-tents used as roofs, added their somber associations to the now desolate scene. The fireplace was generally in the center of the twelve by twenty to thirty-foot hut; the bedstead usually extended the entire length of it; when first built the roof gave a mild, pleasant light, but now the accumulations of vapor, smoke and grease brought darkness, nearly total, on a rainy noon day; of these we had enough to satisfy the laziest hireling that ever steadied the April plow. Says one: "It seemed as if the rains would wash away our dirty continent."

There were rumors and sensations. Occasionally a chimney would be on fire, which gave the fire brigade a chance to halloa itself hoarse; sometimes fifteen or twenty men would "make a brigazee" for the door, and "vamoosed the ranch" as if the deuce were after them, but it was only the smoke, when the wind was the right way and filled the domicile, that caused the scatterment; some showed their knowledge of Bible by quoting the wise man's sayings concerning a brawling wife and a smoky house; others had forgotten the admonitions of the Book, as they heaped curses upon the already tottering chimney; but when the hut was full of smoke, and the rain poured through the roof and filled the remainder, whilst twenty men with weeping eyes and howling throats all tried to cuddle on to one possible dry spot, and no one could do the thing justice by a new set of imprecations, than the whole "menagerie" was "on its ear." Yet how strangely different when, with smoke and rain, midnight darkness also filled the ranch; then there was a lying closer together, blankets drawn over the head until toes were to the weather; meek as a March lamb, shaking and shivering, men waited for the joy that might come in the morning; ere the early dawn some one crawls out, starts "a tremendous smudge with the wet and green pine," and again buries himself in his blanket, woos sleep and comfort until a roaring fire lures and an all-goneness at the stomach compels another venture when it is nearly noon. The days are spent in reading, writing letters, posting the diary, or possibly in a friendly game of "seven-up," or dominoes, sewing on buttons, mending and patching, burnishing guns and bayonets, and watching the pot; in the evening the games may continue, stories are told, "yarns spun," campaigns planned, officers praised or blamed; at "Tattoo" all are expected to quiet, and at "Taps" to have gone off to sleep.

After the 1st of February Colonel Brooks of the Fifty-third Pennsylvania Volunteers, was in command of the brigade for some time, then a Colonel Robinson; afterwards, on the 13th of April, Colonel Carroll gladdened everybody by taking charge of the men who best knew his worth. General Couch was in command of the corps, and reviewed it on the 5th of March, when our regiment was augmented by a large number who had now returned from the hospitals for duty; officers and men appeared in their new clothing with the blue treefoil on their caps.

On the night of the 9th we were routed out and formed into line of battle, and again on the night of the blustering 12th of March, to guard against a cavalry raid. On the evening of the 15th the lightnings flashed and the thunders rolled. The 17th turned out to be a holiday for officers and men of the corps, as the majority spent the day in witnessing the hurdle races, and ludicrous scenes in commemoration of St. Patrick. The nonsense closed with the order to fall in, for the rebel cavalry was making a raid to our rear. During the greater part of the 18th there was firing to our rear. On the 19th it snowed nearly all day, and on the 20th it snowed and rained, ending in rain for the 21st and 22d. On the 27th, Major General French, commanding the division reviewed our brigade of six regiments, in the presence of the Governor of New Jersey, and on the 30th most of the men listened to speeches from Governor Morton and General Meredith to the Fourteenth Indiana.

On the morning of the 31st the ground was covered with snow and slush. On the 6th of April "Honest Old Abe" reviewed the troops near Stoneman's Station; the President rode at the head of the cavalcade, followed by Hooker and Staff, these by corps and division commanders, a detachment of Lancers bringing up the rear, all having moved at a gallop.

On the 14th orders were received to be ready to march at a moment's notice, with eight days' rations in knapsack and haversack, to which was to be added sixty rounds of ammunition. Of course none of the generals were to carry any such amount, and very likely never had, but it did seem to the boys that these dignities had an idea that they were in command of a lot of pack-mules; there was but little complaint, for there was now to be "no more monkeying around," and everybody felt that "Fighting Joe" meant business, and if the rations could not be carried they could easily enough be thrown away when the load became too burdensome; stringent orders were given with reference to the economical use of the sixty rounds of ammunition; the boys believed in less ammunition and more bayonet, and with "Brick-top" as their leader, they were ready to engage an equal number of Louisiana Tigers," or to scoop the "Stonewall Brigade," which they afterward did at Gettysburg, at the point of the bayonet; "Go in on your muscle," was the motto of the "Gibraltar Brigade." Very many of the men would not carry more than forty rounds, because they would not be made pack-mules of for the sake of any general.

The 14th and 15th were rainy days, very much interfering with the movements of our cavalry on rear and flank of the enemy. The week ending with the 24th was very rainy, cold and blustering, making any forward movement entirely impracticable, but the few fine days that followed brought a renewal of the order to be ready, and on the 27th started Meade's, Howard's and Slocum's Corps, the Fifth, Eleventh and Twelfth respectively, up the Rappahannock.

## CHAPTER XVI.

### BATTLE OF CHANCELLORSVILLE.

On Tuesday morning, April 28th, 1863, we were routed out at four, and at six started in the rain up the river, out of sight of the rebel pickets, and reached the United States Ford at eleven and bivouacked, with twenty-one officers and three hundred and forty-five men present for duty.

Early the next morning, April 29th, we relieved the Sixty-ninth New York from picket. The pontoons came up late in the evening, and the Pioneer Corps at once proceeded to put them down, stopping not for the darkness nor the heavy rain of Thursday morning, April 30th. We were mustered for pay. The Eighth Ohio relieved us from picket. About four in the evening we moved with the advance across the river, sent out skirmishers, marched over breastworks, halted until the entire corps had crossed, and then about sunset started into the dense forest; soon met a number of prisoners; continued for several miles, and about ten bivouacked where our road emerged from the woods and crossed the White House plantation, about three-quarters of a mile on the hither side of Chancellorsville.

Chancellorsville was simply a fair-sized brick building, at a cross-road, the intersection of the north and south United States Ford Road with the east and west Turnpike and Orange Plank Road. The plantation was about one mile long, some fifty rods wide at the eastern end, and gradually widening toward the western to about one hundred rods, and lay in a northeast and southwesterly direction, with Fairview Cemetery forty rods south of the plank road in the western center, Hazel Grove, half mile south, and Chancellor House at the cross-road, near the eastern center of the plantation. The plank road passed just south of the house, then entered the woods some seventy rods west,

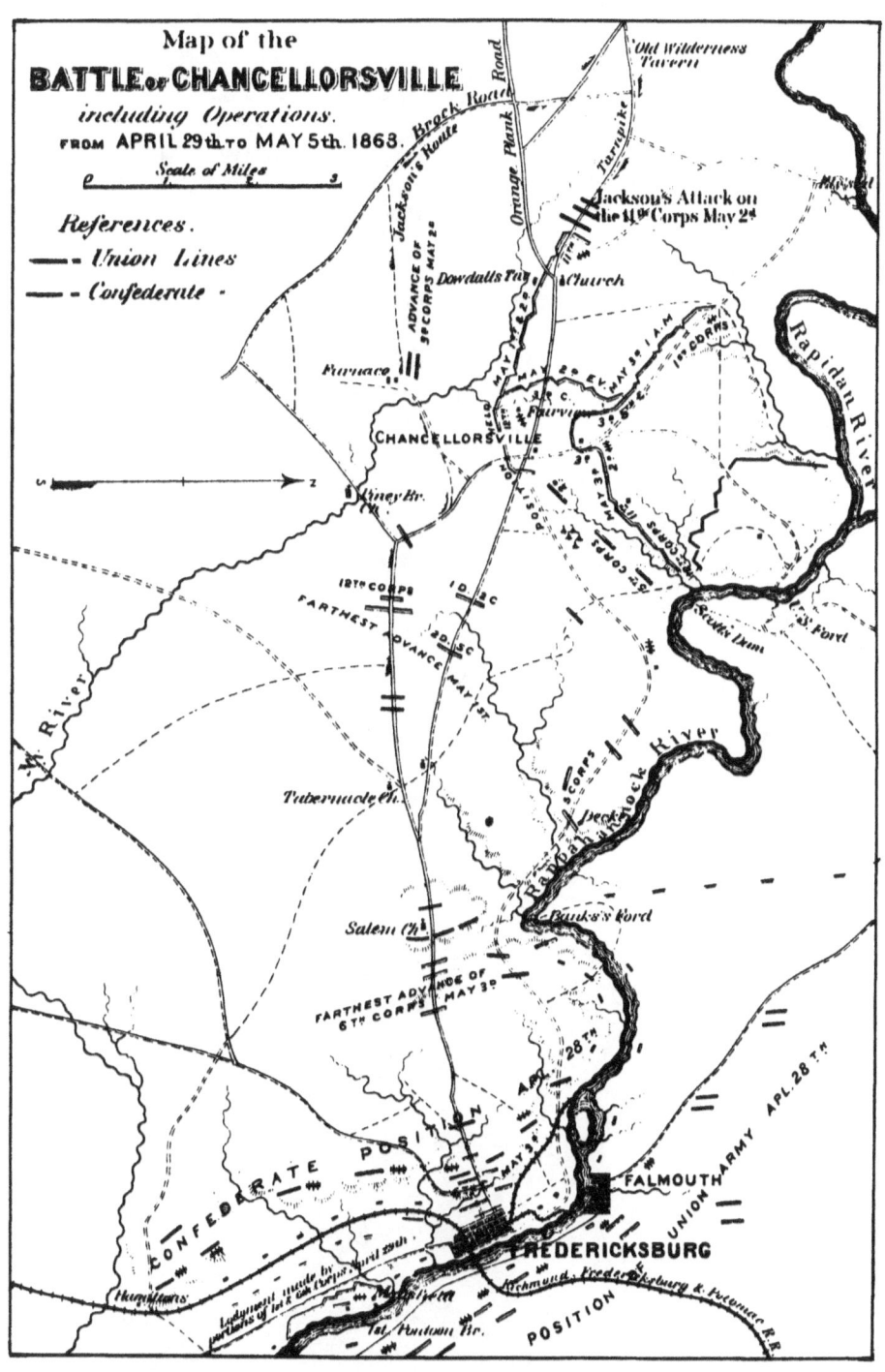

passed down and over a ravine of about sixty rods from crest to crest, by the brow of the western slope where Jackson was wounded, then west one mile to Dowdall's Tavern. For the past hundred years much of the timber throughout this entire region had been cut down for use in mining operations, and had also been burnt over, so that which remained was mostly of a scrubby nature, making a jungle of scrub and burr-oaks, scrub-pines, whortleberries and brambles, in places almost impenetrable, especially to the soldier loaded down like a pack-mule with eight days' rations, sixty rounds of ammunition, blankets, shelter-tents, haversack, canteen and gun; especially would these catch in the hard and spiny branches, hold one to the underbrush, while spines, leaves and branches would take him in the face, head and neck; the haversack was frequently torn from the shoulder, and one must halt to secure his "all," in spite of imperative orders to "Forward."

Friday, May 1, 1863. Every man that had left camp with the regiment answered at roll-call this morning. We retained our position during the greater part of Friday forenoon, while Hancock passed us, drew up his division in line of battle nearly two miles east of the Chancellor House, on the turnpike, with the Twelfth Corps to his right on the Orange Plank Road. About noon these forces were ordered to fall back a mile nearer Chancellorsville. About the same time our brigade had orders to march, passed the White House along the Ford road, and took position sixty rods east of Chancellor House, while heavy firing was going on east of us. After an hour, Carroll, in accordance with orders, massed his brigade in the woods immediately south of the turnpike, and on a slightly easterly slope, where it remained for several hours; the firing in front came nearer, but soon slackened to mere skirmishing. About 4 o'clock, just as the brigade had been ordered to fall back to its old position, the enemy sent shot and shell near the place we had just left, striking consternation among cooks and camp followers, who at once made a "brigazee" to the rear, to the supreme delight of the boys that carried the muskets. The guns were soon silenced by our batteries, and skirmishing continued. By 9 o'clock firing had mostly ceased, and we lay down to rest feeling certain that the morrow would quite likely be a bloody day. The men looked well to the condition of their ammunition and guns, thinking that the booming cannon would doubtless sound the reveille that should wake us from slumber to slaughter. Naught disturbed us during the night.

Saturday morning, May 2d. Morning broke quietly upon the contending forces, that seemed loth to begin the fray, for not a gun was fired before sunrise, when shots were sent after a moving column near the furnace, and a demonstration was also being made to our front and left. At eight we were drawn up in line of battle, one-quarter of a mile to the right and rear of the White House, nearly at right angles to the position just occupied, and skirmishers were thrown forward toward the southeast, on our front. We now joined Hancock's position on the right and Sykes' on the left. About this time Couch, Hooker and others were inspecting the Union position. During the afternoon we felled trees to form an abatis, and dug rifle pits and occupied them until the next day. There were many rumors that the enemy was rapidly retreating, which were generally traced to orderlies and aides, but not believed by the men. Says one "Don't fool yourself; Lee isn't asleep; you'll hear from him soon enough, when he's got a good ready." "Why don't Hooker go for 'em, if they are skedaddling?" asked another. Several hours of quietness having prevailed, greater credence was given the reports, causing considerable laxity, as men left spade and the stacked guns to look about, or were taking a nap. Camp followers, cooks, clerks, post-orderlies, commissary sergeants, quartermasters, hospital stewards and musicians felt assured that it was perfectly safe for one to be with his command.

The sun had already run his course sufficient to begin to hide himself behind the tops of some tall oaks, when the remarkable order of Hooker announcing that the enemy must "fight or ingloriously fly," was wafted by the winds to thousands of ears, and thousands of throats responded with deafening cheers, whilst a band struck up "Hail to the Chief;" scarce had its first echoes died away when ominous sounds were heard toward the setting sun; it was the cannon's boom, and the peculiar reverberations of distant volleys of musketry; soldier looked at soldier in astonishment; we were not left to guess as to what was up, for in a moment more there was the fierce scream of shell in our very midst; men flew to their stacked arms; every man rushed to his post of duty; camp followers scampered for a place of safety; the "bass-hornist," not instantly perceiving the fleet movements of his scared comrades, for a moment played a solo, took in the situation, tore the last note into shreds, grasped frantically the big horn and leaped toward the rear. It was now seven minutes past six; orderlies and aides were hurrying to and fro; shot and shell were straying among us; our guns at once replied; the ground was now cleared, and every man was with his company, awaiting orders; soon a number of troops hurried to our right and front; we expected every moment an order to follow; the rattle of musketry toward the right and west came nearer; skirmishing on our front was getting to the proportions of a battle, whilst some of the enemy's guns seemed to have been silenced; soon men with and without arms, mules, teams, crowds of men, came rushing from the west and south, over the roads and through the woods; we were drawn up in line to stop the panic that had set in; in spite of threats, and soon of fixed bayonets, some poor fellows, with eyes starting from their sockets and the expression of maniacs, rushed through our lines, which had been drawn up athwart their direction of retreat; among them it was evident there were some who had had enough presence of mind to tear off their chevrons and shoulder-straps; the panic had not yet stopped, when guns to the right and front of us opened vigorously upon the enemy, and added confidence to the feeling that we should be able to more than hold our own, for the disaster that had overtaken the Eleventh Corps was now known. Night came on, and for a while to the soft, pale light of the moon was added the cannon's vivid flash, and the fire of bursting shells; by 9 o'clock quiet reigned. We occupied the breastworks during the night, slept but little, while troops were constantly moving; some of us had visited friends in the Eleventh Corps, and were asked to tell the story of their misfortunes. At about midnight there was sharp firing to our right and front; both cannons and muskets soon ceased; it was considered as as only a midnight scare of some nervous pickets, and as of no importance, but it happened to be a sad affair to the enemy, for some three of those shots that had disturbed our rest ended the earthly career of Stonewall Jackson.

Sunday, May 3d. On Sunday morning Hooker had determined to take a new position, that of a triangle, with the base at the river, and the apex at the White House, for he feared a raid on his communications. At daybreak the enemy charged our forces at Fairview and Chancellorsville, where a series of charges and counter-charges were made and guns of another corps captured, which drew our brigade into the fray. Shortly before 7 o'clock in the morning General French, commanding our division, ordered Colonel Carroll to form four of his regiments into line of battle, parallel with the plank road. The Twenty-Fourth and Twenty-Eighth New Jersey remained in the rifle-pits, but were afterward ordered into action; the Eighth and Fourth Ohio, Fourteenth Indiana and Seventh West Virginia were formed in line, but the Eighth was soon detached to French's headquarters, and during the forenoon supported a battery; the remaining three regiments moved forward at 7 o'clock at a quick pace, in as perfect alignment as if on dress parade, to the right of the White House, down a gentle slope, the Fourth entering the timber just to the left of where the southeast corner of the plantation angles into the woods, Captain Jones, riding a white horse, having charge of the right, and Major Grubb, on foot, in command of the left wing.

Our column had gone into the woods about thirty yards when it received the fire of some eight battalions of rebel infantry, killing and wounding a number of our men. We reserved our fire, and sprang forward into the low bushes until we could see the rebels, and before they could load again took deliberate aim and mowed them down, whereupon some of them surrendered, and the rest broke, continuing to load and fire at us as they retreated. Several, after surrendering, raised the gun to shoot, but were knocked and kicked until they were glad to "play fair," but it so aggravated our men that they were not disposed after that to show quarter. We kept up a random fire, taking sure aim, and driving the fellows before us in spite of the desperate efforts made by their officers to make a decided stand; we pursued them down a gentle slope over marshy ground, then up a hillside, where another line gave us a murderous volley, killing and wounding more of our men than at the entrance to the woods; we charged upon them with a feeling of vengeance, mowed them down with a deadly fire, took a number of prisoners, and captured a stand of colors; we still followed them while loading, and came upon another line at the edge of the woods to the west of the Chancellor House; here many of them huddled together, and others ran round and round their comrades, trying to shield themselves, and so bewildered that they hardly knew what they were doing, when we delivered another murderous volley into the thickest of their huddles, literally slaughtering them; it was an awful scene; more surrendered; the rest broke and stampeded across the field, over the road, and were joined by another line that was behind the embankment of a wattling fence, and we let them have another round, and followed after, over the field, to some dead horses, abandoned cannon, dead Union gunners, a large number of small arms and much amunition, at Fairview, which it was impossible to bring away. Here was, also, a regiment of zouaves, whom we at first thought were on hand to help us, but soon learned that we had just saved them from a trip to Libby or Andersonville prisons.

The rebels, seeing that we were not supported, began to rally, and endeavored to flank us on our right, just as the order came to fall back; the boys were loth to do so, feeling sure if we only were supported we could have things our own way, as the rebels were evidently at the point of giving up in despair, and now was the time to end the war, capture the rebels, and not make them "ignominiously fly."

Immediately upon falling back our colors were shot down three times, when Major Grubb seized them, waved them to and fro, singing "Rally Round the Flag, Boys," and was joined in the singing by numbers, as we moved slowly toward the rear, followed by the Confederate skirmishers at long range, while a battery on the plank road enfiladed us with shot and shell, cutting the leaves and branches all around and overhead as we entered the woods.

It was near 11 o'clock when the survivors rallied at the position held in the morning. The New Jersey and Eighth Ohio regiments had also returned. One sergeant and six men had lost their way on the retreat, and did not come in until the middle of the afternoon. Chaplain Strong made his appearance about noon, with gun in hand, cartridge box by his side and face begrimed with powder, having endeavored to carry out the purpose he had had when he enlisted as a private at the breaking out of the war. We had accomplished the work assigned us, to hurl back the rebel tide until our forces could establish themselves in the new line Hooker had chosen when he got shaky

Some of the boys saw him about this time in a half unconscious condition, lying by the roadside, and another officer was sitting by and saying "Ha, ha, the Napoleon of the West!" Alek Hays, who was captured, was seen in a similar condition. Some thought they had "had too much commissary."

The watchword of the enemy was "Remember Jackson," and they fought us with vengeance and desperation; they believed that they would succeed in driving us into the river; that morning their their corps commander was cheered to the echo, when at the head of his troops he sang, "Old Joe Hooker must get out of the Wilderness, out of the Wilderness, out of Old Virginia." To accomplish these ends of vengeance and destruction they fought with a desperation that set no value upon life, and it was no wonder that our loss was so heavy. Of this contest General Doubleday says: "It was a combat of giants; a tremendous struggle of patriotism on the one hand and of vengeance on the other." General Mahone says: "The Federals fought like devils." General French, commanding the division, recommended in his report that the greater part of our brigade "ought to be awarded medals for their gallantry." Colonel Carroll reports: "My men behaved in the most gallant style, and I had more trouble to make them retire when it was found useless to advance than I had to move them forward."

The three regiments captured in this action two stands of colors, one major, five captains, seven lieutenants, and two hundred and seventy enlisted men, and also recaptured a regiment of zouaves. It was difficult to determine who had captured the prisoners, as they were started to the rear and taken in charge by our Brigade Pioneer Corps, whilst the captors kept their places in the ranks; it is also just to remark that the most of the prisoners were glad after their capture to get back out of range of the destructive fire. Thomas McClaren took the flag of the Fourteenth Louisiana Tigers, which he had captured, with him when he was carried back to the division hospital, where he turned it over to Adjutant Wallace. After we had rallied at the rifle-pits we were again formed into line, then moved out of them under a heavy fire, which killed and wounded several in the brigade, which now entered the works that had been occupied by Sykes' Division, on the Mineral Spring Road, at the edge of the woods north of the White House, where we connected with the Eleventh Corps on the left and Hancock's Division on the right. The Chancellor House, and woods we had occupied in the morning, were now on fire, which saddened our hearts very much, because some of our wounded would most likely suffer the untold horrors of being literally roasted alive, and yet we could not go to their rescue. During the afternoon the works were strengthened. About 4 o'clock General Hooker, accompanied only by an orderly, rode along our line, reeling to and fro like a drunken man; historians inform us that he was suffering from a concussion received whilst leaning against a pillar of the Chancellorsville House when it was struck by a cannon ball; it is well that this statement be made here, since many of us believed what was so tersely expressed by some of the boys, who said "Joe Hooker is shot in the neck;" "Hooker has had too much commissary." We all wished to believe that he was sober.

Monday, May 4th. We were several times disturbed during the night by picket-firing. When morning came we hoped more troops would be brought up, and an advance made against Lee's forces, for all felt mortified at what seemed an unnecessary failure to accomplish the purpose of our crossing the river. In the afternoon there was considerable skirmishing, which culminated towards evening in a terrific attack on our lines with shot and shell, which soon subsided after our gunners had replied; several were killed and wounded in the brigade. We again laid down to spend another night on the ground, just in rear of our breastworks; about midnight, when all was silent as the grave, and naught could be heard but the whippoorwill, a volley by some nervous men on the left, fired at an imaginary foe, rent the air; instantly, without a word of command, our brigade arose en masse, with the bedewed rubber blankets glittering in the moonbeams, stood a short time in silence; the firing having ceased all lay down quietly, and were in a moment asleep, barely a word having been spoken. The moon shone brightly, so that that we could distinguish objects for fifteen or twenty rods.

Tuesday, May 5th. At 10 A.M. our pickets were driven back a short distance, but being at once reinforced the line was immediately re-established. A heavy detail assisted the pioneers in repairing the road to the United States Ford. About three the rain began to pour, and at eight we had orders to be ready to fall back to the river; at midnight we started, and crossed the river before day. Colonel Carroll bade good-by to the boys that were left behind on picket, feeling quite sure that they would be captured. At near daybreak Lieutenant Anderson discovered that all our troops had gone, ordered the pickets he had in charge to the rear, and reached the river and crossed just as the pontoons were being taken up. We soon left the river, marched toward camp, and entered our old quarters about noon. Our loss was two officers and fifty-eight men wounded, two missing, and eighteen killed. The brigade lost two officers and thirty-nine men killed, twenty-nine officers and one hundred and seventy men wounded, one officer—Captain Fisk, Aide de Camp —and sixty-four men missing.

The following is a partial list of the killed and wounded:

Company A—C. Runyan, T. H. Shaffer, killed; F. O. Jacobs, wounded.

Company B—F. Beach, P. Ball, D. Fullmer, W. T. Hart, G. W. Parks, G. H. Sargeant, O. L. Stoughton, A. Scott and G. Wilcox, wounded.

Company C—T. Collins, J. Griffin and J. Kempf, killed; Captain J. S. Jones, H. Lamb and D. Thomas, wounded.

Company D—O. McKee, wounded.

Company E—H. Butler, killed; A. Dice, J. Jahala, J. Krug, W. H. McClure, J. Moffitt, E. McKelvey, Thomas McClaren and P. Myers, wounded.

Company F—J. Johnson, J. Rich and G. Sexhaur, killed; T. Scanlan, died of wounds; J. A. Bouer, G. Barth, W. H. Bruce, E. Estep, A. Fournace, F. B. Hane, S. Kauffman, W. Laird, J. Hafer, J. Hays, C. F. Oldfield, J. M. Ricksecker, J. Trownsell, J. Wetzell and C. Yost, wounded.

Company G—W. D. Daniels, F. Hahner and T. McCoy, killed; Lieutenant Edgar, A. Martin, C. Collier, T. J. Carson, W. D. Edgar and W. H. Morrow, wounded.

Company H—H. C. French, William M. Gurley and J. H. Jones, killed; L. Bair and G. H. Smallwood, wounded.

Company I—C. Brooks, killed; J. Brooker, died of wounds; G. Beddow and H. A. Shoub, wounded; Martin Main, missing.

Company K—A. Craig, killed.

## CHAPTER XVII.

MOVE TO A NEW CAMP — GENERAL HANCOCK ASSUMES COMMAND OF THE SECOND CORPS — LEAVE CAMP AS REAR-GUARD OF THE ARMY — MARCH BY WAY OF DUMFRIES, CENTERVILLE, GUM SPRINGS, EDWARDS' FERRY, FREDERICK CITY, TOWARD GETTYSBURG — HOOKER RESIGNS — MEADE ASSUMES COMMAND.

May 6th was a rainy, chilly, and very disagreeable day; the old log huts were again covered by the shelter-tents, and made as comfortable as the water-soaked interior would permit. On the 7th several regiments of nine months' men returned home on account of the expiration of their term of service, which had more of a demoralizing than exhilarating effect upon those that remained. On the 14th, the weather having become settled and the ground dry, the brigade moved camp about two miles to the northwest, where there was an abundance of wood and good water, a grassy plat and desirable shade; two shelter-tents, stretched over a stick, supported by two uprights, constituted the dog-tent; sometimes these tents were secured by two guns with bayonets "fixed," and run into the ground some four feet apart, and the cloth fastened at the gable-ends by the gun-hammers; for better protection from the sun a large number of pine boughs, and even trees, were placed about the tents; many had not even the shelter-tents; these kept themselves protected as much as possible by trees and boughs; it was in reality a camp in a pine grove, and as a change from the dingy log huts, very much enjoyed.

Spring had come; the songsters made the woods ring; many were the men that wandered off alone to write to loved ones, to read or meditate; congenial companions would stroll away, talk over plans and prospects, until they found themselves even beyond the picket's-post; pickets had good times basking in the sun, the outpost as well as the reserve, watching for the officer of the day as much as for the enemy; down at the river there was a suspension of hostilities, whilst men waded the river to exchange coffee and tobacco, and get the latest news. In camp men were reading, writing, sleeping, or discussing the probabilities. Duties were easy; there was plenty to eat and to wear; the regiments were reinforced from the well ones that had returned from the hospitals; bushels of mail came each day for the brigade; the general health of officers and men was very good. There was occasionally the too free use of "commissary" and "stomach bitters," which with "meerschaum pipe" drove dull care away for those who got enough wages to enable them to afford such luxuries. Taken all together the camp out in the grove was happy, and not very anxious for a forward movement. About the 20th came encouraging reports of the condition of things about Vicksburg.

On the 26th came a communication from General French, commanding the division, complimenting the brigade for the part it had taken at Chancellorsville, and recommending that most of the men be presented with medals for their bravery.

Some movement seemed to be on foot in the Confederate camp about the 30th, when preparations were being made by us to meet any attack; surplus baggage was sent to Washington as rapidly as possible; the sick were also removed to the rear, and the troops were under orders to be ready to march at a moment's notice.

By the 5th of June our camp was becoming bare and dusty, and the leaves of the pine boughs dropping, became a nuisance, as they mixed too freely with rations and clothing; camp-life became once more intolerably monotonous. On the 6th some of the troops made a reconnaisance below town, and found the enemy still in force. The burden of letters continued to be "all quiet on the Rappahannock." Designation of companies was as follows: F, G, H, A, K, I, E, D, B, C, the last being the right flank. So dull became camp-life that even the general commanding the brigade would made an effort to be lively; morning after morning rang out his stentorian tones for his aides to "Get up, get up, and hear the little birds sing their praises to God, bless your souls; get up!"

On the 9th General Pleasanton, in a skirmish with cavalry and infantry at Brandy Station, captured some of the Confederate dispatches that indicated a movement on their part up the Shenandoah Valley. On the 10th General Couch, our Corps Commander, having been assigned to the command of the Department of the Susquehanna, General Hancock assumed command of the Second Corps; this gave perfect satisfaction to officers and men, who had learned to know and trust him at Fredericksburg and Chancellorsville.

Many troops had returned home on account of the expiration of their term of service; on the 11th the Twenty-fourth New Jersey left, amid the cheering of the brigade; the Army of the Potomac now numbered about eighty thousand men, whilst Lee's forces reached nearly seventy thousand, who were able to march and fight, making the two about equal in number, since the Confederates did not count those on detailed duty and the Unionists did. Our regiment now numbered about four hundred officers and men present for duty, including those on detached service.

On the 12th Professor Lowe ascended, as usual, in his balloon, was taking his accustomed observations of the Confederates, when there were two puffs of smoke from their cannon on Marye's Heights, the whirring sound of solid shot in the vicinity of the yellow, glittering gas-bag, underneath which in a basket was a lively object that wished to get on terra firma as soon as possible; in a moment all hands that danced attendance had hold of the rope, and by it pulled down balloon, basket and professor; this was the last aeronautic exhibition in the presence of the army; since the destination of the Confederates was now known, and part of our forces on the move, it was useless to waste any more gas; some of our teamsters said that the last they saw of the old balloon was when it was anchored to a tree north of Dumfries. The Confederate Commissary General, it is said, about this time wrote upon Lee's requisition for rations for his troops, that "if Lee wishes rations, let him seek them in Pennsylvania." And it is certain that he was now acting upon the suggestion, for on the 14th of June General Ewell, commanding Jackson's old corps, was at Harper's Ferry, having captured twenty-nine of our cannon, and some four thousand prisoners; Longstreet was at Culpepper and Hill in our front. General Hooker desired at once to fall upon Hill and crush him, but

President Lincoln said to him: "I would not take any risk of being entangled upon a river, like an ox jumping half over a fence, and liable to be torn by dogs front and rear, without a fair chance to gore one way or kick the other." General Halleck also opposed the movement, but preferred a flank attack, the very thing that Lee desired to be done.

On the evening of the 13th of June the Third Corps is at Culpepper Fords, the Fifth near it, the Eleventh at Catlett's Station, the Twelfth at Bealeton, whilst our corps is under orders to march at a moment's notice. On the morning of the 4th we struck tents, watched the rest of our corps moving toward the rear, and at dark we followed, halting near midnight until the pickets, that had remained at their post, could join us; another halt was made early in the morning near Stafford Court House; about noon we started again, on a rapid march through heat and dust for six miles, when we halted at Acquia Creek and camped for the night.

The column moved before daylight on the 16th, halted at Dumfries for breakfast, and drew three days' rations; at noon the march was resumed; clouds of dust arose; the heat was stifling and oppressive; clothing and blankets were thrown away; Ewell was reported as having crossed the Potomac at Harper's Ferry, with his advance at Chambersburg, and Longstreet at Snicker's and Ashby's Gap; it was also reported that the Home Guards had been called out; this was greeted with a "Bully for the Home Guards;" "Bully for Lee."

Guerillas were hanging about our flanks, picking up horses, mules and men; at noon fences, barns and houses were on fire in our immediate rear; it was currently reported that they were set on fire and the owners killed because they had bayoneted one of our men who was too sick to keep up with his command. We reached Woolf Creek Ford, on the Occoquan, before dark, having marched about twenty miles. The First, Sixth and Eleventh Corps were now at Centerville, the Third at Manassas, and the Fifth, Twelfth and advance of the Second at Fairfax Court House; occasional firing could be heard in the west, where Pleasanton was compelling the Confederates to keep west of the mountains, which gave our forces greater freedom of concerted action.

## GHASTLY SIGHTS ON OLD BATTLE-FIELD. 121

At 8 o'clock of the 17th of June we again took up our line of march, as rear-guard of the army; after having passed a line of earthworks many of the men began to straggle across woods and fields, on account of the heat, and helped themselves to cherries, strawberries, and whatever else they could forage, in spite of danger from guerillas. Fairfax Station was soon reached. On the 19th the Twenty-eighth New Jersey started for home, to the delight of the remainder of the brigade, who were getting tired of the continual talk about going home that some indulged in whilst the country was in great danger; yet no one failed to give them credit for what they had done. After enjoying the prolonged rest, we started at 3 o'clock on the afternoon of the 19th, and reached Centerville at nine, just as the rain began to pour; the country was bare, and no top rails could be had; one must either stand up all night or lie down in the mud; all night long somebody was stirring about, or growling about wet hips or leaky blankets. At daybreak everybody was astir; some sought for water, others for wood; soon small fires were covered with black quart cups; occasionally some one would get a blessing because he had upset a cup, and nearly extinguished an already miserably smoking fire. There was an unusual amount of stretching and yawning by those who curled themselves up like hedgehogs under rubber blankets, that afforded very poor ventilation. "Fortune favored the true and brave" when the rain ceased and gave an opportunity to dry our water-soaked garments.

About noon (June 20th) the brigade took the advance, with the Eighth Ohio thrown out as skirmishers; we soon crossed the old battle-ground, where ghastly sights met our gaze; the sod thrown upon bodies of the Union soldiers the year previous had been washed away by the rains, leaving fingers, toes, nose and skull exposed; of some the greater part of the skeleton, with tattered uniforms adhering, could be seen; near a tree was a group of remains, dried and wasted, of comrades who probably had died of wounds and the necessities of life. No inspiration here. Was anyone to blame that these, who had been inside of Union lines for a year, were not yet accounted a decent burial? We thought, heathen Greeks took time and had disposition to bury their dead; a Christian nation might profit by their example. Nature was doing her utmost to mantle the forms of these that had so nobly perished. At 6 o'clock we reached Gainesville, where we remained encamped until the 25th of June; during this time we had a heavy picket-guard, and kept ourselves in readiness for any emergency; guns were examined, ammunition sorted, and cartridge-boxes and haversacks replenished; no one seemed to know definitely the whereabouts of the enemy.

On the 24th General French, having been assigned to the command of Harper's Ferry, General Alexander Hays became commander of our division.

On the 25th Longstreet and Hill had followed Ewell into "Maryland, my Maryland," where they expected a general uprising in their behalf, a glorious victory, and recognition of the Confederacy by the Powers of Europe. While the rebel forces were now near Chambersburg, the Army of the Potomac began to cross at Edwards' Ferry. We had present for duty twenty officers and two hundred and forty-nine men.

We struck tents on the morning of the 25th, and began our march at 10 o'clock, halted at Mountain View to permit teams to pass, and then it was trudge, trudge, through rain and mud, from 3 o'clock until eleven at night, when we bivouacked at Gum Springs. On Friday morning we learned to a certainty that the enemy was in Pennsylvania. About 10 o'clock we started at a rapid gait for Edwards' Ferry, where we arrived at 5 o'clock, took supper, fixed ourselves down for the night, just got into a sound sleep when we were routed out, fell into line, waited awhile for orders to march, marched half a mile, halted about an hour, stood for some ten minutes—some of us getting out of sorts, some kept quiet, others blessed somebody, whilst everybody wondered, "Why don't the Army of the Potomac move?" it didn't move for an hour; that is, our part did not until most of us got comfortably fixed, when we marched slowly across the pontoons, then halted, and stood in or squatted down into the mud for about "an age" (two hours); then moved a few steps, fumbled around in a wheat field; some swore until things "seemed to get blue;" some yelled and all soon stacked arms, lay down, repented and went to sleep. Some of the boys called it "a h—l of a time." Such "briggling about" was almost unpardonable. Who was to blame? No one knew.

Morning was soon at hand; most of us had a late breakfast; happy was the comrade that had not taken off his boots, for it was next to impossible to get the water-soaked "sutler boots" on one's foot; the ripening grain had been laid out by the mud-bespattered men as effectually as though a cyclone had passed over it; the men were in excellent spirits; "we are again in God's country" was the feeling that found vent in expression. Back of us were the rugged mountains; in front, toward the north, a quite level country, with the "Sugar-Loaf Spur" to the right and the South Mountain Range to the left. By 10 o'clock rations were issued, the march resumed at two, and having passed through Poolesville and Barnesville we entered camp, near the "Sugar-Loaf," at eleven at night.

On the next morning, June 28th, we started toward the Monocacy Bridge, where we encamped at 4 o'clock, three miles from Frederick City, at what is now known as Frederick Junction, and on the same spot occupied by the brigade on the 13th of September, just previous to the battle of Antietam; we had hardly stacked arms when mill-race and river were alive with noisy bathers. At this point Colonel Carroll joined us, having been absent nearly two weeks, during which time Colonel Coons, of the gallant Fourteenth Indiana, had command of the brigade; he was loved and much esteemed by all.

On the 29th the corps moved forward at eight, but we were doomed to wait until 1:30 o'clock, when we acted as rear-guard of the wagon train; our course was due north, weather hot, scenery inspiring; before night it rained, and we were forced, sleepy and weary, to trudge through mud and water until near morning, when we entered camp near Uniontown, Maryland, having passed through Frederick City, Liberty, Jamestown and Union Bridge.

On the morning of the 30th we joined the corps north of the town, remained in camp, rested and mustered for pay. The next morning, July 1st, we started northward, toward two mountain spurs that were looming up before us; we moved quite briskly for four miles, when the column was halted, an order read notifying us of the resignation of General Hooker and the appointment of General Meade as Commander in Chief of the Army of the Potomac, also urging the duty of defending our homes and driving back the invader. To this order General Carroll only added, "Do as you always have done." The knowledge of the change of commanders seemed to have no perceptible effect, but the men seemed to think the order too tame, and that we ought to *destroy* the invader instead of driving him back. There was an apparent distrust on the part of the men, who had always seemed more anxious for "real business" than their general officers. The column moved rapidly forward; there was no straggling, no need of commands, no urging to "close up;" the ripening cherries and apples, and abundance of forage, enticed but few from their places; every man was ready to do his duty, now that he knew it as never before, no difference who was in command. Soon the booming cannon could be heard and the smoke seen rising to the right of the two spurs toward which we were hastening. Little was said; every one was thinking; upon every countenance could be seen a settled conviction of duty, and a fixed determination to win or die. About the middle of the afternoon we met the body of General Reynolds; none were disposed to ask questions; but little could be learned, save that he had been killed early in the action, and that nearly the entire of Lee's force was at Gettysburg. There was profounder silence than ever; no more jokes, and as usual before a battle, hundreds of playing cards were strewn along the road. We were passing over a rise of ground, whence the guns could be heard more distinctly and the smoke seen more clearly, when one of the boys, in a sad tone, remarked: "What if they whip us this time?" Instantly a strong, manly voice replied, "They won't; I'll die first." "Here, I," added another; "So will I," said a third; immediately those in hearing closed up, four abreast, and thus it was through a considerable part of the regiment, keeping perfect step, seeming to shake the very earth with their determined tread. The "Old Fourth" was ready to go into the jaws of death and compel a victory. How it stirs our pride, and fires our souls, as in memory we are once more on to the battle with such valiant comrades. Die they did, some of our noblest; multiplied millions will reap the fruits of their heroism.

Firing ceased, and no more smoke was seen to rise; our brigade was in advance of the corps; just at dark we met our Corps Commander, General Hancock, in whose generalship and judgment all had unbounded confidence; the column was halted a few moments after dark. General Hancock informed Colonel Carroll that the enemy was in force at Gettysburg, and hurrying up the rest of his troops, telling them that they had only militia to fight;

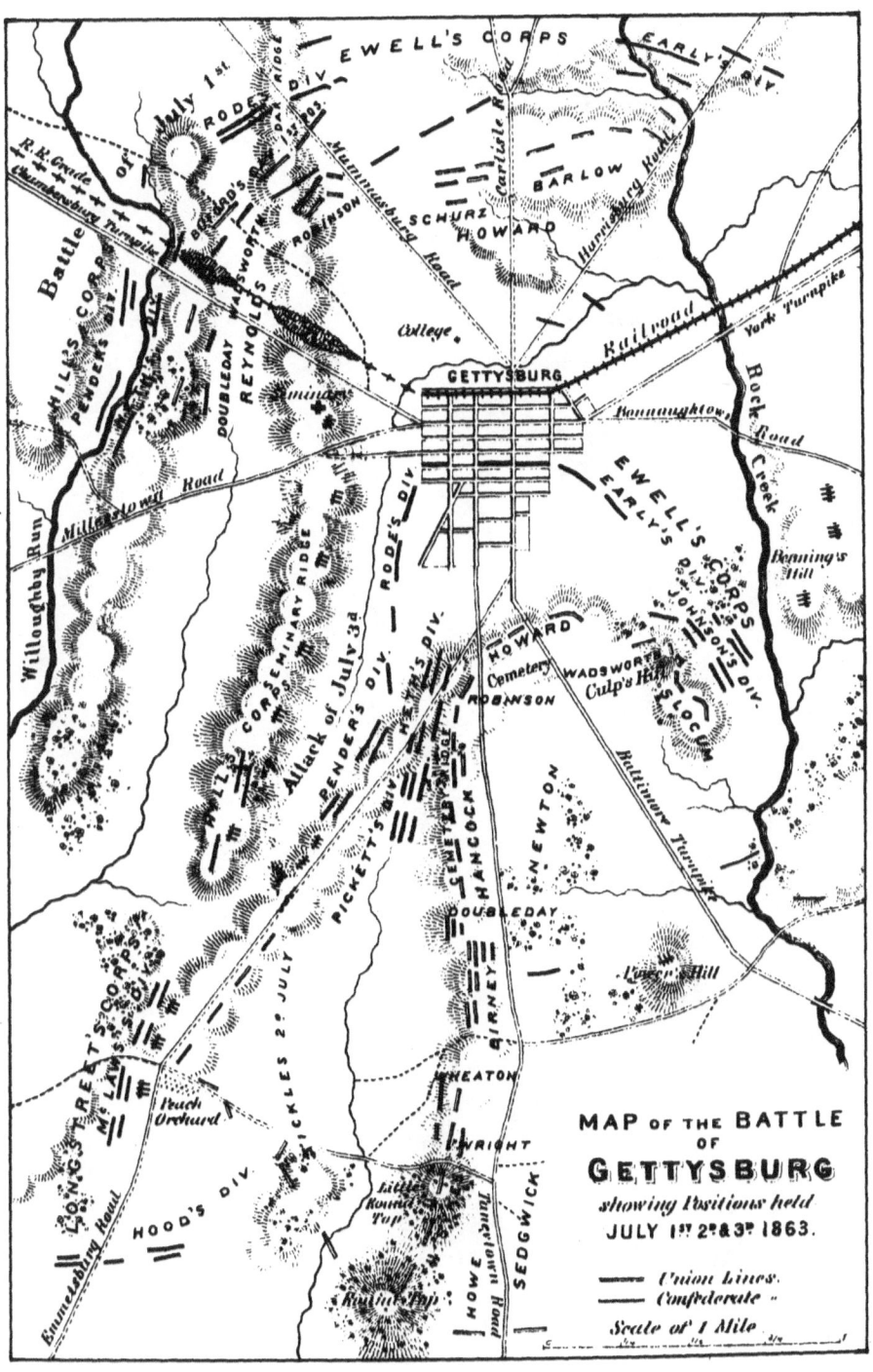

that Reynolds had been killed early in the first onset; that the First Corps had fought hard and lost many men; that the Eleventh had been driven back and lost about five thousand men in the town; that himself had put the remainder of the two corps into position on this side of town; that the Third and Twelfth were coming up and going into position; that no doubt Lee would attack us with his entire force on the morrow; that we could stack arms, rest for the night and take position early in the morning. Just as the General was riding away Carroll asked: "General, have we a good position?" and received the instant reply, in a firm tone, "If Lee does not attack before all our forces are up, we can hold the position I have selected against the whole Confederacy."

We immediately marched into a meadow to the right of the road and a patch of woods near the foot of the two mountain spurs, and stacked arms. The evening was balmy and beautiful, though somewhat hazy, but with sufficient moonlight to enable one to discern any object.

## CHAPTER XVIII.

### THE BATTLE OF GETTYSBURG.

The next morning, Thursday, July 2d, we were roused from our slumbers at about 3 o'clock, ordered to get breakfast and to be ready to go to the front at quarter past four. We started soon after the hour designated, halted shortly after daylight—to the rear and left of Cemetery Hill—for more than an hour, awaiting orders; in the meantime there was a disposition to get a glimpse across the hill, "to see how the land lay" and the position of the enemy; not much could be seen that might indicate the presence of an enemy save an occasional shot fired from a wheatfield, half a mile to the front and left of our position. The flanking, with two other companies, were sent across and down the hill, under the direction of Colonel Carroll, and took position near the Emmitsburg Road, where they remained until relieved by G and I and the Eighth Ohio. The firing became now more frequent, but still continued at long range, as it was not desired to bring on an engagement until the troops were all on hand and in position.

About 8 o'clock the brigade was formed in line of regiments, right in front, with the Fourth Ohio in advance; marched forward into position between Woodruff's Battery and the Taneytown road, on the brow of the hill in Zeigler's Grove, with a rise of ground to the right toward the Cemetery. From this point but little could be seen in any direction, whilst the occasional crack of a rifle could be heard, and whizzing of a ball through the air. The men soon busied themselves getting their arms in the best possible order, blankets and cartridge-boxes into comfortable position. There were present for duty thirteen officers and three hundred and three men.

The position of the brigade was soon changed by the left-flank, until it was clear of a ravine and in the rear of Woodruff's Battery. The skirmishing becoming quite brisk, Companies G and I of our regiment, in command of Captain Grubb, were advanced to the front and somewhat to the left; they soon drove the enemy before them, and took position to the left of an old frame house, shielding themselves behind fence rails and ridges. The entire force of the Eighth Ohio was soon sent to their right, when the enemy was again driven a short distance and a new position occupied. During the afternoon the enemy made a number of unsuccessful attempts to dislodge them. Toward night several Confederate regiments, in their impetuous charge toward the Federal position, swept over our pickets, companies G and I, making increased havoc in their already greatly thinned ranks, and taking several of them prisoners. When night came, and there was a lull, it was found that more than half this heroic band had either been killed or wounded. Among the killed were Lieutenants Shaub and Edgar; Captain Grubb was wounded, and the little band left in command of Sergeant Longworth, who was determined not to leave the field until he had received orders to do so. For some twelve hours had these noble comrades stood the fire of the enemy's pickets. About eleven the remnants joined the regiment on Cemetery Hill, having probably sustained greater loss in proportion than any two companies of any one regiment in the army; Company G had eight killed during the three years and three months; six of these fell during the storm of shot and shell and the charge on this fatal afternoon.

We now return to the regiment, which had retained its position; some were sleeping near the stacked guns, others writing, some wandering away a few rods to get a better view of what was impending. The middle of the afternoon had passed; the pickets had become remarkably quiet; camp followers, clerks, orderlies, aides, colonels and generals, were becoming quite bold—taking observations, watching the smoke of the firing on the picket line and of the occasional booming of a gun on the extreme left, and closely scanning objects a mile or so west of them moving in the deepening shade of the trees; before 6 o'clock the firing on the left was more rapid, accompanied by the whirr of musketry, while troops could be seen hurrying forward over the plain from our side; in a few minutes more there was unusual activity among the strange spectres in the shadow of the trees on our front, then a puff of smoke, a shot went over our heads, then came another, and a third scattered a stack of guns of the rear regiment, the Seventh Virginia, plunging a bayonet into a comrade's side and another cut a comrade of the Fourth in twain; now there was hurrying to and fro, men for their companies and their guns, disinterested eye-witnesses, generals and staff for shelter over the brow of the hill, until each could gain the requisite composure to make his peace with his Maker, comprehend the situation, obtain orders and face the music. There was meager chance for shelter; General Hays and Staff had just dismounted back of us, but across the brow of the hill, when a solid shot plowed through an orderly's horse. The batteries in front of us were now replying vigorously; the enemy's skirmishers were making it hot for our pickets; whizzing shot and whirring shell, plunging and ricocheting among and over us for more than an hour, were making our position uncomfortable; barely a word was spoken. To the direful roar of cannon was added the whirr of musketry, hissing minies, shrieking shell and screaming shot, whilst the air was darkening with clouds of sulphurous smoke, obscuring the hiding sun, lifting occasionally and giving a view of the appalling carnage going on, toward and in front of Round Top, which seemed to draw nearer as daylight hastened away, and threatened to draw us into the fray ere darkness came. We were no longer kept in painful suspense, when there rang out the well known "Attention!" and the three remaining regiments, under a heavy fire, moved rapidly to the left and took position to the left of the Second and Third Brigades of our division, whose position was threatened by a charging column; the charge failing to effect anything save to nearly annihilate our pickets companies G and I. The Fourth retained its place, whilst the Seventh Virginia and Fourteenth Indiana returned to their old position.

As night was lowering its sable curtains over the bloody scene word was received that part of the Eleventh Corps, being taken in front and flank, was compelled to fall back from their support of two batteries on Cemetery Hill. "Attention! Right Face—Double Quick—March!" was instantly obeyed, with Carroll at the head of the Fourteenth Indiana in the lead, the Seventh West Virginia next; a squad of anxious general officers was soon passed, while we hurried by gravestones struck by the spiteful minie ball—toward the cannon's vivid flash and thundering roar; Baltimore Turnpike was crossed, the position of the rebels determined only by their fire; hastening toward them, now by the left flank, the Fourth on the right flank of the brigade, through tanglements of retreating men, caissons and horses, up and along a slope, where maddened gunners of captured batteries raved and swore, or cried in very madness, vowing death to meet rather than give up their guns, striking the rebels with fist, rammer, ammunition and stones; greeting, echoing and re-echoing our cheer upon cheer, saying "It's Carroll's brigade, there'll be no more running; give 'em hell, boys." Bayonets and butts of guns at once joined the efforts of the heroic gunners, then infantry and gunner in a general melee, with flanks of regiments overlaping and every-man-in-as-you-can sort of way, drove the enemy from unhitching horses and spiking guns, down over the hill, under the cross-fire of Stevens' battery on our right, and captured a number of prisoners. Weiderick's and Rickett's batteries were recaptured. Company G of our Seventh West Virginia made sad havoc with their old rebel neighbors. We soon took position by a stone wall, a short distance from the guns toward our right and front, sent out skirmishers and brought in several prisoners; to our right, on Culp's Hill, the terrible racket of musketry continued until near 11 o'clock, by which time the enemy seemed to have withdrawn from our front; having stationed our pickets, those that could endeavored to sleep in spite of the rumbling sounds to our rear, which caused us to fear that our army was falling back, producing much dissatisfaction until it was known that it was the determination of our commanders to fight it out there and then. Aside from this fear the brigade was in the happiest mood, for it knew that it had turned defeat into victory, saved the key to the entire position, thereby averting disaster in compelling us to fall back in confusion, discouraged and disheartened, in case the enemy had held the hill and turned our guns upon us.

It is worthy of notice here that the tremendous cheering of the gunners and the boys had the unintentional effect of keeping Hays' Brigade from joining Hoke's Louisiana Tigers—composed of the Fifth, Sixth, Seventh, Eighth and Ninth Louisiana regiments, which our three small regiments had just routed—and thereby taken us in left and rear before we could have realized our situation. Possibly, in a fit of desperation, we might have changed front in a moment, for above all tumult Carroll's voice could be heard and understood, and charged and driven Hays' force with greater ease than the "Tigers," whom we had just routed more easily than at Chancellorsville. Yet it is well to remember that we should not have had an enemy under cross-fire of Culp's Hill. Possibly the cheering and Carroll's mighty voice saved us, yet the writer has the conviction that most of the men and officers, like their commander of the "Gibraltar Brigade," would sooner have died than have given up this key to the situation. In this affair the loss of the Fourth and Fourteenth Indiana was about the same, but that of the Seventh West Virginia was equal to both in wounded, possibly because they at once recognized their old neighbors and neither showed nor obtained quarter. When all was quiet, some of companies G and I, that had joined us at about 11 o'clock, returned, with several of the Pioneer Corps, to bring off their wounded, bury their dead comrades, and mark their graves.

On Friday, July 3d, at about four in the morning, we were roused by the effort our men were making to dislodge the enemy beyond Culp's Hill. Before nine the sound of cannon and musketry grew fainter, assuring us that our help would not be needed, and that another victory had been scored for the Union. Rations were now getting very short, and many could be seen calculating their allowance for breakfast. Some foraged flour, supplementing by the way of "slap-jacks" the meager store on hand. Rifles and muskets were gathered together, many of them loaded to the muzzle, capped and stood against the stone wall, for use as "grape and canister" into the ranks of any rebels that might make an attempt to climb the hill with belligerent intent. Some time after, this fact of guns loaded to the muzzle was blazed abroad through the dailies, to show that the men who had handled them were so excited during action that they did not know whether their guns had gone off or not, and did not even know whether the ramrod, in loading, extended a few inches or its entire length into the gun. To this nonsense the writer immediately sent a rejoinder setting forth the facts, to which were added short editorials, placing the correspondent in a ridiculous attitude.

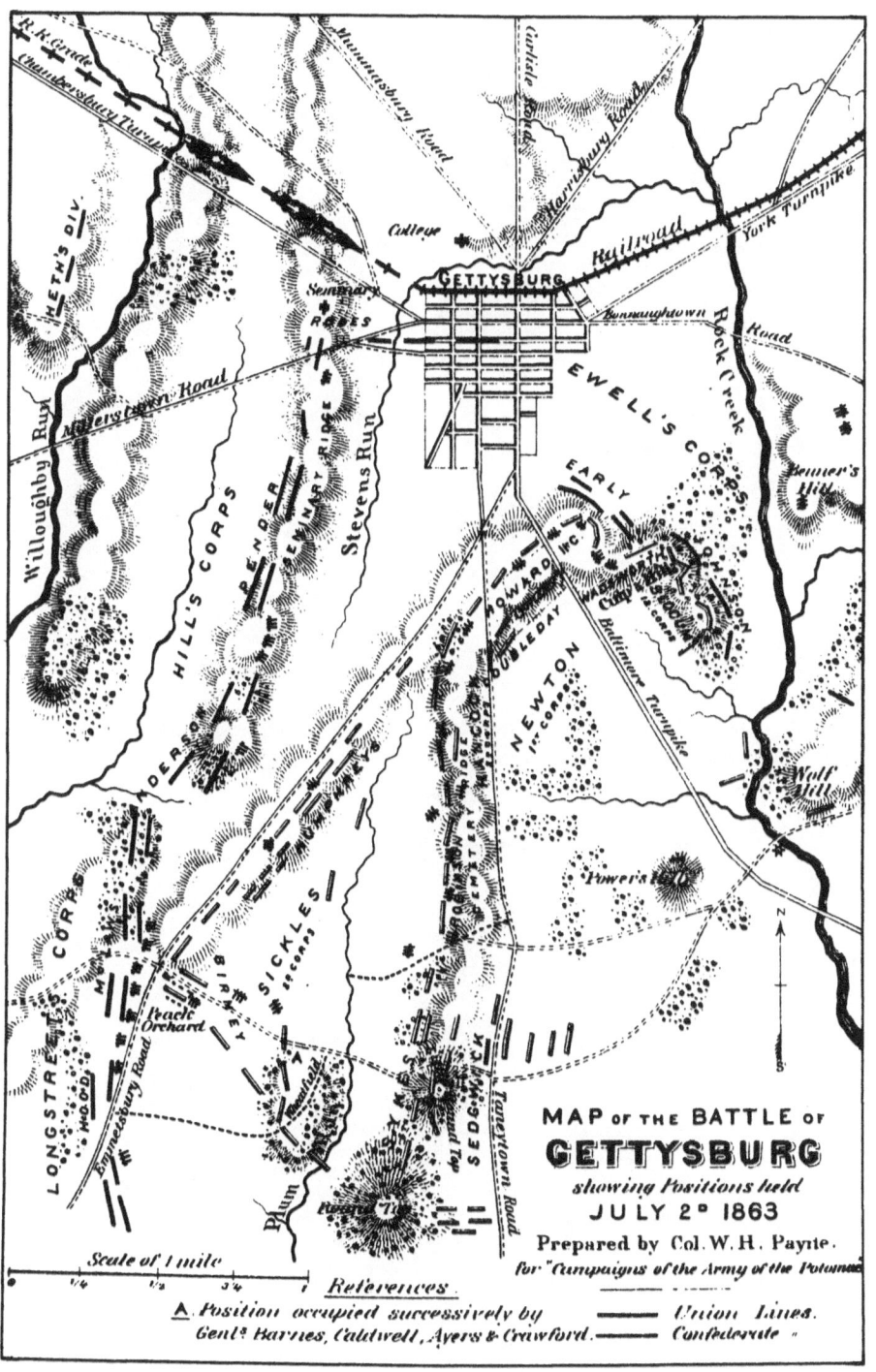

From the top of our hill we had an excellent view of the greater part of the position of both armies. The Union line was in the shape of a fish-hook, of which our brigade occupied part of the bend. From Benner's Hill, on our front and right, Confederate troops could frequently be seen, from half a mile to a mile distant. At about noon there was but little apparent activity on either side. In the edge of the woods to the rear and right of town groups of horsemen could occasionally be seen, as if they were taking a view of our position through spy-glasses; it was evident that some important movement was on foot. The day was lovely; an ominous silence reigned from twelve until one, when a cannon's boom greeted our ears, followed in quick succession by others, so that in a short time it seemed as if pandemonium itself had been turned loose in our very midst, as the two hundred and twenty-five cannon belched forth death and destruction for more than an hour. Occasionally a shell or solid shot found its way into our midst, and many went shrieking and screaming over us, whilst we hugged the earth and kept a lookout for the appearance of the enemy on our front. The firing having mostly ceased, the artillery on the hill had their attention called to the large masses of infantry coming from the woods to left of the town and moving in the direction of the position we had occupied the previous day; it was with difficulty that many of the men could restrain themselves from going to the top of the hill, with the hope of seeing the rebels make their charge; in every direction the skirmishing became very lively, whilst the batteries on our hill began to send shell and canister toward the seminary building; to our left there seemed a lull, then the whirr of musketry told the story of a deadly life or death contest. Now came a time when men held their breath and listened in painful suspense, which was relieved only by the cheering of gunners and comrades on the hill and beyond, as they learned that the enemy was flying toward the rear; the whirring of musketry was terrific, but in a brief time died away; the guns sent only an occasional shot, and hosts of prisoners were seen going to the rear. Everybody was jubilant, and there was many an expressed wish to follow the Confederates in a general charge and put an end to Lee's army. The Eighth Ohio soon made its appearance from the skirmish line—where it had just passed a terrible ordeal—with its trophies of two battle-flags and a large number of prisoners, and was greeted with rousing cheers by their comrades. The contest was ended, and the boys had considerable liberty, yet dared not go any distance, fearing that they might possibly be needed in making a general onset. There began now also a looking after rations, which had entirely given out, and the men were very hungry.

Saturday, July 4th. The Glorious Fourth, and we are still a Nation, and shall most likely continue to be for centuries to come. The old and effete monarchies of Europe dare not recognize the so-called Southern Confederacy, for the "high-water mark of the rebellion" has been reached. Lee has been badly whipped, and is on his way toward Dixie. Just before the break of day a partridge set up a lively "bob-white," which was considered a good omen by the men on picket, who responded with cheering and a sharp lookout for the Johnnies, but could see none; they now urged their way onward into the town, in spite of rain, and found that the enemy had just left. By nine the rain ceased. Special details assisted the Pioneer Corps in burying the dead and removing the wounded to the hospital, in a large barn several miles to the rear, and near Large Round Top. Officers and men wandered over the fields and looked after wounded and fallen comrades, and at the terrible carnage manifest on every hand. The eight companies that had thus far been armed with Springfield muskets now exchanged them for Springfield rifles, which they had gathered from the field. Officers made their report of losses and action. Colonel Carroll said in his report: "Too much praise cannot be given the officers and men."

The loss in the regiment was: Two officers and eight men killed, one officer and sixteen men wounded, and five men missing. In the brigade there were: Three officers and thirty-five men killed, one hundred and forty-seven men wounded, and seven missing.

## LIST OF LOSSES.

The following is the list as shown by the Roster:

Killed—Company A—J. W. Harl.
G—Lieutenant Edgar, W. Bain, D. W. Collins, A. O. Davis, G. H. Martin, A. Myers, G. W. Wilcox.
I—Lieutenant Shoub, S. Roloson, J. Sheak, H. C. Stark.

Wounded—Company C—S. Wells.
F—L. S. Ensign.
G—Captain Grubb, F. Bain, M. Harman, M. V. B. Longworth, H. Pfeiffer, W. Shinderwolf, J. Winstead.
K—J. Boyer, J. Short.

## CHAPTER XIX.

THE CONFEDERATE RETREAT—THE PURSUIT—MARCH TO FREDERICK CITY—THE HUNG SPY—BIVOUAC AT CRAMPTON'S GAP—PASS ANTIETAM—TO WILLIAMSPORT — HARPER'S FERRY — BLACKBERRIES ABUNDANT—TO GREGORY, MANASSAS AND THOROUHFARE GAP—WARRENTON, KELLY'S FORD AND ELK RUN—ACT AS RAILROAD GUARD.

Sunday, July 5th. Officers and men were dissatisfied with our inactivity the previous day, "lying around and doing nothing but see the sickening sights and smelling the miserable smells." But it was soon understood that Sedgwick had pursued and found the enemy entrenched. Rumors of the fall of Vicksburg and the bold utterances of the peace faction in the North, made us anxious to annihilate Lee's forces, cost what it would, and it was a matter of great rejoicing when the order came at two in the afternoon to fall in, although the direction, toward the Two Taverns, did not suit, for it seemed to take us away from the enemy, so that we were glad to halt at ten at night, and cease our wading through the mud.

The beautiful hazy day, the 6th, was spent in writing glowing accounts of our deeds of daring and valor to parents, sweethearts and friends, and in resting, sleeping, or foraging for berries, cherries, pies, bread, cakes and poultry. On the morning of the 7th the entire army seemed to be in motion; we arrived at Taneytown at noon; in the afternoon it rained very hard; we were out of rations and obtained provisions from the citizens, giving vouchers therefor.

On the evening of the 8th, near Frederick City, in spite of rain, mud and a twenty-mile march, we were a lively set, cheering ourselves hoarse, for it was now certain that Vicksburg had been taken, that the Potomac River was rising, and we had a fine prospect of capturing Lee's entire army. Hurrah! Part of his trains and many prisoners had just been taken, and our train was on hand with rations for empty stomachs, and shoes for blistered feet.

Thursday morning, July 9th, at an early hour, our brigade took the advance, marched through Frederick City, then south through the fields at route step, passed the naked body of the rebel spy, Richardson, dangling by the neck from the limb of a tree; Jefferson and Bakersville were left behind, and shortly before dark we bivouacked just beyond Crampton's Gap, having marched about twenty-four miles.

Friday, the 10th, we passed through Keedysville at noon, crossed Antietam Creek at about three in the afternoon, halted, advanced skirmishers, and followed in line of battle over the right of the old battle ground; occasionally a shot was fired at the enemy, who kept himself under cover of the woods on our front.

On the morning of the 11th, Saturday, we advanced some two miles, passed through Tighlmantown, formed in line of battle toward the northeast by Jones' Cross-Roads, where we remained until about four in the evening, when the brigade made a reconnaisance toward Hagerstown and met the retiring Confederates near Funkstown in considerable force; we now fell back into line of battle with the remainder of the division, having out pickets in the meantime. The men were becoming restive, fearing that our movements were too slow and that Lee would give us the slip.

At noon of the next day, Sunday the 12th, we changed front toward the left; about four the line was again changed in a more westerly direction, and advanced a short distance and entrenchments thrown up, although but few of the enemy could be seen by the most advanced pickets; some of our regiment passed beyond the line on foraging expeditions, and learned that Lee was in the act of crossing the river. At a council held at Meade's Headquarters in the evening, it was determined to find out more about the position of the enemy, and Monday, the 13th, was spent in solving this problem and gaining information which a number of privates could have given had they dared to do so.

We continued to throw up works whilst but a handful of the enemy was in front of us.

The next morning, Tuesday the 14th, we early learned what we had suspected, that Lee had crossed the river at Falling Waters. We were at once hurried forward in the rain towards Williamsport to support the cavalry, who succeeded in capturing some stragglers. It was soon discovered that the position held by Lee was fully as strong as the Marye Heights at Fredericksburg, and it was probably wisdom not to force a battle. We spent a very uncomfortable night on the wet ground, with clothing thoroughly soaked, and welcomed the dawn, an early lunch and an immediate march by the way of Sharpsburg to within three miles of Harper's Ferry, and encamped between the canal and river; in the latter floated many bodies of the Confederates. Another miserable night was worried through and the march resumed at six the next morning, Thursday the 16th, and we reached Sandy Hook at nine, entered camp and made out reports and requisitions. The rainy and disagreeable 17th of July was spent in our tents.

At 9 o'clock of the 18th we crossed both rivers at Harper's Ferry, proceeded along Loudon Heights, entered Pleasant Valley and halted at two, then acted as guard for the wagon-train until seven, when we entered camp in a field of dewberries; arms were stacked and order "rest" given; not a moment was lost in determining what general should have credit for such magnificent generalship that brought us to a general charge on the most delicious fruit—medicine to cure the troubles that water-soaked garments and slap-jacks had made; officers and men, saint and sinner, were bowed over or upon their knees, filling stomachs, cups and plates. After a cup of coffee came such a precious night's rest, with an early rally for more berries on Sunday, the 19th. An easy march brought us to Gregory's Gap at four, and in camp by a brook where blackberries were abundant; here several copies "of a contemptible secession sheet, printed in New York City," were purchased of the newsboy and torn into shreds as soon as their character was known, and search was made for the hide of the boy. About this time some officers were detailed on the recruiting service; there were present for duty twelve officers and two hundred and thirty-four men.

HARPER'S FERRY—LOOKING WEST.

On Monday, the 20th, we began the march at 10 o'clock, crossed a number of clear and cold streams with the thermometer around the nineties; hot and weary we entered camp at five, near Bloomville, where we remained until one in the afternoon of the 22d, on the evening of which we bivouacked near Upperville.

At 5 o'clock on the morning of the 23d we resumed our line of march, reached Markham at two, halted whilst other troops advanced and engaged the enemy toward Front Royal; at five we followed, expecting every moment to join in the musketry, which could be distinctly heard beyond Manassas Gap; we halted at eleven at night and bivouacked. It had been a very warm day; our garments, saturated with sweat, made the air rather uncomfortably cool; we had also passed through the worst slough ever encountered on any march, and were mud-bespattered from foot to head.

Being by this time entirely out of rations, there was considerable foraging done, for which many were arrested, but they were released as soon as they came up with their companies; one of the boys, with a "porker" on his back, encountered General Meade, who asked him, "Did you take all of it?" and receiving "Yes, sir," for a reply, further remarked, "Don't waste any," and rode on. "Bully for Meade," was the verdict of all the "boys," whilst officers were glad for a slice. This marching and suffering together did so wonderfully act as a leveler, that officers and men were more on equal footing than in camp, where occasionally some shoulder-strapped dude put on more airs than his known character and bringing up could substantiate, whilst the high-private, on the other hand, was disposed to become lazy and saucy; yet most officers and men, whether in camp, on the march or sanguinary field, felt at all times toward each other as brothers, officers sometimes carrying knapsack for the boys when sick and on the march, and the boys sharing the last hard-tack with a beloved officer; on the field of strife officers and men risked their lives in behalf of a wounded, helpless brother. After all, whether trudging through mud and rain, hungry and weary, languid and sleepy, good humor predominated, and in spite of fate we were a happy set, ofttimes, when wettest and weariest, joining in the chorus—

> "So let the wide world wag as it will,
> I'll be gay and happy still,
> Gay and happy,
> Gay and happy,
> I'll be gay and happy still."

At one in the afternoon of the 24th we started on the return march, and encamped near Markham on the farm of a rebel son of Chief Justice Marshall. On the hot and sultry 25th we reached Rectortown at noon and White Plains at six in the evening. The next morning, the 26th, we moved toward Thoroughfare Gap, and when near it turned toward Warrenton, passed through it at two, then on into the pine woods, sultry as an oven, one's chest seeming to collapse as we hurried along frantically, trying to keep up with some horsemen who knew nothing about carrying knapsacks or marching men, and were only brought to their senses when brigade commanders protested against the murderous proceedings and reported seventeen men prostrated by sunstroke in half an hour; fully one-half were compelled to fall out of ranks, many of them for the first time in their lives: then only in desperation, with throbbing pulse, staggered to the roadside, threw themselves full length, prostrate upon their backs, too much exhausted to speak a word. This was the third time that we had "trotted" over this road, and each time on Sunday. Long before night we entered camp near Warrenton Junction, where we remained several days. On the evenings of the 27th, 28th and 29th it poured. At five on the morning of the 30th we moved at a moderate gait to Elk Run; here two of the boys had nicely ensconced themselves underneath a pine and gone off to sleep, when one of them began patting, rubbing, scratching and slapping—now the back of his neck, then his side, then his legs, until tired nature could endure it no longer—when he broke out: "Jerusalem! say, what in thunder has got into our bed?" The stearine candle on a bayonet having been lighted, revealed the fact that a hillock of black ants had not only sent out skirmishers, but a reconnaisance in force, attacking in front, flank and rear; millions, big and little, flying and crawling, biting and pinching black "varmints," which could not be routed from stockings, pants, shirt and blankets in less than an hour.

The next morning at eight we started for Kelly's Ford; reached it late in the evening, so that many laid down to sleep without going to the trouble of making coffee, and most of those that did threw it away, as the water in the brook drained an old cavalry camp. The next morning, to the delight of many, seventeen men, with cups or canteens in hand, charged for the milk of one cow, and were in turn charged upon by a guard from headquarters, that possibly saw this to be the only chance and way to obtain for itself the much-coveted lactic fluid.

The next day, August 1st, the duty of guarding the railroad was assigned to our division, which returned to Elk Run in the afternoon and encamped on a rocky bluff, where a dreary and monotonous camp life was endured for two weeks with the thermometer ranging for several days along the nineties in the shade, whilst not a breath of air seemed at times to be stirring. Colonel Snider, of the Seventh Virginia, who had taken command of the brigade when we left Maryland, continued in charge.

## CHAPTER XX.

TO ALEXANDRIA—ON BOARD STEAMER ATLANTIC—SAIL TO NEW YORK CITY—JAMAICA PLAINS—RETURN TO ARMY OF THE POTOMAC AT ROBINSON RIVER—RACCOON FORD—VOTING FOR GOVERNOR—RECROSSING THE RAPPAHANNOCK—SKIRMISHING AT AUBURN—BATTLE OF BRISTOE STATION—AT CENTERVILLE—TO BRISTOE—TO WARRENTON.

On the 15th the Eighth Ohio started for New York City, to assist in enforcing the draft. On Sunday, the 16th, the Fourth Ohio and Fourteenth Indiana were ordered to report at Alexandria without delay. All extra-duty men and detachments were ordered to their regiments at once. The cars were taken at Bealeton Station at 2 P.M., and the train bore away a jolly set of boys, that were expecting a good time; locomotive, tender and top of the cars were blue with men, enjoying the breeze and the change and novelty of the situation, not knowing of a certainty their whither, but hoping it might be to help squelch the rioters.

We remained at Alexandria several days, changing camp once, on account of having taken up quarters within a few rods of a brick house containing seven cases of small-pox. The boys, having been paid off on the 6th, were flush, and enjoyed the board at restauants and hotels with those who received better pay. Never did ham and eggs disappear more rapidly, and so many eggs go into a single stomach as then, nor a host more pleased to give great slices of ham and "yust so many eggs as you want, for a quarter, or more, does make no difference."

By noon of the 20th it was certain that we were going on board of the large ocean steamer Atlantic; already the horses of the Fourth and Eighth Ohio, Seventh Michigan, First Minnesota and Fourteenth Indiana were being swung aloft, followed by rations, and soon the regiments named, nearly two thousand strong, lay down on deck, in cabin and hold until five in the morning, when the ship was already moving down the bay, those in the hold crawling on deck "to catch a breath of air." Two more sweltering nights were spent in the hold swarming with "gray-backs," that determined to act as "body-guards" for officers and privates; great was the slaughter of vermin. Adding to this the wretched feeling of being seasick, when a thousand or more were "calling for back rations to come up," made one most heartily glad of having the prospect of once more setting foot on terra firma, as in the early morning a pilot came on board, near Sandy Hook, and took us through the "Narrows." At two in the afternoon we disembarked, a rusty looking set, and took up quarters on Governor's Island, where a dull, monotonous life was led until the 28th, when the brigade headquarters, with most of the regiments, were moved to Fort Greene, or Washinton Park, an eminence overlooking a considerable part of Brooklyn, and the battle-field of General Washington; the Fourth Ohio went by rail and boat to Jamaica Plains, where it quartered some eight days, enjoying the hospitalities of the people. Wherever our troops were quartered the people would gather about them, ask many curious questions concerning our mode of life, watch our cooking and eating, and expressed great surprise that a single one had survived the "sleeping on the cold ground." It was soon evident to all that our services were no longer needed, discipline became lax, men and officers roamed throughout the cities seeing the sights, many indulging to their heart's content, some even beyond moderation.

Thousands of visitors spent part of Sunday, the 30th, with the soldiers; never were men more heartily welcomed; when some of the boys first made their appearance in Wall Street; there were "magnates" that did not stop with the hearty grip of the hand, but hugged the rusty soldier for very joy, exclaiming "God bless you, you are just in time." Privates as well as officers were taken by citizens to their homes, into their magnificent parlors, then after the social tete a tete, adjourned to loaded tables in the dining room, where continued the flow of soul for two or more hours, whilst the fifth to eighth courses followed each other at quite lengthened intervals. Quite a number of the Fourth were present, with many of the Eighth, at the grand festival given at the Carrollton Methodist Episcopal Church on the evening of the 5th.

The next evening, the 6th of September, those of the Fourth who were at Jamaica, and of the Fourteenth Indiana who were in New York City, gathered together at Fort Greene, moved over to New York City the next morning, got aboard the Atlantic in the evening, at the foot of Canal Street, steamed out into the ocean at nine the next morning, and passed by one of the monitors, which excited no little curiosity. On the 9th we were out of sight of land until four, when a storm was brewing toward the west, striking us just as we were entering the bay at night, doing us no damage, only causing a few to look pale and one poor fellow to fasten life preservers to all parts of his body, but the greater number to his legs. At the battle of Fredericksburg this same comrade had taken a position nearer the rebel line than any other man in the Army of the Potomac.

We disembarked at Alexandria at eight on the morning of the 11th, went into camp west of town until seven on the morning of the 12th, when we marched to Fairfax Court House; to Bristoe Station on the 13th, to Bealeton on the 14th, to Brandy Station on the 15th, and rejoined the Second Corps—now in command of General G. K. Warren—at Culpepper Court House, at noon on the 16th, where we advanced in battle array to the left of Cedar Mountain, toward Raccoon Ford, following our skirmishing cavalry.

On Thursday, September 17th, we moved forward some four miles to Robinson River, formed in line of battle, and bivouacked for the night; it rained very hard in the evening and also the next morning.

There had been quite a number of desertions of substitutes and drafted men for several weeks past, from some of the eastern regiments of our division, which was to a considerable extent remedied by the murderous and sickening execution of several of them on the afternoon of the 18th, in the presence of the entire division, drawn up in line at the foot of Raccoon Hill.

On the 19th the brigade went on picket guard on the other side of the river, beginning near the junction of the Rapidan and extending several miles toward Madison Court House, doing considerable skirmishing and foraging, returning to camp on the 23d with an abundance of fresh meat, as the boys had determined to let no hog or sheep turn up their noses at them, much less, "to bite them," nor any squirrels to chuckle or bark at them; General Gibbon ("Long Range") sent a squad of zouaves to arrest the foragers; the boys soon took their guns from them, which so enraged the general that he ordered the brigade to remain in the "rear until the last dog and mule had passed," in case there was danger; it served us a good turn, because the next attacks were not upon us, but upon other brigades, and to do his best the general could not eke out his vengeance, because circumstances seemed determined not to serve his purpose, but himself was brought under fire.

About this time the Eleventh and Twelfth Corps left for the west. On the 24th we received orders to be ready to march at a moment's notice. For more than a week fine weather prevailed, and we had easy times; the scenery was fine, especially from Raccoon Hill, from which the mountains westward could be readily seen. Brigade headquarters were at the house of a Mrs. Garnett.

On Monday, October 5th, we were relieved by the Sixth Corps, and the next day we marched back to Culpepper Court House, and encamped on a red clay hill some two miles northwest of the town. There had been an impression that Lee was falling back, but on the 10th it was determined that he was gaining our right and rear; about ten we received orders to be ready to march immediately, and in fifteen minutes we were on our way to Jeffrey's Saw Mill, where we halted in line, ready for action. On the 11th we marched to Brandy Station, took dinner, crossed the river at three, reached Bealeton at four, bivouacking on a blind road. Rations were very scarce, weather quite cool. Had orders to build no fires and to keep as quiet as possible. Under these circumstances, on the 12th, all in the regiment, with less than half a dozen exceptions, cast our ballots for Brough as Governor of Ohio. At eleven we began a hurried march, recrossed the Rappahannock at noon, went in support of our cavalry, whom we could see making a charge upon the enemy, and at five we bivouacked half a mile north of Brandy Station. We were, however, routed out at 1 o'clock, hurried forward, and again crossed the Rapahannock at four; halted three miles north of Bealeton, got a hot breakfast, rested until one, reached Auburn at ten; laid down without fires, as the enemy was very near us. The Third Corps was now at Greenwich, the Fifth at Catlett's, the Sixth on the railroad between Catlett's and Bristoe, and the First near Bristoe; Kilpatrick's cavalry at New Baltimore, Buford was guarding the wagon-train on its way toward Brentsville, and Gregg was on the left flank of our corps.

The next morning, Wednesday, October 14th, our division was to bring up the rear of the army and guard the wagon-train. We started before day, and were in the act of crossing Cedar Run when a volley came among us from the right and front immediately, without orders, guns were examined and capped, whilst the cannon were hurrying into position; shells burst near at hand, and spiteful minies whizzed over our heads, but in the mist and breaking day no enemy could be seen; skirmishers were immediately advanced with strong supports, whilst our batteries sent their compliments in the direction of the Confederates. Hardly had the firing ceased and our line of march begun when the rear of the division was attacked. We were now hurried forward at a rapid pace, with every man in his place, ready for any emergency, a fight or a lively race to a good position and co-operation with the rest of the army. It transpired that Stuart with his cavalry, hemmed in between our corps and Cregg's Cavalry during the night, in hearing of our camp bustle and being only four hundred yards distant, had fired on our front and right, whilst the firing in the rear was the advance of Lee, which was to help Stuart out of his dilemma. Ewell and Hill were hurrying forward toward Bristoe, to intercept our progress and bring on an engagement, while Meade not knowing the exact whereabouts and intentions of his antagonist, urged all his forces toward Centerville with the utmost speed to give battle there. Having crossed Cedar Run, we hurried forward for some distance, as a guard for the wagon-train, then halted, the train moving out of our way toward Brentsville, after which the march was resumed, moving forward a short distance, halting ready for an attack, whilst other brigades passed us, halted in line, permitting us to pass them in turn. At one point we saw the Confederates on our left, but took them to be our own men.

About 1 o'clock we halted in a dense pine forest, awaiting the arrival of Caldwell's Division, which was assisting the cavalry in repelling an attack of Ewell. Having been faced in line of battle toward the southwest for about an hour, firing was heard in the direction of our line of march, and shells could be seen bursting near the railroad; at once the passing troops were hurried forward at double-quick, and we soon moved rapidly after them, formed in line of battle, along and to the east of the railroad. In a short time a heavy line of skirmishers could be seen advancing rapidly up a hill from the troops on the railroad in advance of us, charge on a battery, take five guns and some four hundred and fifty prisoners; cheer upon cheer went up from the entire line. "We have a good position, let the Johnnies come."

Just before sunset it seemed we should be gratified to our heart's content, as it was certain that something unusual was transpiring on our front as well as in the pines on our right, into which our artillery continued to send their missiles; it was also learned from prisoners that Lee had intended to have his entire force at this point on this afternoon. We were not aware of our real situation, as we numbered only eight thousand, and were about being cut off by Hill's advance, if it had not been so handsomely checked, whilst Ewell was forming on our front and sweeping around our left before dark, making a force of thirty thousand against us. At this juncture the Fifth Corps, followed by the Third, came to Broad Run, connected with our advance, but soon pushed on again toward Centerville, our corps following, our regiment bringing up the rear. Our entire force having crossed Broad Run, we were certain that Lee had been outgeneraled by Meade and Warren, the latter our corps commander, whose praise was in every mouth; during the day all had abundant opportunity to see him give orders, maneuver troops in order to save his trains, yet at the same time not only be ready, but actually did repel front, rear and flank attacks, without making a single mistake, or appearing in the least disconcerted; this young officer was now more than ever admired and loved by all. We moved onward during the night, crossed Bull Run at Blackburn's Ford at 2 o'clock, proceeded about a mile, then bivouacked, just as it began to rain. At about eight (Thursday, October 15th,) we were hurried into line of battle, after which nothing transpired until shortly after noon, when there was slight skirmishing on the front, and some artillery practice. We remained near Centerville during the 16th, without rations, with pouring rain at frequent intervals. Late in the afternoon of the 17th, part of the brigade went in support of cavalry toward Manassas, but found no enemy. At night it was reported that the old movement by the way of Chantilly was being made by the Confederates.

The 18th seemed for once like Sunday, quiet prevailing, and the men enjoying the rest. There were present for duty three hundred and fifty-three. O. C. Knode and James McCollum were missing, and Corporal O. H. Barker wounded.

On the next morning, the 10th, tents were struck at an early hour, line of battle formed near Bristoe in the evening, arms stacked and tents put up. Started next morning, the 20th, at seven, made an easy march to within a mile of Greenwich, where we rested until the 22d, when tents were struck at six in the morning, and soon after entered camp near Warrenton. The next day was cold and stormy; although we were to be ready to march at a moment's notice the men began to make themselves as comfortable as the circumstances would permit.

SURGEON F.W. MORRISON.

## CHAPTER XXI.

TO KELLY'S FORD—SKIRMISH—TO ROBERTSON'S TAVERN—BATTLE—MINE RUN, BATTLE—EXPECTED FORLORN HOPE—GENERAL WARREN'S SENSIBLE DECISION TO SACRIFICE HIS COMMISSION RATHER THAN HIS MEN—RETURN THROUGH THE WILDERNESS TO CAMP NEAR BRANDY STATION.

We were now in the midst of dull camp life once more, going on picket, drawing supplies for the approaching winter, when at seven in the morning of Saturday, November 7th, we started on a forced march to Kelly's Ford, accompanied by the Third Corps; our batteries soon opened upon Rhodes' Confederates, whilst some of the infantry waded across and captured three hundred and forty prisoners. Sedgwick had still better luck, having, with the Fifth and Sixth Corps, charged the enemy at dark and captured nearly the entire of Hays and Hoke's Brigades, the very men who had confronted us on Cemetery Hill at Gettysburg. The next morning we crossed the river and formed in line of battle; after about an hour we marched some distance toward Rappahannock Station and again formed in line of battle; after two hours we marched toward Brandy Station, halted on the spot occupied by us on our return from New York, moved forward a short distance and went into camp at the Station, where we remained during the snowstorm of the next day. On the 10th we marched to Mountain Run and encamped on a Mr. Hamilton's farm. About this time an order was issued by the Secretary of War directing the carrying of no more than five days' rations and forty rounds of ammunition by each man. What a relief! At Centerville we had made the attempt to become veritable camels by loading ourselves with eleven days' rations and sixty rounds of ammunition.

The mountains were now covered with snow, the winds raw and piercing; pine trees were felled, great fires built and chimneys erected. On the 18th we received several months' pay. Early on the 23d tents were struck, but as it began to rain they were put up immediately.

Early on Thursday morning, November 26, 1863, we again struck tents, made a rapid march to Germania Ford, crossed the river and bivouacked in the dense thickets of the Wilderness during the night, and resumed our march early on the 27th, taking a blind road until within about two miles of Robertson's Tavern, where about 10 o'clock we were confronted by some Confederates; the brigade immediately formed in line beyond the Tavern, advanced rapidly with the skirmishers in a field to the left of the pike as well as in the woods on the right; the Seventh West Virginia was on our left, and Carroll's voice could be frequently heard during the firing, "Guide left;" both regiments sent a volley into a house swarming with rebels, making the splinters, glass and clapboards fly and the Johnnies "light out" for the rear; their entire line now fell rapidly back, leaving in our hands a number of prisoners belonging to Gordon's Brigade of Early's Division; our brigade followed them down a slope, but was halted, as it was not desired to bring on a regular engagement, because the corps that was to support us had lost its way and was not yet at hand.

At 4 o'clock General Warren, commanding our corps, ordered an advance from the position held, about a mile from the Tavern, toward Mine Run. The Seventh West Virginia was at once deployed as skirmishers, got into a severe engagement, and they were on the point of being worsted, when our regiment became anxious and requested to go to their assistance, for the boys always felt toward these gallant comrades as if they were brothers; the wish was gratified, as the entire brigade was ordered forward and at once made havoc with the rebels, driving them, after a stubborn resistance, until a good position was reached, when another halt was called, as the support was not yet on hand. There was occasional firing during the night, the enemy seeming to be nervous; he withdrew before daylight; our men had orders not to fire a single gun. Our support was now at hand; the brigade was ordered to advance at an early hour; the skirmishers moved rapidly forward, found no foe until after they had gone more than a mile and had started down into the deep ravine of Mine Run, beyond which could be seen abatis and entrenchments. Toward noon it began to rain, when there was considerable cannonading, mostly by our batteries on the hill back of the brigade, which remained all day and nearly all night on picket. Provisions had become very scarce. We had one man killed and twelve wounded.

In the evening there was "a dispensation of Providence" as one of the boys called it; a sow with a litter of about a dozen good-sized pigs came through the mire over into our skirmishing brigade, and was captured by a captain's cook; hog and shoats were divided among the companies and furnished fresh pork for all. The air was now very chilly and our clothing wet; thoroughly drenched, covered with snow and sleet, did this night on picket find us, so that we had nearly perished before we were relieved early the next morning, Sunday the 29th, just before the break of day.

We were soon with our corps and one division of the Sixth, marching toward the left, reaching Hopewell Church at about two in the afternoon, where our cavalry had a short but spirited contest that in no way hindered our advance, which was continued over two miles; the Second Division had several men wounded in a brief skirmish; turning into the forest and proceeding some distance through underbrush, a position was taken that brought our left to a railroad grade; picks and shovels were brought into lively requisition throwing up entrenchments; poultry and fresh pork was soon brought into camp by the foragers. Just at dark we got into a lively skirmish; during the night two divisions of Sykes' Corps joined us. The disposition of the Union forces on the morning of the 30th was as follows: Sedgwick, with the Sixth Corps, on the extreme right some six miles distant; then Sykes with the Fifth on the immediate right of the turnpike, and Newton with the First on the left; then one division of the Third; then Warren, with the Second Corps, supported by French with two divisions of the Third and one of the Sixth; Sedgwick and Warren were to make a simultaneous attack at 8 o'clock of the 30th.

At an early hour skirmishers were advanced in our front; we followed nearly a quarter of a mile in line of battle. The enemy was now only thirty yards to twenty rods distant on the other side of Mine Run, with its bogs, abrupt banks and steep slope covered with felled trees, followed by lines of rifle-pits, piles of logs and dirt, batteries, and swarms of Confederates. Jackson's old corps had worked like beavers all night and kept themselves in a sweat "to give the Yanks a warm reception in the morning." They were in high glee, full of frolic and anxious to have us venture. Our men knew what was expected of them; they had been given the particulars; because of the cold and the serious work before them the faces of many wore a strange pallid blue; hardly anyone expected to come back alive; some wrote their names on slips of paper, pinned on the outer coat or slipped it under the belt, then each one, looking from the direful task before them to the Eternal Father for strength to do his whole duty, awaited orders.

Eight o'clock came, and with it the boom of the gun that signaled the attack; soon followed the roar of musketry on our right; the Confederate cannon on our right could from some points be seen sending forth its fire and smoke; every man was in line, with gun tightly grasped; time wore away, and half an hour had passed, and the painful suspense was soon over when word was passed along the line that our commander, General Warren, noblest of the noble, had said, "The works cannot be taken, and I would sooner sacrifice my commission in the army than to sacrifice my men." Doubtless many lips spoke the "God bless him;" the Second Corps—the entire army, would follow such a leader to the death. There was to be no more unnecessary slaughtering.

About noon the line fell back a short distance, guns were stacked, knapsacks claimed, fires built and all possible comfort sought for our chilling bodies. The day passed, and the night, and all of Tuesday, December 1st, with nothing unusual transpiring until at half past eight in the evening; the fires having been replenished, knapsacks packed, the blankets and rubbers folded, we fell into line and moved quietly as possible through the brush to the plank road, then tramp, tramp, over plantations, through the seemingly endless Wilderness, passing squads of cavalrymen and smoldering fires, a future battle-field, burning forest, and the spot where was arranged the charge on the Eleventh Corps, reached Culpepper Mine Ford at sunrise, took breakfast, rested until noon, and then started once more for the quarters we had left a week previous, and reached them at seven in the evening. General Meade had intended to winter his troops at Fredericksburg, but General Halleck ordered him to remain at the Rapidan. The Roster shows the following list of casualties:

Killed—J. Sinus, of Company B.

Wounded—R. Kimball of A, T. Beach of B, Captain Jones of C, E. Shannon of D, J. Austin of F, E. T. Shull of G, H. Wilson of H, J. B. Fisher and F. Kopp of K.

John Crawford, of Company C, was killed, and W. G. Morton of F wounded, at Robertson's Tavern.

## CHAPTER XXII.

OUR LAST WINTER QUARTERS—LOG HUTS BUILT—TO MORTON'S FORD—FORDING THE RIVER—BATTLE—CARROLL ON HIS OWN RESPONSIBILITY CHARGES THE CONFEDERATES—ACCOUNT OF CAPTAIN STROUB.

On the 5th of December camp was moved several miles to the southwest, where there was a better location and greater abundance of timber. On the 7th we again changed about one-half mile, at Colonel Carroll's request; went into winter quarters on Cole's Hill, on a branch of Mountain Run, with Brandy Station north of us, Stevensburg two miles south, and Culpepper Court House six miles west. The brigade lay between two hills, sheltered from eastern storms and western gales; streets were laid in regular order, and huts put up in the lines of companies, of sufficient size to hold ten to sixteen men; most of the officers remained in wall tents; for both tents and huts chimneys were built with sticks and clay. On the 11th an order was received granting furloughs and leave of absence, on the same plan as that pursued at Falmouth the year previous. On the 21st there was considerable excitement in reference to re-enlisting, which soon extended to the remaining regiments, and quite a number re-enlisted. A furlough of some sixty days, considerable bounty, with good chance of promotion, were the inducements held out, and thereby retarded as many as it influenced, since many expressed their contempt of re-enlisting from such unworthy motives after having served their country out of pure patriotism for nearly three years. It is probable that numbers would have fallen once more into line if the matter had only been presented in the light of duty.

Christmas came and passed with nothing unusual transpiring, save the imbibing an extra amount of "commissary" by some made camp rather lively, especially on New Year's eve. Cold and blustering weather had thus far prevailed, but Friday, January 1st, 1864, capped the climax, with howling winds that bulged the tents, tore off roofs from the huts and made the chimneys smoke; late in the afternoon it turned to a bitter cold, that caused some who had not a sufficient supply of covering to nearly perish, in spite of roaring fires. Many made themselves comfortable by placing Muster Rolls and other paper between their blankets. The duties during the winter months were not as heavy as the previous winter, since there were more men to perform them. There were occasional drills, the usual brigade and picket guard, chopping and hauling firewood, building roads, and thorough enforcement of police regulations in and about company quarters. Soon neither officers nor men could obtain commissary whisky, save through an order countersigned by regimental and brigade commander.

The greater part of the Seventh Virginia having re-enlisted, the regiment presented Colonel Lockwood, of Moundsville, West Virginia, their commander, with a fine sword and watch on Wednesday, February 3d, in the presence of a number of ladies and a large number of the members of the brigade, and it was made the occasion of witty speeches and a merry time without the help of "commissary."

On the same day General Butler, at Old Point Comfort, sent a telegram to General Sedgwick, who commanded the army in the absence of General Meade, asking him to make a demonstration against Lee, whilst he would with his forces proceed against Richmond. Accordingly, Kilpatrick moved against the enemy at Culpepper Mine Ford, Merritt at Barnett's Ford, Warren with the Second Corps at Morton's Ford, and Newton, with the First Corps, at Raccoon Ford. Caldwell, in the absence of Warren, who was not well enough to take command until late in the day, through some misapprehension of orders, sent a part of his troops wading to their armpits across the river, which captured the enemy's outpost and then pushed forward toward his entrenchments.

The following are the details, as given by the lamented Captain Stroub, in the "*Marsonian Literary Casket:*" "No body of troops, probably, were ever more surprised at receiving that familiar order—'The command will move at six o'clock, with three day's rations in the haversack'—than we of the Second Corps were, as we lay unconsciously snoring in our bunks about 3 o'clock on the cold morning of February 6th, 1864. There had been neither the faintest intimation nor slightest indication of a move of any kind, and hence our surprise. And our surprise was not of the most agreeable nature, either, coming as it did in the 'wee sma' hours ayout the twal,' on a cold, bleak wintry morning, rousing us from our warm bunks, and the enjoyment of a good sleep—which our duties allow us to enjoy not too often at best—and indicating as it did a winter campaign of three days' duration at least. Nevertheless, we 'hustled' out with that prompt obedience that characterizes the gallant soldier, smothering our half-ejaculations of displeasure with the best possible grace, and at the appointed time were ready for the road and the fray. About 8 o'clock we formed a column and moved forward, the Third Brigade of our division in advance, ours (First Brigade) following.

"By 10 o'clock we reached the Rapidan River, and were in the immediate front of the enemy. The whole force, with the exception of the Third Brigade, which was thrown forward, with skirmishers in advance, toward the river, was halted an hour or so under friendly cover of an adjacent wood, and then the artillery was hurried forward to take position so as to cover the crossing of the river, while our brigade pushed rapidly forward to its support, followed promptly by the Second Brigade. As soon as our supporting column emerged from the wood the enemy opened their batteries upon us, and sent shell screaming at and over us, but our brave veteran column moved steadily and unconcernedly along, and took up its position without the loss of a man.

"But we were not allowed to remain here long. In a few minutes we were ordered to forward and cross the river to the support of the Second Brigade, which had forded the river above by wading, under the leadership of its immediate commander, Brigadier General Owen, and our division commander, Brigadier General Hays. The latter brave general dismounted and was the first to wade the river, which was broad and deep, taking a man to the armpits, and ordered his staff to dismount and wade also. It was a brave example for brave men, and it was right bravely followed. After crossing, that brigade made a slight detour to the right, capturing a rebel picket-post of twenty-five men, including two commissioned officers, and then moved to the left and engaged the enemy's skirmishers.

"It was at this stage of the movement that our brave brigade commander, Colonel Carroll, rode along the brigade and intimated the part we were to play, by the laconic words, "Boys, you've got to take water." Cæsar! how our under lip dropped and teeth chattered, and how the cold chills ran through us at the bare prospect of crossing that broad, deep river on a cold wintry day, and without the certainty of being able to dry our clothes when once across. But, notwithstanding, we 'grinned and bore it,' though with many a shiver, and with more than one ejaculation smothered and outspoken.

"Once over the river we moved directly forward over the rolling plain, cut by ravines, which spread out before us for perhaps a mile, and then rose in a succession of wooded and cleared elevations, upon which the enemy was almost impregnably entrenched. About midway of the river and the enemy's position, was an elevated ridge which stretched across the plain and partially covered our advance from the fire of the rebel batteries, directed furiously at us. But in crossing this ridge, and a ravine that cut it transversely and which was completely enfiladed by the guns of the enemy, we were exposed to a terrible fire of artillery, which, however, fortunately for us, went wide of the mark, though close enough for comfort. All the regiments of the division successively ran this furious fire, with the loss of but two or three men. Gaining a cover offered by an advanced knoll, the division was halted and massed, while skirmishers were thrown out to the front, who soon opened a spirited fight, charging and driving the line of rebel skirmishers almost to their works.

"Meanwhile those famous sharp-shooting batteries, Arnold's and Rickett's, directed occasional volleys at the rebel works. Their shells burst, every one, apparently, on the very parapets, and every time scattered the rebel masses that swarmed the works to witness the skirmishing in the valley below. The division lay massed behind the knoll, disturbed only by the whizzing of balls from the skirmish line, and the near bursting of an occasional shell, until about sundown, when all of a sudden the enemy opened upon our masses with all their batteries, while their infantry attacked us heavily along the line, driving back our skirmishers on the right, with the evident intention of getting between us and the ford, and thereby cutting us off from the river.

" 'Fall in—Take arms,' was the order that now passed hurriedly from battalion to battalion. The brave boys of our brigade fell in and took arms under that heavy fire as coolly as if from a rest on drill, and with many a hearty laugh and witticism given because of the timidity and momentary demoralization of the recruits and conscripts, who comprised a considerable proportion of many of the regiments of the division. 'They are flanking us on the right; they are getting between us and the river,' was now the startling cry. 'Have you any orders for me?' coolly asked Colonel Carroll, of one of the aids. 'No, Colonel, but they are flanking us on the right.' 'Then I'll take the responsibility to drive them back,' replied the doughty Colonel, and then commanded, 'Battalion! Right Face!! Forward—March!!!' in those stentorian tones of his, which alone, seemingly, are enough to strike terror into a foe of usual stoicism.

"And forward went our veteran brigade, with the steadiest step and most composed mien imaginable, elbow to elbow, and with guns at right-shoulder-shift, onward to the right where lay the point of danger, not a man dodging or faltering while missiles of death from the enemy's cannon plowed the very ground they trod—screaming, howling and bursting over them, through them, and all around them—and while a deadly musketry-fire poured through their ranks, like swarms of bees and storm of hail combined. Men were struck, fell dead and wounded, but the brave files closed up, and the brave column moved steadily on, men having to be ordered out of the ranks to take care of the wounded. Oh! it was magnificent to behold, and certainly it should be hard to forget, and it would be a gross wrong not to record the sublime behavior of our gallant brigade on that occasion, under that galling fire. Yet we moved down steadily, under that galling fire, toward the river, flanking, moving to the right-about, halting and dressing, until a position was found and taken to counteract the flank movement of the enemy, when skirmishers were thrown out, the rebels driven back, and the old line resumed. Thus our gallant conduct most probably prevented a second Ball's Bluff disaster. But how are your newspaper reports? The First Brigade might as well have been back in camp for all mention it received. Towards midnight we were relieved by parts of the First Division, and withdrawn across the river on an improvised bridge. We were moved back a short distance, and permitted to build fires, dry our wet clothing, warm our chilled frames, and make coffee. Until the evening of the 7th we lay there undisturbed, when we returned to camp. The loss in the brigade was about fifty killed and wounded, out of some five hundred that went into the fight.

"I have ever felt pride at the behavior of our gallant men in every one of the many battles and engagements in which they have participated, but I fairly idolized them on this occasion. 'One should not blow his own horn,' and 'self-praise is no praise,' it is said; but as a faithful chronicler, I feel compelled to tell 'the truth, the whole truth, and nothing but the truth,' even though it should sound like big I and we, and little you. Besides, I find that if we of the First Brigade do not blow our own horn, it won't be blown for some reason, I don't know what, without it's because we're the clodhoppers of the Army of the Potomac. Never but once, at Antietam, it seems, since our connection with the Army of the Potomac, have we received proper mention for distinguished services; and this, too, although our little brigade was resolved into a forlorn hope at Fredericksburg, first took the line and drew the murderous fire of their concentrated batteries, and kept that line for five long hours, losing half our gallant men; and this, too, although at Chancellorsville, when all were faltering and many had been driven, and the flushed foe was surging upon and threatening to annihilate our disorganized masses, our little brigade of seven hundred, unsupported, with serried ranks charged forward through the tangled woods, over enfiladed roads and ravines, fairly driving whole divisions of the enemy from their strong works, and really checking, as it were, the advance of the whole flushed army of treason, thus enabling our broken, shattered line to be reformed, and thus probably saving the entire army; and this, too, although at Gettysburg, when our very center-heart, as it were, was all driven, shattered, pierced, and the guns on Cemetery Hill silenced and taken, our little brigade again saved the day by gallantly charging forward, recapturing the batteries, and driving back the rebel host. We might mention other instances

of our gallant conduct; in fact we have borne a prominent part in every engagement in which we have participated. Our conduct has ever been a theme of praise; but somehow it has always been accorded to somebody else; never but once to us. On our first advent into the Army of the Potomac we pushed to the front, and drove back the batteries and advance of the enemy, who were harassing the weary and fatigued—but still gallant and organized—Army of the Potomac, which had just stood the ordeal of the seven days' battles. Our conduct was glowingly mentioned in the newspaper reports, but ascribed to the praise of some other brigade. I am neither a grumbler nor the son of grumbler, but I do claim to be a lover of justice and fair dealing. But pardon my lengthy digression. WM. S. STROUB,
*Captain Fourth O. V. I."*

The loss in the regiment was reported as: Killed, none; wounded, seventeen. The Roster mentions the following as among the wounded:

Sergeant Major M. E. Haas, mortally.
Company B—J. Conley, V. Glasscock and G. M. Parks.
Company D—J. Burdett and W. Hamblin.
Company F—J. Austin, W. Hershey, J. Ricksecker and L. H. Stands.
Company H—A. Griswold and H. Saiter.
Company K—W. A. Berry.

## CHAPTER XXIII.

SPRING OF 1864 — MARSONIAN LITERARY SOCIETY — *MARSONIAN LITERARY CASKET* — GRAND REVIEW FEBRUARY 23d — WE CHANGE THE BLUE FOR THE WHITE TREFOIL BADGE — REORGANIZATION OF THE ARMY — GENERAL GRANT WITH THE ARMY OF THE POTOMAC — THE CRIMSON-COLORED SAND STORM.

On the 29th of January an adjourned meeting was called and a literary society organized, named the "Marsonian Lyceum of the First Brigade, Third Division, Second Army Corps," of which anyone in the brigade might become a member. A brigade chapel was about this time built, in which the Lyceum held its meetings on each Friday evening, to listen to a lecture or to follow a regular programme of essays and discussions. Twice every Sunday and once during each week religious services were held in the chapel. There was also published a quarto size four-page paper, named the *Marsonian Literary Casket*, with the motto, "Dum Vivimus, Vivamus," and first appeared about the last of February. A history of the brigade from its organization in February, 1862, until May 22d of the same year, occupies nearly two columns. Captain Stroub's account of the affair at Morton's Ford takes up one side; a defense of the morals and morality of the soldiers and a statement of the doings and aims of the Lyceum fill up the greater part of another page; a column is given to the honor of the "Veterans," as those were called who had re-enlisted for another three years; in half a column the editor states how it came that General Sumner, immediately after the battle of Antietam, called ours the "Gibraltar Brigade;" Captain Stroub, as poet, occupies nearly an entire column on "The Gibraltar Brigade of Antietam," whilst one-half of the first column is appropriated to poetic effusions "from the pen of a distinguished field officer of the brigade," entitled "The Night Before the Battle." Aside from these there appeared the following news of the day: that Company B, Fourth Ohio, had erected a dance-house and almost every evening tripped the fantastic toe to the music of the fiddlien; that Captain Brearly had purchased a football, which caused for himself and the boys the "veins to swell, the breast to heave and glow;" that a hall fifty by one hundred feet was being constructed at corps' headquarters, and decorated with national and regimental colors and wreaths of cedar boughs, and lighted by three hundred and fifty star candles; that already officers had gone to Washington to make a requisition for ladies to attend the grand hop, where eight sets could at one time "swing your partner" after having partaken of the magnificent supper, given in honor of Washington; and finally we are informed that, "a few nights since, when the 'wee small hours' were drawing slowly by, two 'shoulder-straps,' evidently having on board more 'commissary' than their weak knees could support, staggered into a *sink* containing about two feet of dish-water and other slops; after floundering about for some time they managed to get out, when one of them, shaking the moisture from his garments, said: '(Hic) Bill, how are the (hic) mighty fallen?'"

It is not manifest that more than one number of the paper was issued; probably it was not a financial success. The Lyceum was well attended, as were the religious services, and the men did make an effort to improve themselves, mentally and morally, and there is no doubt that many officers and men reformed their lives; for much that was done too much credit cannot be given to our indefatigable Chaplain, D. G. Strong, called by the Inspector General the "best chaplain in the Army of the Potomac." This brother of every man was elected to the chaplaincy by the unanimous vote of the regiment when the old fatherly chaplain, Rev. Dr. Lorenzo Warner, was compelled to resign on account of ill health.

Some of our officers attended the corps' ball, which was graced by the presence of Vice-President Hamlin, Meade and his generals, and some two hundred ladies, the most of whom were present at the grand review of the army near Stevensburg, on Tuesday the 23d, when the men stood in the cold "two mortal hours" at attention, waiting for the cavalcade to appear or the procession to move. No one knew the cause of the delay, but one of the married boys remarked, "We are only waiting, as usual, for the women to get their fixings on."

On the 27th we had orders to be ready to move at a moment's notice; this was to give aid, if necessary, to the raid that was being made toward Richmond by our cavalry. During the months of March and April there was more drilling, especially of the conscripts and recruits of other brigades, which so vividly reminded us of our first efforts to keep step and eyes right; there was also a "rivival of music," if one could judge from the "everlasting racket" made by brass horns, fifes and drums, from reveille until tattoo, with their "Too, taw, tee, taw, toot" and "Er'-rub, dub, dub," that threatened to collapse the entire nervous organization of every soul that had to put up with it, however much he might vow to smash the squawking things. Occasionally some one did take dire vengeance, to the utter disgust of the owner of horn or drum.

About the last of March, General Grant made his headquarters with the Army of the Potomac, reviewed the troops, who were eager to see him; General Hancock also resumed command of the Second Corps; the First and Second Divisions of the Third Corps were assigned to our corps, whose brigades and divisions were in turn consolidated. Our brigade was now designated the Third Brigade, Second Division, Second Army Corps, commanded by Colonel S. S. Carroll and composed of the following regiments, in the order named: Fourth Ohio, Seventh West Virginia, One Hundred and Eighth New York, Twelfth New Jersey, Tenth Battalion New York, Eighth Ohio, Fourteenth Connecticut and the First Delaware. We were now required to remove our blue trefoil badge and place in its stead the white trefoil. Our force now numbered, all told, about one hundred thousand men, of all arms, the Confederates possibly sixty-two thousand.

About the last of April officers' wives had returned home, surplus baggage had been turned over and sent to the rear, and a standing order issued to be ready to march with four days' rations in haversacks, and forty rounds of ammunition in cartridge-boxes, and knapsacks.

On the 2d of May there occurred a strange phenomena; about five in the evening, just as many of the troops were returning from drill, a terrible storm loomed up westward toward the mountains and soon hid them from sight; the clouds gathered denser blackness, approached rapidly, rose higher and higher, the highest assuming a fiery redness, so that, above the blackness of darkness, crimson masses rolled over and over and hurried onward until they were directly above us; drops of rain began to fall, the wind to be tempestuous, trees to bend, crack and fall, and a hurricane of sand entered every crevice and hid the day so that one could not discern an object at a distance of four feet. "The world is coming to an end," "Gabriel will blow his horn," was heard when the storm came near, but when upon us in full blast, not a word was heard during the three minutes that the fury of sand continued; the storm gone by, sand covered everything, was everywhere—in everything.

## CHAPTER XXIV.

BATTLE OF THE WILDERNESS — TOD'S TAVERN — BATTLE AT PO RIVER — BATTLE AT LAUREL HILL — CARROLL A BRIGADIER—GRAND CHARGE AT SPOTTSYLVANIA.

Tuesday, May 3d, we received orders to march at eleven at night; at that hour we set out from our last camp and winter quarters with three hundred and seventy-two men and officers ready for duty, crossed the Rapidan at Ely's Ford at nine the next morning, May 4th; the heat being great, overcoats and blankets were strewn along the road as we entered the Wilderness; we made Chancellorsville before noon and the brigade halted; the Fourth, being wagon-guard, accompanied the train to Chancellorsville and bivouacked.

General Hancock had orders to move at five in the morning to Shady Grove Church, extend his right toward the Fifth Corps at Parker's Store; the rest of the brigade with the corps reached Tod's Tavern before nine, and remained near it for some two hours, awaiting orders, which were received near 11 o'clock, when it at once moved to the right, out on the Brock Road, and was soon on the very route taken by Jackson, to the right of the Union position at Chancellorsville; our march was most of the time hurried, at times on the double-quick, with horsemen, guns and caissons obstructing the way. Shortly before 4 o'clock the column halted on an old plantation, where the furrows of an old tobacco-field were thickly covered with pine trees that were from ten to thirty and more feet in height; musketry could now be distinctly heard in the direction we were marching, at the intersection of the Brock and Orange Plank Roads, on the Cook Plantation, some three miles southeast of Parker's Store, two and a half southwest of Chancellorsville, and two west and south of Old Wilderness Tavern, and one-half mile from a railroad bed. In front of our place of halting the Brock Road passed over a high ridge with ravines on either side, the head-waters of the Ny River. On this ridge were several large apple trees, and back of it a run where the boys filled their canteens.

Soon after four the brigade, except our regiment, was hurried forward to and beyond the Plank Road, skirmishers deployed into the dense wood of scrub oaks, with rigid branches reaching from near the roots to the very top, and a position taken to the right of Getty's Division of the Sixth Corps and a general fusilade at once began, the Eighth Ohio and Fourteenth Indiana advancing in support of the skirmishers, who soon recaptured two of Rickett's guns; then rifle-pits were constructed near the road; several had been wounded and killed before the peculiar gloom of approaching darkness made the dense underbrush seem more difficult to penetrate, and the firing was mostly by random in the direction where the enemy could not be seen, but the crack of the musket or rifle revealed his close proximity; at dark firing had mostly ceased, as neither side seemed ready for a general onset.

Friday, May 6, 1864. At break of day, our regiment having been relieved by wagon-guard, hurried forward on the double-quick from its bivouac on the Chancellorsville battle-ground and took its position on the right of the brigade, before 5 o'clock, just as it was joining in the general charge that was to be made, but had been anticipated by a charge of the rebels on the troops on our right and a demonstration on our front that seemed not seriously intended, because there was an immediate falling back, as our brigade moved forward rapidly into the dense underbrush and fired at any rebels that could be seen.

The Confederates constantly fell back on our front until we came near to a field, when about 9 o'clock we were ordered to halt and dress up our lines. The firing was kept up for nearly two hours, when, just as we were ready to advance, a terrific volley, and another, and still others, were poured into our ranks by Longstreet's entire corps, which had been permitted to form in line unobserved on our front. On either side, but especially on the left, the troops fell back, bringing us under an enfilading fire and compelling us to fall back or be captured; many of our boys continued to punish their pursuers after having been wounded. Again did our regiments endeavor to make a

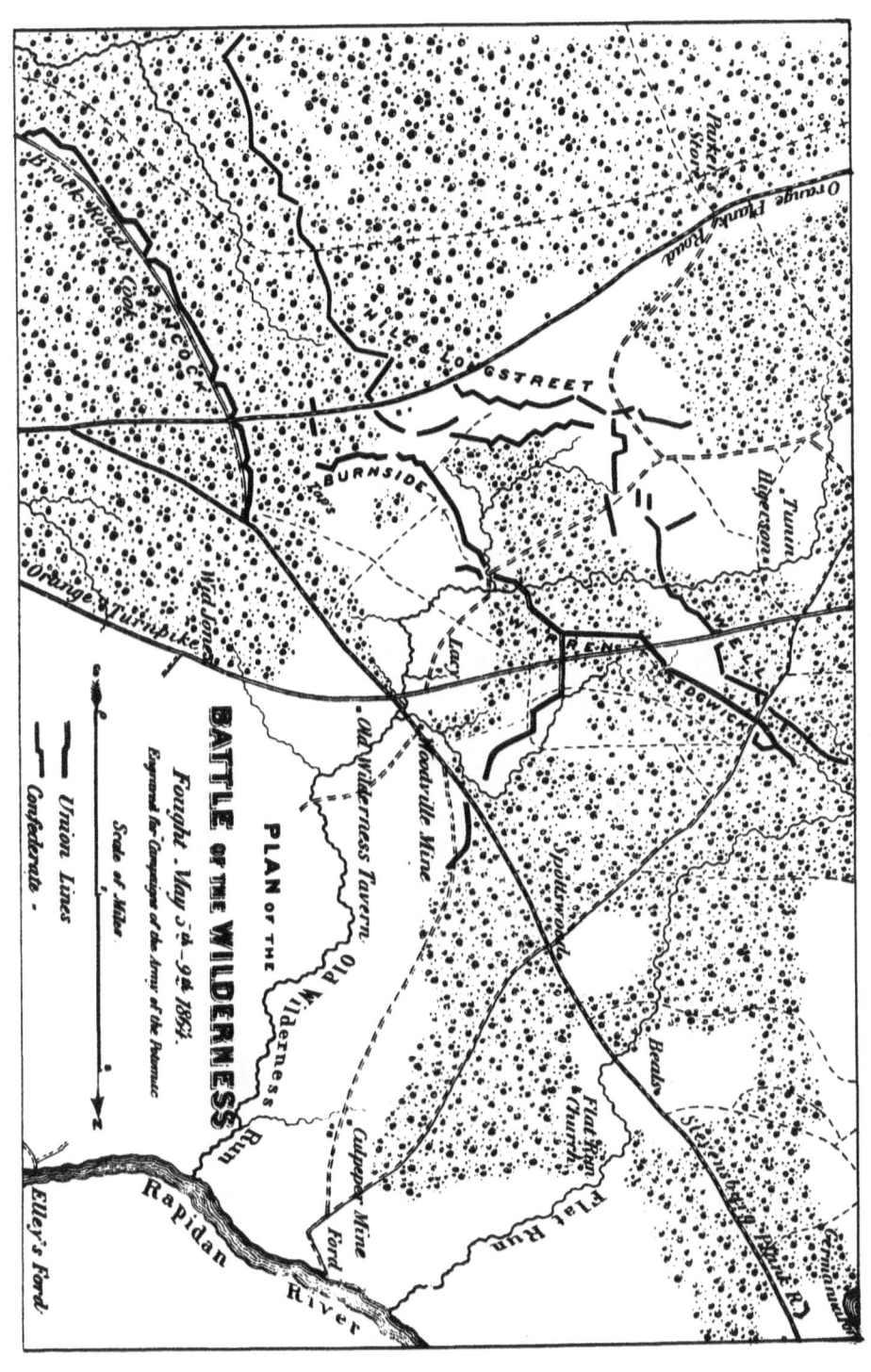

stand, until they were again flanked. Carroll and other officers, on foot and on horseback, gave directions and formed rallying points, only to be again out-flanked, and compelled to retire before a superior force. Once, when the troops on our right began to break from only a front fire, the wrath of our boys waxed hot, and many for the time forgot that there was death and dying all around them, and imprecations were heaped unsparingly upon the men who ran to the rear when there was no great occasion for it; even if their time of service did expire in a few days—so would ours in a month. Good authorities state that the men were out of ammunition; others say that they felt it was useless to make a stand, so back they went, leaving the brigade to contend with Johnnies to the left of them, Johnnies to the front of them, Johnnies to the right of them, compelling it to retire or be captured; the road was reached, troops to the right and left of the brigade were falling rapidly back beyond it, and some of the brigade were disposed to follow, but were ordered by Colonel Carroll to halt and stand their ground; and halt they did, the Fourth being the first to make a stand, probably because it heard the order first, for the rest of the regiments also at once turned upon their pursuers and would not yield another inch; in the meantime Colonel Carroll, although suffering from a wound just received, rode to the fleeing troops and shouted: "For God's sake don't leave me and my men to fight the whole rebel army; stand your ground."

Hancock, Meade and Grant were near and expressed their high appreciation of the services just rendered by the brigade. Some of the boys were halted by a guard as they were going to the creek to fill their canteens. Hancock called out, "Let those men fill their canteens; they are my fighting men." The Confederate onset had already weakened before they came to the road, on account of Longstreet having received a severe wound and Lee having taken command, they were not ready to follow up their advantage until toward night. In the meantime our rifle-pits were strengthened, cartridge-boxes replenished, and all was again in readiness for an advance.

Just before five in the evening the skirmishers began a vigorous firing, and were immediately joined by the troops in the rifle-pits on our front; the woods had been for some time on fire, the dense smoke being driven into our faces, followed by the roaring flames, whirled by the wind, rendering the air for some time stifling hot; of this state of things we were certain the enemy would take advantage, and make a charge upon the line in the pits but a few rods in front of us; the conjecture proved correct, and all were in readiness awaiting the event; presently the "yell" was heard, and on the rebels came, until many of them charged to and over the rifle-pits, which were now being deserted; it was high time for action, and the brigade, with rousing cheers, came to the rescue of the front line, captured a number of prisoners, and sent the remainder reeling back under a well-directed volley, following them beyond the works. After this there was but little more than a random firing of the pickets thrown out; the line was dressed and further events and orders awaited until about 9 o'clock, when we were moved a mile to the right and constructed a line of earthworks during the night.

Saturday, May 7th. There was but little demonstration even on the skirmish-line during the night, which was mostly spent in caring as far as possible for the wounded, who were taken to the corps' hospital, where a large detail of surgeons were busy all night in dressing wounds, amputating limbs and removing the wounded to the rear toward Fredericksburg. Many of the slightly wounded remained with their comrades in the ranks. During the forenoon we were under orders to be ready to march at 12 o'clock; noon came, and also night, when we moved nearly two miles to the right and bivouacked. Our loss in the regiment was eight killed, twenty-six wounded and several missing.

Company A—H. Koontz, killed; R. A. Hall and Ohio Pancoast, wounded.

Company B—V. Glasscock and R. Sebring, killed; A. J. Booze, A. Evarts, J. Fletcher, W. Jones, B. M. Murphy, P. Robinson and J. Ross, wounded.

Company C—N. Conine, killed; Charles Vining died soon of wounds; W. J. Ward, wounded.

Company D—G. V. Devore, killed; A. Ridges and J. Bender, wounded.

Company E—D. Best, H. Cook, J. Johnson, J. Kope, T. McClarren, M. M. Smith, H. Swickey, W. Singer and W. F. Smith, wounded.

Company F—E. W. Alexander and J. Miller, killed; J. G. Darr, B. C. Goodwill, J. Richards, W. M. Shorb and J. Trownsell, wounded.

Company G—J. McArthur, killed; J. Rice, wounded.

Company H—J. French, killed; J. Beckley, wounded.

Company K—J. Rall and S. E. Smith, killed; J. Beaver and L. F. Fullmer, wounded.

Sunday, May 8th. Early in the morning we awoke and found the Fifth Corps passing us; at seven we followed, reached Tod's Tavern before noon, halted at two whilst Warren's Corps was skirmishing with the enemy toward Spottsylvania Court House, some of the shell dropping near us. Again we moved forward until we had gone about three miles, halted for half an hour, moved another half mile and bivouacked for the night. Four days' rations were soon issued and abundance of ammunition furnished and well taken care of by the men, who knew its value now as never before, for a large number had fired not only all the rounds they had, but many that were taken from the boxes of the wounded and dead.

### BATTLE OF PO RIVER.

Monday, May 9th. Early in the morning we moved one and a half miles toward Tod's Tavern, in support of General Birney's Division, until ten, when we marched about three miles toward Spottsylvania Court House, halted on the Hart Farm, near to where a battery was shelling a wagon-train, making it move in a lively and amusing manner and spilling out large quantities of corn and black beans. In the afternoon the brigade moved forward in support of the First Brigade of the Third Division. General Grant was near at hand, sitting upon the grass in silence for more than an hour, save to inquire of General Hancock the propriety of using more artillery. We waded the Po River, which is some fifty feet wide, before dark, and soon the heavens were lit up by blazing rails, making the troops at a distance look like giant spectres; into these the enemy poured a parting volley, but did no harm; unmolested, the night was spent in restful slumbers.

Tuesday, May 10th. Many of the boys enjoyed the contents of an ice-house near at hand; at ten our artillery opened out with telling effect, as we could see the Confederate infantry take to their heels and make off for the rear. We soon marched toward our left to the support of General Warren; in this movement the Second Corps lost its first cannon, which had been mired on account of the horses taking fright at the fires that were raging in the woods. We passed the spot where General Sedgwick was killed on the morning of the 9th, near the crossing on the Alsop Farm, formed in line of battle, and advanced into a dense wood on our right, where our skirmishers were soon involved in a brisk engagement.

### CHARGE AT LAUREL, OR PROSPECT HILL.

At 5 o'clock a general charge upon the enemy's works was ordered; bayonets were fixed and the line moved up the slope under a galling fire, with cheering, over rifle-pits, past Union soldiers into the dense tanglewood of cedars, and were met with terrific volleys of musketry, yet moved onward until some of our boys of the Fourth scaled the breastworks and fell lifeless among the enemy; being without support, the line fell back a short distance; soon after there were many stragglers of other regiments who vowed that they would not take any such risks, as their time of service had nearly expired; Warren and staff urged them in vain to make a stand. Just before dark came another order to charge; the line moved forward a few rods into the impenetrable darkness, up to the breastworks and some upon them, and saw the rebels in some twenty lines deep, heard Carroll's order to fall back, and in so doing the whole Confederate mass riddled us with their fire. Colonel Carroll was this day promoted to a Brigadier Generalship for "gallant and meritorious conduct at the battle of the Wilderness," in which every man in the brigade gloried. Our loss was five killed and thirty wounded.

Company A—R. E. Bigbee and R. Thompson, wounded.

Company B—W. J. Brollier and J. C. Dowling soon died of wounds; J. Armstrong, wounded.

Company C—Samuel Coldflesh and Joseph Tanner, killed; Samuel Traxler soon died of wounds; Captain Byron Dolbear died of wounds several weeks after battle; Benjamin Durfey, Harvey Jennings and Albert Worline, wounded.

Company D—M. Banker soon died of wounds.

Company E—Howard Fishburn, killed.

Company F—Captain Brearley and P. L. Snyder, wounded.

Company G—F. Bain and J. W. Donaldson, wounded.

Company H—L. Grimes, killed; R. Carlyle, J. S. Elliott, J. Grimes, A. Griswold, A. Halstead, J. Kenyon, S. W. Miller and J. Maunasmith, wounded.

Company I—J. M. Finch and Lieutenant C. L. Pettibone, killed; C. Day, wounded.

Company K—J. C. Carter, J. Goodenberger and G. B. Merchant, wounded.

Wednesday, May 11th. There was but little rest during the night, as an attack might be expected at any moment; requisitions for rations and ammunition were filled and the breastworks strengthened; one in passing along our works at any time of day could see men in line behind the works, peering with dilated pupil into the dense underbrush in front of them, having gun ready to bring to an aim should there be the first intimation of a charge on the part of the enemy.

The day wore away with but two sensations; the first was occasioned by a soldier putting the forefinger of his right hand to the muzzle of his gun, springing the trigger with his ramrod, blew off his finger, and was ordered to the front to remain five days, if not sooner shot. He turned out to be a faithful man, and remained by choice on the front after the time of sentence had expired. Another, whilst the ammunition was being distributed, yelled out, "Sergeant, bring your ammunition this way; we are out." The Johnnies heard it, so did the General; the latter called his men to attention while the former began a rapid fire, but soon ceased it when they discovered that those on the front were well provided with ammunition. "That fool ought to be shot," said one in authority.

Darkness came and found the men weary with watching and fighting; many were sound asleep, with gun in hand, when the order came at about 9 o'clock to move back as quietly as possible. The column moved slowly in a drizzling rain until after midnight, toward the left, formed in line of battle on the Landrum Farm, and awaited the break of day.

### BATTLE OF SPOTTSYLVANIA.

Thursday, May 12th. Early in the morning it was quite foggy, so that the advance could not be made at as early an hour as intended; everybody expected a bold and successful movement to be made upon the enemy's works, since the countenances and actions of the general officers showed conclusively to the private soldier that expectation was very high, and the quietness of the enemy, who was known to be near at hand, assured us that we should come upon him unawares. The mist had not yet cleared away when our brigade moved by the right flank over the McCool Farm as the second line of battle, over undulating ground, then up a slope toward the top of which were some felled trees; as the first line entered this abatis it was fired upon by the Confederate pickets, the front line charged, followed closely by our line, which soon came up and mingled with it, and the mass of men went forward irrespective of organizations and location of regimental standards, cheering vociferously; charged over breastworks, sent prisoners to the rear, loaded several guns with grape and sent it after those who were retreating through the pine forest. We had come upon them entirely unexpected, and found some of them rousing from their slumbers, others trying to get on their pantaloons, others trying to slip the feet into their shoes, others looking for their guns; the Johnnies were in almost every attitude and condition—dressed, half dressed and nearly naked. We had caught them napping. Some of the prisoners informed us that their officers had told them we had been so badly whipped that we had started for Fredericksburg the evening previous. One Major General (Johnson), a Brigadier General (Steuart) and many other officers, twenty-two pieces of artillery, with caissons and horses, thirty stand of colors, thousands of small arms, camp equipage, and nearly four thousand prisoners, were the trophies of this most successful sortie.

The danger was not over. Burnside's Artillery threw some of its shot among us and did some damage; some of the boys of the Fourth turned several of the captured guns toward the enemy, loaded and fired for some time before they noticed the danger they were in in firing over open caissons, which might be caused to explode at any moment. The rebels several times tried to rally; they soon brought up more troops and seemed to get ready for a counter attack; in the meantime our artillery

came to our rescue by sending shot and shell into the enemy; we were formed in line on the reverse side of the rebel works, strengthened them as much as circumstances and time permitted while missiles came among us from several directions. Firing and skirmishing was kept up all day; at some points the lines were so near that our men were on one side of the breastworks and the rebels on the other, each endeavoring to capture or drive away the other. Several times during the day did the rebels try to have concerted action and charge upon us, but were so closely watched that each attempt was nipped in the bud; they were not even able to move their wounded that lay thickly on our front. Again and again did the drizzling rain interfere with our comfort. During the night the rebels kept up a constant firing, doubtless to make us believe that they intended to hold that position, when they were, in fact, withdrawing as best they could without provoking a general charge upon their thinned ranks; they made a number of efforts to recapture several guns in our front, but failed, and early in the morning a number of our boys dragged them to our rear.

Our ranks, too, were rapidly thinned out; there were now only four officers present for duty in the regiment; we began to realize that at such a rate of decimation as that to which we had been subjected for less than a fortnight there would be but few remaining to be mustered out of the service in three weeks; although our time was so near out, never did the boys brave danger with greater determination or more fearlessness; they cared more to squelch the rebellion and end the war than to shield themselves from injury and danger. The Fourth lost during this engagement three killed, three missing and thirty-one wounded, of which the following, taken from the rolls at the end of this history, is a partial list:

Company A—A. B. Wallace, wounded.

Company B—F. N. Clayton, killed; L. Morey and G. M. Parks, wounded.

Company C—Lieutenant Anderson, Lieutenant Perry, C. R. Breyfogle, A. Keiser, L. Keiser, H. Lamb, H. Lynn and S. Wells, wounded.

Company D—D. K. Gibbs, E. Wilson and J. White, wounded.

Company E—S. Bird, C. Fogleson, T. M. Lowrey, G. Muchler, J. T. Swearingen and N. Tryon, wounded.

Company F—W. Miller, killed; P. Snyder and J. Thurin, wounded.

Company G—J. W. F. Williams, wounded.

Company H—W. Shendoller, killed; H. Fields, missing; H. S. Kenyon, C. Manly and S. Shertzer, wounded.

Company I—R. Jennings, missing.

Company K—A. Kightlinger, missing; F. Brenneke, H. H. Cunningham, A. P. Freeman, D. Hall, J. Welchonce, wounded; H. J. Shook, wounded and prisoner.

### RECONNAISANCE TOWARD THE NY RIVER.

Friday, May 13th. Overhead the bright sunshine once more greeted us; the enemy had left our immediate front; within a few rods a sickening sight met our eyes which caused us to more fully realize the terribleness of the conflict of the previous day; clothing, small arms, limber boxes, caissons, cannon, dead horses, dead men, wounded men, were heaped together as well as scattered about; the dead were thickly strewn in every direction; in a small compass of about six by sixteen feet lay forty-four Confederate dead and three more were in the last struggles; one poor fellow breathed his last just as four of his dead comrades had been removed from him; numbers of the dead had in their hands an open Bible or Testament, making many of us wish that our deluded brothers would give up the struggle for a bad cause, return to their allegiance, and we would most gladly forgive them. We, too, had sustained sad losses; Colonel Coons, of the Fourteenth Indiana, a noble and brave man, had fallen.

About 8 o'clock came the order, "Fall in! Forward!" The Fourth was deployed as skirmishers, and moved forward over ground that had been partly cleared and burned over the year previous; for some time the firing was very brisk; our column was ordered to halt; we lay for hours on the blackened and charred limbs and leaves; during this time Carroll had his left arm badly shattered above the elbow, and he was compelled to leave the field of strife and carnage for life; the boys had rejoiced with him in the fact that the government had at last recognized his gallant services on the field of battle and made him a brigadier general several days previous, but every heart was saddened because he could not be with us to the end of our time of service, if no longer; every man in the brigade loved him and gloried in him, and would have followed him wherever he might go against the enemy, and he would go wherever he was ordered or die in the attempt; he was as tender in feeling as a woman, whole-souled and true, dearly loved his men, always looked well to their interests, and led them to honor and victory; his fault, if fault it may be called, was that he was too daring, regardless of his own life and welfare; a good fault.

There was considerable murmuring when Colonel Ellis of the Fourteenth Connecticut took command, but much rejoicing when in a few days he was relieved by Colonel Smythe, of the First Delaware, whom the boys had learned to respect from what they had seen of him as a soldier and a gentleman, safe and brave.

One report made on the field gives our loss in the Fourth in the reconnaisance as three killed and one wounded; the rolls give: Girard Durfey, of Company C, and F. Enwright of G, as wounded.

Saturday, May 14th. The brigade having been relieved, remained in a pleasant camp in a ravine in the triangle just back of the breastworks, and in range of the rebel sharpshooters, from whom many a stray shot came uncomfortably near. There were many instances of narrow escapes. Two comrades were arranging a requisition for ammunition; for a moment the one leaned over toward the other, when a ball cut the bark of the sapling at the very point where the middle of his back had been resting. Two comrades had put down their bunk for a good rest after days of excitement, exertion and loss of sleep, laid down, and were just in the act of placing their heads on their knapsacks, when a ball grazed both knapsacks; there instantly came from one, "A miss is as good as a mile," and, from the other, "Can't do that again," and down went both heads and in a moment both were asleep. Another comrade, while asleep, was pierced through the chest by a ball; "never knew what hurt him;" and in a few minutes more he was wrapped in his blankets and placed in his grave underneath his very bed. There were during these days hundreds of like occurrences; there was safety nowhere; men, too, became more serious, careful and determined. All day long the boys could be seen writing letters, cleaning guns or sleeping; there was but little moving about; it was rest day, with the constant expectation of having to make a rapid movement in some direction.

Sunday, May 15th. In the morning we took up our line of march and arrived at the Fredericksburg Pike at about 9 o'clock and remained for several hours; then we went back to support two regiments of the brigade that had been left on picket and had been flanked because some troops whose time was about expiring had given way and did not care to take any further risks "because they wanted to go home." We went into camp on a branch of the muddy Ny River, but had clear water and a good sod.

Monday, May 16th. Remained in camp until toward evening, when we went to the rescue of the Fifth Corps Hospital and brought away over six hundred and fifty wounded, who had been molested by Confederate cavalry. New troops came in during the day.

Tuesday, May 17th. A very warm day; sharpshooters and pickets kept up a fusilade all day and the men were in constant readiness to make or repel an attack or start on a rapid and distant march. At 10 o'clock at night we started and marched to a position near the triangle and works taken on the 12th, the authorities thinking to make another surprise with equal success.

## CHAPTER XXV.

SECOND BATTLE OF SPOTTSYLVANIA, OR THE NY—BATTLE OF NORTH ANNA, OR TAYLOR'S BRIDGE AND JERICKS-FORD—SKIRMISHES ON THE TOTOPOTOMOY—BATTLE OF COLD HARBOR—RELIEVED AND START FOR HOME.

Wednesday, May 18th. As on the 12th, we started at daybreak against the rebel works, but found ourselves at once confronted by a heavy abatis and high breastworks; we moved over one mile beyond the position formerly taken by us; our batteries threw their missiles over our heads but occasionally into our ranks, discouraging and provoking the men who already saw the hopelessness of the task, when the order was given to halt and fall back a short distance. This action was very brief; skirmishing kept up during the entire day, and in the evening we marched several miles toward the left and bivouacked on the Anderson Farm.

The Fourth lost in the Second Spottsylvania or Ny River battle eight killed and four wounded.

Company A—R. Kimball, wounded.

Company B—W. Case, M. Craven and M. Fry, killed; L. Hutcheson, wounded.

Company C—S. H. Orton, killed; W. H. Owsten, wounded.

Company D—A. K. Lewis, soon died of wounds.

Company H—Hiram Fields, killed.

Company I—Reuben Jennings and A. Potter, killed; H. W. Alexander, wounded.

Thursday, May 19th. An attack was made on the wagon train in the evening and we were ordered out to help repel it, but our services were not needed and we returned to camp. Reports up to this time showed our losses in the brigade to have been one thousand and forty-eight since we left our winter quarters.

Friday, May 20th. We had orders to march early in the morning; they were countermanded, but we held ourselves in readiness to march at a moment's notice, and in the meantime to rest as much as possible. At eleven at night the column moved southward, passed Massaponax Church at midnight, reached Guinea Station shortly after daylight the next morning, (Saturday, May 21st,) Bowling Green at ten, and Milford Station at one in the afternoon; crossed the Mattapony and entrenched ourselves at once a short distance beyond the river. The pickets soon had a skirmish with some Confederate cavalry. Colonel Smythe and his Adjutant General, Captain Reed, came near being captured. By night our works looked quite formidable, for out of the sandy loam they were easily constructed.

Sunday, May 22d. The brigade made a reconnaissance a distance of three miles; returned at 3 P.M., having found only a few cavalrymen; several of our officers returned from recruiting service. Rations, ammunition and clothing were issued after midnight, and gave the first opportunity for change of attire since we had left camp.

### BATTLE OF NORTH ANNA RIVER, OR FAYLOR'S BRIDGE AND JERICKSFORD.

Monday, May 23d. Early this morning we started for Hanover Court House, crossed Polecat Creek at ten, arrived at the bridge over the North Anna River at two in the afternoon; immediately there was an artillery duel, and skirmishing became brisk, and continued until 9 P.M., our regiment being in the advance; three of the men who had volunteered to go down to the railroad bridge, to determine its condition, were wounded by a volley from the other side of the river, viz: W. T. Hart of B, B. McPherson of C, and A. Ustick of H.

Tuesday, May 24th. Late in the previous evening the enemy destroyed the bridge; early on this morning our brigade crossed the river a short distance below the Chesterfield bridge over pontoons, under the fire of the enemy, threw out skirmishers, advanced in line some distance, and at once constructed earthworks, within about six hundred yards of the Confederate works, on the Dawswell or Dowsdell Plantation, noted for its race-course and fast horses. At six in the evening the brigade got into a severe skirmish, drove the enemy a short distance. The day was warm.

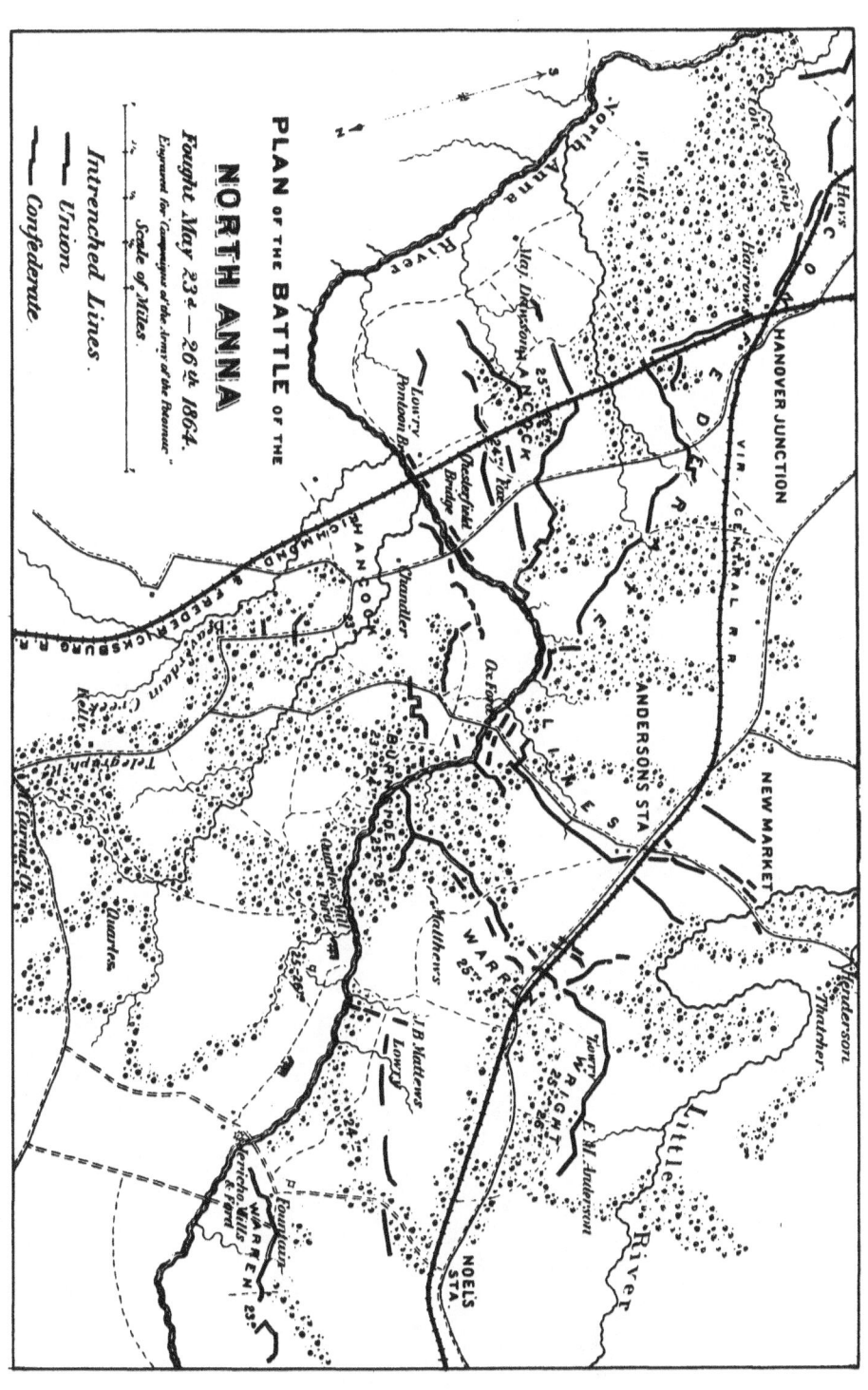

Wednesday, May 25th. New lines were constructed during the night. There was but little sleeping; the entire brigade again moved forward, drove the enemy from the first and then from the second line of works, and continued skirmishing all day.

Thursday, May 26th. There was but little firing during the night; we were on the skirmish line the entire day, and toward night the brigade again advanced under a severe fire, drove the Confederates once more, sustaining a loss of two killed and five wounded. At about 8 o'clock at night the army began to recross; the brigade followed at ten, in pitch darkness, the men staggering about against the comrade in front, then in a moment taken arrears; having reached the position we held before crossing the river we settled down gladly, and were soon asleep.

Friday, May 27th. Nothing transpired during the early morning save the moving troops of the Fifth, Ninth and Second Corps passing us. The pickets of the brigade, detailed from regiments, were yet on the other side of the river, until about ten, when as they recrossed the Confederates began to shell us, until we started, soon after eleven, when we rapidly brought up the rear of the army; took dinner about noon. The division soon moved out, and not receiving orders for two hours to follow, we were compelled for more than that length of time to make a forced march in order to close up, then proceeded slowly, in the immediate rear of the division, until eleven at night, when we bivouacked.

Saturday, May 28th. The usual day's rations of beef having been cooked and stored in haversacks, breakfast eaten, the march was resumed at 7 o'clock. Frequent halts were made in a low, swampy country, where one could see but a short distance. Roads and by-ways were numerous. We crossed the Pamunky at about 3 o'clock, moved forward some three miles, and then arranged ourselves in battle array, on the Huntley Farm, to the left of the Sixth Corps, at once dug entrenchments, near a road leading from Crump's Creek to Hawes' Shop. Rations, except beef and coffee, were getting very scarce. We held our position and rested until at noon on the next day.

### SKIRMISH ON TOTOPOTOMOY (May 29-31.)

Sunday, May 29th. At noon our brigade supported the advance of the other brigades. The day was very warm, and the skirmishing brisk until night set in, the enemy evidently being in front of us in force. The ground was low and wet.

Monday, May 30th. At seven in the morning the Seventh Virginia took the advance as skirmishers; our progress was very slow, over a good road by a 40x60 church; a halt was called at four in the afternoon, about three miles distant from the last camp. Rations having been brought from the White House Landing, there was once more plenty to eat. Flour and bacon, currant and ginger wines, and onions, were found in considerable quantities at a low mansion on the plantation over which we now extended our skirmish line. An attack in force, which it was intended should be made here at this time, failed because the Sixth Corps became entangled in almost impassable swamps on our right; in front there was considerable skirmishing, and on our left it assumed the magnitude of a general engagement, whilst the cannon were active in silencing the guns of the enemy, making us think that we were getting into the very midst of affairs.

Tuesday, May 31st. We remained in our breastworks the greater part of the forenoon; shortly before noon we moved forward, occupied the works of the enemy, and supported the First and Second Brigades of the division, in their advance over the marshy ground toward the enemy beyond Totopotomoy Creek. Entrenchments were hastily constructed and the position held until the next evening, nothing of note happening, the men taking a rest during the cool day.

Wednesday, June 1st. Lieutenants Spalter, Brophy, Watkins, Dickerson and Patton returned to the regiment, with recruits and furloughed veterans, who now began their three years of service. We were under artillery fire all day. Toward night the entire brigade went to the front, leaving pickets on the line. At half past nine at night, we began the march toward the left, through oppressive heat, choking dust, and pitch darkness; halted occasionally on account of some obstructions, getting but little sleep or rest; the men were more in a mood to sleep than to do any hard fighting, and began to feel that "Grant, or any other man" who was responsible for such constant drudging of his men, ought to begin to be made to feel that they were human, and absolutely needed rest.

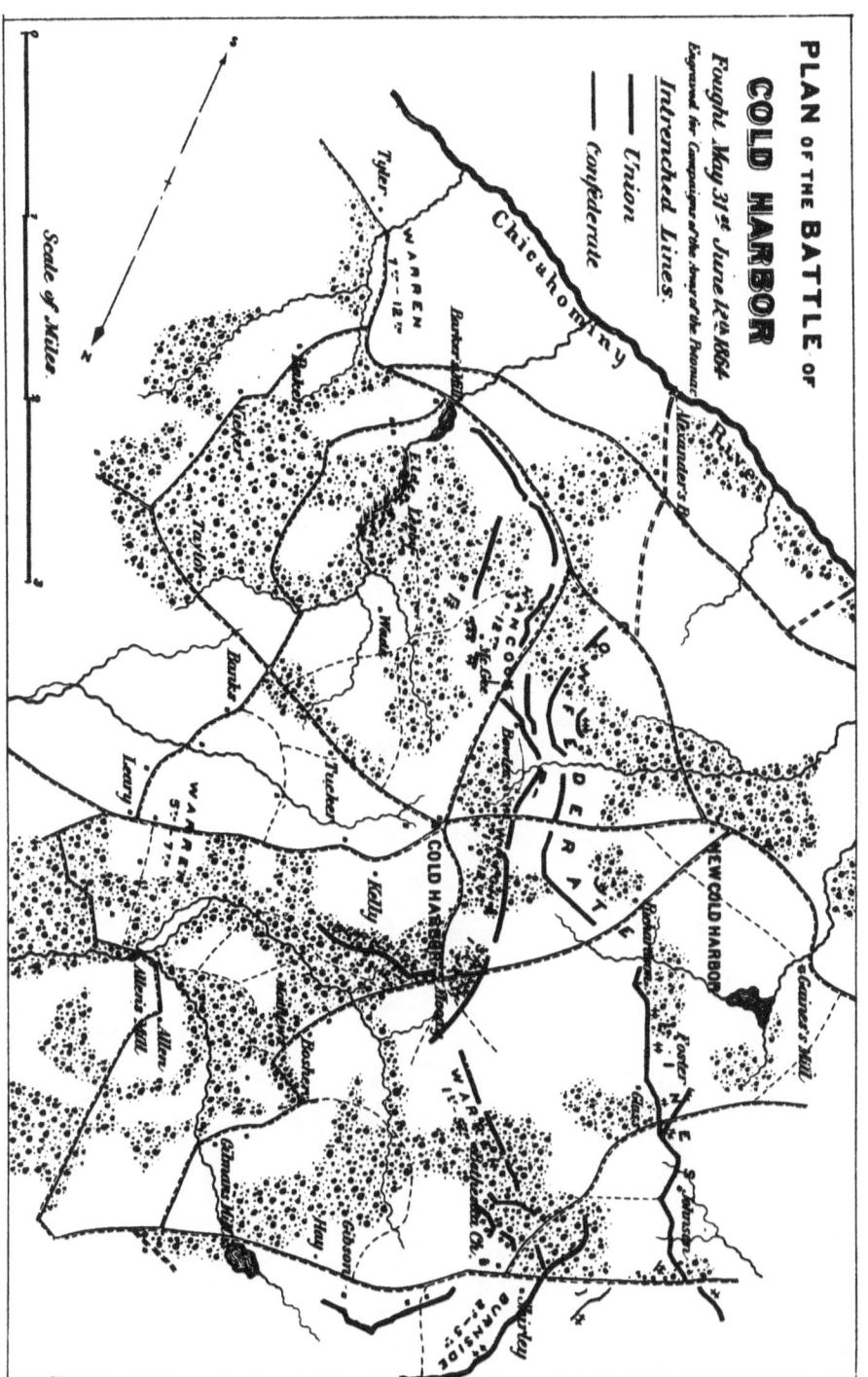

## BATTLE OF COLD HARBOR.

Thursday, June 2d. After a lengthened halt, and before the ration of beef was distributed or crackers could be "crunched down, without water," the brigade was formed with other troops in line of battle about 7:30, and being immediately attacked by the Confederates, moved rapidly forward under flying balls, took up a position and constructed huge earthworks, from which a constant fire was kept up until far into the night. There was an effort made to save ammunition, take good aim, and to fire only when it was very certain that a Johnny's head was in range, or his position made very uncomfortable. All began to turn themselves into sharpshooters, beginning to think that the only way to whip the Confederacy was to kill off the soldiers, for every man that was disabled counted one less of a force with which to contend. The order to attack at 5 P. M. was countermanded on account of a wind and rain storm.

Friday, June 3d. Just at dawn the entire brigade advanced quietly, moved rapidly over a field, up a slope, and we were at once met by shot, shell and canister; nothing daunted, most of the men hurried forward, drove in the skirmishers and sharpshooters of the enemy, captured their riflepits, came within a few rods of the Confederate earthworks, but being without support, fell back a few rods, formed a new line, in the edge of a wood, in the first line of captured riflepits, threw up breastworks of timber and whatever came first to hand and could be made available. The lines, now but a few rods apart, held each other as in a vise; neither Confederate nor Unionist dare show his head above the parapets lest he be "peeled," nor was it safe for either to attempt to leave the works, nor for any one to go to them; neither had ever been in closer quarters to remain any length of time. It was soon evident that the men that opposed us were new, on account of their incessant firing, which old troops would not have indulged in for so long a time without intermission. Tricks were sometimes played on them; some of the boys raising hats on ramrods whilst others watched with guns at an aim through holes in the parapet, peeled the fellows that shot at the hats. The works themselves were virtually bullet-proof, and there was no danger save when one gave way to the provocation induced by "the everlasting shooting," raised his head to see where the nonsense came from, determined on vengeance, and was himself pecked. There was more disposition to fun than seriousness, as some of the nervous ones juked and dodged when the balls had passed and danger was over; then there was such a scatterment made among the Johnnies, when the howitzers dropped an occasional round of shot among them, and furnished us a good opportunity for rifle-practice as their heads went bobbing, back into their trenches.

Toward night there was a lull, and a charge upon our works was anticipated, so that the men not only reserved their fire, but many put in extra charges. Soon after sunset a terrific cannonading began, and the ground to the rear of our works was raked by a cross-fire from some five or more directions, but few reaching the men because the cannon could not be sufficiently depressed, and there was as great danger to their men as to ours. Soon the infantry, some three lines deep, came over their entrenchments, crept noiselessly toward our works, received a volley from our first line, then immediately from the second, whilst the first loaded and again fired, took the guns of the second, and with a keen outlook, kept up an accurate firing at the objects on their front, whilst others continued to load as rapidly as possible, and handed over the loaded pieces and in return received and reloaded the empty guns. This method proved very destructive to the enemy, killing and wounding many, whilst numbers, not daring to return to their works, surrendered themselves as prisoners. This was the first time we had an opportunity to repel a charge whilst occupying breastworks. After the enemy had been hurled back all along the line, cheer upon cheer rent the air. During the attack, when it was almost certain death to leave the breastworks, Adjutant Wallace went to the rear and soon returned with a detail from the Ordnance Corps loaded with ammunition. There was now no picket-guard, but some kept a watch of every move beyond the breastworks while others slept; thus the night passed slowly by, with no disturbing cause save the ceaseless crack of the rifle, that became more frequent as soon as the darkness began to flee before the earliest dawn. This "eternal whacking" was always an evidence of new troops on our front, as the old soldiers on either side had given up the practice long ago, and were disposed to censure such of their comrades as engaged in it, since it did but little good in the way of deciding anything, and permitted no opportunity for the much-needed rest. But if the Johnnies wanted to keep pecking away, the same arrangement was kept up by the boys during the day that they had previously, some resting while others kept the enemy dodging. Thus was Saturday, June 4th, spent, the boys keeping up the maneuvers of the previous day, yet with greater caution, although the temptation was greater than ever to "peel" the new recruits on our front.

Just at dark the Confederates opened as usual with cannon, and for some twenty minutes the heavens were lurid with the flash of the guns, the brigade in the meantime holding itself in readiness to meet another charge. Quietness soon reigned.

Our regiment lost during the day three killed and seventeen wounded:

Company A—H. C. Pollock, wounded.

Company B—F. Beach, wounded.

Company C—T. Williams, mortally wounded.

Company D—H. Ries, killed; C. L. Baily, H. Heater, H. White and F. K. Yarger, wounded.

Company E—H. Brown and C. M. Line, wounded.

Company F—J. Hafer, killed; F. L. Ensign, J. McCauley and C. E. Yaley, wounded.

Company I—F. J. Winstead, wounded.

Company K—D. D. Booher and J. C. Carter, wounded.

Just before the "ball opened," and all was quiet, a colored servant was riding pompously through the rear line of works, with rations of beef, tack and sweet potato for his "Massa," when the ricochet of a solid shot, passing uncomfortably near, so frightened him that he tumbled from his horse, followed by the rations and horse's heels, scrambling on his knees, hands, nose and toes, blubbering with his mouth, his face turning from a jet black to an ashen hue, flung himself upon two "shoulder straps" that were reclining behind the breastworks, hugged their legs together until they roared with pain, and for some minutes he could not be persuaded, "cussed," or pulled from his deathlike grip.

Sunday, June 5th. The morning was quite damp. Skirmishing was more vigorous and uncomfortable than ever, and the more so since the order relieving the regiment from duty had been received, and yet there was no possible opportunity for it to go to the rear in a body. Some had very narrow escapes, yet only two were wounded; and one of the recruits was pierced through by a rifle ball. Toward evening the boys began to bid "good-by" to the recruits and veterans, as singly and in squads of half a dozen, under cover of darkness, they moved cautiously to the rear and halted, out of danger, waited until all had come up, and then with a feeling of relief—a very strange feeling, that is indescribable, fell into line and marched toward the wagon-train, and camped near it for the night. In the meantime an artillery duel lit up the heavens.

Our ranks had been greatly thinned, since the beginning of the campaign just thirty days previous; during the greater part of the time we had been under fire, even when not in a regular engagement nor on the skirmish line, the guns of sharpshooters having the camps in range; during the thirty days we had sustained a loss of twenty-four killed, and one hundred and twenty-one wounded, and about twenty missing, out of a total of three hundred and thirty-five men and officers present for duty subject to detail when we left winter quarters.

---

The Colonel commanding our brigade of nine regiments issued the following order, from his position on the front line:

HEADQUARTERS THIRD BRIGADE, SECOND DIVISION,
SECOND ARMY CORPS, June 5, 1864.

GENERAL ORDERS, No. ——

The term of service of the Fourth Ohio Volunteers having expired, the Colonel commanding Brigade desires to express his appreciation of their valuable services, rendered whilst he has been associated with them.

The Fourth Ohio has nobly sustained its well-earned reputation—won upon many a battle-field—until the last hour of its term of service, whilst many other regiments, similarly situated, have been sent to their respective States to be mustered out.

The Colonel commanding prides himself that he commands one of the best, if not the best brigade in the service, and he takes pleasure in saying that the Fourth Ohio has contributed in a good measure towards establishing its reputation.

The commanding officer, in his own name, and in behalf of the several regiments composing this Brigade, tenders to the officers and men of the Fourth

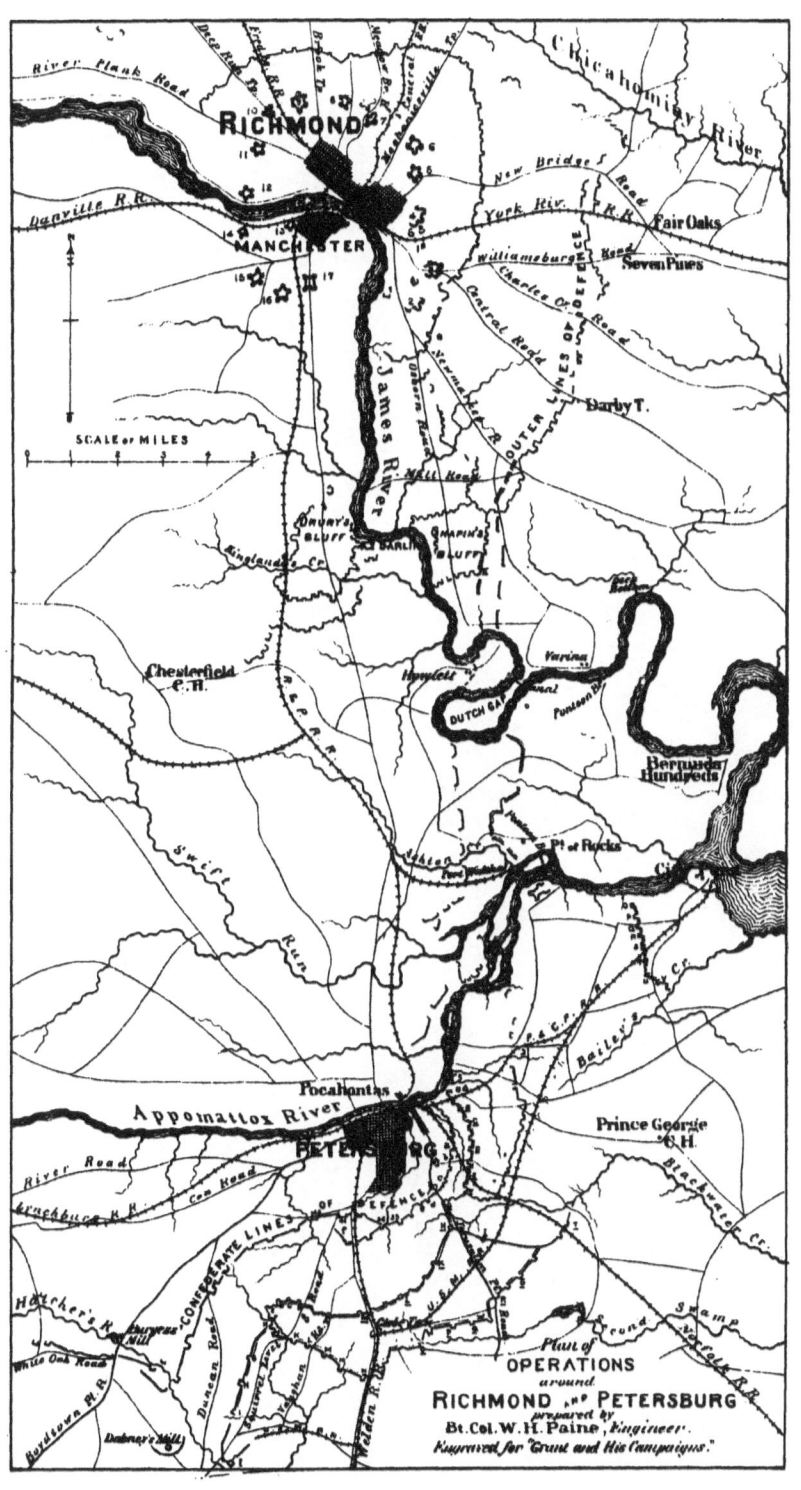

Ohio his and their heartfelt wishes for their future prosperity, and sincerely trusts that "when this cruel war is over," we may all meet around the festive board and renew old associations.

By order of
COLONEL THOMAS A. SMYTHE,
*Commanding Brigade.*

JNO. J. REID,
*Acting Assis't Adj. General.*

Colonel Smythe's wish was never realized. This dearly beloved man was finally breveted a Major General of Volunteers, was mortally wounded April 7th, 1865, at Farmville, Virginia, and died on the very day of Lee's surrender.

The Fourteenth Indiana was relieved on the 6th, and the Eighth Ohio on the 24th of this month, leaving behind only Company I of the Eighth, the Seventh West Virginia, and the Veterans of the Fourth and Eighth, a remnant of the old brigade; the Ohio Veterans were merged into an organization, known as Fourth Ohio Veteran Volunteer Infantry, continued in the Second Corps, and were in a few months nearly annihilated.

On Monday, June 6th, we left camp, four miles from the front, reached White House Landing at two in the afternoon of the 7th, and turned over our arms and accoutrements. The next morning we boarded the steamer Highland Light, reached West Point at two, Yorktown about four, and the bay in another hour, passed Fort Washington at about eight on the 9th, and reached Washington City at ten, went ashore at once, marched to the Baltimore & Ohio Railroad Depot, near the Capitol, where we remained until 11 o'clock of the 11th, when we boarded the cars, reached Point of Rocks at night, Martinsburg in the morning of the 12th, Piedmont in the evening, Fairmount the next morning, Monday, June 13th; Bellaire at ten, Columbus near midnight, where we were marched to some lousy, dirty barracks that were near at hand, where every soldier was to remain until the authorities gave him permission to go elsewhere. Most of the officers, dissatisfied with such a reception, set out for more comfortable and decent quarters; non-commissioned officers and privates felt that such treatment was not in accordance with the dignity of their soon-to-be-citizenship of a great republic, which they had helped to make great, and sought quarters more in harmony with their tastes. Some went to the depot and took the first train home; some took up their abode at the first hotel or boarding house; others, weary and worn, gave themselves to sleep as best they could in the old board tents; most of the latter marched to Camp Chase the next day.

Before noon of the 14th work on the Muster-Out Rolls was begun in earnest and within one week the regiment was ready to be discharged. The boys came again and again from boarding places and camps for several days to inquire in regard to the time they could be mustered out. They received the answer that only two companies could be discharged each day. This was too much. The paymaster seemed to insist upon taking his own time. The boys knew that at the front when danger was near it took only a few hours to pay off the entire regiment, and insisted that payment could be more speedily made now than on the front; threats of arrest were made; the boys determined not to put up with these, and after disarming every guard that confronted them, carried their point and were rapidly furnished their arrearages and one hundred dollars bounty, and mustered out of the service. By Wednesday evening, June 22d, 1864, we were citizens once more.

The old flag was turned over to Governor John Brough by Captain George F. Laird. On the flag was the following inscription: "4th Regt. O. V., U. S. A., Romney, Blue's Gap, Front Royal, Harrison's Landing, Fredericksburg, Chancellorsville, Gettysburg, Bristoe, Mine Run, Morton's Ford, Wilderness, Spottsylvania, Po River, North Anna River, Prospect Hill, Cold Harbor."

With tearful eyes, glad hearts and hearty good-bys, the boys took the first train for home, many never to meet again on earth. Several years passed before the first reunion of the regiment. In one of the cities where one or two companies of the Old Fourth were organized, the "old boys" meet each year soon after harvest time, to greet each other and talk over the joys and trials of the days of yore. Each year will they thus meet, with ever thinning ranks, until the last platoon, yea the last man, with silvered hair and faltering step, comes alone. What memories will crowd that brain of victories won and comrades brave and true! What feelings storm that heart as it longs to join the yonder thousand and answer the roll-call of our Supreme Commander in the reunion eternal. Who shall be that last comrade, that with quivering voice can truthfully say, "I, am the Old Fourth Ohio?"

"The boys in blue are turning gray,
    Thin grows our ranks and thinner;
We played death's game full many a day,
    But death to-day is winner.

Mid whistling shot and screaming shell,
    When stoutest hearts must quiver,
Facing the battery's belching hell,
    Some crossed death's silent river.

Some mangled, moaned with tortured breath,
    Till death in mercy freed them ;
In prison-pens some starved to death,
    With only foes to heed them.

And some "God's Country" gained at last,
    Died 'mid the dear home faces ;
Of limbs torn off by war's fierce blast,
    Their empty sleeves are traces.

We list no more the shrieking shell,
    No more the bullet's rattle ;
But comrades fall while tolls the bell,
    As once they fell in battle.

Then close the ranks as years roll on,
    As life's dim sun grows colder ;
Face death to come as death that's gone,
    With shoulder firm to shoulder.

What though above our wasting ranks
    No battle-flag is gleaming,
God's red and white in morning light
    O'er Heaven's vault is streaming.

Though scant the muster-roll below,
    Above 'tis growing longer;
Though faint on earth our voices grow,
    In heaven they'll swell the stronger."

# LIST OF SKIRMISHES AND BATTLES

### IN WHICH PART OR ALL OF THE FOURTH OHIO VOLUNTEER INFANTRY PARTICIPATED.

| | | |
|---|---|---|
| 1861— | Rich Mountain, | Wednesday, July 10 |
| | Rich Mountain, | Thursday, July 11 |
| | Petersburg, W. Va., | Tuesday, September 10 |
| | Petersburg, W. Va., | Thursday, September 12 |
| | Mechanicsburg Gap, | Monday, September 23 |
| | Mechanicsburg Gap, | Tuesday, September 24 |
| | Romney, | Wednesday, September 25 |
| | Romney, | Saturday, October 26 |
| | Blue's Gap, | Tuesday, November 5 |
| 1862— | Blue's Gap, | Monday, January 6 |
| | Winchester, | Sunday, March 23 |
| | Cedar Creek, | Tuesday, March 25 |
| | Woodstock, | Tuesday, April 1 |
| | Edinburg, | Wednesday, April 2 |
| | Mount Jackson, | Thursday, April 17 |
| | Rood's Hill, | Thursday, April 17 |
| | New Market, | Thursday, April 17 |
| | Front Royal, | Friday, May 30 |
| | Near Port Republic, | Monday, May 9 |
| | Harrison's Landing, | Thursday, July 3 |
| | Evlington Heights, | Friday, July 4 |
| | Centerville, | Monday, September 1 |
| | Leesburg, | Wednesday, October 1 |
| | Snicker's Gap, | Sunday, November 2 |
| | Banks' Ford, | Tuesday, November 18 |
| | Fredericksburg, | Friday, December 12 |
| | Fredericksburg, | Saturday, December 13 |
| 1863— | Chancellorsville, | Friday, May 1 |
| | Chancellorsville, | Satruday, May 2 |

## BATTLES AND SKIRMISHES. 187

| | |
|---|---|
| 1863—Chancellorsville, | Sunday, May 3 |
| Chancellorsville, | Monday, May 4 |
| Chancellorsville, | Tuesday, May 5 |
| Gettysburg, | Thursday, July 2 |
| Gettysburg, | Friday, July 3 |
| Funkstown Heights, | Saturday, July 11 |
| Robinson's River, | Thursday, September 17 |
| Robinson's River, | Wednesday, September 23 |
| Brandy Station, | Sunday, October 11 |
| Rappahannock, | Monday, October 12 |
| Auburn, or Cedar Run, | Wednesday, October 14 |
| Bristoe Station, | Wednesday, October 14 |
| Centerville, | Thursday, October 15 |
| Centerville, | Friday, October 16 |
| Kelly's Ford, | Saturday, November 7 |
| Robertson's Tavern, | Friday, November 27 |
| Mine Run, | Saturday, November 28 |
| Mine Run, | Sunday, November 29 |
| Mine Run, | Monday, November 30 |
| 1864—Morton's Ford, | Saturday, February 6 |
| Wilderness, | Friday, May 6 |
| Tod's Tavern, | Monday, May 9 |
| Po River, | Monday, May 9 |
| Laurel Hill, | Tuesday, May 10 |
| Spottsylvania, C. H., | Thursday, May 12 |
| Spottsylvania Reconnaisance, | Friday, May 13 |
| Ny River, | Wednesday, May 18 |
| North Anna River, | Monday, May 23 |
| North Anna River, | Tuesday, May 24 |
| North Anna River, | Wednesday, May 25 |
| North Anna River, | Thursday, May 26 |
| Huntly's Farm, | Sunday, May 29 |
| Totopotomoy, | Sunday, May 29 |
| Totopotomoy, | Monday, May 30 |
| Totopotomoy, | Tuesday, May 31 |
| Pamunky River, | Wednesday, June 1 |
| Cold Harbor, | Thursday, June 2 |
| Cold Harbor, | Friday, June 3 |
| Cold Harbor, | Saturday, June 4 |
| Cold Harbor, | Sunday, June 5 |

## CHAPTER XXVI.

EXPERIENCE IN REBEL PRISONS — ANDERSONVILLE AND SALISBURY.

We have taken the liberty to give the following from the statement of Sergeant J. S. Rice's "Experience as a Prisoner:"

In the forenoon of the battle of the Wilderness, Sergeants Rice, Trownsell and George Musser, having been wrongly directed by an officer, were, with about one hundred and fifty men of different regiments, entirely surrounded and taken prisoners. Our three comrades were first sent to Gordonsville, thence to Lynchburg, Danville, and on the 23d of May entered Andersonville Prison, witnessed all its horrors, and endured its starvation and barbarism until the 13th day of September. Having been located near the north gate of the prison they happened to be among the first to be removed, and placed on box-cars, reached Macon the next morning. Having no faith in the statements of the guard that they were on their way to be exchanged, they resolved to escape, so, with eight others, while the guard was on the top of the car and the train in motion, they made a hole in the bottom of the car, and when the train halted at a small station near the southern boundary of South Carolina, they slid down on the track and hid away under the station platform until the train had gone and all was quiet, when they divided into two squads. Our comrades with two others bade the six adieu, not to see them nor hear from them again. Night after night they traveled northward, rested in some secluded spot during the day, living on sweet potatoes, chickens, ducks and such other articles as could be obtained from the colored people. Musser getting sick, was with much regret left behind. The Pee Dee River was reached, and while waiting to be ferried over by a negro they built a fire in a deep ravine, which attracted the attention of some rebel guards in a town near at hand, who surrounded and captured them. They were at once taken to Albemarle, and exhibited for a day and night in a jail to hundreds of people who had never seen a "Yank," as "the only living curiosities in the country." They were then removed to Salisbury, about the middle of October, where the cold, chilly winds, rains of autumn and winter, and with but little covering and most of the men barefoot—many with legs frozen black to the knees—made this last prison pen more horrible than Andersonville. Many had no other shelter day nor night than that found under the floor of the hospital building. As day after day one or more of this number died from exhaustion and starvation others were heartily glad to get their places, and thus be sheltered from the wintry heavens. Day after day a wagon-load of dead were hauled out, and sometimes a four-mule team was not able to draw the wagon-load of dead, so some were dumped out into the mud.

An effort of the prisoners to secure their release was discovered by the guard, who shot down the men for some time as fast as they could load and fire, then, without anything to soothe their pain, they were turned over to the tender mercies of rebel surgeons—probed, cut, slashed and sawed, without let or mercy.

For food enormous prices were paid. A sweet potato, pie or cake, cost one dollar; an onion, egg, apple or spoonful of salt was fifty cents. No wonder our comrade, when released March 1st, 1864, calls it—just as its doom was forever sealed—"THE ACCURSED CONFEDERACY."

## MEMOIRS.

### COLONELS ANDREWS AND CANTWELL—SURGEON McABEE—SURGEON MORRISON—CHAPLAIN WARNER—CAPTAIN WALLACE—CAPTAIN McMILLEN.

LORIN ANDREWS was born in Ashland County, Ohio, April 1st, 1819, and spent his early life on his father's farm, in the common school and in obtaining a collegiate education. As a teacher of youth he early displayed such qualities, and took such an intelligent interest in the cause of morals and education, that he became at once a prominent leader in many reforms. In 1851-52, he was agent for the Ohio Teacher's Association; in 1853 its choice for State School Commissioner, and in 1854 its President, and soon thereafter he was elevated to the Presidency of Kenyon College, a Protestant Episcopal institution that had sent forth from its Halls those who held high rank in the councils of the Nation. When the call was made for volunteers to defend the country's honor, Lorin Andrews was the first man in the great State of Ohio to offer his services, and in any desired capacity, which he had done three months before the President's call for troops.

He was Captain of the first company organized in his county, went with it to Camp Jackson at Columbus, and in the organization of the Fourth Ohio Volunteer Infantry he was appointed its Colonel, took his regiment to Camp Dennison, and at once arranged for the comfort of his men, and with the aid of his associates rapidly pushed forward officers and men towards the highest proficiency in field maneuverings and drill-manual of of arms. Many re-enlisted for three years longer with the express understanding that their Colonel should retain command of the regiment. He had the entire confidence of his men as well as subordinates in command. On "Dress Parade" as well as elsewhere, he commanded respect, and his men felt a just pride in his fine, commanding person, rich and powerful intonations of his voice, that revealed his nobility of soul and lent inspiration to effort. Tact, mild firmness, self-possession, courage of opinion and action, ease and frankness of expression, intelligence and loftiness of purpose, were prominent characteristics.

He possessed versatility of talent, the power of comprehensive grasp as well as mastery of details that indicated the ability and disposition to be on the front line in National councils or on the field of battle.

It was a very sad day in Camp Pendleton, near Oakland, Maryland, when the flag was lowered to half-mast, and the regiment informed that our beloved Christian commander had passed from earth, at his home in Gambier, Ohio, on Wednesday, September 18th, 1861, after a promising military career of only five months. He was buried with military honors and mourned by thousands.

The following is the epitaph on his monument in the cemetery at Gambier:

LORIN ANDREWS,

PRESIDENT OF KENYON COLLEGE,

EMINENT

AS A

TEACHER, PATRIOT AND CHRISTIAN.

The first in Ohio to answer the call of his Country in 1861, he served as Colonel of the Fourth O. V. I. in the First Campaign against the Great Rebellion, and Died a Martyr to the Union, September 18th, 1861, aged 42 years, honored and beloved by all.

JAMES CANTWELL was born in Jefferson County, Ohio, December 8th, 1810, and removed to near Mansfield at the age of eleven, where he grew to an honored manhood. He was a Lieutenant in the Mexican War; became a member of the House and Senate. At the call for troops he enlisted a company, and on the 26th of April, 1861, was elected Lieutenant Colonel of the Fourth Ohio, which position he retained until the 22d of October of the same year, when he resigned to become Colonel of the Eighty-second Ohio Volunteers.

There was in his bearing the evidence of having earnestly fought life's battles; that he was possessed of much hard sense as well as good nature, and a faithfulness unto death. He seemed ever cool and collected, able not only to take in, but also to be master of the situation. He was a doer, rather than a talker; kind-hearted, generous, faithful and true. Although his resignation had already been accepted, and he was ready to start for home, he determined "to go with the boys once more," and accompanied the regiment on its second expedition to Romney, and proved himself of considerable service by his knowledge of localities, his coolness, good judgment and bravery. He soon returned home, was appointed Colonel of the Eighty-Second Ohio, led his regiment through the campaigns of Milroy and Fremont in West Virginia, then with Sickles, in Pope's forward march and retreat. On the 22d of August, 1862, he had command of Sickles' line of skirmishers, moved forward gallantly to the railroad, changed front under a galling cross-fire, "and fell from his horse dead, with words of command and encouragement upon his lips," a minie ball having pierced his head. Thus ended too soon the career of another brave, fearless and valuable officer. His body was brought to Mansfield, Ohio, and buried with the military honors due to his rank.

H. M. McABEE, M. D., son of Rev. I. M. McAbee, was born May 12th, 1827, in Westmoreland county, Pennsylvania; graduated from the Cleveland, Ohio, Medical College in 1851; several years after he entered the ministry and at the outbreak of the rebellion he was pastor of the First Methodist Episcopal Church in Beaver, Pennsylvania; was among the first that offered his services to the Governor of Ohio—for years his adopted State—was appointed Surgeon of the Fourth Ohio May 1st, 1861, resigned September 16th, 1863, and was killed soon after in a railroad accident near Painesville, Ohio. His reputation as a man, surgeon and physician had preceded him, on which account he was on detatched duty the greater part of the time, acting as Surgeon in Chief of the Department of West Virginia under Generals Kelley and Lander; had charge of Camp Ohio until March, 1863, and of over a thousand wounded men after the battle of Gettysburg, having been for some time Surgeon in Chief on the Staff of General Reynolds.

He was possessed of an intensely affectionate yet highly sensitive nature. He was a hard worker, and good organizer. His many plans for the welfare of the sick and wounded, his reports to his superiors from subordinates, of examinations into a large number of cases, his letters to and from friends of the sick and wounded that had been under his care and treatment, convince one that Surgeon McAbee was most assiduous in his attentions to the needs of those in his charge. He expected well men to be men, and had a supreme contempt for the man who tried to play off sick. For the truly sick, in his intense desire to do his whole duty, he ofttimes gave his eyes but little sleep or his weary body the needed rest. He cared for his wounded even though he had to go inside of the enemy's lines, and hazarded a conflict with his superiors for the sake of the comfort of his sick.

His letters are characteristic of one who had noble purposes, firm resolves, high ideals, and lofty conceptions of Christian duty. The following is a specimen from his letter of resignation, written to Secretary Stanton:

"After the battle of Gettysburg, with but three assistants, I was left in charge of a thousand badly wounded men, not a few of whom, I fear, absolutely died for want of appropriate and good professional care. And it is my deliberate opinion that the failure to furnish a sufficient number of medical officers on that occasion has cost the country more good men than did the charge of any rebel brigade on that severely contested field. I have no candidates to urge for places, and have nothing to ask for myself. I have been in the field since May 1st, 1861, and although I believe now, as I did then, that a place in the army in times like these is the most honorable to which a citizen can aspire, yet I have so entirely despaired of seeing the medical staff of the army made what the country and age have a right to expect, that I shall accept it as a personal favor to be allowed honorably to retire to the quiet of private life."

The following from the pen of Frank B. Nickerson, Sergeant Eighth Ohio, is of value:

"On the afternoon of July 2d, 1863, at Gettysburg, I was carried back badly wounded, to the hospital of the Second Corps, near Round Top, and placed with hundreds of desperately wounded. Surgeon McAbee was constantly at work, and it was midnight before he reached me; having asked a few questions and promised to specially care for me at daybreak, he turned to a mere boy on my left—a Confederate—not more than seventeen years old; death's pallor was on his brow and the blood flowing from his mouth; he was moaning pitifully, in striking contrast to the silent way so many were suffering and dying all around. Dr. McAbee seemed touched with his youthful appearance and disquietude of mind, and said to him, "My poor fellow, you cannot be helped; you can live but a little time." The boy broke out in a despairing cry, "My poor mother, what will she do? I cannot die, I cannot die. She will never know what became of me. I was shot on the skirmish line and no one knows it." The Surgeon wrote into his notebook his name as a member of a Georgia regiment, and his mother's address, and promised, if possible, to write to his mother, and then knelt down by his side, holding the lantern in his blood-stained hand; with the other he took a pocket Bible from his pocket and read the first fourteen verses of the Fourteenth of St. John, and then offered up a prayer for the soul that was passing away, in such simple, earnest language that helped the faith of all. Twenty-two years have passed and I still have a tender memory for the heartfelt ministrations of that man that night. Last summer, in visiting the battle-field, I rode to that barn, noticed the blood stains upon its sills, and asked the owner if any Confederates were brought here. He replied, "Yes, one boy—and I buried him across that little rolling by the fence. I miss the place when I plow. He is there.'

---

REV. LORENZO WARNER, M. D., was born in Waterbury, Connecticut, and removed with his parents to Medina, Ohio, at the age of five, where he grew to young manhood. After having nearly completed his collegiate course in the Western Reserve College at Hudson, Ohio, he entered and graduated from a Cincinnati Medical College, with honors. He practiced for some ten years, then represented his county two years in the Ohio Legislature, after which he entered the ministry of the Methodist Episcopal Church, and remained an honored member, always filling important appointments; served six years as Chaplain in the Ohio State Penitentiary; Chaplain of the Fourth Ohio from June 15th, 1861, until March 17th, 1863, when he resigned on account of failing health, but continued his work as a preacher until the day of his sudden and unexpected death, at his home in Galion, Ohio, on the 12th of April, 1876.

Dr. Warner was one of nature's noblemen, and drew about himself a host of friends and admirers wherever he went. Having added to great natural abilities early culture, he was a power for good in the way of moral reforms, and possessed the unusual gift of presenting his thoughts and convictions in that happy and fluent manner that convinced the judgment of his hearer, and a mildness of spirit that won the esteem and love of those who differed with him.

On account of his age and fatherly bearing the boys called him Father Warner, a title of which he had reason to be and was proud, for it was a token of their love for their Chaplain, with whom they felt on as familiar terms as a son can with his father. Although his few years with the boys were among the happiest of his life, yet the stern realities of war brought to death at the battle of Pittsburg Landing a dearly beloved son who had been a member of our regiment, and honored with a commission, and another son having been severely wounded at Fredericksburg, his cup of sorrow began to overflow, and to the regret of all "Good Father Warner," with rapidly silvering locks, hastened to his home to help a beloved companion to bear the cruel pangs of this earthly life, which could not even then be borne save with the indwelling of that heavenly and higher.

---

After a long illness, Dr. FRANCIS W. MORRISON died March 16th, 1886, at his residence on East Central avenue, Delaware, Ohio.

FRANCIS W. MORRISON, M.D., of Delaware, was born near Mansfield, Ohio, July 13th, 1831, and is the son of James and and Ruth (Billings) Morrison. He entered college at Delaware in the spring of 1853, and graduated in June, 1856. Being without means, he earned what he could by manual labor and teaching school, both to carry him through college and while in pursuit of his medical education. He graduated at the medical schools of Cincinnati in the spring of 1860, when he commenced the practice of his profession with his former preceptor, Dr. Blymyer. In the spring of 1861 he enlisted as a private in Company I of the Fourth Ohio Volunteers, in the three months' service. He again, July 7th, 1861, enlisted for three years in the Eleventh Ohio Volunteer Infantry as Hospital Steward, and continued with that command in West Virginia until August, 1862, when he was commissioned Assistant Surgeon of the Fourth Ohio Volunteer Infantry, and was ordered east to join his new command, with which he was ever present on active service. In November, 1863, the doctor was commissioned Surgeon of the regiment, in which capacity he served until his regiment was mustered out of service in June, 1864. He then married Miss Elizabeth Willey, of Delaware, Ohio, June 29th, 1864, and on the 10th of July following entered the contract service as Surgeon at Camp Dennison, Ohio, where he continued until September 20th, when he was commissioned Surgeon of the One Hundred and Seventy-fourth Ohio Volunteer Infantry, and in this position he faithfully served until January, 1865, when he was detailed as Brigade Surgeon, on the Staff of General Minor T. Thomas, where he continued until ordered home to be mustered out with his regiment in July, 1865, at the close of the war.

Since then he has continued to reside in Delaware, except four years of residence in his native place.

Dr. Morrison was a member of the Delaware County Medical Association, was twice annually chosen its Secretary and finally President. He was independent and self-reliant; like many others made his own fortune unaided, and was thus in a position to comprehend the obstacles and inconveniences which beset the pathway of the youth who would obtain an education and a competency in life. He left a family of three children and a wife to mourn his loss.

---

CAPTAIN JAMES WALLACE was born at Ravenna, O., August 9, 1838; his father dying in 1844 and his mother in 1848, he came to Canton to live with his uncle, John Harris, Esq. Young Wallace's educational opportunities were excellent and well utilized; he was a lover of books, especially of the exact sciences, in which he excelled; he attended the Michigan University, and subsequently, in 1856, entered the Military Academy at West Point, where in less than a year ill health compelled him to surrender his cadetship and to close his books.

Although he was of slender build and in fickle health, his was a restless, prying disposition; his seasons of recreation were of short duration, and we hear of him now assisting in the lake survey with General W. F. Raynolds and now in the work of building lighthouses on the coast of Florida. About 1860 he returned once more to Canton and entered upon the study of law; while thus engaged he organized and drilled the Canton Zouaves, the crack military company in his section of the country at that day; he was popular, energetic, of pure character and Christian affiliations, highly talented and finely educated, and, with youth on his side, seemed to be just entering upon a career in civil life in which honor and distinction surely awaited him, when the call for troops found him the first man from Stark county to offer his services in defense of the Union to the Governor of Ohio, from whom, as early as April 17, 1861, he was in possession of his commission to raise a company; volunteers came forward and filled the company to the limit in a very few days; many of the Captain's old Zouaves put off the gay toggery in which they had played soldier and donned the blue uniform of the Nation's defenders; a number of Canton's oldest families

CAPTAIN JAMES WALLACE.

contributed one or more members; more promising and patriotic young men could not have been selected than those who freely offered to follow the young captain to the awful conflict, from which many of them, including their heroic leader, were never to return.

He was the model soldier, without fear or reproach, never shrinking from hardship or danger and never absent from his regiment, the Fourth Ohio, until December 12, 1862, the date of the dreadful battle and Union repulse at Fredericksburg; in that memorable assault, and while leading his men in the advance skirmish-line, he was struck by a rebel shell on the left knee. During the first few days the surgeons gave him reason to hope, though he would inevitably be a cripple for life, but by December 26th the limb swelled and became intensely painful; four days later the leg had to be amputated, as a last effort to save his life.

In his last days the wounded captain received the tenderest care from the loving hands of his affianced wife, Miss Henrietta Schneider, a lady whose beauty and excellence of character made her every way worthy of his love. On January 4th, at 1 P.M., the prostrate soldier and his plighted bride were united in marriage by the Chaplain of the Seventh Ohio Regiment; about 6 P.M. the same day the nurse observed a single drop of blood upon the bandage of the amputated limb; the surgeon was called, and the startling discovery was made that an artery had been ruptured; a few moments after he gave to his country the life he had staked in its defense; he made the sacrifice in the full exercise of his consciousness and passed into the sleep of death without a moan or a complaint.

His remains were buried in the Canton Cemetery, with most impressive ceremonies, on January 8th. A friend suggested a monument over the grave, built by the joint offerings of the Captain's old townsmen, a proposition that was immediately responded to by subscriptions to the required amount; but the young soldier's widow interposed; she craved the precious privilege of being alone in paying this last tribute of love, and begged the subscribers to receive back their money; and thus this beautiful shaft was made yet more beautiful by its typification of wifely devotion, while it marks the last resting-place of one of the purest and bravest of men.

### DEATH OF CAPTAIN McMILLEN.

At Alexandria, Virginia, on Sunday night, June 29th, 1862, Company E had the great misfortune of losing their Captain by drowning in the Potomac River. The regiment was preparing to embark on the steamer "South America," to join General McClellan before Richmond, and had lain two or three hours on the wharf in the rain. The night was very dark and many lantern-lights flickered on shore and river, deceiving one as to the whereabouts of danger, making the least misstep fatal. It seems that about midnight Captain McMillen became tired of the delay in getting aboard and went alone in advance of his company toward the vessel, a distance of about one hundred and fifty yards. He evidently kept a straight course for the light at its bow instead of diverging to the right and passing around men, horses, mules, artillery and baggage-wagons that blockaded the way, The sad result was that in the darkness he accidentally stepped off and fell into the water at the mouth of a canal running from the river. Several men of the Fourteenth Indiana, of our Brigade, heard him fall, and as speedily as possible took him from the water. Life was extinct. They recognized him as a Fourth Ohio officer, and not knowing his name, called out for our regiment. Captain Crawford, of Company C, and Lieut. Lemuel Jeffries, of D, were among the first to quickly respond and identify the body. Colonel Mason was informed, and at once detailed Captain Wallace, of Company F, and six men of Company E to take charge of the remains. The body was conveyed to the Government Hospital in Alexandria, and the next day, with all care, it was forwarded by express to Wooster relatives by Captain Wallace, Charles W. McClure and R. B. Spink. No efforts of the members of Company E were successful in procuring a furlough so as to accompany the remains home, and in a few hours all were steaming down the river in an opposite direction. Captain McMillen was greatly liked by his own company, and every man felt his death as a personal loss. The whole regiment—officers and men—esteemed him highly as a man and soldier, and expressed it that in him one of the best officers and most congenial of comrades had departed. The Captain died a widower in the 41st year of his age, having been born at Wooster, Ohio, March 22d, 1823. He served in the Mexican War in 1846-7, as Second Lieutenant of Company E, Third Regiment O. V. I.

# CHRONOLOGICAL RECORD.

## 1861.

*April—*

12. F. Confederates fire upon Fort Sumter.
14. S. Fort Sumter evacuated. The wildest excitement everywhere.
15. M. President Lincoln calls for 75,000 volunteers.
16. T. Martial music, patriotic speeches and enlistments.
26. F. Excitement unabated. Many troops report at Columbus. Our regiment organized at Camp Jackson to serve three months.

*May—*

2. Th. Regiment goes by rail to Camp Dennison, O.; 86 miles.
3. F. Builds barracks. Rain and mud in abundance.
4. Sa. Mustered into U. S. service by Lt. Granger, for three months.
5. S. Rain and mud; guard armed with clubs.
6. M. Rainy and dreary; men in bunks, asleep.
7. T. Sunshine. Afternoon squad-drill. Pleasant evening.
8. W. Pleasant. Provisions arrive from friends.
9. Th. Hot. Many prostrated during drill in the forenoon.
10. F. Moderate. Were furnished old muskets.
11. Sa. A man of C drummed out of camp. Pleasant weather.
12. S. Rain and mud. Rations scarce; men are complaining.
13. M. Shower in morning; drill in afternoon.
14. T. Were armed with old muskets. Boys had "funeral" over bad beef.
15. W. Tried to "present" and "shoulder arms." Are on bread and water.
16. Th. Major Anderson, hero of Fort Sumter, on rear platform of car and is greeted with immense cheering by some 6,000 troops.
17. F. Fine weather; drilling; troops arriving.
18. Sa. Police duty and but little drill. More troops arrive.
19. S. Religious services. Showers in afternoon.
20. M. Rainy, drowsy and dreary day.
21. T. Sunshine and mud. No drilling to-day.
22. W. Drill. Addresses by Genl. Cox, Col. Andrews and others.
23. Th. Three-year re-enlistment excitement begins.
24. F. Many re-enlist for three years or during the war.
25. Sa. Beautiful day. Re-enlistment continues.
26. S. Rev. Wm. Harris, a future bishop, preaches.
27, 28, 29, 30 and 31, re-enlistment and reorganization.
29. W. Coats, dark blue, were furnished the regiment.

*June—*

- 2. S. Services, attended by regiment in front of quarters.
- 3. M. Rain continues; camp life very monotonous.
- 4. T. Rain, hail and fearful storm; bunks, everything, wet.
- 5. W. Light-blue pants furnished. Furloughs granted those that re-enlist.
- 6. Th. Were mustered into U. S. service for three years or during the war. Most of the men that re-enlisted leave for home on furlough.
- 12. W. Most of furloughed men return to camp.
- 13. Th. Those that did not re-enlist leave for home.
- 14. F. Hot and dusty; too hot for drill.
- 15. Sa. Dress parade. Heat and dust. L. Warner appointed Chaplain.
- 16. S. Quarters becoming filthy. Services. Rest, if flies permit.
- 17. M. Reviewed by McClellan. Rumors and canards the rage.
- 18. T. Hot, dry and dusty. Vigorous drilling with new arms.
- 19. W. Drill. Flanking companies get an "extra dose of Zouave."
- 20. Th. Begin to get ready to go; cook two days' rations.
- 21. F. Leave our filthy habitations at 5 P.M. On board of box-cars.
- 22. Sa. Reach Columbus at 3 A.M., have bread and coffee for an early breakfast; reach Bellaire at 5 P.M. Quartered in machine shop.
- 23. S. Breakfast on coffee and crackers; into Virginia in afternoon; on box-cars at 3 P.M.; reach Fetterman at 10 P.M.; rode 305 miles.
- 24. M. Remained near Grafton. Saw first rebels, and first soldier's funeral.
- 25. T. Onward by rail to Clarksburg, in leaky cars; 22 miles.
- 26. W. Draw camp and garrison equipage, wagons and horses.
- 27. Th. Awaiting troops and orders; take view of hills and breastworks.
- 28. F. March 10 miles to Camp Elk Creek on a long slope.
- 29. Sa. Rain. Scouts sent out for miles over the hills.
- 30. S. March to Camp Ewing, 6 miles.

*July—*

- 1. M. Rain. Remain at "Camp Starvation."
- 2. T. March with several regiments to Buckhannon, 15 miles.
- 3. W. Fine day. Farmers, with their daughters in their "dimities," call.
- 4. Th. Beautiful day. McClellan's Grand Review astonishes the natives, while cannon on the right and left of them celebrate the "Glorious Fourth." Were brigaded with the Ninth O. V. I. and Howe's Battery, Col. Cook in command. Camp Rosecrans.
- 5. F. March 3 miles toward Beverly; camp in a wheat-field.
- 6. Sa. Fifteen miles to Middle Fork Bridge. Excitement. Enemy routed. See Mr. Johns, killed by rebels. "Johns', or Dead Man's Camp."
- 8. M. Scare in camp. Fall into line. Bathers disconcerted.
- 9. T. Marched to Roaring Run, 15 miles over hills on a pike.
- 10. W. Rich Mountain. Reconnaisance, 2 miles, into laurel bushes.
- 11. Th. Move near to enemy's works, then flank them. Receive round of shot. Hear for first time volleys of musketry and cannonading.
- 12. F. Pursue Confederates to Beverly; 1,000 prisoners; 8 miles.
- 13. Sa. Continued pursuit to Huttonsville, 10 miles.

14. S. Pursue to top of Cheat Mountain and return, 28 miles.
15. M. Cold nights, hot days. Rest in camp in the valley.
16. T. Return to Beverly, 10 miles, along a beautiful valley.
17. W. In camp. Prisoners, paroled, leave; men stroll and rest.
18. Th. In camp. Mr. Cooper, of the Band, first man of regiment killed.
19. F. Fine day. Funeral of Cooper. Scenery grand. Inspection.
20. Sa. More excitement. Man of Ninth Ohio bushwhacked.
21. S. Beautiful day. Chaplain Warner preached.
22. M. In camp. Beautiful day. Wash and rest.
23. T. Cross Laurel Hill. Camp; 20 miles. Meet cavalry with prisoners.
24. W. Marched through Philippi, 19 miles. See battle-field.
25. Th. To Webster, 6 miles; on cars to Oakland, Md., 52 miles.
26. F. In camp all day; rain at night. Ignorant of our destination.
27. Sa. Under arms in rain two hours. Two men stunned by lightning.
28. S. On cars to New Creek, now Keyser; 33 miles. Fine day.
29, 30, 31. Warm. Guard railroad for 100 miles.
31. W. Part of Company C goes to Oakland to guard train.

*August—*
6. T. Companies gathered from different places they were guarding.
7. W. Marched to Stone House, 20 miles. Fine day.
8. Th. Marched to Camp Pendleton, Md., 14 miles. Rain.
9 to 15. Rain and mud. In camp near covered bridge.
15. Th. Moved camp to Fort Pendleton, 1 mile.
16 to 23. At work on entrenchments; fine weather. Rain on 22d.
24. Sa. Hot. Blackberries abundant. Clear, moonlight evening.
25 to 31. Felling trees and entrenchment work. Fine weather.

*September—*
1 to 8. Fine weather; work nearly completed.
8. S. Several companies march to Greenland. Bivouac.
9. M. They advance toward Petersburg. Bivouac.
10. T. Skirmish at PETERSBURG. Return to Greenland.
11. W. Other companies go in support. Bivouac at Greenland.
12. Th. Rout of the Confederates at PETERSBURG. Return.
13. F. Return to Greenland before dark. Fine day.
14. Sa. Return to Camp Pendleton with spoils at 5 P.M.
15. S. Sermon by the Chaplain. Fine weather.
16. M. Guard duty every other day.
17. T. Rain. Men attacked with fevers and rheumatism.
18. W. Death of Col. Andrews at Gambier, O.
19. Th. Flag at half-mast. A beautiful day.
22. S. Under Lt. Col. Cantwell we march to New Creek, 34 miles.
23. M. Skirmish at Mechanicsburg Gap. March 16 miles.
24. T. Skirmishing in the Gap. Eighth O. V. I. at Hanging Rock Pass.
25. W. Battle of Romney, and retreat to New Creek; 20 miles.
26. Th. Oakland on cars; Pendleton at night. March 14 and ride 33 miles.
27 to 30. Rainy and dreary. Footsore and weary, we rest.

*October—*

1 to 24. Monotonous life. Fishing. Weather cool. Snow on mountains.
16. W. Col. Mason assumes command of our regiment.
25. F. March to New Creek, 34 miles, over the mountains.
26. S. March to, and second battle of, Romney; 18 miles.
27 to 31. Troops arrive. Genl. Kelley Commander of Department.

*November—*

1 to 30. Remain at Romney. Some 600 on picket out of division daily. Almost daily foraging; occasional scouting.

*December—*

1 to 31. A repetition of guard and picket duties. Latter part of the month snow deep and weather cold. Much fun on New Year's Eve.

## 1862.

*January—*

1 to 5. Weather milder; thawing and freezing. Heavy guard duty.
6. M. March to Blue's Gap, 18 miles. Sleet, rain and snow.
7. T. Battle of Blue's Gap, and return in the evening; 18 miles.
8. W. Weather moderating; ground bare. Baggage sent toward railroad.
9. Th. Rumors of Jackson's attempt to hedge us in. Leave camp as rearguard. Lander joins us. Thin, frozen crust over mud.
10. F. Reach Springfield at 3 A.M.; 8 miles. Rain.
11. Sa. Reach Patterson's Creek, 15 miles. Rain and mud.
12. S. Remained camped in the mud, near the bridge.
13. M. Letters in abundance. Weather colder.
14. T. Rain in forenoon; freezing in the afternoon.
15. W. Sunshine; ice thin. Cleaning guns.
17 to 21. Rain and mud. Scouts sent out in different directions.
20, 21. Six companies go to Green Springs, 16 miles.
22. W. Move camp out of the mud. Lander in command of troops.
23. Th. Deep snow collapses several of the Sibley tents during the night.
24. F. Col. Mason in command of Artillery Brigade of Lander's Division.
25 to 30. Milder weather; mud; tents, clothing and blankets wet.
31. F. Move camp over a mile again out of the mud.

*February—*

1. Sa. Snow three inches deep, covering the mud.
2. S. Troops moving down the river. Scouting.
5. W. Preparing to leave; cars ready.
6. Th. Rain. Hope soon to leave our foul-smelling tents.
9. S. Chaplain preached in forenoon; left on board cars in evening.
10. M. Reach Pawpaw Tunnel at 3 A.M.; 15 miles.
11. T. More snow on mud; life a misery.
12. W. Sunshine, slush and mud. Nicknacks from home.
13. Th. Expedition starts for Bloomery Gap. Weather colder.

| | | |
|---|---|---|
| 14. | F. | Expedition returned. More snow and mud. |
| 17. | M. | Rain after cold days. News of surrender of Fort Donelson. |
| 22. | Sa. | Salute fired. Mud. Lander's Grand Review. |
| 28. | F. | General inspection. Mustered for pay. Colder. |

*March—*

| | | |
|---|---|---|
| 1. | Sa. | Marched to Sideling Mountain; 11 miles. Colder. |
| 2. | S. | Lander dies; expedition returns; 11 miles. Large flakes of snow. |
| 3. | M. | Cold, muddy and dreary. Lander's body taken to Washington. Col. Kimball in command of the division. Troops in line. |
| 6. | Th. | Struck tents at 4 P. M.; without cover all night; wretchedness. |
| 7. | F. | Remained in camp until 2:30 P.M. Took cars. Many sick. |
| 8. | Sa. | Reached Hancock in the morning; Back Creek in the evening; 46 miles. Camp in the woods; crossed a wire bridge. |
| 9. | S. | Old Fort in sight. To Martinsburg, 15 miles. Leave baggage. |
| 10. | M. | Rain. Camp in the woods, near Martinsburg. Rations scarce. |
| 12. | W. | March toward Winchester 16 miles, and camp in a cemetery. |
| 13. | Th. | Winchester at 5 P.M. Meet Eastern troops. Camp in a meadow. |
| 14. | F. | Companies F and C go to Harper's Ferry, and A, D, H and K to Berryville; B and I are in Winchester. |
| 18. | T. | Eighty men go from Berryville on a scout to Millwood. |
| 23. | S. | Battle of Winchester. Companies at Berryville start for Winchester. |
| 24. | M. | Col. Mason with eight companies pursue Jackson to Cedar Creek. |
| 25. | T. | Again advanced. Fine weather continues; spring-time has come. |
| 26. | W. | Awaiting action of enemy. Banks on hand with Williams' Division. |
| 27. | Th. | Reconnaisance 6 miles toward Woodstock. Apple trees in bloom. |
| 31. | M. | Regiment advances toward Woodstock; in the evening at Strasburg. |

*April—*

| | | |
|---|---|---|
| 1. | T. | Fourth, in advance, leaves Strasburg; reaches Woodstock at 4 P.M. Artillery duel at Stony Creek. |
| 2 to 5. | | Artillery exchange occasional shots. Skirmishing. |
| 4. | F. | Considerable skirmishing across the creek. Rain. |
| 5 to 9. | | Rain; snow on 9th. Fun on picket on high bank north of creek. |
| 12. | Sa. | Change camp to Stony Creek, by high bridge and strong spring. |
| 13. | S. | Ordered to attend service. Molluscous fossils in bed of creek. |
| 14, 15. | | Rainy. Lively times on picket. Firing over heads of rebel bathers. |
| 16. | W. | Under orders to be ready to march at a moment's notice. |
| 17. | Th. | Skirmish to Mount Jackson; 15 miles; left in front. Fine weather. |
| 18. | F. | Advance 11 miles. On picket near bridge over Smith's Creek. |
| 19, 20. | | Occasional showers. |
| 23. | W. | W. B. Drown, of H, mortally wounded by an accidental shot. |
| 24. | Th. | Cold, rainy and stormy. In camp east of and near a creek. |
| 25. | F. | March toward Harrisonburg, 6 miles; camp in a meadow. |
| 26. | Sa. | Beautiful day. In camp. Wheat-fields very green. |
| 27. | S. | March to Camp Cave, Virginia, over an excellent pike, 10 miles. |
| 28, 29. | | Weyer's Cave is explored. Weather very delightful. |
| 30. | W. | Mustered for pay. Dress parade and division-drill south of camp. |

*May—*

4. S. Company and Regimental Inspection. Weather fine. Men rest.
5. M. Return to New Market, 10 miles; march at easy gait.
6. T. Move camp near midnight east of the town, between Smith's Creek and Massanuten Mountains, north of a covered bridge.
7. W. Inspection; 8th, 9th and 10th warm; baggage turned over on 9th.
11. S. Review by General Shields. Weather fine. Delightful valley.
12. M. Warm and dusty. March to Luray, through forests; 16 miles.
13. T. Toward Front Royal, over hills, onion and garlic fields; 19 miles.
14. W. To Front Royal, 6 miles. Camp near the railroad.
15. Th. Heavy showers. In camp. Spy "Belle Boyd" on the streets.
16. F. Started in rain at 10:30 A.M., through Chester and Manassas Gaps.
17. Sa. Start at 6:30, in fog; pass Flint Hill and Gaines' Cross Roads.
18. S. Start at 6; camp at Warrenton, 11 miles. Only ladies and darkeys.
19. M. March to Catlett's Station, 15 miles. Forests and wood-ticks.
20. T. Warm. Food scarce. In camp. Poor gravel soil. Bristly grass.
21. W. March toward Fredericksburg, 16 miles, through barren country.
22. Th. Start at 6 A.M.; reach Falmouth just before a shower; 15 miles.
23. F. Were reviewed by Lincoln and Stanton. Cloudy day.
25. S. Toward Catlett's Station, 17 miles. Back to Shenandoah Valley.
26. M. To Turkey Creek, 23 miles. Fine day. Hard march.
27. T. To Manassas by noon, and Hay Market before dark, 20 miles.
28. W. Start at 6:30; Thoroughfare Gap at 9; by grist and saw-mill, along railroad; leave Salem to left; camp at Rectortown; 20 miles.
29. Th. Start at 7 P.M.; make 10 miles through mud; camp in clover-field.
30. F. At 6:30 start through Manassas Gap. Deploy as skirmishers. Pass through Markham. Charged into Front Royal at noon; skirmishing. Take 150 prisoners. B and C are provost-guards.

*June—*

1. S. Battle anticipated. March 2 miles; return and march 3 miles south.
2. M. Start at 7, through mud and rain; camp without supper; 16 miles.
3. T. On half rations; 9 miles. Camp at Luray. Rain.
4. W. Camp on Culpepper Pike, 1 mile from Luray. Fresh pork and flour.
5. Th. To Columbia Bridge; 6 miles. Shields' curious order. Footsore.
6. F. Confederate pickets in sight. Flour, pork, honey and fowls.
7. Sa. Back to Luray; 6 miles; route step, arms at will.
8. S. Columbia Bridge; just as camp becomes settled are ordered forward.
9. M. At 4:30 continue to push toward Port Republic. About noon move forward. Flanking companies deployed. Covered retreat of brigades that had a fearful struggle at Port Republic. Fremont beyond the enemy. Return to near Shenandoah Furnace.
10. T. At 7:30 onward to Columbia Bridge. Early shower and mud.
11. W. Footsore and many shoeless, reach Luray; round trip 62 miles.
12 to 15. Rested. Some strawberries find their way to camp.
15. S. Start at 11 and march 12 miles. Camp in a clover-field.
16. M. Reach Front Royal at dark; 16 miles. Camp east of town.

17. T. Receive pay for two months at sunset. Fine day.
18. W. Drew clothing. Showers. To be ready to march.
20. F. Leave at 3 and arrive at Bristoe by cars at 7 P.M.; 54 miles.
22. S. Band received its new instruments. Fine weather.
29. S. By rail to Alexandria, 34 miles. Capt. McMillen drowned.
30. M. On board "South America," go to Harrison's Landing, 266 miles.

*July—*
2. W. Disembarked. Assist in covering retreat of McClellan's Army.
3. Th. Skirmish; number wounded by shell; 1 killed; gunboat shells over us.
4. F. In battle-line advance on pickets. Skirmish. National salute fired.
8. T. Hot. Get our baggage. Lincoln reviews army on the gallop.
16. W. Join Sumner's Corps—Second Corps. Kept in broiling sun 8 hours.
22. T. Reviewed by McClellan. Weather very hot; many are sick.

*August—*
1. F. Booming cannon, bursting shell and lurid heavens at night. Confederate batteries across the river soon silenced.
10. S. Join reconnaisance to Malvern Hill, 10 miles. With the reserve.
11. M. Return. Days hot, nights pleasant. Knapsacks are sent to boat.
12. T. Heat more intolerable; most of men sick; camp horribly filthy.
13 to 16. Under marching orders. March 6 miles on 16th down Peninsula.
17. S. To Charles City; over Chickahominy on pontoons; 18 miles.
18. M. March 8 miles through dust. Green corn plenty for two days.
19. T. Through dust to Williamsburg; 11 miles. Health of men better.
20. W. Reach near Yorktown; 9 miles. Boys fish for clams and bathe.
21. Th. Pass Cornwallis' and recent works to Big Bethel; 15 miles.
22. F. Through rain and mud to Newport News, 11 miles. Peaches.
25. M. Transported by "Canonicus" to "Cahawba;" marched 3 miles.
26. T. Leave at 6. New Ironsides. Porpoises. Enter Potomac at 1 P.M.
27. W. Leave boat at Acquia Creek at 1; on board "Long Island" at 8 P.M.
28. Th. Disembarked at Alexandria at 11; leave toward Centerville at 1; orders to cook four days' rations; 3 miles; on vessel 175 miles.
29. F. For Arlington Heights at 5 P.M.; 240 present for duty; 8 miles.
30. Sa. Furnished with ammunition and rations. Start suddenly on forced march toward Centerville; halt near Fairfax; 20 miles.
31. S. To Centerville before day; in line to front, then to right; 5 miles.

*September—*
1. M. Moved to the right. Supported Fourteenth Indiana skirmishers. In two hours recalled. At 11 P.M. marched 4 miles in nine hours; 168 men present for duty.
2. T. Halted 3 miles east of Fairfax at 4 P.M., then move rapidly toward Chain Bridge. Stragglers fire into each other. Night dark as pitch. Our rear shelled; marched 21 miles.
3. W. Falls Church at 2:30 A.M. To Fort Gaines. Cross river; 4 miles.
4. Th. Change camp; many sick; beseiged by hucksters.

5. F. Go into camp at 10 P.M., toward Rockville; 10 miles. Fine day.
6. Sa. March beyond Rockville nearly 2 miles; 11 miles; very warm.
7. S. The 132d P. V. takes our place in brigade. Fort Gaines, 10 miles.
8. M. Reach Fort Gaines at 9 A.M.; 300 sick on hand; 11 miles.
28. S. Reach Baltimore & Ohio Depot at 7:30; on board cars at 2. Chas. Gray, of C, injured by falling from a car; march 6 miles.
29. M. Harper's Ferry during night; camp on Bolivar Heights; 102 miles.

*October—*
1. W. Forced march by Lovetsville and Waterford, to Leesburg, 28 miles.
2. Th. Return via Wheatland and Hillsborough. Reviewed by Lincoln and McClellan. Three-fourths of the men sick. 24 miles.
4. Sa. Reconnaisance to Halltown; picket and skirmish; 5 miles.
6. M. Return to camp; 5 miles. Many sick and dying. "Camp Diarrhœa."
13. M. Battalion-drill. Wormy crackers and spoiled bacon. Warm.
14. T. Most of men serve as provost-guard in town and quarter at a hotel.
16 to 18. On picket. Some more skirmishing. Warm weather.
18. S. Several enlist in the Regular Service in artillery companies.
24. F. On inspection with knapsacks.
26. S. Return from picket. Rain.
28. T. Drill. Men vexed with the doings of the peace party in the North.
30. Th. Orders at 4; strike tents at 10; march at 4 P.M. across Shenandoah.
31. F. March down Pleasant Valley, 4 miles. Muster for pay.

*November—*
1. Sa. Start at 10; deployed at Gregory's Gap, after cavalrymen, 13 miles.
2. S. Up the valley to Snicker's Gap. Deploy as skirmishers. Several, with Lt. Jones, are in sight of rebel camps; 10 miles.
3. M. March to Ashby's Gap, 16 miles. Cannonading. Fine weather.
6. Th. Rectortown and Piedmont, 20 miles. Mason in com. of brigade.
7. F. Move camp during snow-storm. Burnside relieves McClellan.
8. Sa. Camp 5 miles southeast of Salem, 18 miles. Snow melting.
9. S. Beyond Warrenton and return; go into camp 2 miles northeast of town, 8 miles, among pines; good water. Mules raise bedlam.
10. M. McClellan reviews troops. Tremendous cheering. Dissatisfaction.
12. W. Picket; rainy and cold; nights frosty. More bedlam among mules.
13. Th. Fine day. Return from picket at night. Walnuts and hickorynuts.
15. Sa. Camp 4 miles beyond Warrenton Junction; 13 miles. Fine day.
16. S. Start at 11 as wagon-guard; camp near midnight; 14 miles.
17. M. March at 8; camp 2 miles from Falmouth; 14 miles; rain.
18. T. On double-quick after raiders. Roll-call every hour. Raining.
19. W. Rain. Roll-call every hour. Heavy picket begins.
20. Th. Move camp. Rain. Firing south of Fredericksburg.
21. F. Clearing off. Cold. Picket duty. Regimental guard.
24. M. In readiness to march. Constant duty. Picket, cutting wood, etc.

## CHRONOLOGY.

*December—*
1. M. Cold. But few able for duty. Duty heavy. Rations execrable.
6. S. After a week of sunshine, now three inches of snow.
9. T. "Be ready to march at a moment's notice, with three days' rations."
10. W. Building huts. Clear, cold. "Be ready to march in the morning."
11. Th. Started at 5 and halted to the rear of Phillips House. At 4 P.M. advanced to rear of Lacy House; were shelled and fell back. Cannonading for an hour. Pontoons laid.
12. F. Roused at 4:30. After breakfast crossed the river, deployed as skirmishers, advanced beyond the town, drove in the enemy's skirmishers, and bivouacked in the town.
13. Sa. Battle of FREDERICKSBURG. Near noon advanced as skirmishers, established line near a stone wall at foot of Marye's Heights, and were relieved at 5 P.M.; survivors bivouac in town.
14. S. Remain in the town. Groans and shrieks on the field can again be heard at night. Northern lights are visible.
15. M. Make reports of casualties. Draw rations. Send the wounded recovered during the night to the rear. Leave camp by the river bank, recross the river and enter the old camp and huts at near midnight; 8 miles.
16. T. Inspection in forenoon; line of battle to repel rear attack in afternoon.
17. W. Snow, picket duty, and burying the dead.
18. Th. Some of the huts finished. Men "have the blues."
20. Sa. Picket every other day. Stood two hours at Division Headquarters before receiving orders. Some threaten to take "French leave."
25. Th. Camp lively for the first time since the battle.
29. M. "Ready to march at a moment's notice."
30. T. Order is continued. Fine weather as usual.

### 1863.

*January—*
1 to 16. Orders to march. Variable weather; cold, clear, rain and storm.
17. Sa. Corps reviewed. Weather fine.
18. S. Col. Mason, promoted to Brigadier-General, still commands brigade.
19. M. Ready to move. The Twenty-fourth and Twenty eighth New Jersey are assigned to our brigade.
20. T. Cold. Infantry and artillery move up the river.
21. W. Troops continue to move up the river. Raining, pouring.
22. Th. Army returns. "Burnside stuck in the mud." Rain and cold.
23. F. Orders to move countermanded. Rainy. Troops still returning.
24. Sa. Sunshine; hazy. Heavy picket duty.
25. S. Sunshine; 26th, rain; 27th, showers; 28th, stormy, driving snow.
29. Th. Snowstorm and drift; 30th, snow melting; 31st, fine day.

*February—*
1. S. Mason on leave; Col. Snyder, of 7th W. Va., in command of brigade.
2. M. Many applications for "leave of absence." Fine day.

3. T. Cold; 4th, coldest day; 5th, rain and snow; 6th, rain; 7th, cloudy.
8. S. Moderating; 9th, spring-like; 10th, sultry. Heavy duties.
11. W. Sunshine and clouds; 12th, rain; 13th, beautiful; 14th to 16th, fine.
17. T. Rain and snow. Men on duty every day.
18. W. Men are granted "furloughs," and officers "leave of absence."
25. W. Hooker relieves Burnside. Men are delighted.

*March—*

1 to 9. Weather variable. A number of sick absentees return to duty. The troops are reviewed by Genl Hooker.
9, 10, 11. Stormy and very disagreeable. Under arms.
12. Th. Brigade under arms to repel a rear attack. Rainy day.
13. F. Sunshine. Col. Carroll in command of brigade. 14th, blustering.
15. S. Stormy; thunder in the evening. More return from hospital camp.
16. M. Storm and hail in the night. 18th, heavy firing down the river.
19. Th. Snowing; 20th and 21st, rainy and cold.
23. M. Sunshine; 24th, rain; 25th, fine; 27th and 28th, rain; 29th, windy.
30. M. Gov. Morton in camp and makes a speech. 31st, snow and sunshine.

*April—*

1, 2. Fine; 3d, stormy in the evening.
4. Sa. Stormy and cold. Col. Brooks in command of the brigade.
5, 6. Weather beautiful; 7th, windy yet spring-like.
8. W. Troops reviewed near Stoneman's Station by President Lincoln.
9 to 13. Fine weather. Preparations for a movement.
14. T. Five days' rations in haversacks, three days in knapsacks, and sixty rounds of ammunition for enlisted men. Tents struck.
15. W. Many slept in the rain. 16th to 21st, variable, mostly sunshine.
22. W. Very stormy and disagreeable. Brigade Band organized.
23, 24. Cold and windy; 25th to 27th, fine weather and expecting to move.
27. M. Troops are moving; we are under orders to march.
28. T. Up at 4 and start at 6 A.M. for United States Ford; 10 miles.
29. W. On picket on the north bank awaiting the laying of pontoons.
30. Th. Cross the river and march to White House near Chancellorsville.

*May—*

1. F. In support of first line, which begins skirmishing at 10 A M. About 2, fall back from Chancellorsville to near White House.
2. Sa. Construct earthworks. Still in reserve. Fine day.
3. S. In grand charge in the morning drive the enemy back through the woods, coming out twenty rods to right of Chancellor House. Held the enemy at bay by counter-charge and random fire until ordered to fall back about 10:30 A.M.
4. M. Remain in earthworks. Are shelled. Picket skirmishing.
5. T. Near daybreak cover retreat of army. Return to camp during rain.
6. W. Rain; 7th, cold; 8th, cloudy; 9th, sunshine; 12th and 13th, sultry.
14. Th. Brigade moves camp.
31. S. Extra baggage sent to the rear. Orders to be ready to march.

## CHRONOLOGY. 209

*June—*

10. W. Couch goes to Dept. of Susquehanna. Hancock in charge of corps.
12. F. The 24th N. J. leaves for home with best wishes of entire brigade.
13. Sa. Suffocating; rain in evening. Dr. Morrison has ambulance train.
14. S. Leave at 8:30 P.M. and march greater part of the night; 9 miles.
15. M. To Dumfries in dust and heat, marching slow and tiresome; 6 miles.
16. T. Maryland reported invaded. Rations. Col. Coons in command of the brigade. Camp at Wolf Run Shoals, 20 miles. Rapid marching; occasional half-hour halts.
17. W. Near Fairfax Station; 7 miles. Hot. Cavalry with us part of time.
18. Th. The 28th New Jersey start home. In camp. Rain. Confederates reported to be in Maryland and Pennsylvania.
19. F. Rained hard at 3 P.M.; march at 6 P.M. and reach Centerville in a disagreeable rain at 9 o'clock; 5 miles.
20. Sa. Started at 1, weather pleasant; passed over old battle-field and saw skeletons exposed; reach Gainesville at 6 P.M.; 12 miles.
25. Th. Marched to Gum Springs; mud and rain from 3 P.M.; 15 miles.
26. F. To Edwards' Ferry; went into camp at dark, in rain and mud; were roused as soon as asleep, worried through mud and over river, and went into camp at daylight all "out of sorts;" 15 miles.
27. Sa. Through Poolesville and Barnesville; camp at 11 P.M.; 12 miles.
28. S. Frederick Junction by Monocacy Bridge; bathe; fine day; 12 miles.
29. M. Col. Carroll in command. March, via Frederick City, Liberty, Jamestown and Union Bridge, to near Uniontown, Md.; 30 miles.
30. T. March beyond Uniontown; 3 miles.

*July—*

1. W. Via Uniontown and Taneytown, Md., to near Gettysburg; 20 miles.
2. Th. Took position west of Cemetery Hill. Under fire all day. In the evening repulsed the charge of Hoke's and Hays' Brigades on Cemetery Hill; 3 miles. Battle of GETTYSBURG.
3. F. Under fire all day on right hand slope of Cemetery Hill.
4. Sa. Gather arms. Arm with Springfield rifles found on field. Rain.
5. S. March near Two Taverns. Delightful country; pleasant; 6 miles.
6. M. In camp. Make reports and requisitions; wash clothing and rest.
7. T. Marched to Taneytown, Md., over fields; warm; 11 miles.
8. W. Via Woodbury and Walkerville to near Frederick City; 20 miles.
9. Th. Via Frederick City, passed the nude body of a hanging spy. March rapidly to Jefferson and Bakersville, near Rohrersville; 24 miles.
10. F. March through Rohrersville, cross Antietam Creek at 1 P.M., pass through Keedysville over right of old battle-field, and form in line of battle; 12 miles.
11. Sa. Advance in line of battle about 2 miles in the morning, make a reconnaisance toward Hagerstown, meet the enemy, and skirmish near Funkstown Heights; 4 miles.

| | | |
|---|---|---|
| 12. | S. | Rained hard in the afternoon. Changed position at noon toward the left, and again at 4 P.M. Throw up entrenchment and do some scouting and foraging. |
| 13. | M. | Change again to left and front, construct earthworks and skirmish. |
| 14. | T. | Were just ready to pounce upon enemy, but they had crossed the river. Hurry after to Williamsport; rain and mud; 8 miles. |
| 15. | W. | Uncomfortable night. March to Harper's Ferry and camp between river and canal. Dead Confederates in the river. 20 miles. |
| 16. | Th. | Camp near Knoxville, 5 miles. 17th, make reports and requisitions. |
| 18. | Sa. | Cross the Potomac and Shenandoah Rivers and march up Pleasant Valley; 12 miles. Beautiful valley. Fine weather. |
| 19. | S. | Camp near Gregory's Gap in a blackberry patch; 6 miles. |
| 20. | M. | March to near Bloomfield and camp at 5 P.M.; fine day; 12 miles. |
| 22. | W. | Start at 1 and camp at Upperville at 5 P.M.; fine day; 10 miles. |
| 23. | Th. | Via Markham, Manassas Gap, near Front Royal; skirmish; 20 miles. |
| 24. | F. | Return to Markham in the afternoon by a rapid march; 10 miles. |
| 25. | Sa. | Start at 5 A.M., pass Rectortown at 11, and reach White Plains at 6 P.M.; 16 miles. Thousands of wagons in sight. |
| 26. | S. | Start at 5 toward Thoroughfare Gap, through Warrenton at 2 P.M., and camp, nearly exhausted, near Warrenton Junction; 21 miles. |
| 27. | M. | In camp, weary and footsore. Rain in evenings of 27th, 28th, 29th. |
| 30. | Th. | Started at 5 P.M. and marched rapidly to Elk Run; 8 miles. |
| 31. | F. | For Kelly's Ford at 8 A.M. Fine day. 7 miles. |

*August—*

| | | |
|---|---|---|
| 1. | Sa. | Return to Elk Run to guard the railroad; 8 miles. From this day until the 15th the heat was intense. In camp; nights cool. |
| 16. | S. | To Bealeton Station; 8 miles. On cars to Alexandria; 38 miles. |
| 17, 18, 19, 20. | | Feasting in Alexandria; ham and eggs, etc. |
| 20. | Th. | On steamer "Atlantic" in evening with three other regiments. |
| 21. | F. | Left the wharf at 5 A.M. Down the river and bay into the ocean. |
| 23. | S. | New York Harbor at 6 A.M., and landed on Governor's Island at 2 P.M.; 500 miles. Camp near Castle William. |
| 28. | F. | By boat and rail to Jamaica, L. I.; 12 miles. Do guard duty. |

*September—*

| | | |
|---|---|---|
| 6. | S. | Move by rail to Fort Greene, Brooklyn, L. I.; 9 miles. |
| 7. | M. | Marched to New York City and embarked on "Atlantic;" 4 miles. |
| 8. | T. | Steamer left the wharf at 9 A.M. Passed the "Monitor." |
| 9. | W. | Out of sight of land until 3 P.M. Before entering the bay a storm threatens. Many seasick. Anchored for the night. |
| 10. | Th. | Alexandria at 3 P.M. Soldiers and "gray-backs" too numerous. |
| 11. | F. | Disembarked at 8 A.M. and go into camp 2 miles west of town. |
| 12. | Sa. | March to Fairfax. Sunshine and bracing air. 14 miles. |
| 13. | S. | March to Bristoe Station. Delightful weather. 16 miles. |
| 14. | M. | March to Bealeton Station. Pass old-time camps; 12 miles. |

15. T. March to Brandy Station. Fine day. 12 miles. Baggage on cars.
16. W. March to Cedar Mountain. New and delightful scenery. 13 miles.
17. Th. To Robinson's River. In line of battle. Rain in evening. 4 miles.
18. F. Showers. Two deserters of 14th Conn. executed in afternoon.
19 to 13. On picket along the river. Fine weather. Rations scarce. Boys forage, shoot squirrels, get zouaves after them and disarm them.
23. W. Skirmish on picket line. Suspect a movement toward our rear.
24 to 30. Fine weather. Two corps leave for the West. Under orders.

*October—*

1 to 5. In camp. Relieved by Sixth Corps on 5th. March to corps' camp.
6. T. March at 7, reach Culpepper at 1, and camp on red clay; 12 miles.
10. Sa. Hurry to Jeffrey's Saw Mill. Enemy near. Expect battle. 4 miles.
11. S. Brandy Station at noon; Bealeton at 4. Race with enemy. 18 m.
12. M. No fires, no noise. Vote for Governor. Recross the Rappahannock and bivouac half a mile north of Brandy Station. 9 miles.
13. T. Started at 1 A.M., recrossed the Rappahannock at 4, and halted 3 miles north of Bealeton. Picket skirmish. Onward at 1 P.M. and camp at Auburn at 10. Fires. Night cool. 16 miles.
14. W. Cedar Run Skirmish. March to Bristoe. Battle of Bristoe Station. March to Blackburn's Ford and camp at 2 o'clock the next morning. Exciting times. 22 miles.
15. Th. Began to rain at 2 A.M.; hurried into line at 8. Skirmish.
16. F. At Centerville awaiting movements of enemy. Rain. Rations scarce.
17. Sa. Part of brigade support cavalry toward Manassas. Skirmishing.
18. S. Quiet Sunday, save picket racketings. Cool nights.
19. M. Start at 6 A.M. In line of battle at Bristoe. Camp at night. Fine day. 7 miles. Skirmish toward Auburn.
20. T. March at 7 toward Gainesville, then south; camp near Auburn. 18 miles. Enemy acknowledges himself out-generaled.
21, 22. Remain in camp. Fine weather. Rest.
23. F. March at 6 and halt at Turkey Run Bridge, near Warrenton; 4 miles.
24. Sa. Cool and stormy. "Ready at a moment's notice to repel attacks."
25. S. Occasional sunshine. Cavalry skirmishing toward Bealeton heard.
26 to 31. Growing colder; sun most of the time.

*November—*

1 to 7. Sunny; dry and cold air. Begin to wish for winter quarters.
7. Sa. Start at 7 on forced march to Kelly's Ford; 19 miles.
8. S. Crossed the river, drew up in line, halted an hour, moved 3 miles to the right, halted two hours, advanced to Brandy Station and camped; 10 miles. Confederate camp-fires in sight.
9. M. Cold. First snow. Picket duty severe and frequent.
10. T. March to Mountain Run and camp on Hamilton Farm; 4 miles.
11 to 22. In camp; variable weather; rain on 20th; paid off on 18th.
23. M. Struck tents, then the rain poured most of the day; tents up again.
24. T. Cloudy. "'Twill rain if we strike tents." Growing colder.

26. Th. Cross the Rapidan at Germania Ford and bivouac in thicket of the Wilderness 3 miles beyond the Ford. Cold, cloudy. 12 miles.
27. F. To Robertson's Tavern and Cross Roads. Drive enemy's pickets. Severe skirmish. 10 miles. Drive enemy again at 4 P.M.
28. Sa. Move on the advance to Mine Run. Skirmish. Rain at 10 A.M. Cannonading at noon. Kept on picket. Nearly perish in snow, rain and sleet. Confederate lines in sight.
29. S. Relieved near daybreak and march to left of line. Near Hopewell Church as skirmishers, take position and entrench. 6 miles.
30. M. General attack abandoned, as Warren had sooner lose his commission and sacrifice his position in the army than expose his men in useless assaults. Men wet and shivering with cold.

*December—*

1. T. Remain until 8:30 P.M., build fires, steal quietly to rear and away toward the river, and pass fires and cavalry pickets through the forests. 21 miles. No skirmishing. Cold weather.
2. W. Culpepper Mine Ford at sunrise and camp at 7 P.M. 16 miles.
5. Sa. Move camp 3 miles nearer Stevensburg. Dr. Morrison takes the wounded to Washington.
7. M. Move camp a mile, to Cole's Hill, on Mountain Run, and go into winter quarters.
11. F. Furloughs are granted the men, and leave to officers.
12 to 17. The first half of the month cold and sunshine.
17. Th. Rainy and disagreeable; worst day of season. Huts mostly finished.
21. M. Re-enlistment in the Fourteenth Indiana causes a sensation. 17th to 26th, sunshine. Hilarious Christmas Eve.
27. S. Rain. Re-enlistment inducements. Furloughs and big bounties.
28, 29. Rain; 30th, cloudy; 31st, rain; a happy New Year's Eve.

## 1864.

*January—*

1. F. Strong winds until after 12 M., and intense cold during the night.
2, 3. Cold, clear; 4th, snow, and sleet at 10 P.M.; 5th to 7th, clear, cold.
8. F. Moderating; snowing, three inches deep. Picket duty heavy.
9 to 12. Clear and cold; 13th, cold and damp.
14 to 17. Moderating; sunshine. Picket and police duty heavy.
18. M. Rain at 6 A.M.; 19th, strong winds, evening cold; 20th, high winds.
21 to 23. Sunshine; 24th, cloudy; 25th to 30th, more sunshine.
29. F. Brigade Lyceum formed. Brigade Chapel arranged for. *Marsonian Literary Casket* dates its beginning; 30th, fine; 31st, cloudy.

*February—*

1, 2. Rain and cloudy.
3. W. Stormy forenoon and clear afternoon. Sword presentation to Col. Lockwood, of 7th W. Va. Most of his men re-enlisted.

6. Sa. Orders at 4 A.M.; march at 8. Cross river. Battle at Morton's Ford.
7. S. Reach old winter quarters at 8 P.M. Wounded brought in earlier.
9. T. Seventh West Virginia goes on furlough; 7th to 15th, fine days.
15 to 18. Cold and strong gales from mountains. Heavy picket duty.
22. M. Corps' Headquarters Ball; 23d, Grand Review by Genl. Meade.
26. F. Marsonian Literary Society has its usual Friday evening lecture.
28. S. "Ready to march at a moment's notice," in support of Kilpatrick.

*March—*

1. T. Rain; 2d, cloudy, cold; 3d to 10th, fine; 10th, very disagreeable.
11 to 15. Beautiful days; red-birds singing; 15th, cold; 16th, fine.
17. Th. St. Patrick's all day. Hurdle races, etc., in the Irish Brigade visited by everybody. Cloudy, yet pleasant.
18. F. Fine. Conscript drilling. Fall into line in the evening.
20. S. Chaplain Strong preaches against swearing as useless and degrading.
21. M. Fine. Duty lighter. Police regulations very strict. Lecture.
22. T. Snow at 10 P.M. ten inches deep; 23d, sunshine; snow melting.
24. Th. Cold rain. Army is consolidated. Exchange blue for white trefoil.
25. F. Camp all life; fife, drums, band and squad-drills; fine day.
26. Sa. Very disagreeable, but does not squelch squawking brass bands.
29. T. Genl. Grant's Grand Review postponed on account of rain.

*April—*

1 to 7. Rainy and cloudy. Nine regiments in the brigade.
7, 8. Fine days. The Seventh West Virginia back from furlough and received with hearty greetings. A class in phonography.
8 to 13. Variable. Get ready for forward movement. Ladies return home.
13. W. Parks, of C, killed by a citizen in the sutler's tent. Cloudy.
14. Th. Review of brigade by Gibbon, Division General. Fine day.
15. F. Reviewed by Hancock, commanding corps. Infantry, artillery and cavalry in line. Rain in the evening. 16th, rain.
17 to 22. Fine days. Snow nearly off of the mountains.
22. F. Second Corps reviewed by Grant. Horns squawk and drums "Rub-dub eternally." All is life and activity. Expect hard fighting and signal victories with Carroll, Hancock, Meade and Grant.
23. Sa. Fine. Dust flying in camp. Roads drying. Getting in readiness.
25. M. Division "en masse" witnesses the hanging of an enlisted man.
25 to 30. Fine. Dull monotony. Expect to move.

*May—*

1. S. A dozen men in a regiment stack arms and stand up for their rights. Do not get them, or possibly soldiers have none.
2. M. Sand-storm and crimson clouds in afternoon. Magnificent sight.
3. T. Receive orders to be ready and march at 11 P.M.. Fine day.
4. W. Cross the Rapidan at Ely's Ford at 8:30 A.M., and reach Chancellorsville at noon; 16 miles.
5. Th. Were roused at 3:30, marched at 4 A.M., and act as wagon-guard.

6. F. Battle of the Wilderness. Start from Chancellorsville; join brigade at 4:45 A.M. Brigade advances shortly before 5 A.M. and drives the enemy 1½ miles by 9. At 11, troops on flanks giving way, was compelled to fall back to road. Charge in afternoon to meet that of enemy. Fires on our front. Heat and smoke.
7. Sa. Care for the wounded at night. To be ready to march at noon. At night move to the right and rear. Fine weather.
8. S. At 7 follow Fifth Corps, reach Tod's Tavern before noon, halt until 2, move 3 miles, halt half an hour, move ½ mile, bivouac, and draw rations and ammunition. 10 miles.
9. M. March toward Tod's Tavern in support of Birney. About 10 march toward Spottsylvania, 3 miles, and in afternoon cross the Po River. Camp fired into. 5 miles. Obtain ice from ice-house and gather black beans spilt from skedaddling rebel wagons.
10. T. Start shortly after noon toward the left, beyond Alsop Crossing, form in line, charge enemy at 5:30, were repulsed, and charge again at 6:30. Battle of Prospect Hill. 5 miles.
11. W. Throw up breastworks. Ready to repulse a charge. Move to the left at night, 4 miles.
12. Th. Spottsylvania. Battle. Grand charge, capturing works, cannon, prisoners, etc.
13. F. Skirmish and reconnaisance. Carroll wounded. Col. Coons, of the Fourteenth Indiana, killed. Col. Ellis in command of brigade.
14. Sa. Col. Smythe in command of brigade. Rest toward left and rear.
15. S. Skirmish on picket line. Fine day. On reserve line.
16. M. In camp. Help to rescue the wounded. Slight skirmish.
17. T. March at 10 P.M. to battle-ground of the 12th. 3 miles.
18. W. Move against enemy at daybreak. Repulsed. Battle of Ny River.
19. Th. Helped repel an attack on wagon-train. Fine day.
20. F. Orders to march. Start at 11 P.M. to left and south; move rapidly.
21. Sa. Reach Guinea Station at daylight, Bowling Green at 10, Milford at 1, cross Mattapony, skirmish and entrench. 30 miles.
22. S. Made reconnaisance over low and wet ground; 6 miles.
23. M. Start early, cross Polecat Creek at 10, and reach bridge over North Anna River at 2. Under fire until dark. 12 miles.
24. T. Cross the river early. Skirmish. Drive enemy over 2 miles.
25. W. Drove the enemy from their first and second line of works. Skirmish nearly all day.
26. Th. On skirmish line all day. Advance line in the evening. Fall back to the river at 10 P.M. 3 miles.
27. F. Recrossed the river at 10 A.M. Shelled by the enemy. Bring up the rear of our army by starting at 11 down the river and halting at 11 P.M. 16 miles.
28. Sa. Resume march at 7 A.M., Cross Pamunky at 3 P.M., march 3 miles, form in line of battle on Huntly's Farm, to left of Sixth Corps, and entrench. Rations, except beef and coffee, scarce. 10 m.

29. S. Advance nearly a mile at noon and entrench. Skirmish on picket.
30. M. Advance at 7 A.M. and support 7th W. Va. as skirmishers. 3 m.
31. T. Advance near Totopotomoy Creek to support skirmishers.

*June—*
1. W. Recruiters, recruits and veterans return. Brisk skirmish at dark. Start at 8:30 to the left and move all night. Very dark. 8 m.
2. Th. After breakfast advance a mile. Skirmish all day. Charge countermanded.
3. F. Battle of Cold Harbor. Charge on rebel works at 4:30 A.M. Entrench. Repulse rebel charge in the evening. Constant firing.
4. Sa. Skirmishing all day. Cannonading at noon and evening.
5. S. Skirmishing all day. Receive an order relieving us from duty. At dark bid good-bye to veterans and recruits, go in squads to the rear, and camp near wagon-train. 4 miles.
6. M. Reach White House Landing at 2 P.M.; 14 miles.
7. T. Turn over arms and accoutrements to the Government.
8. W. On board the steamer "Highland Light." Down the York and up the Chesapeake.
9. Th. Reach Washington at 10 A.M. Camp near the Capitol.
10. F. In camp awaiting transportation. Anxious to go home.
11. Sa. Board Baltimore & Ohio box-cars at 11 A.M., all huddled together.
12. S. Reach Martinsburg at 6 A.M., and Piedmont in the evening.
13. M. Reach Fairmount in the morning, Bellaire about 10, and Columbus at night. Try to "bunk" in Tod Barracks. "Break for" the hotels and boarding houses.
14. T. Begin making out muster-out rolls and filling out discharge papers. Most of the men remain in Camp Jackson until the 22d, when we received our pay, bounty and discharge papers, and then took the first train for home.

# CORRESPONDENCE

## IN REGARD TO FAILURE OF HOWARD TO RECOGNIZE OUR PART AT GETTYSBURG—TABULAR VIEW OF CASUALTIES IN BRIGADE AT FREDERICKSBURG, CHANCELLORSVILLE AND GETTYSBURG—TABULAR VIEW OF ORGANIZATIONS IN U. S. ARMY—NUMBER OF MEN IN THE UNION SERVICE, KILLED, ETC.—NATIONAL CEMETERIES, ETC.—GREATEST LOSSES, ETC.

The following, from Captain John C. Reid of the Eighth Ohio, and Acting Assistant Adjutant General upon the Staff of Generals Carroll and Smythe, in regard to the part taken by the Fourth and other regiments in the battle of Gettysburg, is certainly worthy a place in this record. It was written for and printed in the *National Tribune*, a soldier's paper published at Washington City:

*To the Editor:*
From reading the so-called "Personal Reminiscences" of General Howard concerning the attack on the evening of July 2d, on that portion of his corps stationed on Cemetery Hill, and the repulse of the same, as published in your issue of the 1st instant, it is apparent he still, as in his essay or article published in *The Atlantic* of July, 1876, tries to convey the false impression that he did not call for any aid, and that Carroll's Brigade was sent to him without solicitation, and then only assisted in restoring his line, etc. As stated by James Beale, in his article appearing in the same issue of your paper: "After the many times that General Howard's fictions have been upset by appeal to historic facts, one views with amazement his continuance in the errors so often demolished."

It is charitable to call his omissions, misstatements, etc., "errors," but they are so numerous, and his persistency in them is such, that one is forced to believe they were purposely made. General Howard has from the first been unwilling to admit that there was any actual break in his line on the evening of July 2d, or that his infantry failed properly to support his batteries, and hence he failed in his report, made within the next few days, to give General Carroll (then Colonel commanding) and his Brigade the credit of saving same. The fact is, three regiments of Carroll's Brigade, (Fourth Ohio, Fourteenth Indiana and Seventh West Virginia) recaptured two of his batteries, re-established his line, and had to hold same that night and all of the following day, because [some of] his infantry had "fallen back" to find a better position, and he was unable to bring them to the front until the evening of July 3d, when the battle was over.

The following letter from General Gibbon and Captain Huntington, as well as the letter of General Howard, are interesting at the present time, whilst the latter is narrating his "Personal Reminiscences"—his revised edition of same: and, lest I may be accused of making garbled extracts, I give them in full, promising, however that General Carroll has no knowledge of my intention so to do.

In the *Army and Navy Journal* of March 12th, 1864, there appeared the following communications from "Adjutant" and General Gibbon:

### COLONEL CARROLL'S BRIGADE AT GETTYSBURG.

*To the Editor.*

SIR--In your issue of February 20th, "Truth," in a letter on Congress and General Howard, says that "General Hancock sent seven regiments * * * to report to General Howard." In this respect he is mistaken. Three regiments of this brigade, under Colonel Carroll's command, were first sent, and sometime afterwards two more from the Second Division. The two latter did not come to the same part of the field as our brigade, which *alone* drove the enemy from Cemetery Hill, out of our batteries, and held that portion of the line from which part of the Eleventh Corps had been driven. As a corroboration, I inclose a letter from General Gibbon, who commanded the Corps at that time.

Respectfully, your obedient servant,

"ADJUTANT."

Headquarters First Brigade, Third Division,
Second Corps, March 6, 1864.

### GENERAL GIBBON'S LETTER TO COLONEL CARROLL.

[Official Business.]

HEADQUARTERS, RENDEZVOUS FOR DRAFTED MEN,
PHILADELPHIA, PA., Feb. 23, 1864.

*Colonel:*

It has recently come to my notice that you have failed to receive from Major-General Howard the official acknowledgement to which you and your brigade are entitled by your services with his corps at Gettysburg on the night of the 2d and day of the 3d of July. I am very sorry to learn this, more especially at so late a day, as, had I been present with my command, I should probably have been able to do you and your gallant brigade an act of justice, which would have atoned in some measure for your misfortune in being sent away from your own corps, where your services would have been fully acknowledged, to the relief of another, where, although I am told they were appreciated and acknowledged at the time, you failed to obtain that public and official acknowledgment which every soldier has a right to expect to receive as freely and frankly as it should be his duty to give it. As I happened to be in command of the Second Corps when your brigade was, at the suggestion of Major-General Hancock, detached to the assistance of the Eleventh, I am, of course, cognizant of the circumstances attending the transaction, and I feel it incumbent upon me, as your then commanding officer, to do what I can to repair what I am led to believe is an act of injustice to a portion of my command. I know nothing, of course, officially of your services whilst detached from the Second Corps, but I am not presuming too much when, considering your reputation as a soldier, the character of your command, and the reports which reached me at the time and afterwards of your timely arrival at and prompt recovery of a critical point, I suppose them to have been of the utmost importance in preventing the enemy from obtaining a foothold on the key to our position—Cemetery Hill. You are at liberty to make what use you deem proper of this communication, and I shall be much gratified if it aids you in any way in obtaining a just acknowledgment of the services of yourself and your command at the battle of Gettysburg.

I am, sir, very respectfully, your obedient servant,

JOHN GIBBON,
*Brigadier General Volunteers.*

The following letter was also published, but I have forgotten the date:

### ANOTHER TRIBUTE TO CARROLL.

MARIETTA, O., March 25, 1864.

*Brigadier General John Gibbon:*

GENERAL—Though I have not the honor of your personal acquaintance, I cannot refrain from expressing the gratification afforded me by your letter to Colonel S. S. Carroll in regard to his services at the battle of Gettysburg, which has just fallen under my observation. I commanded a brigade of artillery reserve, posted on Cemetery Hill, and have a personal knowledge of what was done by Colonel Carroll and his brigade. The Colonel called to me as soon as he arrived on the hill, having, as he said, no precise orders, and asked me where the enemy were; and that point ascertained, he needed no further information. I say, and I believe it can be proved, that the prompt and gallant action of Colonel Carroll saved the hill that Thursday evening. The value of that service it is hard to overestimate. The enemy were actually in one of the batteries of my command (Rickett's, F and G, Pennsylvania Artillery), and that portion of the Eleventh Corps who should have supported it were too busy "redeeming" themselves to attend to that duty. I had the honor of serving under Colonel Carroll in the Shenandoah campaign, and only echo the opinion of all who knew him there, in saying that a braver or more thorough soldier never wore the uniform. In the matter of promotion, I consider him the worst used man in the United States Army. As I have been compelled to leave the service from injuries sustained in it, I trust there is no impropriety in thus addressing you, the first general officer who, as far as I am aware, has done public justice to Colonel Carroll.

I am, General, most respectfully, your obedient servant,

I. F. HUNTINGTON,
*Late Captain First Ohio Light Artillery.*

These publications brought forth the following from General Howard, which appeared in the Washington *Daily Chronicle* of April 5th, 1864:

### HE DID NOT INTEND TO SLIGHT CARROLL.

HEADQUARTERS ELEVENTH CORPS,
LOOKOUT VALLEY, TENN., March 27, 1864.

*To the Editor of the Chronicle.*

SIR—In the *Army and Navy Journal* of March 12th, 1864, also in the Cincinnati *Commercial* March 24th, 1864, letters appear from Brigadier General John Gibbon, commanding Second Corps, complaining that the services of Colonel S. S. Carroll at the battle of Gettysburg have not been acknowledged in the proper official manner. It is with painful regret that I find it appearing that I have not complimented the gallantry and efficiency of Colonel Carroll in such manner as was my purpose. The letter I wrote Colonel Carroll was in no sense intended as a private letter. I have a copy in my official record, which I most gladly have now transmitted to Major-General Meade, and will be pleased if you will publish the same. I would also furnish you an extract from my official report relative to Colonel Carroll's Brigade, had I permission to publish it. I wish to say, in excuse for *apparent* negligence, that I supposed his own corps commanders completely cognizant of the doings of this brigade at Gettysburg. I warmly subscribe to the sentiment of General Gibbon's letter so far as it concerns Colonel Carroll, and publicly disclaim any intention to do an injustice to him or any other gallant soldier. I will add that I have omitted to commend several worthy officers who were connected with me and rendered the most honorable and timely service. I acknowledge this with sorrow, but am determined to make all possible amends for such omissions.

On the second day of the battle, towards evening, my line being pressed, I sent an Aid-de-Camp to General Meade requesting re-enforcements. The same Aid was intrusted with an order, or request, from General Meade to General Gibbon, commanding Second Corps, to the same effect. I believe, also, that I sent Lieutenant-Colonel Meysenberg directly to General Hancock, commanding a wing, with a similar request; this being done to save time. At any rate, with generous promptitude, a brigade under Colonel Carroll was dispatched to the point most endangered, moving up in the manner described in my letter. Colonel Carroll not only repulsed the enemy at that point, but remained that night and the next day, holding an important position of the line between Generals Ames and Wadsworth (First Corps). Colonel Carroll was exceedingly disappointed at being retained after the position became one of inaction. He was eager to participate in the glorious operations where the Second Corps had so prominent a part on the third and last day of the battle. For fearlessness and energetic action, Colonel Carroll has not a superior.

Respectfully,

O. O. HOWARD,

*Major-General.*

## A LETTER OF THANKS TO CARROLL.

HEADQUARTERS ELEVENTH CORPS,
WARRENTON JUNCTION, VA., July 29, 1863.

*Colonel S. S. Carroll, Commanding Brigade, Second Corps.*

COLONEL—I wish to thank you for the prompt support you gave me on the evening of the 2d of July at Gettysburg, on the extreme right of General Ames' Division. I was particularly weak at that point, having only a single thin line, through which the enemy were just breaking. You came up quickly, deployed and moved into position after your old style. For this and your subsequent patience in strengthening that position until the close of the attack on the 3d of July, I tender you my hearty thanks.

Respectfully,

O. O. HOWARD,

*Major-General.*

The repeated calls for help appearing in General Howard's letter of March 27th, 1864, are hardly reconcilable with the statement, in substance, that Carroll's Brigade was sent to him without solicitation, and the fact that Carroll was compelled to remain on the line of the Eleventh Corps until the 3d, when in fact the battle was over, shows how he "was enabled to shorten my front." Further comment is unnecessary; suffice it to say that General Howard does not, and perhaps cannot, write "history."

JOHN REID,

*Chicago, Illinois.*

---

[The above is embraced in this History without the knowledge of Captain Reid.—WILLIAM KEPLER.]

TABULAR VIEW OF CASUALTIES IN THE BRIGADE IN BATTLES OF FREDERICKSBURG, CHANCELLORSVILLE AND GETTYSBURG, TAKEN FROM DIARY OF THE AUTHOR.

| Regiment. | Fredericksburg. | | | | | | | | Chancellorsville. | | | | | | Gettysburg. | | | | | |
|---|---|---|---|---|---|---|---|---|---|---|---|---|---|---|---|---|---|---|---|---|
| | Officers killed. | Officers wounded. | Officers missing. | Men killed. | Men wounded. | Men missing. | Officers in action. | Men in action. | Officers killed. | Officers wounded. | Officers missing. | Men killed. | Men wounded. | Men missing. | Officers killed. | Officers wounded. | Officers missing. | Men wounded. | Men killed. | Men missing. |
| 4th Ohio | 1 | 4 | ... | 6 | 34 | 2 | 19 | 98 | ... | 2 | ... | 14 | 58 | 4 | 2 | 1 | ... | 8 | 16 | 5 |
| 14th Indiana | 1 | 9 | ... | 3 | 58 | 4 | 19 | 254 | ... | 8 | ... | 7 | 42 | 7 | ... | 3 | ... | 6 | 20 | ... |
| 7th West Virginia | ... | 4 | ... | 4 | 26 | 3 | 19 | 190 | 1 | 1 | ... | 4 | 18 | 13 | ... | 1 | ... | 5 | 38 | 1 |
| 8th Ohio | ... | 2 | ... | 6 | 24 | 1 | 17 | 175 | ... | ... | ... | 1 | 10 | ... | 1 | 10 | ... | 17 | 73 | 1 |
| *24th New Jersey | 1 | 6 | ... | 4 | 94 | ... | 26 | 556 | 1 | 2 | ... | 2 | 17 | 14 | ... | ... | ... | ... | ... | ... |
| *28th New Jersey | ... | 10 | ... | 13 | 146 | ... | 28 | 600 | ... | 2 | ... | 2 | 30 | 26 | ... | ... | ... | ... | ... | ... |

*24th and 28th New Jersey had been discharged the month previous on account of expiration of term of service.

## TABULAR STATEMENT OF ORGANIZATIONS IN THE SERVICE OF THE UNITED STATES DURING THE REBELLION.

| STATES AND TERRITORIES. | CAVALRY. | | ARTILLERY. | | | INFANTRY. | | TOTAL. | | |
|---|---|---|---|---|---|---|---|---|---|---|
| | Regiments. | Companies. | Regiments. | Companies. | Batteries. | Regiments. | Companies. | Regiments. | Companies. | Batteries. |
| Maine | 2 | .... | 1 | 3 | 7 | 30 | 22 | 33 | 25 | 7 |
| New Hampshire | 1 | .... | 1 | ... | 1 | 17 | 4 | 19 | 4 | 1 |
| Vermont | 1 | .... | 1 | 1 | 3 | 17 | .... | 19 | 1 | 3 |
| Massachusetts | 5 | 4 | 4 | 8 | 19 | 68 | 47 | 77 | 59 | 19 |
| Rhode Island | 3 | 2 | 3 | ... | 1 | 8 | 1 | 14 | 3 | 1 |
| Connecticut | 1 | .... | 2 | ... | 3 | 21 | .... | 30 | .... | 3 |
| New York | 27 | 10 | 15 | ... | 35 | 252 | 15 | 294 | 25 | 35 |
| New Jersey | 3 | .... | .... | ... | 5 | 38 | 4 | 41 | 4 | 5 |
| Pennsylvania | 23 | 28 | 4 | 5 | 19 | 227 | 62 | 254 | 95 | 19 |
| Delaware | .... | 8 | .... | 1 | 1 | 9 | 4 | 9 | 13 | 1 |
| Maryland | 4 | 4 | .... | ... | 6 | 20 | 1 | 24 | 5 | 6 |
| District of Columbia | 1 | 1 | .... | ... | .... | 2 | 33 | 3 | 34 | .... |
| West Virginia | 7 | 2 | .... | ... | 8 | 17 | 2 | 24 | 4 | 8 |
| Virginia | .... | .... | .... | ... | .... | .... | 1 | .... | 1 | .... |
| North Carolina | 2 | .... | .... | ... | .... | 2 | .... | 4 | .... | .... |
| Georgia | .... | .... | .... | ... | .... | .... | 2 | .... | 2 | .... |
| Florida | 2 | .... | .... | ... | .... | .... | .... | 2 | .... | .... |
| Alabama | 1 | 5 | .... | ... | .... | .... | .... | 1 | 5 | .... |
| Mississippi | .... | 2 | .... | ... | .... | .... | .... | .... | 2 | .... |
| Louisiana | 2 | .... | .... | ... | .... | 3 | .... | 5 | .... | .... |
| Texas | 1 | 9 | .... | ... | .... | .... | .... | 1 | 9 | .... |
| Arkansas | 4 | .... | .... | ... | 1 | 3 | 2 | 7 | 2 | 1 |
| Tennessee | 21 | 7 | .... | ... | 5 | 9 | .... | 30 | 7 | 5 |
| Kentucky | 16 | 10 | .... | ... | 7 | 45 | 1 | 61 | 11 | 7 |
| Ohio | 13 | 18 | 3 | ... | 27 | 218 | 11 | 234 | 29 | 27 |
| Michigan | 12 | 2 | 2 | ... | 11 | 36 | 7 | 50 | 9 | 11 |
| Indiana | 13 | 1 | 1 | ... | 26 | 123 | 16 | 137 | 17 | 26 |
| Illinois | 17 | .... | 2 | ... | 8 | 157 | 9 | 176 | 9 | 8 |
| Missouri | 30 | 26 | .... | ... | 6 | 64 | 20 | 94 | 46 | 6 |
| Wisconsin | 4 | .... | 1 | ... | 12 | 53 | .... | 58 | .... | 12 |
| Iowa | 9 | .... | .... | ... | 4 | 46 | .... | 55 | .... | 4 |
| Minnesota | 2 | 10 | 1 | ... | 3 | 11 | .... | 14 | 10 | 3 |
| California | 2 | 4 | .... | ... | .... | 9 | .... | 11 | 4 | .... |
| Kansas | 9 | .... | .... | ... | 3 | 10 | 5 | 19 | 5 | 3 |
| Oregon | 1 | .... | .... | ... | .... | 1 | .... | 2 | .... | .... |
| Nevada | .... | 6 | .... | ... | .... | .... | 3 | .... | 9 | .... |
| Washington Territory | .... | .... | .... | ... | .... | 1 | .... | 1 | .... | .... |
| New Mexico Territory | 2 | 5 | .... | ... | .... | 6 | 11 | 8 | 16 | .... |
| Nebraska Territory | 2 | 4 | .... | ... | .... | .... | 2 | 2 | 6 | .... |
| Colorado Territory | 3 | .... | .... | ... | 1 | .... | 2 | 3 | 2 | 1 |
| Dakota Territory | .... | 2 | .... | ... | .... | .... | .... | .... | 2 | .... |
| U. S. Vet. Volunteer Infantry | .... | .... | .... | ... | .... | 10 | .... | 10 | .... | .... |
| U. S. Volunteer Infantry | .... | .... | .... | ... | .... | 6 | 1 | 6 | 1 | .... |
| United States Colored Troops | 6 | .... | 11 | 4 | 10 | 102 | 18 | 119 | 22 | 10 |
| *U. S. Army, Regulars | 6 | .... | 5 | ... | .... | 19 | .... | 30 | .... | .... |
| Total | 258 | 170 | 57 | 22 | 232 | 1666 | 306 | 1981 | 498 | 232 |

*Nine of the U. S. Army Regulars had 24 companies each. Allowing for these and errors, it may be said there were in the war organizations the equivalents of 2,050 regiments.

## STATISTICS.

**NUMBER OF MEN IN THE UNION SERVICE AT DIFFERENT TIMES:**

January 1, 1861, 16,367. July 1, 1861, 185,751. January 1, 1862, 575,917. March 31, 1862, 637,126. January 1, 1863, 918,191. January 1, 1864, 860,737. January 1, 1865, 959,460. March 31, 1865, 980,086. May 1, 1865, 1,00,516.

**THE LOSSES WERE AS FOLLOWS:**

Killed, 61,362. Died of wounds, 34,773. Died of disease, 183,287. Accidentally killed, 306. Missing in action, 6,749. Honorably discharged, 174,577. Discharged for disability, 224,306. Deserted, 199,045. Resigned, 22,281.

Of the 6,049,648 cases treated in hospitals, 185,353 died; 26,164 are known to have died as prisoners of war; 29,336 died of typhoid fever; 35,127 of diarrhœa; and about half as many, or 16,487, were discharged for the same cause; 33,949 died of, and 34,209 were discharged for, gunshot wounds; 5,177 died of measles; 7,058 of small-pox; 6,497 of consumption; 19,971 of inflammation of the lungs, and 5,360 of malarial fever.

Authorities calculate that on an average only 662 men out of every 1000 were effective, and probably in action. Of this effective total, 1 out of 38.1 died of wounds; 1 out of 6.7 was wounded; 1 out of 7 prisoners; 1 out of 9 that enlisted died.

There are 80 National Cemeteries, in which are buried 171,302 whose names are known and 147,568 unknown. Of these there are buried at Andersonville 12,793 known and 921 unknown; at Salisbury, North Carolina, 94 known and 12,032 unknown; at Arlington, Virginia, 11,915 known and 4,349 unknown; at Cold Harbor, 673 known and 1,281 unknown; at Fredericksburg 2,487 known and 12,770 unknown; at Gettysburg 1,967 known and 1,608 unknown; at Memphis 5,160 known and 8,817 unknown; at Vicksburg 3,896 known and 12,704 unknown; at Chalmette, Louisiana, 6,837 known and 5,674 unknown.

There were 2,261 battles, skirmishers and affairs, distributed by years as follows: 158 in 1861, 564 in 1862, 627 in 1863, 779 in 1864, 135 in 1865.

There were were 2 Lieutenant Generals. Major Generals in U. S. Army in full rank 11, and by brevet 152. Major Generals of Volunteers in full rank 128, and by brevet 288. Brigadier Generals in U. S. Army in full rank 36, and by brevet 187. Brigadier Generals of Volunteers in full rank 561, and by brevet 1,170.

Of General Officers, 38 were killed, 29 died of wounds, and 35 of diseases and other causes.

THE GREATEST LOSSES IN ACTION WERE AS FOLLOWS:

| Date. | Name. | Killed. | Wounded. | Missing. | Total. | Estimated Confederate Losses. |
|---|---|---|---|---|---|---|
| 1861 | | | | | | |
| July 21. | Bull Run. | 481 | 1,011 | 1,460 | 2,295 | 1,752 |
| 1862 | | | | | | |
| Feb. 14–16. | Ft. Donelson. | 446 | 1,735 | 150 | 2,331 | 15,067 |
| April 6–7. | Shiloh. | 1,735 | 7,882 | 3,956 | 13,573 | 10,699 |
| May 31 June 1 | Seven Pines and Fair Oaks. | 890 | 3,672 | 1,222 | 5,739 | 7,997 |
| June 25 July 1 | Seven days retreat. | 1,582 | 7,709 | 5,959 | 15,294 | 17,583 |
| August 30. | Bull Run. | 800 | 4,000 | 3,000 | 7,800 | 3,700 |
| September 17. | Antietam. | 2,010 | 9,146 | 1,043 | 12,469 | 25,899 |
| October 8. | Perryville. | 916 | 2,943 | 489 | 4,384 | 7,000 |
| December 13. | Fredericksburg. | 1,180 | 9,028 | 2,145 | 12,353 | 4,576 |
| December 31. | Stone's River. | 1,533 | 7,245 | 2,800 | 11,578 | 25,560 |
| 1863 | | | | | | |
| May 2. | Chancellorsville. | 1,512 | 9,518 | 5,000 | 16,030 | 12,281 |
| To July 4. | Siege of Vicksburg. | 543 | 3,688 | 303 | 4,536 | 31,277 |
| July 2 to 4. | Gettysburg. | 2,834 | 13,709 | 6,643 | 23,186 | 31,621 |
| September 20. | Chickamauga. | 1,644 | 9,262 | 4,945 | 15,851 | 17,804 |
| 1864 | | | | | | |
| May 7. | Wilderness. | 5,597 | 21,463 | 10,677 | 37,737 | 11,400 |
| May 8–18. | Spottsylvania. | 4,177 | 19,687 | 2,577 | 26,461 | 9,000 |
| June 1–5. | Cold Harbor. | 1,905 | 10,570 | 2,456 | 14,931 | 1,700 |

# ROSTER

## OF THREE MONTHS' SERVICE, AS DETERMINED AT CAMP JACKSON.

[First date is that of rank; second date is time of commission.]

*Colonel*, Lorin Andrews, April 26, 1861; April 26, 1861.
*Lieutenant Colonel*, James Cantwell, April 26, 1861; April 26, 1861.
*Major*, James H. Godman, April 26, 1861; April 26, 1861.
*Surgeon*, H. M. McAbee, May 2, 1861; May 2, 1861.
*Assistant Surgeon*, J. Y. Cantwell, May 1, 1861; May 1, 1861.
*Adjutant*, B. R. Durfee; 1st Lt. April 21, 1861.
*Quartermaster*, I. Underwood, 1st Lt. April 26, 1864; April 26, 1861.

*Captains—*
    Company A—James C. Irvine, April 27, 1861; April 27, 1861.
    Company B—H. B. Banning, April 20, 1861; April 20, 1861.
    Company C—James M. Crawford, April 16, 1861; April 16, 1861.
    Company D—George Weaver, April 18, 1861; April 18, 1861.
    Company E—James McMillen, April 19, 1861; April 19, 1861.
    Company F—James Wallace, April 21, 1861; April 21, 1861.
    Company G—J. S. Robinson, April 19, 1861; April 19, 1861.
    Company H—E. B. Olmstead, April 27, 1861; April 27, 1861.
    Company I—E. Powell, April 21, 1861; April 21, 1861.
    Company K—A. H. Brown, April 22, 1861; Apirl 22, 1861.

*First Lieutenants—*
    Company A—L. W. Carpenter, April 27, 1861; April 27, 1861.
    Company B—W. C. Cooper, April 20, 1861; April 20, 1861.
    Company C—J. S. Jones, April 16, 1861; April 16, 1861.
    Company D—Gordon A. Stewart, April 18, 1861; April 18, 1861.
    Company E—Jacob Shultz, April 19, 1861; April 19, 1861.
    Company F—Percy S. Sowers, April 21, 1861; April 21, 1861.
    Company G—Peter Grubb, April 27, 1861; April 27, 1861.
    Company H—Wm. S. Stroub, April 27, 1861; April 27, 1861.
    Company I—N. W. Scott, April 21, 1861; April 21, 1861.
    Company K—M. J. Lafever, April 22, 1861; April 22, 1861.

*Second Lieutenants—*
Company A—F. A. Coates, April 27, 1861; April 27, 1861.
Company B—George Rogers, April 20, 1861; April 20, 1861.
Company C—Byron W. Dolbear, April 16, 1861; April 16, 1861.
Company D—Daniel Timmons, April 18, 1861; April 18, 1861,
Company E—Reason B. Spink, April 19, 1861; April 19, 1861.
Company F—Geo. F. Laird, April 21, 1861; April 21, 1861.
Company G—Wm. Surgeson, April 19, 1861; April 19, 1861.
Company H—J. R. Pritchard, April 23, 1861; April 23, 1861.
Company I—Wm. Constant, April 21, 1861; April 21, 1861.
Company K—Wm. H. Garrett, April 22, 1861; April 22, 1861.

—————:o:—————

## MUSTER ROLLS

### OF THREE MONTHS' SERVICE.

#### COMPANY A, KNOX COUNTY GUARDS.

*Captain*, Lorin Andrews.
*First Lieutenant*, I. Underwood.
*Second Lieutenant*, L. W. Carpenter.
*First Sergeant*, F. A. Coates.
*Second Sergeant*, C. V. Johnson.
*Third Sergeant*, C. B. Church.
*Fourth Sergeant*, F. M. Ball.
*First Corporal*, J. C. Long.
*Second Corporal*, A. Gilliam.
*Third Corporal*, Robert McDowell.
*Fourth Corporal*, William Stoyle.

| | | |
|---|---|---|
| G. W. Anderson | David Hawkins | H. H. Pollock |
| William Atherton | Richard A. Hall | H. P. Pyle |
| Samuel Aisel | John Hanegan | J. Phifer |
| Josiah Bell | J. G. Irwin | D. W. Parke |
| S. C. Beach | R. W. Kerr | P. S. Patterson |
| Geo. D. Bergin | Wm. Knight | J. W. Rowley |
| Dr. W. B. Beardslee | James Logsdon | Timothy Rogers |
| Thomas Cameron | Robert Larkins | Leander Reed |
| R. E. Bigbee | R. J. Thompson | John Shaffer |
| D. M. Craig | Shannon Taylor | William Seacord |
| Isaac Cole | William Welsh | Richard Sutton |
| Thomas Dixon | Byron Ward | Amos Evans |

Harry Davy
Jacob Mefford
James McGiffin
David McKay
John A. Mitchell
T. J. O'Neal
Emanuel Phillips
Richard Pickard
Robert Pate
C. Porter
Henry Price
Thomas Robinson
C. H. Runyon
Thomas Roberts
Jackson Taylor
Thomas Sharp
Thomas Scott
J. F. Sweny
Geo. W. Elliott
John W. Fry
Jefferson Foos
C. D. Glasgow
Bernard Griffis
Monroe Haller

B. F. Weaver
George B. Jones
J. F. Young
B. F. Horner
L. B. Welsh
A. Armstrong
Moses Adler
W. H. Alling
S. C. Bartlett
Smith Bunn
J. B. Brown
Thomas Barry
W. Buchanan
S. D. Church
W. H. Bigbee
William Clark
Thomas Clayton
W. E. Doty
Samuel Magill
Lewis H. Mitchell
M. M. Murphy
Homer G. McClelland
E. S. Miller
John K. O'Neal

B. D. Evans
W. D. Furlong
D. F. Gardner
C. E. Gardner
James W. Hall
Orvill Hill
Jack Hollabaugh, Jr.
J. Headington
Burr Headington
Henry Irwin
Robert Kimball
W. F. Lynch
Jacob Silley
Austin Stanton
A. H. Taylor
Samuel Tipton
Alfred Upfold
John W. White
Jonas Ward
C. H. Walker
Joseph Yager
Charles Wood
Charles Wright
William Kidwell

Total, 119

---:o:---

## COMPANY B, UNION GUARDS.

*Captain*, H. B. Banning.
*First Lieutenant*, W. C. Cooper
*Second Lieutenant*, George Rogers.
*Orderly Sergeant*, Wm. Thos. Patton.
*First Sergeant*, E. W. Meunscher.

*Second Sergeant*, Morgan Barr.
*Third Sergeant*, Charles G. Jennings,
*First Corporal*, Alfred Angel Covilla.
*Second Corporal*, Henry N. Davis.
*Third Corporal*, Wm. A. Gillespie.

*Fourth Corporal*, David Bonar.

George David Bergin
George Rigler
Charles Hamilton Bush
Gilbert Martin Park
Ephraim Boyle
Ewalt Fullman
Jeremiah Stinger

Walter Bryant Bergin
John Alonzo Alson
Alexander Shaffer
Jos. Wilson Workman
Thomas F. E. Clayton
William Alfred Bell
Gustavus A. Melhorn

Steven Black Parks
Valentine Glasgow
Martin Craig
John Stevens
Samuel O. Thomas
Joshua H. Van Ruden
Henry D. Callihan

Daniel Stinger
Henry Martin Williams
Wm. Cornelius Mealy
John Mantle Dunn
Robert Dunbar Sands
Amos DeHaven
Wm. Henry Conden
Levi Banning Brice
John Conley
Rolland Critchfield
Benjamin F. Greer
Henry Smith
Morgan Beaver
George William Cooley
Samuel Beeny
John Armstrong Dill
Charles Camp Walker
Abraham W. Lippitt
Thomas Clayton
Ulysses Newton Sapp
Daniel Baker
Wilson Barnes
Archibald Dyer
Timothy Rogers
Samuel Earl
Thomas McEwen
John Worman
John Francis Peak
William Barrable
Phillip J. Mc N. Kelly
William Stevens
Erastus Cake
Henry Rayham
Henry Graff
W. Harvey Remington
George L. Wilcox
John Burr Bevans
James Head
Byron Selby
James Andy Tilton
Michael Coughlin
Benjamin F. Shaffer
John Delany Randall
William Seth Neal
Hyram Lynch
Edwin Freeman
Abraham Doty
William Taylor Hart
Levi Hazen
Joseph A. R. Sapp
John Tyler DeWitt
William H. Everts
John K. Hawk

Total, 85

―――:o:―――

## Company C, Delaware Guards.

*Captain*, James M. Crawford.
*First Lieutenant*, John S. Jones.
*Second Lieutenant*, Byron Dolbear.
*First Sergeant*, Jacob Kruck.
*Second Sergeant*, Andrew M. Anderson.
*Third Sergeant*, Llewellyn Powell.
*Fourth Sergeant*, Albert H. Perry.
*First Corporal*, James Mickle.
*Second Corporal*, William Warner.
*Third Corporal*, Chas. J. Windship.
*Fourth Corporal*, W. O. Welch.

Gillis J. Anderson
George W. Armstrong
Thearon A. Beach
Lorenzo M. Burkholder
Leroy S. Barnes
Charles A. Brown
Robert H. Brown
Charles A. Buckley
Chas. R. Breyfogle
John Birdsall
Thomas Cox
Samuel Colflesh
John A. Crawford
Henry Conklin
Adam Keiser
Joseph Kimball
William Kepler
Hiram Lynn
Silas Long
Philip Lyman
James D. Cellars
William T. Dart
John E. Jewett
Henry A. Welch
William Irvine
Charles Williams
Jasper Burroughs
Lyman Carpenter
Amos L. Parks
Jackson Pugh
Ambrose A. Plotner
George Pearce
George Perry
George B. Ropp
Addison Roloson
Wesley H. Roloson
George Smith
Edward P. Shafer
Isaac Sigfried
David Thomas
Elias G. Traxler
Joseph Tanner

| | | |
|---|---|---|
| Joseph Conway | Henry Stark | George Tipton |
| Timothy Collins | Howard Lamb | Alexander A. Veer |
| William Davis | Joseph W. Lindsey | Charles Vining |
| John Dale | John Munsell | Girard Welch |
| Benjamin Durfey | Francis W. Mills | L. Byron Welch |
| John Evans | Watson C. McCullough | Samuel Wells |
| William B. Fritz | James McEntire | William J. Ward |
| Luther Freeman | John F. Martin | James D. Wetherbe |
| Joseph Griffin | John F. Moses | Elias Heller |
| Daniel Gangway | William H. Munnell | Charles H. Gray |
| Henry H. Hatch | Erwin McElroy | Robert D. McCarter |
| David M. Howe | David F. Nash | William McDermott |
| Ezra Hickenbottom | Levi Olney | David R. Tipton |
| Richard Humphrey | Samuel Prior | George Bartlett |
| Robert P. Jennings | Cornelius Parks | William Donelson |
| Johnathan Kempf | James O. Pearse | William H. Bailor |
| Levi Keiser | | Total, 102 |

———:o:———

## COMPANY D.

*Captain*, George Weaver.   *First Lieutenant*, Gordon A. Stewart.
*Second Lieutenant*, Byron W. Evans.

| | | |
|---|---|---|
| Theodore J. Young | Harrison Stout | Hugh O'Neal |
| Joseph Dickelman | Daniel Swank | George W. Owens |
| Pembroke Z. Snow | Mark Scott | Joseph Ridgeway |
| Hugh White | John W. Baker | John C. Rose |
| Franklin Herbert | John Brum | Enos Shannon |
| Joseph Holloway | William Clark | Adam D. Shriner |
| Amos Briggs | Franklin Day | George W. Stanley |
| Charles A. Stockton | Jeremiah Nevill | George W. Swank |
| John Burdett | George W. Quimby | Francis H. Swizert |
| John H. Reeves | Comfort Stanley | Thomas J. Weirick |
| John A. Beam | Lafayette McCreary | John J. Wright |
| Jacob Butcher | Jefferson H. Darrah | Charles C. Calahan |
| Hurd Carney | Isaac J. Atkinson | Ossian McKee |
| David K. Cribbs | Joseph F. Moore | Calvin L. Bailey |
| George V. Devore | Sylvester McCann | Matthew Briggs |
| William Hamblin | David Snodgrass | John Cassidy |
| Reuben H. Johnson | William Albright | George Davis |
| Joseph M. Musser | John C. Bailey | Stephen Funk |
| Thomas H. Pierson | David W. Black | Edward George |
| Christian Ries | Albert W. Bunyan | Henry Heater |

Calvin T. Warner
John W. Wenner
Philip H. Wickiser
Isaac E. Wilson
Franklin R. Yarger
Henry Ries
George W. Lewis
James M. Clark
Hiram Linniger
Gotlieb Pracker
John Anderline
Milo Banker
Archibald Cooper
Jacob Devore
Joseph Dunson
Joseph Myers
Samuel McFarland
Morgan V. Shaffer

Samuel Burnhimer
Charles Case
Joseph Davis
Thomas C. Duncan
Joseph A. Furgeson
David Furney
John Furney
Harvey Garbeson
John C. Guiney
Charles Herron
Conrad H. Hoit
Wesley Kesler
John Moxwell
Amos J. Moore
Martin McCartney
Byron McKee
John J. McKnight
Martin Ohler

Marshal M. Helveson
John W. Hendershott
Elias Keys
Francis S. Layton
George Michaels
William Stout
Benjamin White
John Ross
Isaac Switzer
Thomas Petty
N. G. Case
Roland Parks
Cyrus Herrick
William Switzer
James Bender
Jacob Wetzel
Joseph White

Total, 113

———:o:———

## Company E, Given Guards.

[Note.—In the order in which each signed his name to the paper calling for volunteers. The 26 marked * did not re-enlist when the Company organized for three years, but returned to Wooster from Camp Dennison.]

Jacob Shultz,
   *First Lieutenant*
R. B. Spink,
   *Second Lieutenant*
*L. H. Scoby,
   *First Sergeant*
*Wm. M. Lightcap,
   *Second Corporal*
Howard Fishburn,
   *Second Sergeant*
George Patterson
John Fitch
John I. Hoke
Levi Graybill
J. B. Sanford
Wm. H. Hanson,
   *Fifth Sergeant*
Henry Cutter

William H. McClure,
   *Fourth Sergeant*
William Brighton,
   *First Corporal*
Joshua W. McClarran,
   *Third Sergeant*
Robert McElhenie
Thomas C. Warner
Daniel Y. Black
George Sowers
Marion E. France
Robert Segner
*Robert Kennedy
David Flack
*James Black
William Cline,
   *Fourth Corporal*
Jonas Kope

Joseph D. Bodine
William Eberly
David S. Pollinger
Cyrus Gray
*Alex Gray
Orlando Dyarmon
Aaron Kope
George Musser
Charles F. Line
*Joseph J. Lake
Matt M. Smith
John Walduck
*Francis M. Anderson
*Jacob Wilson
William Singer
David Best
George W. Carey
D. S. Cassiday

ROSTER.   231

*Thomas Dice
John Jahala
Lemuel Jeffries
John H. Wain
Ed. Smedley
James Moffitt
George Cline
Sylvester R. Heffelfinger
John F. Barrett
Daniel O. Brinkerhoff
Alfred B. Chapman
*Joseph D. Pratt,
    *Third Corporal*
H. O. McClarran
*Thomas J. Cole
Harmon Helt
James McMillen,
    *Captain,*
Frank Keehn
Corodon Fogleson
Addison S. McClure
Charles W. McClure
Joseph H. Carr

*James M. Shaffer
William McGlenen
George Mutchler
Peter O. Vannatta
James Snyder
*Benjamin Kramer
Louis S. Lehman
Hiram Arnold
*Henry Hedrick
*Daniel Mohn
James S. Swearengen
*John Springer
Arch H. Dice
W. W. Sands
*John Groff
Clifford A. Lewis
Frank Miller
*L. Reamer
Thomas W. Bucher
*Harmon Smyser
Edward McKelvy
Joseph O. Young

John Johnson
Hiampsel Shreve
W. H. Baumgardner
W. H. Bucher
Henry Swickey
Evan Everly
George C. Francis
*I. U. Patterson
*Anthony A. Black
J. C. Brandt
George Stewart
Thomas McClarran
Harvey H. Cook
*William G. Eberman
Levi Arnold
Alex. A. Carr
William Osborne
Hubbard Brown
*Joseph Egbert
*John C. Pritchard
*William Lawrence
*Ezra M. Hoag

Total, 109

——:o:——

## COMPANY F, CANTON ZOUAVES.

*Captain*, James Wallace.
*First Lieutenant*, Percy S. Sowers.
*Second Lieutenant*, George F. Laird.
*First Sergeant*, R. B. Treat.
*Second Sergeant*, Samuel Brearley.
*Third Sergeant*, William C. Kimball.
*Fourth Sergeant*, T. S. Lambert.
*Fifth Sergeant*, William Walker.
*First Corporal*, N. S. McAbee.
*Second Corporal*, George S. Lester.
*Third Corporal*, William F. Raynolds.
*Fourth Corporal*, John Ricksecker.

E. W. Alexander
Edward Balmat
Preston Barber
W. Bateman
Joseph P. Balmat
Robert Black
Thad K. Cock
Wellington Douds
George W. Dearing

Charles W. Gerwig
Joseph W. Hostetter
John Hafer
L. D. Hane
W. Hanneford
William H. Hershey
T. F. Hilbert
S. H. Hoover
Marshall E. Haas

Marcus T. Meyer
John McAuley
A. Moffit
H. Moonshower
A. J. Price
C. T. Penny
W. G. Reeves
J. Frank Raynolds
Joseph Stuckey

William Deckman
Conrad Deckman
Byron Eaby
Lyman S. Ensign
Edwin Estep
Michael Foehl
Frank Friedy
Peter L. Frailey
Joseph C. Flickinger
Bradley C. Goodwill
Dan H. Gotshall
C. H. Granville
B. F. Greek
James E. Graham
James Johnson
Aaron Kille
William Kingsworth
Jefferson Koontz
J. H. Kille
William Laird
Charles A. Leiter
Marshall Lohm
S. R. Lemmon
Philip Lallo
David Lee
D. M. Warren
Ed. S. Meyer
Joseph Miller
Frank J. Spalter
Charles Strong
Frank Sell
L. Shepperd
William M. Shorb
William Smith
David Sell
James Trownsell
Julius Thurin
J. Trump
A. Wernet
Andrew Youngblood
H. E. F. Yaley
A. H. Yaley

Total, 81

———:0:———

## Company G.

Luther Furney
Asa B. Carter
Charles Pool
John H. Bales
J. B. Pool
David McConnel
Jacob E. Holmes
Samuel Weise
Augustus Fosket
A. W. Jamison
James R. Cutting
Thomas McCoy
Henry W. Keefer
Thomas Wran
D. Griner
William Noel
W. B. Hatch
Jerome L. Beach
Peter Boswick
William Crabill
Thomas Gordon
Amos Joy
Jacob Sergeson
George Elsesser
Baily Wilcox
W. W. Williams
John Watters
L. Krysher
J. P. Cook
W. F. Wilkin
Samuel Collins
P. H. Mahan
S. C. Wooley
F. McGinnis
J. W. Jeffries
Thomas Birch
Rezin Gilmore
A. H. Edgar
Isaih Larkins
John P. Lehn
N. Kirkpatrick
James Wilkin
William Cameron
Samuel Glucker
Samuel Griner
Arthur Newcomb
Charles Collier
Henry Bechtel
William Shindewolf
Henry Pheiffer
Charles Bramble
Frederick Fisher
Isaac Bolenbaugh
Jacob W. Bowman
Joseph M. Musser
David Donnelly
G. W. Smith
A. J. Smith
James A. Atkinson
N. S. Weaver
W. H. Morrow
J. S. Philbrick
Archibald Cooper
Andrew Gorder
Richard Shaffer
Henry M. Simens
George H. Martin
William M. Danields
Cornelius Unger
Lucas H. Walden
N. S. Ritzler
William Talmer
Jacob R. Johnson
Robert G. Russel
Hays Gaskell
Wash Bowers
M. Bowers
Asa O. Davis

Asher Rice
Robert Stevenson
Michael Herrmann
J. S. Robinson
A. V. Curtis
Samuel Stevenson
William S, Sergeson
Jacob A. Holmes
John C. Smith
Graham Jones
M. B. V. Longworth
William West
Aaron Scott
Albert Winsett
Samuel H. Davis
D. O. Hagerman
G. W. Wooley

George W. Wooley
George Crabill
Thomas Goodman
Charles A. Smith
Joseph Stanford
Jacob Sherman
Rudolph Newcomb
Isaac Thrailkin
Charles Martin
Bernard Mayer
Alexander Jones
Rudolph Renfer
James Crawford
Leonard Beacock
John Gibson
David Mentzer
Peter Grubb

W. D. Porterfield, Jr.
Edward Shuey
William Meredith
Henry Bunn
Jacob Andrick
Henry Price
Fred Beck
Mc. F. L. Lisles
Sylvanus P. Morey
Samuel Andrews
Edward Sorgen
James Cantwell,
*Captain*
William J. Dickson
John E. Ward
Charles Griner

Total, 127

———:o:———

## COMPANY H.

*Captain*, E. B. Olmstead.
*First Lieutenant*, W. S. Stroub.
*Second Lieutenant*, John R. Pritchard.
*First Sergeant*, T. H. Dickason.
*Second Sergeant*, G. A. Mouser.

*Third Sergeant*, R. I. Strawbridge.
*First Corporal*, H. L. Boyd.
*Second Corporal*, C. C. Godman.
*Third Corporal*, W. Z. Davis.
*Fourth Corporal*, J. W. King.

J. Alexander
E. S. Baker
A. Blocksom
E. Boyer
J. S. Brady
Levi Bair
S. E. Ball
W. R. Baker
C. J. Barnett
P. J. Blondon
William Clements
S. Chambers
H. H. Cory
F. M. Carn
J. V. Culp

A. Griswold
A. Halstead
B. Honaker
William Hatch
Jasper Jones
J. E. Jonson
E. D. Jones
J. H. Jones
C. S. Knapp
H. Kenyon
John King
William Kennedy
J. R. Knapp
W. H. Kline
M. S. Knapp

G. H. Smallwood
William Stockwell
J. A. Sapington
H. G. Sayter
John Short
J. S. Stockwell
J. A. Smallwood
W. H. Selanders
H. Saiter
J. Seares
M. Stull
G. W. Swanks
Silas Schertzer
F. W. Stone
C. Thompson

| | | |
|---|---|---|
| J. E. Crow | J. M. Kenyon | T. E. Tillettson |
| W. B. Drown | J. M. Lee | J. W. Tatman |
| J. Dewey | O. Lane | C. G. Thompson |
| E. J. Dane | M. Lane | B. A. Virdin |
| J. H. Dennison | P. Lumioe | H. Winslow |
| A. Elkhart | T. C. Likens | J. B. Wolfe |
| J. Elliott | Milton Marsh | C. Warner |
| H. C. French | G. H. May | J. M. West |
| Hiram Fields | D. McClarry | A. J. Ward |
| A. Farrin | William Porter | Allen Willis |
| Bryant Grafton | Washington Porter | J. Webber |
| J. Grimes | Benjamin Rainey | Joshua Wortman |
| J. M. Godman | John Rhoads | P. Yeo |

Total, 74.

---:o:---

## COMPANY I, OLENTANGY GUARDS.

*Captain*, Eugene Powell.  
*First Lieutenant*, A. W. Scott.  
*Second Lieutenant*, W. F. Constant.  
*First Sergeant*, Samuel J. Shoub.  
*Second Sergeant*, E. A. Willey.  
*Third Sergeant*, Channing L. Pettibone.  
*Fourth Sergeant*, F. W. Morrison.  
*First Corporal*, Hosea A. Alexander.  
*Second Corporal*, G. W. Scott.  
*Third Corporal*, Henry A. Shoub.  
*Fourth Corporal*, J. Gregg.

| | | |
|---|---|---|
| Peter Aigan | E. Gray | A. E. Plunkett |
| M. Allen | J. W. Gray | J. R. Plunkett |
| Daniel Bills | H. Gribble | James Powers |
| J. Brooker | W. M. Howard | E. Root |
| J. Beckwith | S. Hummell | S. Rolloson |
| O. H. Barker | W. C. Helford | J. N. Stark |
| R. Bell | F. Hickenbottom | J. L. Snyder |
| J. Bogan | R. Hickenbottom | D. Shindollar |
| J. R. Bassinger | J. Hooper | B. A. Sherer |
| E. H. Chase | J. Hardman | M. Snell |
| G. B. Carpenter | J. Harrington | T. E. Stark |
| George W. Cowles | W. Hahn | J. Spalding |
| George Conklin | J. T. Hoard | Wm. Stephens Dorn |
| P. Courtes | W. Harrington | T. W. Scott |
| B. Closson | W. Keesey | A. S. Scott |
| C. Closson | J. H. Krogman | E. St. Clair |
| F. Case | Thomas Lindsay | J. Shauk |

G. Divan
W Davy
D. Deppin
D. Evans
J. Furguson
J. M. Finch
W. Fleckner
George W. Farris
J. O. Fowler

D. S. Lee
I. C. Lewis
B. Lower
A. Lybrand, Jr
O. McCreary
A. Myers
George H. Purdy
J. A. Pendleton

W. Traxler
J. Taylor
L. B. Vanatta
J. Wilson
C. H. Wigton
Frederick P. Welch
Demas Wise
John Welch

Total, 87.

——:o:——

COMPANY K.

*Captain*, Albert H. Brown.
*First Lieutenant*, M. J. Lefever.
*Second Lieutenant*, Wm. H. Garrett.
*First Sergeant*, Samuel Cutter.
*Second Sergeant*, Byron Thomas.
*Third Sergeant*, William Camp.
*Fourth Sergeant*, Franklin Saiter.
*First Corporal*, John F. Uhler.
*Second Corporal*, Abner Ustick.
*Third Corporal*, Albert White.
*Fourth Corporal*, Sampson Apt.

Joshua Armstrong
John Anslow
Isaac Bacon
Michael Beckle
B. Abel Brockett
Ansona Buenevento
William Berry
David Bell
William Boyd
Solomon Boyer
Samuel Boyer
John Beaver
Daniel Booher
Melvin Crowl
Cyrus H. Carpenter
John C. Carter
Cyrus Carter
Henry H. Cunningham
Alfred W. Dunt
Solomon Epley

Charles Foss
Richard Fields
Samuel E. Hain
William Huggins
John G. Hiner
Simon Huggins
Jonathan J. Hall
John Hardy
Theodore C. Gross
James Imboden
David Joy
John Knable
John Kightlinger
Edward C. Kistler
Jacob Kise
Samuel Kise
John J. Kade
Edward Kirby
Abraham Kightlinger
James Kennedy

George B. Merchant
John P. Marquis
William Martin
Thomas F. Moon
Thomas McColloch
Daniel Mather
John O'Brien
John L. Patten
John Rall
John Ringle
William H. H. Reed
Harvey W. Rhodes
Theoderick Reed
John Rush
William Robinson
Ralph Spring
William H. Strade
Joseph Short
George W. Slack
Charles Sprague

| | | |
|---|---|---|
| Samuel Epley | Lewis Kightlinger | Harvey Wheeler |
| Christian Erline | Melvin A. Lilly | Wallace W. Wilson |
| James English | John L. Loyd | Lafayette Welchhonce |
| Asa P. Freeman | Philo F. Leatherby | Isaac Welchhonce |
| Wesley Free | Hiram Meily | David T. Yager |
| Timothy Fell | Allen Mutchler | Jacob Yauger |
| Frank M. Filler | Richard Morris | Philip Yox |

Total, 92.

# ROSTER OF THREE YEARS' SERVICE

## IN THE ORDER OF RANK, NAME, TIME OF APPOINTMENT, TIME OF COMMISSION—REMARKS.

*Colonels—*

Lorin Andrews, June 5, 1861; June 5, 1861; died September 18, 1861.
John S. Mason, Oct. 3, 1861; Oct. 3, 1861; Brig. Gen'l, Nov. 29, 1862.
James H. Godman, Nov. 29, 1862; April 9, 1863; hon. dis. July 28, 1863.
L. W. Carpenter, July 28, 1863; August 19, 1863; mustered out.

*Lieutenant Colonels—*

James Cantwell, June 5, 1861; June 5, 1861; appointed Col. 82d O. V. I.
James H. Godman, Jan. 9, 1862; Jan. 9, 1862; wounded Dec. 13, 1862.
L. W. Carpenter, Nov. 29, 1862; April 9, 1863; Colonel, July 28, 1863.
G. A. Stewart, July 28, 1863; August 9, 1863; mustered out, July 28, 1863; retained.

*Majors—*

James H. Godman, June 5, 1861; June 5, 1861; Lieut. Col., Jan. 9, 1862.
George Weaver, January 9, 1862; Jan. 9, 1862; resigned Nov. 6, 1862.
L. W. Carpenter, Nov. 6, 1862; Dec. 26, 1862; Lieut. Col. Nov. 29, 1862.
G. A. Stewart, November 20, 1862; April 9, 1863; mustered out.
Peter Grubb, July 28, 1863; August 29, 1863; mustered out.

*Surgeons—*

H. M. McAbee, May 2, 1861; May 2, 1861; resigned September 16, 1863.
F. W. Morrison, September 16, 1863; November 7, 1863; mustered out; Surgeon 174th O. V. I.

*Assistant Surgeons—*

J. Y. Cantwell, June 7, 1861; June 7, 1861; resigned August 20, 1861.
A. Longwell, August 21, 1861; August 21, 1861; resigned October 27, 1862.
F. W. Morrison, July 31, 1862; July 31, 1862; promoted from Hospital Steward 11th O. V. I.
J. B. Laird, November 29, 1862; February 13, 1863; resigned July 11, 1864
B. Gray, April 22, 1864; April 22, 1864; mustered out.

*Chaplains—*

L. Warner, M.D., June 15, 1861; Aug. 26, 1861; resigned Mar. 17, 1863.
D. G. Strong, March 25, 1863; May 6, 1863; mustered out.

*Captains—*

L. W. Carpenter, June 4, 1861; June 4, 1861; Major, November 6, 1862.
H. B. Banning, June 4, 1861; June 4, 1861; Col. 87th O.V.I., June 25, 1862.
J. M. Crawford, June 4, 1861; June 4, 1861; resigned August, 1862.
George Weaver, June 4, 1861; June 4, 1861; Major, January 9, 1862.
J. McMillen, June 4, 1861; June 4, 1861; drowned at Alexandria, Va.
James Wallace, June 4, 1861; June 4, 1861; died of wounds Jan. 6, 1863.
J. S. Robinson, June 4, 1861; June 4, 1861; Major 82d O. V. I.
E. B. Olmstead, June 4, 1861; June 4, 1861; resigned October 17, 1862.
E. Powell, June 4, 1861; June 4, 1861; Major 66th O. V. I.
A. H. Brown, June 4, 1861; June 4, 1861; resigned June 11, 1862.
G. A. Stewart, January 9, 1862; January 9, 1862; Major, Nov. 29, 1862.
Peter Grubb, January 9, 1862; January 9, 1862; mustered out.
William Constant, January 9, 1862; Jan. 9, 1862; resigned Nov. 22, 1862.
F. A. Coates, June 11, 1862; Sept. 12, 1862; hon. disch. Oct. 15, 1862.
J. S. Jones, June 25, 1862; September 12, 1862; mustered out.
George F. Laird, June 29, 1862; September 12, 1862; mustered out.
J. Ferguson, November 22, 1862; December 11, 1862; died of wounds.
John Green, June 11, 1862; Dec. 26, 1862; promoted by President, 1863.
W. S. Stroub, August 31, 1862; December 26, 1862; mustered out.
D. Timmons, October 17, 1862; December 26, 1862; mustered out.
I. Underwood, November 6, 1862; December 26, 1862; declined promotion.
B. W. Dolbear, November 6, 1862; January 26, 1863; died of wounds.
S. L. Brearley, January 10, 1863; February 10, 1863; mustered out.
William Wallace, April 29, 1863; May 18, 1863; declined promotion.
William M. Camp, March 1, 1863; May 18, 1863; mustered out.
J. R. Pritchard, April 1, 1863; May 23, 1863; mustered out.
B. W. Evans, April 1, 1863; June 17, 1863; died in Salisbury Prison.

*First Lieutenants—*

F. A. Coates, June 4, 1861; June 4, 1861; resigned October 15, 1862.
John Green, June 4, 1861; June 4, 1861; Captain, June 11, 1862.
John S. Jones, June 4, 1861; June 4, 1861; Captain, June 25, 1862.
G. A. Stewart, June 4, 1861; June 4, 1861; Captain, January 9, 1862.
Jacob Shultz, June 4, 1861; June 4, 1861; resigned June 1, 1862.
George F. Laird, June 4, 1861; June 4, 1861; Captain, June 25, 1862.
Peter Grubb, June 4, 1861; June 4, 1861; Captain, January 9, 1862.
William S. Stroub, June 4, 1861; June 4, 1861; Captain, August 21, 1862.
William Constant, June 4, 1861; June 4, 1861; Captain, January 9, 1862.
B. R. Durfee, June 4, 1861; June 4, 1861; Lieut. Col. 82d O. V. I.
W. H. Garrett, August 9, 1861; August 9, 1861; resigned Dec. 7, 1862.
D. Timmons, January 9, 1862; January 9, 1862; Captain, Oct. 17, 1862.
I. Underwood, Jan. 9, 1862; Jan. 9, 1862; Q. M.; resigned April 29, 1863.

A. W. Lippett, January 9, 1862; January 9, 1862; died Dec. 26, 1862.
J. Ferguson, January 9, 1862; January 9, 1862; Captain, Nov. 22, 1862.
B. W. Dolbear, January 9, 1862; January 9, 1862; Captain, Nov. 6, 1862.
William M. Camp, June 21, 1862; Sept. 12, 1862; Captain, Mar. 1, 1863.
S. L. Brearley, June 31, 1862; Sept. 12, 1862; Captain, Jan. 10, 1863.
George Lester, September 30, 1862; September 30, 1862; mustered out.
L. Jeffries, June 25, 1862; September 12, 1862; resigned January 7, 1867.
R. B. Spink, November 22, 1862; Dec. 11, 1862; resigned Mar. 23, 1863.
J. R. Pritchard, June 11, 1862; Dec. 26, 1862; Captain, April 1, 1863.
William T. Patton, August 31, 1862; December 26, 1862; mustered out.
T. H. Dickerson, October 17, 1862; December 26, 1862; mustered out.
B. W. Evans, November 6, 1862; Dec. 26, 1862; Captain, April 1, 1863.
William Welch, Dec. 7, 1862. Dec. 26, 1862; Colonel of Colored Troops.
Byron Thomas, Dec. 26, 1862; Feb 16, 1863; resigned August 12, 1863.
William Wallace, November 6, 1862; February 10, 1863; mustered out.
Joseph H. Carr, January 7, 1863; Feb. 10, 1863; resigned Nov. 3, 1863.
A. M. Anderson, March 24, 1863; July 20, 1863; mustered out.
G. O. Hill, January 10, 1863; May 18, 1863; resigned November 28, 1863.
George Brophy, March 1, 1863; July 20, 1863; mustered out.
C. L. Pettibone, April 29, 1863; July 20, 1863; killed May 10, 1864.
F. J. Spalter, January 1, 1863; July 20, 1863; Major 4th Ohio Battalion.

*Second Lieutenants—*

I. Underwood, June 4, 1861; June 4, 1861; promoted.
A. W. Lippett, June 4, 1861; June 4, 1861; promoted.
B. W. Dolbear, June 4, 1861; June 4, 1861; promoted.
D. Timmons, June 4, 1861; June 4, 1861; promoted.
H. Cutler, June 4, 1861; June 4, 1861; resigned June 21, 1862.
S. L. Brearley, June 4, 1861; June 4, 1861; promoted.
W. F. Sergeson, June 4, 1861; June 4, 1861; resigned November 7, 1862.
J. R. Pritchard, June 4, 1861; June 4, 1861; promoted.
J. Ferguson, June 4, 1861; June 4, 1861; promoted.
W. H. Garrett, June 4, 1861; June 4, 1861; promoted.
W. M. Camp, August 9, 1861; August 9, 1861; promoted.
A. Gilliam, August 9, 1861; August 9, 1861; resigned July 13, 1862.
L. Jeffries, December 20, 1861; December 20, 1861; promoted.
I. Larkins, January 9, 1862; January 9, 1862; resigned October 31, 1862.
W. T. Patton, January 9, 1862; January 9, 1862; promoted.
George S. Lester, January 9, 1862; January 9, 1862; promoted.
T. H. Dickerson, January 9, 1862; September 12, 1862; promoted.
B. W. Evans, June 11, 1862; September 12, 1862; promoted.
William Welch, June 13, 1862; September 12, 1862; promoted.
Byron Thomas, June 21, 1862; September 12, 1862; promoted.
William Brighton, June 25, 1862; Sept. 12, 1862; killed in Fredericksburg.
R. B. Spink, June 29, 1862; September 12, 1862; promoted.
C. L. Pettibone, November 22, 1862; December 11, 1862; promoted.
A. M. Anderson, October 31, 1862; December 26, 1862; promoted.

Joseph H. Carr, June 11, 1862; December 31, 1862; promoted.
S. J. Shoub, August 31, 1862; February 10, 1863; killed July 2, 1863.
W. McCullough, October 17, 1862; December 31, 1862; died of wounds March 29, 1863.
Frank J. Spalter, November 6, 1862; December 31, 1862; promoted.
George O. Hill, December 7, 1862; December 31, 1862; promoted.
George Brophy, December 26, 1862; February 16, 1863; promoted.
J. Dunlap, November 6, 1862; March 30, 1863; resigned.
William F. Lynch, January 7, 1862; March 30, 1863; resigned.
W. A. McDermott, December 13, 1862; April 29, 1863.
J. R. Knapp, June 10, 1863; May 18, 1863; mustered out.
A. H. Edgar, Mar. 29, 1863; May 25, 1863; killed at Gettysburg, July 2, 1863.
J. G. Evans, April 29, 1863; May 28, 1863.
W. W. Williams, March 24, 1863; July 20, 1863; mustered out.
J. Watkins, January 1, 1863; July 20, 1863; mustered out.
A. H. Perry, March 1, 1863; July 20, 1863; mustered out.

# EXPLANATION OF, AND STATEMENT CONCERNING, THE ROSTERS.

The Rosters were made up from the following sources: "List of names furnished by the Secretary of War;" Muster-Out Rolls in the office of the Secretary of State, at Columbus, Ohio; from "Ohio in the War;" from the "Adjutant's Record" of Adjutant William Wallace of Omaha, Nebraska. Much information was also furnished by comrades at Reunions of the Regiment. Several members of every company had the advance sheets of their company in possession for some time and did their utmost to correct them and add information.

The first date after each enlisted man's name has reference to the day he enlisted or re-enlisted for three years.

"Mustered out" means, "Mustered out with the regiment on the expiration of the term of service, June 22, 1864, at Columbus, Ohio."

"Discharged," if the cause is not stated, means, "Discharged on account of physical disability."

Where there is no statement as to time of having been mustered out, it is to be understood that such comrade was mustered out June 22, 1864, at expiration of term of service.

The following abbreviations are used: U. S. Art. for United States Artillery. I. C. for Invalid Corps. V. R. C. for Veteran Reserve Corps. O. B. for Ohio Battalion. Tr. for transferred. Re-en. for re-enlisted. Dis. for discharged. Res. for resigned. Ad. for address. Corp. for Corporal. Sergt. for Sergeant. Lt. for Lieutenant. Capt. for Captain. Assist. Sur. for Assistant Surgeon. Lt. Col. for Lieutenant Colonel. Col. for Colonel.

The Roster was rearranged and written three times with typewriter at the expense of much labor and time. An honest effort has been made to do each comrade justice.

WILLIAM KEPLER.

# ROSTER OF THREE YEARS' ORGANIZATION OF THE FOURTH OHIO VOLUNTEER INFANTRY.

### FIELD AND STAFF.

Lorin Andrews—Colonel; promoted from Captain of the Knox County Guards, or Company A, April 26, 1861, to command the three months' organization. Commissioned Colonel of three year's organization June 5, 1861. Died of typhoid pneumonia, September 18, 1861, at his home in Gambier, Knox county, Ohio.

John S. Mason—Captain of Eleventh U. S. Infantry; Colonel of the Fourth O. V. I. Oct. 3, 1861. Brigadier General Nov. 29, 1862. Is Colonel of U. S. Infantry and located in California.

James H. Godman—Captain; Major April 26, 1861; Lt. Col. Jan. 9, 1862; Col. Nov. 26, 1862; wounded at Fredericksburg Dec. 13, 1862, in rear of the city at the opening of the battle, resigned July 28, 1863, on account of disability resulting from the wound. Auditor of State in 1863, 1865 and 1867. Brevet Brig. Gen. March 13, 1864. Address, Columbus, O.

Leonard W. Carpenter—Elected First Lieut. April 27, 1861; Captain Co. A, June 5, 1861; Major, Nov. 6, 1862; Lt. Col. Nov. 29, 1862; Colonel July 28, 1863. Address, Logansport, Ind.

James Cantwell—Lt. Col. April 26, 1861; resigned Dec. 10, 1861; Colonel of the 82d O. V. I.; killed in second battle of Bull Run, Aug. 21, 1862.

George Weaver—Captain of Company D; Major, Jan. 9, 1862; resigned Nov. 6, 1862. Deceased.

Gordon A. Stewart—Captain of Co. D, Jan. 9, 1862; Major, Nov. 29, 1862; Lt. Col., July 28, 1862. Died in 1884, after having been in Government service for some years in Washington, D. C.

Peter Grubb—Captain of Co. G; Major, July 28, 1863; wounded at Gettysburg July 2, 1863; at Chancellorsville May 3, 1863. Died in 1883.

Bradford R. Durfee—Adjutant, April 26, 1861; First Lieut. Com. B., Nov. 1, 1861; resigned Dec. 10, 1861; Lt. Col. of the 82d O. V. I. Deceased.

John Green—Adjutant, Nov. 1, 1861; Captain, June 11, 1862; A. A. A. Gen. to Gen. Mason, Jan. 14, 1863.

Lemuel Jeffries—Of E, Acting Adjutant. Address, Wooster, O.

William Wallace—Of F, Adjutant Nov. 6, 1862. Address, Omaha, Neb.

Abram W. Lippett—Quartermaster, Jan. 5, 1862; died at home in Mount Vernon, O. ~~Jan. 5, 1862.~~ Dec. 26,

Israel Underwood—Quartermaster, June 5, 1861; Jan. 9, 1863; res. April 29, 1863. Address, Mt. Vernon, O.

Henry M. McAbee—Surgeon, May 2, 1861; res. Sept. 16, 1863. Killed soon after in railroad accident near Painesville, O.

Jacob Y. Cantwell—Assistant Surgeon, June 7, 1861; res. Aug. 20, 1861.
Francis W. Morrison—Assist. Sur. from Hospital Steward of 11th O. V. I., July 31, 1862; Surgeon Nov. 7, 1863. Surgeon 174th O. V. I.; Brigade Surgeon. Died at Delaware, O., March 16, 1886.
Albert Longwell—Assistant Surgeon, Aug. 21, 1861; res. Oct. 27, 1863. Died soon after the war.
John B. Laird—Assistant Surgeon, Feb. 13, 1863; res. July 11, 1864.
Barzillia Grey—Assistant Surgeon, April 22, 1864.
Lerenzo Warner—Chaplain, Aug. 26, 1861; res. March 17, 1863. Died of apoplexy at Galion, O., April 12, 1866.
Daniel G. Strong—Corporal; Chaplain, May 6, 1863. In ministry of Methodist Episcopal Church in Wyoming Territory.
Marshall E. Haas—Corp.; Serg., Oct. 13, 1862; Serg. Major, Sept. 1, 1863; mortally wounded at Morton's Ford, Feb. 6, 1864.
Charles W. McClure—Quartermaster Serg. July 10, 1863. Ad. Wooster, O.
John R. Knapp—Commissary Serg. Sept. 1, 1861. Quartermaster Serg., Aug. 1, 1862; 2d Lt., May 26, 1863; Quartermaster June 9, 1863.
Robert D. McCarter—Commissary Serg., Aug. 2, 1862. Ad., Columbus, O.
David T. Bruck—Hospital Steward, June 17, 1861.
John L. Loyd—Quartermaster Sergeant, June 27, 1861. Dropped from rolls Dec. 1861.
Addison McClure—Serg. Major, June 27, 1861; Capt., in 16th O. V. I. Oct. 1, 1861. Member of Congress several years. Address, Wooster, O.
Lemuel Jeffries—Serg.; Serg. Major, Oct. 1, 1861; 2d Lieut., Dec. 26, 1861; 1st Lieut., June 25, 1862. Address, Wooster, O.
Joseph H. Carr—Serg. Major, Actg. Adjt., Dec. 26, 1861; 2d Lt., Dec. 31, 1862; A. D. C. to Carroll; 1st Lt., Feb. 10, 1863; res. Nov. 3, 1863; Lt. Col. 169th O. V. I. Address, Indianapolis, Ind.
William A. McDermott—Serg. Major, Jan. 16, 1863; 2d Lt., May 11, 1863.
Joseph W. Watkins—Serg. Major, May 9, 1863; 2d Lieut., July 28, 1863. Address, Chattanooga, Tenn.
Richard Humphries—Serg. Major, May 1, 1862; 2d Lieut. 45th O. V. I., Aug. 1, 1862. Address, Columbus, O.
John Clark—Principal Musician, June 5, 1861; in Co. F, Oct. 1, 1862.
Frederick Olenhausen—Principal Musician, June 18, 1861. Leader of Band.
Wellington Douds—Principal Musician, March 1, 1864.

## Company A.

Carpenter, Leonard W., Capt. June 4, 1861; Major, Nov. 6, 1862; Lt. Col., April 9, 1863: Colonel, Aug. 19, 1863. Address, Logansport, Ind.

Green, John, Capt. Jan. 14, 1863; assigned to Gen. Mason's Staff as A. A. A. Gen. Address, Council Bluffs, Ia.

Pritchard, John R., 2d Lt., June 5, 1861; 1st Lt.. Dec. 26, 1862; Capt., May 23, 1863. Address, Galion, O.

Coates, Foster A., 1st Lt., June 4, 1861; Capt. Sept. 12, 1862; resigned Oct. 15, 1862. Deceased.

Brearly, Samuel L., 2d Lt., June 4, 1861; 1st Lt., Sept. 12, 1862; Capt., Feb. 10, 1863. Address, Minneapolis, Minn.

Welsh, William, Serg.; 2d Lt., June 13, 1862; 1st Lt., Dec. 4, 1862; of Co. K; Colonel 19th Colored Volunteers.

Underwood, Israel, 2d Lt., June 4, 1861; 1st Lt. Jan. 9, 1862; Capt., Dec. 26, 1862; declined promotion; appointed Quartermaster, and res. April 29, 1863; Serg. at Arms at Columbus, O. Address Mount Vernon, O.

Gilliam, Algernon, 2d Lt., Aug. 9, 1861; res. July 13, 1862 Ad., Canton, O.

Lynch, William F., 2d Lt., Mar. 30, 1863; resigned. Capt. 25th Col. Vols.

Addler, Moses, June 5, 1861; dis. near Warrenton, Va., Nov. 9, 1862. Address, Goshen, Ind.

Bendle, William, June 3, 1861: died at Cincinnati, Aug. 1, 1861.

Bell, Josiah, G., June 5, 1861; dis. at Romney, Va., Nov. 16, 1861.

Bigbee, Robert E., June 5, 1861; wounded at Po River, May 10, 1864.

Briggs, John, June 5, 1861; dis. at Washington, D. C., Jan. 3, 1863.

Brown, Jacob, June 5, 1861; dis. Oct. 18, 1862. Re-enlisted and killed at Chickamauga.

Browning, George E., Sept. 13, 1861; dis. at Camp Kelley, Va., Feb. 3, 1862; re-enlisted and killed at Sabine Cross Roads.

Bronscombe, William, June 3, 1861.

Brollier, Willard J., June 3, 1861; died at Fredericksburg, of wounds received at Po River, May 20, 1864.

Brumm, Addison S., June 5, 1861; Corp., June 5, 1861; transferred to Invalid Corps, Feb., 1864.

Church, Berry F., June 5, 1861; dis. at Harper's Ferry, to enlist in 4th U. S. Artillery, Oct. 18, 1863.

Church, Stephen D., June 5, 1861; transferred to Invalid Corps Feb., 1864. Address, Baltimore, Md.

Corder, Elias, June 3, 1861; dis. at Washington, D. C., Dec. 5, 1862.

Crawford, Henry, June 3, 1861; died of camp fever, at Pendleton, Maryland, Sept. 17, 1861.

Cooper, Jay D., June 3, 1861; Corporal, June 5, 1861; discharged at Beverly, Va., July 24, 1861.

Cummins, James M., or Cunningham, June 3, 1861; disch. at Cumberland, Maryland, August 4, 1862.

Davy, Isaac, June 3, 1861; died at Back Creek, of congestion of the lungs, March 10, 1862.

Degrote, George H., June 5, 1861; disch. at Harper's Ferry, Oct. 18, 1862, to enlist in 4th U. S. Artillery.

Dixon, Thomas, June 5, 1861; discharged at Washington, Sept. 19, 1862.

Dowling, John C., June 3, 1861; Sergeant, Nov. 21, 1863; died in Fredericksburg, Va., of wounds received at battle of Po River.

Eggleston, Adoniram, June 5, 1861; disch. at Washington, Sept. 19, 1862.

Erwin, Jacob, June 3, 1861; disch. at Harper's Ferry, Oct. 27, 1862.

Furlong, William D., June 5, 1861; disch. at Washington, Sept. 20, 1862.

Foos, Jefferson, June 5, 1861; prisoner of war at Richmond, Nov. 30, 1863.

Gates, Lewis, April 1, 1862; disch. at Philadelphia, Aug. 15, 1862.

Gilliam, Algernon, June 5, 1861; Serg., June 5, 1861; 2d Lt., Aug. 8, 1861.

Griffis, Bernard, June 5, 1861; Corporal, Jan. 26, 1863; wounded at Chancellorsville and Spottsylvania. Address, Pagetown, O.

Grimwood, William J., June 3, 1861. In N. Y.

Glaze, Columbus D., June 5, 1861; discharged at Columbus, O., May 9, 1863. Address, Mount Vernon, O.

Hargrave, Richard, M. J., June 5, 1861; discharged at Camp Pendleton, Md., Sept. 14, 1861.

Harden, Cornelius, June 5, 1861; discharged at Harper's Ferry, Oct. 18, 1862, to enlist in 4th U. S. Artillery.

Hall, Richard A., June 5, 1861; wounded in the neck at Wilderness, May 6, 1864. Address, Ada, O.

Haller, James, June 5, 1861; Corp., June 5, 1861; Sergeant, Aug. 18, 1861; disch. at Columbus, O., Jan. 31, 1862. Died and was buried at Mount Vernon, O., by comrades, on reunion day, some ten years since.

Hill, George O., June 5 1861; 1st Sergeant, Oct. 1, 1862; 2d Lieut., Dec. 7, 1862. Deceased.

Headington, Murry B., June 5, 1861; discharged at Harper's Ferry, Oct. 18, 1862, to enlist in 4th U. S. Artillery.

Harl, James W., June 3, 1861; died of wounds, July 5, 1863, received at Gettysburg, July 2, 1863.

Harl, Tramel W., Sept. 13, 1861; transferred to 4th Ohio Battalion.

Henry, Daniel J., June 3, 1861; disch. Jan. 29, 1863, at Washington, D. C.

Horner, Benjamin F., June 5, 1861; Corp., June 5, 1861; disch. at New York, Dec. 1, 1862. General Passenger Agent of the "Nickle Plate" Railroad. Address, Cleveland, O.

Hollabach, Jacob, June 5, 1861. Regimental Clerk.

Hull, James W., or Joseph W., June 5, 1861; was prisoner at Richmond. Address, Mount Vernon, O.

Huntley, Emmons, June 3, 1861; taken prisoner, paroled. Ad., Columbus, O.

Ingram, A., Corp., July 20, 1861; Sergt., Jan. 1, 1863; 1st Sergt., Nov. 1, 1863; wounded at Wilderness, May 6, 1864.

Jacobs, Francis O., June 5, 1861; disch. on account of wounds received at Chancellorsville, May 3, 1863. Address, Newark, O.

Kerr, Robert W., June 5, 1861; disch. at Convalescent Camp, May 6, 1863 In War Department. Address, Washington, D. C.
Kimball, Robert, June 5, 1861; wounded at Mine Run, Nov. 28, 1863; in the hand at second Spottsylvania, May 18, 1864
Knode, Oliver C., June 3, 1861.
Koontz, Henry C., Aug. 16, 1861; killed at Wilderness, May 6, 1864.
Langham, Alexander, March 24, 1862.
Lawton, Austin, June 5, 1861. Address, Cincinnati, O
Logsdon, James W., June 5, 1861; disch. at Columbus, O., June 9, 1863 Address, Mount Vernon, O.
Lybarger, George H., June 10, 1861; disch. at Camp Pendleton, Md , Oct 12, 1861. Address, Monroe Mills, O
Lynch, William F., June 5, 1861; Corporal, June 5, 1861; Sergeant, Oct. 8, 1861; Second Lieutenant, January 7, 1863. Address, Waco, Texas.
Long, Isaiah C., June 5, 1861; Sergeant, June 5, 1861; First Sergeant, May 9, 1863; disch. at Alexandria, Va., Nov. 21, 1863. Address, Newark, O.
Miner, Benjamin D., June 3, 1861; Corp., June 1, 1861; Serg., May 9, 1863,
McClellan, Homer G., June 5, 1861; Corporal, May 5, 1862; Sergeant, March 1, 1864. Deceased.
Magill, Samuel W., June 5, 1862; Corporal, July 28, 1862; disch. at Harper's Ferry October 7, 1863. Address, Howard, Knox county, O.
Mahaffey, Joseph, June 3, 1861. Deceased.
McGuggin, James N., June 5, 1861; Sergeant, June 5, 1861; discharged at Beverley, Va., July 24, 1861.
McKenzie, Caleb, June 3, 1861; discharged at Columbus, O., May 9, 1863. Address, Mt. Vernon, O.
Miller, Edward S., June 5, 1861; discharged at Falmouth, Va., February 7, 1863. Address, Mt. Union, O.
McKenzie, Joseph C., June 3, 1863; discharged at Morris' Farm, Va., May 3, 1862; wounded at Petersburg, W. Va. Address, Mt. Vernon, O.
McKenzie, William F., October 19, 1861.
McKenzie, John L., October 19, 1861; died at Camp Ohio, of typhoid fever, September 11, 1862.
McDowell, William E., June 5, 1861; died of chronic diarrhœa, at Harper's Ferry, November 19, 1862; buried at Mt. Vernon, O.
McGiffin, James N., June 5, 1861; Sergt, Aug. 18, 1861; dis. Sept. 5, 1862
Morris, William H., June 3, 1863.
Montis, John, June 3, 1861; transferred to Invalid Corps February 27, 1864. Address, Mt. Vernon, O.
Murphy, Marshall N., June 5, 1861. Buried at Mt. Vernon, O.
Neeley, William, Feb. 8, 1862; disch. at Mt. Pleasant, O., Aug. 5, 1861.
O'Neil, Thomas, June 5, 1861; disch. at Harrisonburg, Va , Aug. 8, 1862.
O'Neil, John K., June 5, 1861; discharged at Washington, Dec. 11, 1862.
Pancoast, Ohio, June 3, 1861; wounded in right shoulder, at Wilderness, May 6, 1864. Druggist in Ashland, O.
Pollock, Henry G., June 5, 1861; Corporal, October 18, 1862; wounded at Cold Harbor, June 3, 1864. Address, Cardington, O.

Parks, John L., June 5, 1861; died at Washington, D. C., of chronic diarrhœa, November 7, 1862; buried at Mt. Vernon, O.

Pate, Robert A., June 5, 1861; died at Cleveland, O., of chronic diarrhœa, April 10, 1863; buried at Gambier, O.

Peaks, John T., August 17, 1861; died at Old Point Comfort, Va., of gastritis, August 25, 1862.

Phifer, Leroy, Aug. 22, 1861; died of lung fever, at Grafton, Va., Mar. 14, 1862.

Phifer, James W., June 5, 1861; died of chronic diarrhœa, at Newark, N. J., September 9, 1862.

Phillips, Emanuel, June 5, 1861; re-enlisted as veteran February 2, 1864, and transferred to the Fourth Ohio Battalion.

Powers, James L., re-enlisted as vet. Feb. 2, 1864, and transf. to 4th O. B.

Phifer, Eleazer P., June 3, 1861; discharged at Columbus, O., June 28, 1862. Address, Mt. Vernon, O.

Pyle, Henry P., June 5, 1861; Corporal, June 29, 1861; disch. at Washington, D. C., January 1, 1863. Address, North Liberty, Knox Co., O.

Roberts, John, June 3, 1861; Corporal, March 6, 1862; Sergeant. Address, Kingston Center, O.

Robinson, Thomas, June 5, 1861. Address, Danville, Knox county, O.

Roberts, Thomas, June 5, 1861. Address, Springfield, O.

Russell, William, June 5, 1861; discharged at Camp Pendleton, Md., October 12, 1861. Address, Hartford, O.

Rogers, Percival, June 3, 1861; Corporal, January 1, 1863.

Runyan, Charles M., June 5, 1861; killed at Chancellorsville, May 3, 1863.

Seacord, William, June 5, 1861; transferred to Invalid Corps November 13, 1863. Address, Newark, O.

Scott, Thomas, June 5, 1861; discharged at Columbus, October 4, 1862.

Sharp, Thomas, June 5, 1861; discharged at Fortress Monroe, Sept. 22, 1862.

Smith, Henry, August 22, 1861; transferred to Invalid Corps Nov. 13, 1863.

Taylor, Adam H., June 5, 1861; discharged at Washington, D. C., January 20, 1863; enlisted in the United States Cavalry.

Thompson, Randall, June 3, 1861; wounded at Po River, May 10, 1864.

Thompson, William H., June 5, 1861; transferred to Brigade Band April 17, 1863. Buried at Mt. Vernon, O., in 1883.

Watkins, Joseph W., June 10, 1861; Sergeant, March 30, 1863; Sergt. Major, May 9, 1863. Address, Chattanooga, Tenn.

Wallace, Alfred B., August 22, 1861; wounded in right arm at Spottsylvania, May 12, 1864; transf. to Fourth Ohio Battalion. Address, Chesterville, O.

Ward, Byron W., June 5, 1861. Address, Mt. Vernon, O.

Welsh, William, June 3, 1861; Sergeant; promoted to Second Lieutenant.

Welsh, Zephaniah B., June 5, 1861; disch. at Washington, D. C., October 29, 1862. Address, Mt. Vernon, O.

Welshymer, William, June 3, 1861. Address, Mt. Vernon, O.

Whittington, William, June 3, 1861; discharged at Harper's Ferry, October 18, 1862, to enlist in the Fourth United States Artillery.

Whitworth, John T., June 3, 1861. Address, Monroe Mills, O.

White, John W., June 5, 1861; transferred to V. R. C. March 23, 1864.

Wolverton, John B., June 3, 1861; Corp., July 20, 1861; Sergt., Jan. 1, 1863; wounded at Fredericksburg, Dec. 13, 1862. Address, Mt. Vernon, O.
Yager, Joseph, June 5, 1861. Address, Soldiers' Home, Dayton, O.

———:o:———

## Company B.

Banning, Henry B., Captain June 4, 1861; Major 52d O. V. I.; Colonel 87th O. V. I.; Colonel 125th O. V. I.; Colonel 121st O. V. I.; Brig. Genl. in 1865; Member of Ohio Legislature; Member of Congress. Deceased.
Green, John, First Lieutenant, June 4, 1861; Captain, December 22, 1862; A. A. Genl. to Genl. J. S. Mason.
Lippett, A. W., Second Lieut., June 4, 1861; Quartermaster, June 3, 1861; First Lieutenant, January 9, 1862. Died December 26, 1862.
Underwood, Israel, Second Lieutenant, June 4, 1861; First Lieutenant, January 9, 1862; Captain, December 26, 1862, but declined commission, and was appointed Quartermaster, January 4, 1863; for some years Sergeant-at-Arms of the House, at Columbus, O. Address, Mt. Vernon, O.
Patton, William T., Second Lieut., Jan. 18, 1862; First Lieut., Jan. 4, 1863.
Jones, John S., Captain from Co. C, October 5, 1862. (See Co. C Roster.)
Brophy, George, Sergeant, Oct. 5, 1862; Second Lieut., Feb. 16, 1863; First Lieut., July 20, 1863; wounded at Fredericksburg, Dec. 13, 1862.
Armstrong, J., Feb. 23, 1864; wounded May 10, 1864; transf. to 4th O. B.
Alson, John, June 1, 1861; died at Frederick City, of chronic diarrhœa, November 20, 1862.
Bergen, George D., June 1, 1861; Sergeant, December 29, 1861; discharged at Washington, D. C., September 24, 1862.
Barnes, George W., June 5, 1861. Address, Centerburg, O.
Barnes, Albert, June 5, 1861; disch. at Camp Dennison, O., Oct. 22, 1861.
Barber, Aquila, June 5, 1861; discharged at Camp Ohio, April 10, 1863. Address, Centerburg, O.
Barker, William H., June 5, 1861. Address, Ada, O.
Barker, Joseph M., Oct. 14, 1863; transf. to 4th O. B. Ad., Mt. Vernon, O.
Beach, Franklin B., June 5, 1861; wounded at Chancellorsville, May 3, 1863, at Mine Run, November 28, 1863, and in left arm and right shoulder at Cold Harbor, June 3, 1861. Address, Gambier, O.
Brophy, George, August 27, 1861; Sergeant, October 5, 1862; Second Lieutenant, February 16, 1863.
Beardsley, W. B., June 1, 1861; dis. at Paw Paw Tunnel, Va., Feb. 4, 1862.
Bergen, Charles, June 5, 1861; Corporal, Dec. 13, 1862; wounded at Fredericksburg, Dec. 13, 1862; discharged on account of wounds March 26, 1862. Deceased.
Beckholdt, William, June 5, 1861; disch. at Camp Keys, Nov. 6, 1861.

Ball, Pliney, June 5, 1861; wounded at Chancellorsville, May 3, 1863. Deceased.

Boley, Jacob, June 5, 1861; disch. Oct. 19, 1862, to enter Regular Army.

Booze, Andrew J., June 5, 1861; wounded at Wilderness, May 6, 1864.

Brown, Henry D., June 2, 1861; dis. at Camp Pendleton, Md., Oct. 22, 1861.

Bush, Charles H., June 1, 1861; discharged Oct. 22, 1861.

Case, Wilber, June 5, 1861, killed at Spottsylvania, May 18, 1864.

Cassidy, Edward, June 5, 1861.

Chandler, John, June 1, 1861; Sergeant, May 5, 1862; 1st Sergeant, October 10, 1862. Deceased.

Claytor, Thompson C., June 1, 1861. Address, Perry, Dallas county, Iowa.

Claytor, Thomas N., June 1, 1861. Died May 18, of wounds, at Spottsylvania, May 12, 1864.

Clayton, Nelson E., Dec. 25, 1868; transferred to 4th Ohio Battalion.

Conley, John, June 1, 1861; Corporal, December 15, 1863; wounded at Morton's Ford, February 6, 1864.

Covella, Alfred A., June 1, 1861; discharged November 25, 1861; promoted in Seventh West Virginia.

Cline, John M., June 5, 1861; wounded at Romney, Sept. 24, 1861.

Colgan, Francis, June 5, 1861; disch. Oct. 19, 1862, to enter U. S. Artillery

Craven, Malen, June 5, 1861; killed at Spottsylvania, May 18, 1864.

Craven, James W., June 5, 1861.

Dunlap, John M., June 1, 1861; 2d Lieutenant Co. K. March 8, 1863; discharged February 8, 1864.

Davis, William, June 5, 1861. Address, Tama City, Iowa.

Davis, John W., June 5, 1861; disch. at Camp Pendleton, Md., Oct. 22, 1861.

Deabolt, June 5, 1861; Corp., May 3, 1863; killed at Gettysburg, July 2, 1863.

Dunn, Michal, Aug. 23, 1863; transferred to 4th Ohio Battalion. Deceased.

Evarts, Andrew, March 31, 1862; trans. to 4th Ohio Battalion; wounded in the hand at Wilderness, May 6, 1864.

Evans, Byron W., June 1, 1861; 2d Lieut., June 29, 1862. Deceased.

Earl, Samuel, June 1, 1861; disch. Oct. 18, 1862, to enter Regular Army.

Fletcher, Jacob P., June 1, 1861; wounded at Wilderness, May 6, 1864. Address, Brandon, Ohio.

Fulmer, Dewalt, June 1, 1861; Corporal August 5, 1863; wounded at Chancellorsville, May 3, 1863.

Foot, Burnly, June 3, 1861; disch. at Camp Pendleton, Md., Oct. 22, 1861.

Fry, Martin, June 5, 1861; died at Fredericksburg after amputation of arm wounded at Spottsylvania, May 18, 1864.

Gillespie, John W. A., June 1, 1861; Sergeant; discharged November 6, 1862; Captain in an Ohio regiment.

Gordon, Henry B., June 1, 1861; Corporal, November 1, 1862; died at Frederick City, Md., of chronic diarrhoea, December 1, 1862.

Glasscock, Valentine, June 1, 1861; taken prisoner at Chancellorsville, May 3, 1863; wounded at Morton's Ford, February 28, 1864; killed at Wilderness, May 6, 1864.

Graff, Henry, June 1, 1861; discharged near New Creek, West Virginia, October 24, 1861. Deceased.

Galbreath, George W., June 5, 1861; killed June 18, 1862.

Graham, Archie, Feb. 18, 1862; transferred to 4th Ohio Battalion.

Hart, William T., June 1, 1861; Sergeant, May 3, 1863; wounded at Chancellorsville, May 3, 1863; in the right leg at North Anna River, May 24, 1864. Address, Gambier, Ohio.

Hoey, William C., June 5, 1861; discharged October 19, 1862, to enter Regular Army. Address, Fredericktown, Ohio.

Hunt, Milton, June 5, 1861; discharged at Harper's Ferry, November 9, 1862. Address, Rich Hill, Ohio.

Hutcheson, Leander, June 4, 1861; wounded at Spottsylvania, May 18, 1864. Address, Mount Vernon, Ohio.

Harrington, Joseph W., June 5, 1861; discharged October 19, 1862, to enter the Regular Army.

Hull, Joseph, August 10, 1861; discharged October 19, 1862, to enter the Regular Army. Address, Mount Vernon, Ohio.

Jackson, William, June 5, 1861; in Brigade Band, June 23, 1863. Address, Columbus, Ohio.

Jones, William, June 5, 1861; Corporal, May 3, 1863; wounded in the left hip at Wilderness, May 6, 1864.

Johnson, William, June 5, 1863; wounded in left hip at Wilderness May 6, 1864. Address, Uniontown, Ohio.

Jewells, Lewis, February 22, 1864. Transferred to 4th Ohio Battalion.

Kile, William, June 5, 1861; discharged at Fort Gaines, D.C., Dec. 11, 1862.

Kibler, Joseph, June 5, 1861; discharged October 19, 1862, to enter Regular Army. Address, Kirkersville, Ohio.

Kimball, Isaiah, June 5, 1861; Corporal, May 3, 1863.

Lucas, Elisha, June 5, 1861; died of chronic diarrhœa, at Frederick City, Md., December 1, 1862.

Lyons, Albert, June 5, 1861; died of chronic diarrhœa, at Newark, N. J., October 27, 1862.

Listenberger, George, discharged at Camp Denison, Ohio, in 1861.

Milhone, Gustave A., June 1, 1861; discharged at Falmouth, Va., February 27, 1863. Deceased.

McCune, Thomas, June 1, 1861; drowned at Piedmont, Va., Nov. 4, 1861.

McDonald, Ronald, June 5, 1861; died of inflamation of the bowels at Camp Pendleton, Md., August 21, 1861.

McHorter, Francis, June 5, 1861; discharged at Romney, Va., Nov. 6, 1861.

Montanya, Alonzo M., June 5, 1861; Address, Chicago, Ill.

Morey, Lorin, June 5, 1861; wounded in left leg, May 12, 1864, at Spottsylvania. Address, Centerburg, Ohio.

Michael, George, Oct. 12, 1861; trans. to Invalid Corps, Nov. 18, 1863.

Myers, David, February 28, 1862; discharged Nov. 27, 1862.

Murphey, Bryant M., Oct. 14, 1861: Corporal; wounded in right leg at Wilderness, May 6, 1864.

Nixon, William, June 5, 1861; died of smallpox at Camp Ohio, Feb. 3, 1863.

Patton, William T., June 1, 1861; 1st Sergeant, August 31, 1861; 2d Lieutenant, January 9, 1862.

Patterson, Hutchinsan, Oct. 12, 1861; died of conjestion of the lungs at Romney, Va., December 27, 1861.

Pay, William, discharged at Romney, Va., Nov. 6, 1861.

Parks, Gilbert M., June 1, 1861; wounded at Chancellorsville, May 3, 1863; Morton's Ford, Feb. 28, 1864; at Spottsylvania, May 12, 1864.

Pinkerton, Benjamin F., June 1, 1861; discharged at Camp Pendleton, Md., October 22, 1861.

Pergh, Henry, June 6, 1861; discharged Nov. 6, 1861.

Poland, William, June 5, 1861; Corporal, Jan. 22, 1862; Sergeant, May 3, 1863. In Missouri.

Pritchard, William F., Feb. 20, 1864; transferred to 4th Ohio Battalion.

Remington, William H., June 1, 1861; Corporal, March 6, 1862; Sergeant, August 25, 1862.

Robertson, Henry, H. June 5, 1861; Address, Mount Liberty, Ohio.

Robertson, Phillip, June 5, 1861; wounded at Wilderness, in the left arm, May 6, 1864. Address, Centerburg, Ohio.

Rowley, Simon B., June 5, 1861; discharged at Camp Ohio, Dec. 20, 1862.

Rockwell, William, June 3, 1861. Address, Brandon, Ohio.

Rockwell, Lewis, June 5, 1861.

Rial, John, June 1, 1861; wounded at Prospect Hill, June 4, 1864.

Ross, Jacob, February 20, 1864; transferred to 4th Ohio Battalion.

Russell, Thomas J., March 31, 1864; transferred to 4th Ohio Battalion.

Sargeant, George H., March 17, 1862; wounded at Chancellorsville, May 3, 1863; transferred to Invalid Corps.

Shaffer, Alexander H., June 1, 1861; discharged at Camp Pendleton, Md., October 22, 1861.

Shaffer, Benjamin F., June 1, 1861. Died in 1884.

Shaffer, Isaac, Oct. 12, 1861; discharged at Fort Gaines, Dec. 2, 1862. Address, Bolivar, Ohio.

Shaffer, Lyman, October 16, 1861; discharged at Fairfax Seminary, Va,. August 11, 1862. Deceased.

Shaffer, Thomas H., Feb. 22, 1862; killed at Chancellorsville, May 3, 1863.

Sapp, Joseph R., June 5, 1861; discharged at Philadelphia, Oct. 22, 1862.

Sanford, Josiah B., June 3, 1861; disch. at Fort Gaines, Sept. 19, 1862.

Stinger, Daniel A., June 1, 1861: Sergeant; discharged October 14, 1862; 2d Lieutenant in 125th Ohio Volunteer Infantry.

Stoughton, Omar L., June 1, 1861; Corporal, June, 1861; Sergeant; wounded at Fredericksburg, December 13, 1862; at Chancellorsville, May 3, 1863. Address, Mount Vernon, Ohio.

Shipp, William, June 5, 1861; discharged November 7, 1861.

Smith, Charles, June 5, 1861; Corporal, Aug. 10, 1863; died at Alexandria, Va., Dec. 14, 1863, of wounds received at Mine Run, Nov. 28, 1863.

Stephens, William, June 5, 1861; discharged at Frederick City, Maryland, May 23, 1863. Address, Mount Vernon, Ohio.

Simms, Jesse, June 5, 1861; Corporal, Aug. 10, 1863; died at Alexandria, Va., Dec. 14, 1863, of wounds received at Mine Run, Nov. 26, 1863.

Stump, James B., June 5, 1861.

Scott, Archibald, June 5, 1861; Corporal, May 3, 1863; wounded at Chancellorsville, May 3, 1863.

Seymore, Henry S., June 5, 1861; died at Mount Liberty, Ohio, of chronic diarrhœa, January 17, 1863.

Seymore, Charles S., June 5, 1861; discharged at Falmouth, Va., Jan 2, 1863.

Shank, Theoderick, June 5, 1861.

Sebring, Robert, February 22, 1864; killed at Wilderness, May 6, 1864.

Taylor, Henry, June 5, 1861; discharged December 5, 1862.

Taylor, Hezekiah, June 5, 1861; discharged October 19, 1862, to U. S. Army. Address, Mount Vernon, Ohio.

Trimble, Thomas O., June 5, 1861; discharged at Camp Kelley, January 26, 1862. Deceased.

Updike, Edgar, June 5, 1861; discharged at Falmouth, Va., December 21, 1862. Address, Red Oak, Iowa.

Van Voorhees, William O., June 5, 1861; wounded at Romney, Va., Sept. 24, 1861, resulting in blindness, and disch. at Fort Gaines, Dec. 25, 1863.

Walden, Lucas H., June 5, 1861; died of chronic diarrhœa at Frederick City, November 22, 1862.

Wilcox, Edward, June 5, 1861. Address, Davenport, Iowa.

White, William, June 5, 1861. Corporal, August 31, 1861; Sergeant, May 3, 1863. Address, Kirkersville, Ohio.

Worley, Douglass, June 5, 1861; drowned at Piedmont, Va., Nov. 4, 1861.

Wilcox, George, June 1, 1861; wounded at Chancellorsville, May, 3, 1863; transferred to Invalid Corps. Address, Davenport, Iowa.

Young, Squire H., June 3, 1861; Serg., Aug. 31, 1861; disch. Sept. 24, 1862.

:o:

## Company C.

Crawford, James M., Captain, June 5, 1861; resigned November 14, 1862; received first commission as Captain, issued by Governor; Colonel 145th O. V. I. Address, Delaware, O.

Jones, John S., 1st Lt., June 5, 1861; A. D. C. to Shields; Capt., Sept. 12, 1862; Actg. Maj. at Chancellorsville; wounded at Mine Run, Nov. 28, 1863; declined nomination as candidate for Legislature; Colonel 174th O. V. I., Sept. 21, 1864; Brigadier General, June 27, 1865; Member of Ohio Legislature; Member of Congress. Address, Delaware, O.

Dolbear, Byron, 2d Lt., June 5, 1861; 1st Lt., Jan. 9, 1862; Capt. Co. C, Nov. 6, 1862; died at Delaware, O., June, 1864, of wounds received at Po River, May 10, 1864. Buried at Delaware, O.

Anderson, Andrew M., Sergeant; Second Lieut., Dec. 26, 1862; First Lieut., July 20, 1863; wounded in the thigh, at Spottsylvania, May 12, 1864; Quartermaster 189th O. V. I. Address, Delaware, O.

Perry, Albert H., Sergeant; Second Lieutenant, July 20, 1863; wounded in right leg at Spottsylvania, May 12, 1864. Address, Columbus, O.

Evans, Byron W., Second Lieutenant of Co. C, August 31, 1862; First Lieutenant, November 1, 1862; transferred to Co. D.

Carr, Joseph H., 1st Lieut. Co. C, June 25, 1863; resigned Nov. 3, 1863.

Anderson, Andrew M., June 3, 1861; Sergeant, June 4, 1861; Second Lieutenant, August 31, 1862.

Armstrong, George, Corp., June 5, 1861; Sergt. Died in Kansas, Jan., 1886.

Anderson, Gillis J., June 3, 1861. Died June 15, 1867; buried at Delaware, O.

Arthur, Napoleon B., June 3, 1861; Corp., Jan. 14, 1863. Ad., Delaware, O.

Allen, Aaron P., Sept. 1, 1862; transf. to 4th O. B. Address, Marion, O.

Aigen, Stephen P., October 6, 1862; transferred to Invalid Corps; taken prisoner at Reams Station.

Barger, William H., Sept. 21, 1861; disch. at Columbus, O., Nov. 21, 1862.

Beach, Theron A., June 3, 1861; discharged at Camp Pendleton, Md., November 7, 1861. Address, Gambier, O.

Beard, Truman, June 3, 1861. Address, Galena, O.

Burkholder, Lorenzo M., June 3, 1861.

Brown, Robert O., June 3, 1861; discharged at Fortress Monroe, October 19, 1862; died soon after. Buried at Delaware, O.

Bryfogle, Charles D., June 3, 1861; Corp., Jan. 14, 1863; wounded May 12, 1864; Captain in 174th O. V. I. Deceased; buried at Delaware, O.

Bryfogle, Joshua D., June 3, 1861; disch. at Harper's Ferry, November 5, 1862; in Tenth Ohio Cavalry. Deceased; buried at Delaware, O.

Bryfogle, William D., June 3, 1861; transferred to Fourth Ohio Battalion; was not at first accepted on account of youth; wounded at First Romney Race. Deceased; buried at Delaware, O.

Birdsall, John, June 3, 1861. Address, Las Vegas, New Mexico.

Bailor, William, June 3, 1861; re en. as Veteran and transf. to 4th O. B.

Barnes, Leroy S., June 3, 1861. Address, Laramie City, Wyoming.

Bartlett, George, June 3, 1861; discharged at Columbus, O., December 22, 1862. Deceased; buried at Delaware, O.

Benton, Erastus, June 3, 1861; discharged at Columbus, O., July 1, 1872.

Burns, John, June 3, 1861; discharged at Columbus, O., Nov. 14, 1862.

Bieber, John, June 3, 1861. Address, Lakewood, Shelby Co., Ill.

Cox, Thomas, June 3, 1861.

Collins, Timothy D., June 3, 1861; killed at Chancellorsville, May 3, 1863.

Crawford, John A., June 3, 1861; killed at Robertson's Tavern, Nov. 27, 1863.

Conklin, Henry, June 3, 1861; disch. at Fort Gaines, April 12, 1863.

Cellars, James D., June 3, 1861. In Kansas.

Chandler, Robert L., June 3, 1861. Died October 14, 1862.

Conine, Nelson H., June 3, 1861; Corporal, October 1, 1862; killed at Wilderness, May 6, 1864.

Converse, George, June 3, 1861; transferred to Invalid Corps, July 16, 1863. Address, Delaware, O.

Colflesh, Samuel W., June 3, 1861; Corporal and Sergeant; killed at Po River, May 10, 1864.

Dart, William T., May 20, 1861; transferred to Invalid Corps, February 16, 1864. Address, McKeesport, Pa.

Durfey, Girard, Oct. 16, 1861; wounded May 13, 1864; re-en. as Vet., Feb. 19, 1864; transf. to 4th O. B. Address, Sodliers' Home, Dayton, O.

Dale, John, June 3, 1861. Died at Sandy Hook, Md., in 1865; buried at Delaware, O.

Durfey, Benjamin, June 3, 1861; wounded in right shoulder at Po River, May 10, 1864. Address, Delaware, O.

Eager, Thomas, June 3, 1861. Address, Delaware, O.

Fritz, William D., June 3, 1861; discharged at Columbus, O., March 5, 1863. Address, Delaware, O.

Ganway, Daniel, June 3, 1861. Address, Delaware, O.

Griffin, Josiah, June 3, 1861; killed at Chancellorsville, May 3, 1863.

Goddard, Harrison, June 3, 1861; transferred to Invalid Corps, January 14, 1864. Address, Delaware, O.

Grey, Charles, June 3, 1861; Corporal, October 1, 1862; injured by fall from the cars while in motion, near Washington, having fainted, and died soon after at Harper's Ferry, November 23, 1862, of typhoid fever.

Gaylord, Charles R., June 12, 1861; transf. to I. C., Sept. 16, 1863.

Gaylord, George M., June 3, 1863; Sergeant.

Goodrich, Wellington, June 3, 1861; discharged.

Hatch, Henry H., June 3, 1861; discharged at Camp Pendleton, Md., November 7, 1861. Address, Ostrander, O.

Howe, David M., June 3, 1861; Corporal, Jan. 14, 2863; Captain in 174th O. V. I. Died in Pittsburg, Pa., in 1881; buried at Delaware, O.

Humphreys, Richard, June 3, 1861; Sergeant Major, July, 1862; discharged, to become Quartermaster of 86th O. V. I. Address, Columbus, O.

Heller, Elias, May 20, 1861; died in New York City, in December, 1862, of chronic diarrhœa.

Kruck, Jacob, Orderly Sergeant from April 16, 1861, until June, 1865, having probably served before, and longer in this office, than any other Volunteer for 1861 to 1865. Address, Delaware, O.

Jennings, Harvey, October 16, 1861; Corporal, May 3, 1863; wounded in the right hand at Po River, May 10, 1864; transferred to Fourth Ohio Battalion. Address, Winfield, Kan.

Kempf, Jonathan, June 3, 1861; killed at Chancellorsville, May 3, 1863.

Keiser, Adam, June 3, 1861; wounded in the right shoulder at Spottsylvania, May 12, 1864; at Chancellorsville, May 3, 1863. Ad., Larwill, Ind.

Keiser, Levi, June 3, 1861; wounded at Spottsylvania, in left shoulder, May 12, 1864. Address, Larwill, Ind.

Kimball, Joseph, June 3, 1861; died at Cumberland, Md., January, 1862.

Kepler, William, June 3, 1863; wounded in left shoulder at Harrison's Landing, Va., July 3, 1862; Historian of the Regiment. Address, Berea, O.

Lamb, Howard S., June 3, 1861; wounded at Chancellorsville, May 3, 1863, and in the hand, May 12, 1864, at Spottsylvania. Ad., Laclede, Mo.

Lynn, Hiram, June 3, 1861; re-en. as Vet., Feb. 12, 1864; wounded in right arm at Spottsylvania, May 12, 1864; transf. to 4th O. B.; Captain.

Mickle, James, Sergeant, June 3, 1861. Address, Douglass Grove, Neb.

McCarter, Robert D., June 3, 1861; Q. M. Sergt. Address, Columbus, O.

McDermott, William A., June 3, 1861; Corporal, Sergeant and Sergeant Major; Second Lieutenant, April 29, 1863.

Munsell, John, June 3, 1861; discharged at Romney, Va., January, 1861. Address, Marion, O.

Martin, John F., June 3, 1861.

Moses, John F., June 3, 1861; transferred to Battery A, Fourth U. S. Artillery, June 5, 1862. Address, Rushville, Ind.

McCullough, Watson, June 3, 1861; wounded on skirmish line in the rear of Fredericksburg, December 12, 1862; died of wounds at Delaware, O., March 29, 1863; 2d Lt. shortly before death. Buried at Delaware, O.

McElroy, Erwin, June 3, 1861; discharged at Columbus, O., February 23, 1863. Address, San Jose, Cal.

McPherson, Benjamin, May 20, 1861; wounded in left elbow at North Anna River, May 23, 1864. Night watchman at Depot, Delaware, O.

Mickle, Robert, June 3, 1861. Address, Delaware, O.

Markle, Jacob, Oct. 16, 1861; dis. at Columbus, O., Feb. 16, 1864. Deceased.

Nash, David T., June 3, 1861.

Only, John, June 3, 1861; transferred to Battery A, Fourth U. S. Artillery, October 18, 1862. Address, Delaware, O.

Orton, Smith H., June 3, 1861; killed at Spottsylvania, May 18, 1864.

Owsten, William H., Oct. 16, 1861; wounded in the chest at Spottsylvania, May 18, 1864; transferred to 4th O. B. Address, Delaware, O.

Prior, Samuel, June 3, 1861. Address, Cedar Run, Muskingum Co., O.

Parks, Cornelius, June 3, 1861; murdered by Sutler's Clerk, at Coles' Hill, Va., April 13, 1864. Body taken home.

Perry, Albert H., June 3, 1861; Sergt., June 5, 1861; 2d Lt., July 28, 1863.

Parks, John, June 3, 1861; died at Delaware, O., of wounds received at Romney, September 25, 1861.

Pugh, John H., June 3, 1861; discharged at Camp Ohio, January 14, 1863. Address, Richmond, Ind.

Plotner, Ambrose A., June 3, 1861; discharged at Alexandria, Va., November 26, 1862. Address, Santiago, Chili, South America.

Rolloson, Wesley, June 3, 1861. Address, Delaware, O.

Richerts, Everett, June 3, 1861; died at Harper's Ferry, November 23, 1863, of chronic diarrhœa.

Smith, George, June 3, 1861. Address, Delaware, O.

Shafer, Edwin P., June 3, 1861; died at Nashville, Tenn.

Siegfried, Isaac, June 3, 1861; died of typhoid fever, at Cumberland, Md., December 8, 1861.

Shearer, George W., June 3, 1861. Address, Terre Haute, Ind.

Staunton, Benjamin, June 3, 1861; died at Grafton, Va., August 17, 1861, of typhoid fever.

Stewart, Thomas C., June 3, 1861; disch. at Columbus, O., July 11, 1863; Member Tennessee Legislature. Ad., 518 East St., New York City.

Steuver, Oliver, June 12, 1861; died at Cumberland, Md., in 1862.

Thomas, David, June 3, 1861; wounded in shoulder at Chancellorsville, May 3, 1863; disch. at Washington, Dec. 13, 1863. Address, Delaware, O.

Traxler, Elias, June 3, 1861; died of wounds received in the left arm at Po River, May 10, 1864.

Tanner, Joseph, June 3, 1861; Corporal, December 1, 1861; killed at Po River, May 10, 1864.

Torrence, George, June 12, 1861; Corporal, Oct. 12, 1881; killed at Fredericksburg, December 13, 1862, while acting as Color Bearer; fell with the colors in hand, his blood and brains staining the flag.

Tipton, Samuel, June 3, 1861.

Trout, Andrew, June 12, 1861; re-enlisted as Veteran; transferred to Fourth Ohio Battalion; taken prisoner at Reams Station.

Veer, Alexander A., June 12, 1861; discharged at Columbus, O., July 2, 1862. Address, Delaware, O.

Vining, Charles, June 3, 1861; died, May 8, 1864, of wounds received in the left leg, at Wilderness, on May 6, 1864.

Welch, Girard, June 3, 1861; Corporal, May 3, 1863; re-en. as Veteran, Feb. 19, 1864; transf. to 4th O. B.; Captain. Address, Star Prairie, Wis.

Welsh, L. Byron, June 3, 1861; Corporal in 1862; discharged February 20, 1863. Is a paralytic in San Francisco, Cal.

Ward, William J., June 3, 1861; wounded in right shoulder, May 6, 1864, at Wilderness. Address, Kansas City, Mo.

Wells, Samuel, June 3, 1861; wounded at Gettysburg, July 3, 1863; in right thigh, at Spottsylvania, May 12, 1864. Address, Delaware, O.

Walker, Augustus P., June 12, 1861. Buried at Delaware, O.

Worline, Albert, June 12, 1861; re-enlisted as Veteran; wounded in the abdomen, at Po River, May 10, 1864; transferred to Fourth Ohio Battalion; taken prisoner at Reams Station.

Warner, William H., June 3, 1861; discharged, to become Second Lieutenant in 48th O. V. I. Killed at Pittsburgh Landing.

Warner, Thomas C., June 3, 1861; wounded at Fredericksburg, December 13, 1862, in the hip; discharged at Camp Ohio, on account of wound, March 23, 1863; Chaplain G. A. R. of Ohio in 1864; Pastor Methodist Episcopal Church at Chattanooga, Tenn., in 1886.

Williams, Thomas, March 23, 1864; shot through the chest and killed, at Cold Harbor, June 4, 1864.

Winship, Charles J., Corporal; died of congestion of the lungs, at Romney, Va., November 25, 1861. Buried at Galena, O.

Ropp, George D., June 3, 1861; Corp.; killed at Fredericksburg, Dec. 13, 1862.

Welch, William O., Corporal; discharged at Columbus, O., September 23, 1862. Address, Delaware, O.

Jennings, Robert P., June 3, 1861; discharged at Romney, Va., December 31, 1861. Address, Winfield, Kansas.

Lambert, Thomas, June 3, 1861; transferred from Co. F and promoted to Sergeant; discharged to accept promotion in 66th O. V. I.

———:o:———

## Company D.

Weaver, George, Captain, June 4, 1861; Major, January 9, 1862. Died at Patterson, O., soon after the close of the war.

Stewart, Gordon A., First Lieutenant, June 4, 1861; Captain, Jan. 9, 1862; Major, April 9, 1863; died at Washington, D. C., in 1884, after having served in Department offices for some years.

Evans, Byron W., Second Lieutenant, September 12, 1862; First Lieutenant of Co. D, December 26, 1862; Captain Co. D, June 17, 1863; taken prisoner at Wilderness, May 6, 1864; kept awhile at Macon, Ga.; with others, cut a hole through the bottom of the box-car in which they rode, escaped when near Charlotte, and shot by a guard when a few rods from the car; a leg was amputated by Dr. Ashby, brother of General Ashby of cavalry fame; after a few days Evans died from exhaustion, at Salisbury, N. C. In the fall of 1884, Dr. Morrison, formerly of the Fourth O. V. I., happened upon his grave, learned the particulars of his death from Ashby, and was given his Bible and other effects, which were by Dr. Morrison and Lieutenant Patton returned to the bereft wife.

Timmons, Daniel R., Second Lieut., June 4, 1861; First Lieut., Jan. 9, 1862; Captain, Dec. 26, 1862, and assigned to Co. E. Ad., Patterson, O.

Jeffries, Lemuel, transferred from Co. E as Second Lieutenant, December 26, 1861; afterward transferred to Co. E.

Spink, R. B., Second Lieutenant, June 29, 1862, from Co. E; transferred to Co. I, December 19, 1862.

Spalter, Frank J., Second Lieutenant, December 31, 1862; First Lieutenant, July 20, 1863; Major, Fourth O. B.; killed near Petersburg, 1864.

Albright, William, June 4, 1861; disch. at Falmouth, Va., May 12, 1863.

Anderline, John, June 4, 1861; died of chronic diarrhœa, at Harper's Ferry, November 5, 1862.

Atkinson, Isaac G., June 4, 1861; Corporal; discharged at Camp Pendleton, Md., October 22, 1861.

Burdett, John, June 4, 1861; Corporal, May 1, 1863; wounded at Morton's Ford, February 6, 1864. Address, Patterson, O.

Baker, John, June 4, 1861.

Brum, John, June 4, 1861; wounded at Romney, Va., September 25, 1861.

Bunyan, Albert, June 4, 1861; disch, at Columbus, O., April 27, 1863.

Brigg, Matthew, June 4, 1861; transferred to Invalid Corps.

Banker, Milo, June 4, 1861; died at Fredericksburg several days after having been wounded in the hip at Po River, May 10, 1864.

Baily, Calvin L., wounded at Cold Harbor, June 3, 1864; transf. to 4th O. B.
Baily, John G., June 4, 1861; wounded at Fredericksburg, December 13, 1862; discharged as Corporal, April 20, 1863. Address, Patterson, O.
Beam, John A., June 4, 1861.
Black, David W., June 4, 1861; discharged at Wheeling, July 14, 1862.
Butcher, Jacob, June 4, 1861. Deceased.
Briggs, Amos D., June 4, 1861; Corporal; wounded at Wilderness, May 6, 1864. Address, Patterson, O.
Burnheimer, Samuel, October 27, 1861; discharged August 12, 1862.
Clark, James W., June 4, 1861; Corp., May 1, 1861. Died in New York City.
Clark, William S., June 4, 1861.
Case, Charles, June 4, 1861; disch. at New York City, October 27, 1862.
Carney, Hurd, June 4, 1861.
Cooper, Archibald, June 4, 1861; died of chronic diarrhœa, at Canton, O., April 16, 1863.
Cassaday, John, June 4, 1861; transferred to Invalid Corps, Sept. 1, 1863.
Clucker, Charles, June 4, 1861; transferred at Harper's Ferry to U. S. Artillery, October 19, 1862.
Cory, Benjamin F., June 4, 1861; disch. at Columbus, O., Feb. 13, 1863.
Cribbs (or Gibbs), David K., June 4, 1861; wounded at Spottsylvania, May 12, 1864.
Callahan, Charles C., June 4, 1861; Corporal; Sergeant, May 1, 1863; transferred to 4th O. B., from which he was mustered out as Lieut. Colonel.
Darrah, Jefferson H., June 4, 1861; Sergeant, June 4, 1862; discharged at Camp Ohio, November 30, 1862.
Cook, Charles A. E., January 24, 1864; transf. to Fourth Ohio Battalion.
Devore, Jacob, June 4, 1861; died of chronic diarrhœa, at Patterson, O., December 6, 1862.
Devore, George V., June 4, 1861; wounded and missing at Wilderness, May 6, 1864. Probably dead.
Devore, Robert, October 4, 1861; discharged at Fort Gaines, January 9, 1863. Address, Patterson, O.
Dunson, Joseph, June 4, 1861; died of chronic diarrhœa on board Steamer Spaulding, August 18, 1862.
Davis, George, June 4, 1861; re-enlisted as Veteran; transferred to 4th Ohio Battalion.
Davis, Joseph, June 4, 1861; disch. at Frederick City, Md., Dec. 29, 1862.
Duncan, Thomas, June 4, 1861; discharged at Fort Gaines, Oct. 28, 1862.
Day, Franklin, June 4, 1861.
Deckleman, or Dickerman, Joseph L., June 4, 1861; 1st Sergeant, October 1, 1862. Address, Sandusky, Ohio.
Ferguson, Joseph A., June 4, 1861; discharged October 18, 1862, to enlist in United States Artillery.
Furney, David, June 4, 1861; discharged at Fort Gaines, January 19, 1863; died at Sandyville, Ohio, 1884.
Furney, John, October 12, 1861; disch. at New Market, Va., May 11, 1862.
Funk, Stephen, March 18, 1864; transferred to 4th Ohio Battalion.

Garbeson, Harvey, June 4, 1861; discharged at Washington, July 3, 1862. Address, Kenton, Ohio.

George, Edward, June 4, 1861; transferred to Invalid Corps.

Guiney, John C., October 12, 1861; discharged at Washington, July 3, 1862.

Herron, Charles, June 4, 1861; discharged at Fort Gaines, November 5, 1862. Address, Smithsonian, Washington, D. C.

Hamlin, William, June 4, 1861; wounded at Morton's Ford, Feb. 6, 1864.

Heater, Henry, June 4, 1861; wounded at Fredericksburg, Dec. 13, 1862; in left thigh at Cold Harbor, June 3, 1864. Trans. to 4th Ohio Battalion.

Herbert, Franklin, June 4, 1861; wounded at Fredericksburg, December 13, 1862; Corporal, December 12, 1861. In Kansas.

Hoyt, or Hoist, Conrad, June 4, 1861; disch. at Fort Gaines, Oct. 28, 1862.

Holloway, Joseph, June 4, 1861; Corporal, May 1, 1862; wounded at Gettysburg, July 3, 1863; at North Anna, May 23, 1863.

Hendershott, John W., June 4, 1861; re-enlisted January 24, 1864; transferred to 4th Ohio Battalion.

Helverson, Marshall, February 23, 1864; transferred to 4th Ohio Battalion.

Johnson, Reuben, June 4, 1861; wounded. Address, Dunkirk, Ohio.

Keyes, Elias, January 28, 1864; transferred to 4th Ohio Battalion.

Lewis, Alvi K., June 4, 1861; Sergeant, June 4, 1861; wounded at Spottsylvania, May 18, 1864; died of wounds, May 19, 1864.

Layton, Francis S., March 29, 1864; transferred to 4th Ohio Battalion.

Lewis, Orlando E., June 4, 1861; discharged March 9, 1863.

Lininger, Hiram, June 4, 1861; Corporal, June, 1861; died of typhoid fever, December 8, 1861, at Romney.

Lininger, Wilson, Sept. 17, 1861; dsich. at New Market, Va., May 11, 1862.

Kestler, Wesley, October 1, 1861; discharged at Philadelphia, May 31, 1863.

Myers, Joseph, June 4, 1861; died of chronic diarrhoea at Harper's Ferry, November 19, 1862

McKee, Byron, June 4, 1861; discharged October 18, 1862, to enlist in United States Artillery. Deceased.

McKee, Ossian, Corporal, May 1, 1863; wounded at Chancellorsville, May 4, 1863; transferred to Invalid Corps.

Maxwell, John, June 4, 1861; discharged at New Market, Va., May 3, 1862.

Musser, John M., June 4, 1861; Musician, March 2, 1862.

McCrary, Lafayette, June 4, 1861; Sergeant, September 10, 1861; discharged at Fort Gaines, September 19, 1862.

McCan, Madison, June 4, 1861; wounded at Fredericksburg, December 13, 1862; re-enlisted and transferred to 4th Ohio Battalion, and killed while carrying its colors at Petersburg.

McCan, Socrates, January 28, 1864; transferred to 4th Ohio Battalion.

McCan, Sylvester, October 6, 1861; Corporal May 1, 1863; discharged at Camp Dennison, Ohio, October 22, 1863. Address, Patterson, Ohio.

McFarland, Samuel, June 4, 1861; died of chronic diarrhoea, in New York City, September 21, 1862.

McKnight, John J., July 4, 1861; wounded at Harrison's Landing, Virginia, July 3, 1862; discharged at Detroit, Michigan, July 19, 1863.

Moore, Joseph F., June 4, 1861; trans. to U. S. Artillery, October 19, 1862.
Moore, Amos J., June 4, 1861; discharged November 20, 1862, to accept commission in 118th Ohio Volunteer Infantry.
McCartney, Martin, June 4, 1861; disch. at Columbus, O., January 20, 1863.
Mafus, Aaron W., June 4, 1861; wounded. Address, Fort Wayne, Indiana.
Michaels, George, Oct. 12, 1861; transferred to Co. B, February 20, 1862.
Neville, Jeremiah, June 4, 1861.
Ohler, Martin, June 4, 1861; discharged at New Market, Va., May 11, 1862.
Owens, George W., June 4, 1861; disch. at Columbus, Ohio, Oct. 20, 1862.
O'Neil, H., July 17, 1861; disch. Oct. 18, 1862, to enlist in 4th U. S. Artil.
Pracker, Gottleib, June 4, 1861; Regimental Bugler, died quite suddenly at Falmouth, Va., December, 18, 1862.
Pierson, Thomas H., June 4, 1861; address, Forest, Ohio.
Quinby, George W., June 4, 1861.
Ries, Henry, June 4, 1861; shot through the larynx and killed at Cold Harbor, June 3, 1864.
Ries, Christian, June 4, 1861. Address, Ada, Ohio.
Rose, John C., June 4, 1861; discharged at Columbus, O., January 24, 1863.
Ridgeway, Joseph, June 4, 1861; disch. at Harper's Ferry, Oct. 23, 1862.
Reeves, John H., June 4, 1861; Musician, then Brigade Bugler.
Render, James, June 4, 1861; wounded at Wilderness, May 6, 1864. Transferred to 4th Ohio Battalion.
Smalley, Henry, June 4, 1861; discharged at Camp Pendleton, October 27, 1861. In Kansas.
Stockton, Charles A., June 4, 1861; Corporal, October 4, 1862, Address, Little Rock, Arkansas.
Scott, Mark, June 4, 1861; died of chronic diarrhoea, at Frederick City, Maryland, November 26, 1862.
Switzer, Francis H., June 4, 1861; discharged at Fort Gaines, September 19, 1862. Address, Patterson, Ohio.
Stanley, George W., June 4, 1861; discharged at Fort Gaines, November 13, 1862. Deceased.
Snodgrass, David, June 4, 1861; Corporal; discharged February 20, 1862, to accept commission in 74th O. Volunteer Infantry. Address, Kenton, O.
Stout, Harrison, June 4, 1861; died September 28, 1862.
Simpson, Samuel N., June 4, 1861. Address, Van Wert, Ohio.
Shannon, Enos, June 4, 1861; wounded at Mine Run, November 28, 1863 discharged at Columbus, Ohio, January 9, 1864.
Snow, Beverly W., June 4, 1861; discharged to enlist in 4th United States Artillery, October 9, 1862.
Snow, Pembroke, June 4, 1861. Sergeant, May 1, 1863.
Sandford, Joseph F., February 4, 1864. Transferred to 4th Ohio Battalion.
Souls, Charles, February 20, 1864. Transferred to 4th Ohio Battalion.
Schriver, or Schriner, Adam D., June 4, 1861; discharged to enlist in 4th United States Artillery, October 9, 1862.
Swank, Daniel, June 4, 1861; died at Romney, Virginia, November 26, 1861, of erysipelas.

Switzer, William, June 4, 1861; transferred to 4th Ohio Battalion.
Stanley, Comfort, June 4, 1861; 1st Sergeant; discharged October 1, 1862, to accept promotion in 45th Ohio Volunteer Infantry. Killed in action.
Stout, John A., August 26, 1861; transferred to 4th Ohio Battalion.
Snyder, Samuel, October 26, 1861.
Swank, George W., October 12, 1861; discharged at Romney, Jan. 1, 1862.
Sprague, Thomas S., Oct. 12, 1861; transferred to Co. I, February 20, 1862.
Shaffer, Isaac, October 12, 1861; transferred to Co. B, February 20, 1862.
Shaffer, Morgan V., October 12, 1861; died of measles at Cumberland, Maryland, February 21, 1862.
Shaffer, Thomas H., October 12, 1861; transferred to Co. B, Feb. 20, 1862.
Steward, George W., December 25, 1863; transferred to 4th Ohio Battalion.
Warner, Calvin T., June 4, 1861.
Wenner, John W., June 4, 1861. Address, Forest, Ohio.
Wickhiser, Phillip H., June 4, 1861. Deceased.
Wright, John J., June 4, 1861; disch. Oct. 10, 1862. Ad., Belle Center, O.
White, Hugh, June 4, 1861; Corporal, May 1, 1861; Sergeant, May 1, 1863; wounded in the neck at Cold Harbor, June 3, 1864.
Weirick, Thomas J., June 4, 1861; disch. at Columbus, Ohio, April 27, 1863.
Wilson, Isaac E., June 4, 1861; wounded in the shoulder at Spottsylvania, May 12, 1864. Infirmary Director at Kenton, Ohio.
Wetzel, Jacob, October 12, 1861; transferred to Co. F, February 20, 1862.
Williams, John L., August 30, 1862; transferred to 4th Ohio Battalion.
White, Joseph, February 24, 1864; wounded at Spottsylvania, May 12, 1864.
Yarger, Franklin K., June 4, 1861; wounded at Cold Harbor, June 3, 1864. Address, Waynesburg, Stark county, Ohio.

―――:0:―――

## Company E.

McMillen, James, Captain, June 4, 1861; drowned at Alexandria, Virginia, in Potomac River, June 29, 1862.
Coates, Foster A., for a time Captain; resigned, October 5, 1862. Deceased.
Timmons, Daniel R., Captain, January 3, 1863.
Shultz, Jacob, 1st Lieutenant, June 4, 1861; resigned, June 24, 1862. Address, Wooster, Ohio.
Cutter, Henry, 2d Lieutenant, June 4, 1861; resigned, June 24, 1862.
Jeffries, Lemuel, 1st Lieutenant, September 30, 1862; discharged, June 14, 1863, and assigned to 20th Veteran Reserve Corps as 1st Lieutenant; Captain; mustered out, April 30, 1866. Address, Wooster, Ohio.
Carr, J. H., 1st Lieutenant of Co.; Aid-de-Camp to Colonel Carroll; discharged, November 3, 1863; Colonel 169th Ohio Volunteer Infantry. Address, Washington, D. C.
Spink, Reason B., 2d Lieutenant, June 4, 1861; 1st Lieutenant and transferre to Co. I; res. March 23, 1863. Died in 1882, and buried at Wooster, O.

Brighton, William, 2d Lieutenant; killed at Fredericksburg, Dec. 13, 1862.
Pettibone, Channing L., 1st Lieutenant; killed at Spottsylvania, May 12, 1864.
Dickerson, Theodore H., 1st Sergeant of Co. H; 2d Lieutenant; 1st Lieutenant. Address, Marion, Ohio.
Arnold, Hiram W., June 4, 1861; died at Fort Gaines, November 26, 1862.
Arnold, Levi, June 4, 1861. Address, Orrville, Ohio.
Andrett, Hiram, June 4, 1861; discharged, February 28, 1862.
Barrett, John F., June 4, 1861; Corporal; wounded at Romney, September 25, 1861; discharged, July 11, 1862. Address, Wooster, Ohio.
Brinkerhoof, Daniel O., June 4, 1861; Corporal; died of fever at Wooster, O., December 23, 1861.
Brighton, William, 1st Sergeant, June 4, 1861; 2d Lieutenant.
Brown, Hubbert, June 4, 1861; re-enlisted as Veteran; wounded in face at Cold Harbor, June 3, 1864; transferred to 4th Ohio Battalion.
Best, David, June 4, 1861; wounded at Wilderness, May 6, 1864.
Bordine, Joseph D., June 4, 1861; discharged, October 25, 1861.
Brant, Jacob C., June 4, 1861; died at Harper's Ferry, October 26, 1862.
Baumgardner, William H., June 4, 1861; discharged March 10, 1863. Address, Wooster, Ohio.
Bucher, Thomas W., June 4, 1861; discharged March 7, 1863.
Bucher, William H., June 4, 1861; Adjutant 176th Ohio Volunteer Infantry. Address, Cincinnati, Ohio.
Black, Daniel Y., June 4, 1861; Address, Wooster, Ohio.
Butler, Harmon, Aug. 28, 1862; killed at Chancellorsville, May 3, 1862
Beckley, Andrew, October 4, 1862; discharged, January 1, 1863. Deceased.
Bechtel, James W., Oct. 4, 1862; disch., Feb. 3, 1863. Ad., Peoria, Ills.
Bolus, Christian, Oct. 4, 1862; trans. to 4th Ohio Battalion. Ad., Wooster, O.
Bird, Sparks, October 8, 1862; wounded in the head at Spottsylvania, May 12, 1864; transferred to 4th Ohio Battalion. Address, Mohican, Ohio.
Cassiday, Benjamin F., August 22, 1862. Address, Wooster, Ohio.
Cassiday, David S., June 4, 1861; discharged in 1863. Deceased.
Cline, William, June 4, 1861; wounded at Romney, September 25, 1861; died February 11, 1863, at Fort Gaines, of smallpox.
Carr, Alexander A., June 4, 1861; disch. Dec. 17, 1862. Ad., Wooster, O.
Carr, Joseph H., June 4, 1861; Sergeant-Major, November 1, 1861; 2d Lieutenant, June 11, 1862.
Cook, Harvey, June 4, 1861; wounded in the shoulder at Wilderness, May 6, 1864.
Carl, John F., June 4, 1861; disch. to enlist in 4th U. S. Art., Oct. 18, 1862.
Cameron, William J., June 4, 1861; transferred to Vet. Res. Corps in 1863.
Chapman, Alfred B., June 4, 1861; transferred to Inv. Corps, Sept. 12, 1863.
Cline, George W., June 4, 1861; disch. Oct. 28, 1862. Ad., Canton, Ohio.
Carey, George W., June 4, 1861; discharged, April 18, 1862.
Coates, Samuel F., Aug. 30, 1862; trans. to Vet. Res. Corps, Sept. 12, 1863.
Caswell, Daniel, June 4, 1861; discharged in 1863.
Cline, George W., June 4, 1861; transferred to 4th U. S. Art., Oct. 18, 1862.

Dyarmon, Orlando, June 4, 1861; Corporal; transferred to Veteran Reserve Corps, October 2, 1863. Address, Defiance, Ohio.

Dunlin, Thomas B., June 4, 1861; prisoner at Front Royal; disch. in 1863.

Dice, Archibald, June 4, 1861; wounded at Fredericksburg, December 13, 1862, and Chancellorsville, May 6, 1863. Address, Wooster, Ohio.

Eberly, William, June 4, 1861; Corporal; prisoner at Mine Run. Address, Smithville, Ohio.

Everly, Evan, June 4, 1861; died at Newark, N. J., December 10, 1862.

Fishburn, Howard, June 4, 1861; Sergeant; killed at Po River, May 10, 1864. Had been in the Mexican War.

Fogleson, Corydon, June 4, 1861; Corporal; Sergeant; wounded at Spottsylvania, May 12, 1864. Deceased.

France, Marion E., June 4, 1861; disch., March 3, 1863. Deceased in 1884.

Flack, David, June 4, 1861; discharged, Oct. 20, 1862. Ad., Cleveland, O.

Fitch, John, June 4, 1861. Address, Millersburg, Ohio.

Francis, George, June 4, 1861; transferred to Vet. Res. Corps, July 28, 1863.

Fleck, William H., June 4, 1861; disch. Oct. 26, 1862. Ad., Ogden, Utah.

Grabill, Levi, June 4, 1861; Sergeant; discharged September 11, 1863.

Gray, Cyrus, June 4, 1861; discharged Oct. 2, 1862. Deceased.

Greenwood, Van B., June 4, 1861; Corporal; wounded at Wilderness, May 6, 1864. In Jasper county, Missouri.

Gruber, George, September 4, 1862; transferred to 4th Ohio Battalion.

Held, Harmon, June 4, 1861; Sergeant. Address, Chicago, Illinois.

Heffelfinger, Sylvester E., June 4, 1861; discharged October 18, 1862, to enlist in 4th United States Artillery.

Hankey, John B., June 4, 1861; transferred to Invalid Corps, July 28, 1863. Address, Bowling Green, Ohio.

Haun, Henry, June 4, 1861.

Holliday, William, June 4, 1861; Sergeant; killed at Spottsylvania, May 18, 1864.

Hanson, William H., June 4, 1861; Sergeant; discharged May 1, 1863. Address, Jeromeville, Ohio.

Hoke, John S., June 4, 1861; Corporal.

Hummer, Daniel, October 4, 1862; killed at Fredericksburg, Dec. 13, 1862.

Jeffries, Lemuel, June 4, 1861; Sergeant Major, October 16, 1862; 2d Lieutenant and Acting Adjutant.

Jahala, John, June 4, 1861; wounded at Chancellorsville, May 3, 1863; discharged September 21, 1863.

Johnson, John, June 4, 1861; wounded at Wilderness, May 6, 1864.

Kope, Aaron J., June 4, 1861; discharged October 18, 1862, to enlist in 4th United States Artillery. Address, Archibald, Ohio.

Kope, Jonas, June 4, 1861; wounded at Wilderness, May 6, 1864. Deceased.

Keen, Frank, June 4, 1861. Deceased

Klepper, John M., June 4, 1861; discharged, November 20, 1862.

Krug, John H., June 4, 1861; wounded at Chancellorsville, May 3, 1863. Address, Granville, Ohio.

Line, Charles M., June 4, 1861; wounded at Cold Harbor, June 3, 1864. Address, Rochester, Pa.

Lewis, Clifford A., June 4, 1861; dis. Dec. 5, 1862. Address, Wooster, O.

Lehman, Lewis S., June 4, 1861; discharged October 26, 1862.

Lapp, John, June 4, 1861; discharged October 26, 1862.

Lowry, Thomas, June 4, 1861; Corporal; wounded at Spottsylvania, May 12, 1864; re-enlisted as Veteran and transferred to Fourth Ohio Battalion.

McClure, Addison S., June 4, 1861; Sergeant Major; Captain in 16th O. V. I., September, 1861; member of Congress. Address, Wooster, O.

McClure, William H., Sergeant; wounded at Chancellorsville, May 3, 1863. Address, Wooster, Ohio.

McClure, Charles W., June 4, 1861; Corporal; Quartermaster Sergeant. Address, Wooster, Ohio.

McClarren, Joshua, June 4, 1861; Corporal and Sergeant; discharged January 23, 1863. Deceased.

Moffitt, James, June 4, 1861; wounded at Chancellorsville, May 3, 1863.

Miller, Frank, June 4, 1861; discharged to enlist in Fourth United States Artillery, October 18, 1862.

McKelvey, Edward A., June 4, 1861; wounded at Chancellorsville, May 3, 1863; discharged June, 1863.

McClaren, Harrison O., June 4, 1861. Address, Wooster, Ohio.

McClarren, Thomas M., June 4, 1861; wounded at Chancellorsville, May 3, 1863; at Wilderness, in the left leg, May 6, 1864; practicing physician at Wellington, O.; State Medical Examiner for Knights of Honor of Ohio; Medical Examiner for G. A. R. of Ohio.

Muchler, George, June 4, 1861; wounded in leg at Spottsylvania, May 12, 1864.

McElhenney, Robert, June 4, 1861; discharged February 16, 1863.

McCoy, Thomas, June 4, 1861; discharged February 14, 1863.

Musser, George, June 4, 1861; prisoner at Wilderness, May 6, 1864; taken to Andersonville; exchanged. Address, Kent, Ohio.

Myers, Daniel, October 4, 1862. Died at Cumberland, Md., June 24, 1862.

Myers, Patrick, October 4, 1861; wounded at Chancellorsville, May 3, 1863; prisoner at Mine Run, November 28, 1863, and died in Andersonville Prison, August, 1864.

Osburn, William, June 4, 1861. Address, Red Haw, Ashland Co., O.

Patterson, James H., June 4, 1861; discharged to enlist in Fourth United States Artillery, October 18, 1862. Deceased.

Patterson, George, June 4, 1861; discharged to enlist in Fourth United States Artillery, October 19, 1862.

Pollinger, Davis S., June 4, 1861. Address, South Pittsburg, Pa.

Powell, Anthony, June 4, 1861. Address, Kent, Ohio.

Rahm, Darvey E., June 4, 1861; prisoner at Cold Harbor, June 3, 1864; kept in Belle Isle and Andersonville until December, 1864. Ad., Wooster, O.

Rouch, George, June 4, 1861. Died September 13, 1861.

Smith, Matthew M., June 4, 1861; Corporal; prisoner at Chancellorsville, May 3, 1863; wounded at Wilderness, May 6, 1864. Address, Wooster, O.

Stewart, George W., June 4, 1861; re-enlisted as Veteran and transferred to Fourth Ohio Battalion.

Sowers, George, June 4, 1861.

Segner, Robert, June 4, 1861.

Segner, Peter, August 28, 1862; transferred to Fourth Ohio Battalion.

Sands, William H., June 4, 1861; discharged October, 1862.

Shreve, Hyampsell, June 4, 1861; transferred to Veteran Reserve Corps in 1863. Address, Nashville, Ohio.

Snyder, James, June 4, 1861. Address, Wooster, Ohio.

Smedley, Edward, June 4, 1861; transferred to Fourth United States Artillery, October 18, 1862.

Swearengen, James T., June 4, 1861; wounded in the hip at Spottsylvania, May 12, 1864. Address, Ashtabula county, Ohio.

Swickey, Henry, June 4, 1861; wounded at Wilderness, May 6, 1864. Is in the Regular Army.

Singer, William, June 4, 1861; wounded in the right thigh at Wilderness, May 6, 1864. In Illinois.

Shirk, Harrison C., June 4, 1861; discharged January 4, 1863; Captain in 169th O. V. I. Address, Allegheny City, Pa.

Smith, William F., October 8, 1862; wounded in the side at Wilderness, May 6, 1864. Address, Wooster, Ohio.

Tryon, Nathan, August 21, 1862; wounded in the leg at Spottsylvania, May 12, 1864; died of wounds.

Vannatta, Peter O., June 4, 1861. Deceased.

Wayne, John H., June 4, 1861; disch. May 3, 1862. Address, Wooster, O.

Warner, Thomas C., June 4, 1861; transferred to Company C. Address, Chattanooga, Tenn.

Warner, Samuel J., June 4, 1861; prisoner at Front Royal, Va.; discharged in 1863. Address, West Salem, Ohio.

Walduck, John, June 4, 1861. Died at Frederick City, Md., Nov. 26, 1862.

Winans, Henry H., October 4, 1861; transferred to Fourth Ohio Battalion.

———:o:———

## Company F.

Wallace, James, Captain, April 21, 1861; June 4, 1861; wounded at Fredericksburg, December 13, 1862; died of wounds, in hospital at Georgetown, D. C., January 4, 1863.

Brearley, Samuel L., Sergeant, April 21, 1861; Second Lieutenant, June 4, 1861; First Lieutenant, September 12, 1862; Captain, February 10, 1863; wounded, May 26, 1864, at Po River. Address, Minneapolis, Minn.

Laird, George F., Second Lieut., April 21, 1861; First Lieut., June 4, 1861; Captain, June 29, 1862, and assigned to Co. K. Address, Canton, O.

Lester, George S., Corporal, April 21, 1861; Sergeant, June 4, 1861; Second Lieutenant, January 9, 1862; First Lieutenant, June 30, 1862; Aid de Camp to General Mason, January 14, 1863; declined promotion to Captain. Died, at Painesville, O., April 20, 1864.

Wallace, William, Sergeant, April 21, 1861; First Sergeant, June 4, 1861; Second Lieut., June 21, 1862; First Lieut., November 6, 1862; Adjutant, November 6, 1862; declined promotion to Captain. Ad., Omaha, Neb.

Spalter, Frank J., Second Lieutenant, January 17, 1862; First Lieutenant Company D, July 27, 1863; Major, then Lieutenant Colonel, of Fourth Ohio Battalion; killed at Petersburg, Va., September, 1864.

Alexander, Edward W., June 5, 1861; wounded at Wilderness, May 6, 1864.

Austin, Jacob, June 5, 1861; wounded at Mine Run, November 21, 1863; at Morton's Ford, February 6, 1864; at Po River, May 10, 1864.

Balmot, Edward, June 5, 1861; discharged at Columbus, O., July 1, 1862.

Balmot, Joseph P., June 5, 1861; discharged at Washington, April 17, 1863.

Barber, Preston, June 5, 1861. Address, Akron, Ohio.

Bour, Joseph A., June 3, 1861; wounded at Chancellorsville, May 3, 1863; transferred to Invalid Corps, November 15, 1863.

Barth, George, August 19, 1862; wounded at Chancellorsville, May 3, 1863; arm amputated at shoulder; discharged at Washington, June 20, 1863. Address, Canton, Ohio.

Bowland, Joseph, March 31, 1862; disch. at Columbus, O., January 4, 1863.

Brownell, Jasper, June 3, 1861; died at Frederick City, Md., Dec. 24, 1862.

Buch, Aaron, June 3, 1861.

Bruce, William H., June 3, 1861; wounded at Chancellorsville, May 3, 1863. Address, Canal Fulton, Ohio.

Cable, Jonathan, June 3, 1861; appointed Wagoner.

Cock, Thaddeus K., June 5, 1861; Sergeant, June 5, 1861; discharged to accept promotion in 51st U. S. Colored; captured February 14, 1864; tied to a tree, tantalized, cursed and shot by Confederates, because he dared to be a commander of colored troops.

Cock, George B., June 5, 1861; discharged February 16, 1863, at Columbus, O.; Major 5th U. S. Colored. Address, Canton, Ohio.

Cassidy, Edward, June 3, 1861; discharged at Columbus, O., October 17, 1862. Address, Canal Fulton, Ohio.

Criss, Albert J., June 3, 1861; discharged at Romney, Va., January 2, 1862.

Clark, John, June 5, 1861; Musician, Jan. 5, 1861; disch. Dec. 13, 1862.

Darr, Isaiah G., June 3, 1861; Corporal, September 22, 1862; wounded at Wilderness, May 6, 1863.

Dearing, George W., June 5, 1861; discharged at Harper's Ferry, October 18, 1862; in Fourth United States Artillery.

Deckman, Conrad, June 5, 1861; transferred to Invalid Corps, Jan. 5, 1864.

Deckman, William, June 5, 1861; discharged at Harper's Ferry, October 18, 1862; in Fourth United States Artillery.

Deweese, Eli, June 5, 1861; discharged at Harper's Ferry, October 18, 1862. in Fourth United States Artillery.

Deweese, Isaac B., August 18, 1862; transferred to Fourth Ohio Battalion. Address, Canton, Ohio.

Douds, Wellington, June 5, 1861; Musician, March 4, 1864.

Eaby, Byron, June 5, 1861; died at Fortress Monroe, Va., September 4, 1862.

Ensign, Lyman S., June 5, 1861; Corporal, March 11, 1862; wounded at Gettysburg, July 3, 1863; in the left shoulder, at Cold Harbor, June 3, 1864. Address, Canton, Ohio.

Estep, Edwin, June 5, 1861; wounded at Chancellorsville, May 3, 1863; transferred to Invalid Corps. Address, Akron, Ohio.

Ferguson, William, June 5, 1861; Corporal, January 1, 1862; Sergeant, October 1, 1863; wounded at Romney, October 26, 1861. Ad., Canton, O.

Flickinger, June 5, 1861; Corporal, December 16, 1861; discharged September 4, 1862. Address, Minerva, Ohio.

Flora, Frank, June 3, 1861; discharged at Washington, October 28, 1862.

Flora, Jacob, June 3, 1861; discharged at Beverly, Va., July 21, 1861.

Foehl, Michael, June 5, 1861; appointed teamster.

Fournace, Abraham, August 16, 1862; wounded in the arm and leg, at Chancellorsville, May 3, 1863; transferred to 4th O. B. Address, Canton, O.

Fogle, John, June 3, 1861; disch. at Camp Pendleton, Md., October 19, 1861.

Fogle, Henry, October 18, 1861; detailed as Clerk to Surgeon; discharged, December 7, 1862, at Washington. Address, Canton, Ohio.

Garman, Jeremiah J., June 5, 1861; re-enlisted as Veteran, February 25, 1864; transferred to Fourth Ohio Battalion. Address, Greensburg, O.

Garman, Harrison, June 5, 1861; discharged, at Washington, January 8, 1863. Address, Akron, Ohio.

Gotshall, Daniel H., June 5, 1861; disch., at Columbus, O., January 3, 1863.

Goodwill, Bradley C., June 5, 1861; wounded, May 6, 1863. Ad., Canton, O.

Goodwill, Lewis F., Oct. 16, 1861; disch., at Columbus, O., Dec. 7, 1862.

Granville, Charles H., June 5, 1861; left regiment at Romney, Nov. 10, 1861.

Greek, Benjamin F., June 5, 1861; disch., at Huttonville, Va., July 15, 1861.

Haas, Marshall E., June 5, 1861; Corporal, June 5, 1861; Sergeant, October 15, 1862; Sergeant Major, September 1, 1863; wounded, at Morton's Ford, Va., February 6, 1864. Died at Canton, O., July 26, 1876.

Hafer, John, June 5, 1861; wounded at Chancellorsville, May 3, 1863; at Prospect Hill, Va., June 4, 1864. Address, Akron, Ohio.

Hane, Lenions D., June 5, 1861; Corporal, June 5, 1861; Sergeant, January 1, 1862; First Sergeant, October 13, 1862; missing at battle of Fredericksburg, December 13, 1862.

Hays, Joseph, June 3, 1861; wounded at Chancellorsville, May 3, 1863; discharged February 18, 1864. Address, Akron, Ohio.

Hershey, William, June 5, 1861; wounded at Morton's Ford, February 6, 1864; in left foot, at Spottsylvania, May 18, 1864. Address, Canton, O.

Hilbert, Frank F., June 5, 1861; disch., October 28, 1862, at Washington.

Hane, Fernando B., October 18, 1861; wounded at Fredericksburg, December 13, 1862; at Chancellorsville, May 3, 1863. Address, Bryan, O.

Hibshman, Oliver S., June 5, 1861; Corporal, October 1, 1861; prisoner at Spottsylvania, May 12, 1864; died on Fair Grounds, in Charleston, S. C., a rebel prison, in the arms of Comrade H. J. Shook, of Co. K.

Hostetter, Joseph, June 5, 1861; Corporal, December 16, 1861; Sergeant, October 1, 1863. Address, Orrville, Ohio.

Johnson, James, June 5, 1861; killed at Chancellorsville, May 3, 1863.

Krug, Benaniah, June 5, 1861; discharged at Washington, October 28, 1862.

Kingsworth, William, June 5, 1861; discharged at Harper's Ferry; in Fourth United States Artillery. Address, Canton, Ohio.

Koontz, Jefferson, June 5, 1861; discharged at Columbus, O., November 14, 1862. Address, Canton, Ohio.

Kunneman, Benedict, June 5, 1861. Address, Mansfield, Ohio.

Kauffman, Samuel, October 16, 1861; wounded at Chancellorsville, May 3, 1863; transferred to Veteran Reserve Corps. Address, Canton, O.

Lester, George F., June 5, 1861; Sergt., June 5, 1861; 2d Lieut., Jan. 9, 1862.

Lahm, Marshall, June 5, 1861; discharged at Harper's Ferry, October 18, 1862. Died on the cars on his way home.

Leiter, Charles, June 5, 1861; discharged, January 28, 1861, at Patterson Creek, to accept promotion in 61st O. V. I. Address, Monroeville, Ind.

Laird, William, June 5, 1861; wounded at Chancellorsville, May 3, 1863; First Lieutenant in 186th O. V. I. Address, Canton, Ohio.

Lemmon, Samuel R., June 5, 1861; discharged at Columbus, O., February 28, 1863. Address, Canton, Ohio.

Little, David R. P., June 5, 1861; disch. at Camp Dennison, May 20, 1862.

McAbee, Newton S., June 5, 1861; Corporal, June 5, 1861; discharged, June, 1861, to accept promotion in 11th O. V. I. Address, Cleveland, O.

Meyer, Edward S., June 5, 1861; Sergeant, June 5, 1861; discharged, September 6, 1861, to accept promotion in 32d O. V. I.; Captain in 107th O. V. I., November 11, 1862; Major, November 3, 1864; Colonel Fifth Regiment of First Army Corps; Brevet Brigadier General, March 13, 1865. Address, Cleveland, Ohio.

Meyer, Marcus T., June 5, 1861; discharged, September 6, 1861, to accept promotion in 32d O. V. I. Address, Canton, Ohio.

Meredith, Isaac, June 5, 1861; wounded at Romney, and lost an arm, October 26, 1861; discharged at Patterson Creek, January 20, 1862.

McCauley, John K., June 5, 1861; wounded at Cold Harbor, June 3, 1864. Address, Canton, Ohio.

Miller, Joseph, June 5, 1861; killed at Wilderness, May 6, 1864.

Miller, William, June 3, 1861; re-enlisted as Veteran, January 3, 1864; killed at Spottsylvania, May 12, 1864.

Miller, Samuel, June 3, 1861; discharged at Washington, March 26, 1863.

Morton, William G., June 3, 1861; wounded at Robinson's Tavern, November 28, 1862.

Nixon, George L., June 3, 1861; transferred to Invalid Corps, September 20, 1863. Address, Bolivar, Ohio.

Ogden, Samuel, October 18, 1861; discharged at Columbus, O., July 3, 1862.

Oldfield, Charles T., June 3, 1861; Corporal, January 1, 1862; wounded at Chancellorsville, May 3, 1863; transferred to Invalid Corps; First Lieutenant 186th O. V. I. Address, Canton, Ohio.

Penny, Calvin T., June 5, 1861; left regiment at Romney, Nov. 10, 1861.

Peters, Jacob, June 3, 1861; discharged at Columbus, O., October 28, 1862.
Raynolds, James Frank, June 5, 1861; discharged June 10, 1862. Address, Cameron, Missouri.
Raynolds, Jefferson, September 9, 1861; discharged, February 24, 1864, to enlist in United States Army. Address, Las Vegas, New Mexico.
Raynolds, William T., Corporal, June 5, 1861; discharged, January 2, 1862, to accept promotion in Sixth Ohio Cavalry. Address, Las Vegas, N. M.
Reeves, William S., June 5, 1861; died at Harrison's Landing, July 16, 1862.
Rich, John, June 3, 1861; killed at Chancellorsville, May 3, 1863.
Ricksecker, John M., June 5, 1861; Corporal, March 5, 1862; wounded at Chancellorsville, May 3, 1863; at Morton's Ford, February 6, 1864; at Wilderness, in right arm, May 6, 1864.
Russell, William, June 3, 1861; disch., at Trenton, N. J., March 25, 1863.
Rank, John, August 27, 1862; transferred to 4th O. B. Address, Canton, O.
Spalter, Frank J., June 5, 1861; Clerk at Brigadier Headquarters; Second Lieutenant, December 31, 1862.
Sell, Franklin, June 5, 1861; wounded at Fredericksburg, December 13, 1862; died of wounds, December 28, 1862, at Lincoln Hospital.
Sines, James S., June 3, 1861; wounded at Romney, October 26, 1861; discharged at Columbus, O., September 26, 1862.
Senders, Junius G., June 5, 1861; Corporal, June 6, 1861; Sergeant, January 1, 1863; First Sergeant, January 1, 1863.
Shorb, William M., June 5, 1861; Corporal; Sergeant, March 5, 1862; wounded in the head at Wilderness, May 6, 1864. Address, Canton, O.
Steel, Jabez C., June 5, 1861; Corporal, December 16, 1861; transferred to Invalid Corps, September 1, 1863.
Scanlan, Thomas, June 5, 1861; died at Potomac Creek Hospital, May 18, 1863, of wounds received at Chancellorsville, May 3, 1863.
Sheppard, Louis, June 5, 1861; Corporal.
Shively, Seraphim, June 5, 1861; Sergeant and First Sergeant, October 1, 1862; discharged October 13, 1862. Address, Canton, Ohio.
Shroyer, Leonard, June 3, 1861; died at Alexandria, Va., October 2, 1862.
Snellbaker, Joseph, June 3, 1861. Address, Sandyville Ohio.
Stands, Levi H., June 3, 1861; wounded at Morton's Ford, February 6, 1864. Address, Canton, Ohio.
Stands, John B., June 3, 1861. Address, Canton, Ohio.
Strong, Charles R., Bugler; discharged at Fortress Monroe, September 3, 1862. Address, Lagonda, Ohio.
Swift, George, June 3, 1861.
Sylvester, Stephen P., June 5, 1861; wounded at Fredericksburg, December 13, 1862; transferred to Invalid Corps, July 1, 1863.
Sexhauer, Gotleib, October 18, 1861; killed at Chancellorsville, May 3, 1863.
Simmerman, Elza, March 24, 1862; transferred to V. R. C., March 2, 1864.
Simmerman, Erastus, March 4, 1862; disch. at Washington, Nov. 14, 1862.
Snyder, Peter L., August 18, 1862; wounded in the hip, at Po River, May 10, 1864; transferred to Fourth Ohio Battalion. Address, Louisville, O.
Seigle, Andrew, August 19, 1862; transferred to Fourth Ohio Battalion.

Squires, Jacob, August 27, 1862; transferred to Fourth Ohio Battalion.

Squires, Washington, August 27, 1862; transferred to Fourth Ohio Battalion. Address, Massillon, Ohio.

Thomas, Henry W., June 3, 1861. Address, Canton, Ohio.

Thurin, Julius, June 5, 1861; wounded in the hip, at Spottsylvania, May 12, 1864. Address, Louisville, Ohio.

Trownsell, James, June 5, 1861; Corporal, June 5, 1861; Sergeant, October 1, 1862; wounded at Chancellorsville, May 3, 1863; wounded and taken prisoner at Wilderness, May 6, 1864. Address, Tuscola, Illinois.

Wallace, William, First Sergt., June 5, 1861; Second Lieut., October 1, 1862.

Wernet, Adolphus A., June 5, 1861.

Wise, Andrew M., June 3, 1861; disch., November 14, 1861, at Romney.

Wetzel, Jacob, October 12, 1861; wounded at Chancellorsville, May 3, 1863; transferred to Fourth Ohio Battalion. Address, Carrollton, Ohio.

Yaley, Henry C. F., June 5, 1861.

Yaley, Christian E., August 28, 1862; wounded at Cold Harbor, June 3, 1864; transferred to Fourth Ohio Battalion.

Yost, Charles, June 3, 1861; wounded at Chancellorsville, May 3, 1863; transferred to Invalid Corps. Address, Akron, Ohio.

Youngblood, Andrew, June 5, 1861; discharged at Camp Pendleton, Maryland, October 17, 1861. Address, Canton, Ohio.

———:o:———

## Company G.

Robinson, James S., Captain, April 19, 1861; October 26, 1861; Major 82d Ohio Volunteer Infantry; Lieutenant Colonel, April, 1862; Colonel, August 29, 1862; Brigadier General, January 12, 1865; Brevet Major-General, March 13, 1865; member of Congress; Secretary of State of Ohio, 1885. Address, Columbus, or Kenton, Ohio.

Grubb, Peter, 1st Lieutenant, June 4, 1864; Captain, January 9, 1862; Major, August 29, 1863; wounded at Gettysburg, July 2, 1863; at Chancellorsville, May 3, 1863. Deceased; buried at Tiffin, Ohio.

Sergeson, William S., 2d Lieutenant, June 4, 1861; resigned November 7, 1862. Died in hospital near Cincinnati.

Larkins, Isaiah, 1st Sergeant; 2d Lieutenant, January 9, 1862; discharged for disability, October 31, 1862. Address, McPherson, Kansas.

Edgar, Addison H., 2d Sergeant; 2d Lieutenant, June 15, 1863; wounded at Chancellorsville, May 3, 1863; killed at Gettysburg, July 2, 1863. Before he fell he requested comrades to return to his parents his watch and sword, and assure them that he had been true to his trust.

Williams, William W., Sergeant, October 1, 1862; 2d Lieutenant, July 20, 1863. Deceased.

Jeffries, Lemuel L., 2d Lieutenant from Co. E, December 20, 1861; transferred to Co. D, January 9, 1862.

Dickerson, T. H., 1st Lieutenant of Company, January 5, 1863.
Camp, William M., 1st Lieutenant of Company, May 26, 1863.
Andric, Jacob, June 6, 1861; discharged October 22, 1862, to enlist in United States Artillery. Died in Andersonville prison.
Albert, Martin, June 3, 1861; wounded at Chancellorsville, May 3, 1863.
Arbogast, George W., June 3, 1861; taken prisoner at Spottsylvania, May 12, 1864. Address, Round Head, Ohio.
Bechtold, Henry, June 6, 1861; Sergeant; transferred to Invalid Corps, November 1, 1863. Address, Rochester, N. Y.
Bingham, William H., June 6, 1861; died of chronic diarrhoea, at Stevensburg, Virginia, April 20, 1864.
Busby, Paul, June 6, 1861. Killed near Lima, Ohio, on railroad, in 1872.
Bales, John A., June 6, 1861; Corporal, July 4, 1861; discharged at Frederick, Maryland, January 10, 1863. Address, Kenton, Ohio.
Bain, William, June 6, 1861; killed at Gettysburg, July 2, 1863.
Bain, Finley, October 6, 1861, wounded, July 2, 1863, at Gettysburg; wounded in side, May 10, 1864, at Po River; transferred to 4th Ohio Battalion. Deceased.
Beach, Jerome L., June 6, 1861; disch. at Williamsport, Md., June 2, 1862.
Bowman, Jacob W., June 6, 1861; discharged, October 22, 1862, to enlist in Regular Army.
Beck, Frederick, June 6, 1861; wounded at Romney, September 25, 1861; at Fredericksburg, December 13, 1862; transferred to Invalid Corps, July 1, 1863. Deceased.
Birch, Thomas, June 6, 1861; died of chronic diarrhoea, at Bolivar Heights, November 26, 1862.
Black, Samuel, June 3, 1861; wounded at Romney, October 26, 1861. Died at Camp Chase, Ohio, March 13, 1863.
Brant, Thomas F., June 12, 1861; killed at Fredericksburg, Dec. 13, 1862.
Born, John U., June 3, 1861; wounded in the hip at Cold Harbor, June 3, 1864. Address, Kenton, Ohio.
Collier, Charles, June 6, 1861; wounded at Chancellorsville, May 3, 1863 (which place, with family, he visited in 1884); discharged at Washington, March 31, 1863. Address, Kenton, Ohio.
Collins, Samuel M., June 6, 1861; wounded at Cold Harbor, June 3, 1864. Practicing physician at Sidney, Ohio.
Collins, David W., June 12, 1861; killed, July 2, 1863, at Gettysburg.
Campbell, Charles, June 3, 1861.
Campbell, William D., June 3, 1861. Address, Round Head, Ohio.
Campbell, Patrick H., June 3, 1861.
Campbell, Daniel H., June 3, 1861. Dropped from the rolls, Feb. 5, 1862.
Colckglazer, Zurah S., June 3, 1861; discharged at Falmouth, February 11, 1863. Deceased.
Clary, James, June 13, 1861; transferred to 4th Ohio Battalion; prisoner at Gettysburg, July 2, 1863.
Cutting, James R., Jne 6, 1861; Sergeant, July 4, 1861; discharged at Newark, N. J., October 27, 1862.

Carson, Thomas J., October 6, 1861; wounded at Chancellorsville, May 3, 1863; transferred to 4th Ohio Battalion. Deceased.

Carson, James J., October 6, 1861; discharged June 2, 1862, at Williamsburg, Pa. Address, Eagle Post Office, Ohio.

Daniels, William M., July 26, 1861; Corporal; discharged, October 22, 1862; enlisted in U. S. Artillery; killed at Chancellorsville.

Davis, Asa O., December 3, 1861; killed July 2, 1862, at Gettysburg.

Daniels, Jacob, June 6, 1861; discharged at Moore's Farm, Va., May 3, 1863. Address, Kenton, Ohio.

Davis, Samuel H., June 6, 1861; transferred to Regimental Band, June 8, 1861; died at Kenton, Ohio, September 14, 1861.

Donaldson, James W., June 6, 1861; or August 17, 1861; wounded in finger, May 10, 1864, at Po River; transferred to 4th Ohio Battalion.

Edgar, Addison H., June 6, 1861; 2d Sergeant; 2d Lieut., June 15, 1863.

Elsessor, George, June 6, 1861; discharged at Romney, Va., November 13, 1861. Address, Kenton, Ohio.

Enright, Thomas, June 6, 1861; wounded in the side at Spottsylvania, May 12, 1864; killed on railroad at Lima, Ohio, in 1882.

Edgar, William D., June 6, 1861; Corporal, July 4, 1861; wounded in right arm at Chancellorsville, May 3, 1863; transferred to Invalid Corps, September 30, 1863. Address, Dunkirk, Ohio.

Edgar, Daniel, Musician; trans. to 4th O. Battalion. Address, Dunkirk, O.

Gordon, Thomas, June 6, 1861.

Gaskill, Hayes, June 6, 1861; discharged October 22, 1862, at Harper's Ferry to enlist in 4th United States Artillery.

Gilmore, Reason, June 6, 1861; died about the year 1868.

Griner, Charles, June 6, 1861; injured by the falling of a tree at Fort Pendleton, Md.; wounded at Fredericksburg, December 13, 1862. Address, Beaver Falls, Pennsylvania.

Griner, Daniel, June 4, 1861; wounded at Fredericksburg, December 13, 1862, in the side; Corporal, July 1, 1863. Address, Ada, Ohio.

Herman, Michael, June 6, 1861; wounded at Gettysburg, July 2, 1862; transferred to Invalid Corps.

Hatch, William B., June, 1861; re-enlisted as a Veteran; transferred to 4th Ohio Battalion. Address, Kenton, Ohio.

Hinebaugh, Shew, June 6, 1861; discharged at Romney, Va., November 30, 1861. Address, Dunkirk, Ohio.

Hufnagle, Lewis, June 6, 1861. Address, Huntington, Indiana.

Hahner, Frederick, June 6, 1861; killed at Chancellorsville, May 3, 1863.

Herbst, William, June 6, 1861. Address, Belle Center, Ohio.

Hagerman, Dayton O., June 6, 1861; Corporal; discharged at Harper's Ferry, October 26, 1862.

Holmes, Jacob A., June 6, 1861; 4th Sergeant; discharged at Moore's Farm, Va., May 11, 1863. Address, Kenton, Ohio.

Jones, Graham, June 6, 1861; discharged at Newark, N. J., December 30, 1862, on account of wounds received at Fredericksburg, Dec. 13, 1862.

Jameson, Alfred W., June 6, 1861; lost a leg at Fredericksburg, December 13, 1862; discharged at Columbus, Ohio, December 24, 1863, after having leg amputated the second time.

Johnson, Jacob, August 17, 1861; disch. at New Market, Va., May 11, 1862.

Jeffers, George W., June 6, 1861; 3d Corporal; discharged at Frederick, Md., January 15, 1863. Address, Malone, Mich.

Keifer, Henry W., June 6, 1861; discharged at Washington, Dec. 2, 1862.

Larkins, Isaiah, 1st Sergeant, June 6, 1861; 2d Lieutenant, January 9, 1862.

Longworth, Martin V. B., June 6, 1861; Corporal; Sergeant, July 4, 1861; 1st Sergeant, September 1, 1863; wounded in the hand at Gettysburg, July 2, 1863, when in command of two companies of skirmishers after commissioned officers had been killed. Address, Bucyrus, Ohio.

Lehn, John P., June 6, 1861; Corporal; discharged at Cumberland, Maryland, September 2, 1861.

Leslie, William, June 6, 1861; re-enlisted as Veteran, and transferred to 4th Ohio Battalion. Address, Dunkirk, Ohio.

Leslie, Eli M., June 6, 1861; killed on railroad near Van Wert, O., in 1866.

Martin, George H., June 6, 1861; killed at Gettysburg, July 2, 1863.

McGinnis, Franklin, June 6, 1861. Address, Forest, Ohio.

Myers, Andrew, June 6, 1861; killed at Gettysburg, July 2, 1863.

Myers, John F., June 6, 1861; discharged at Fortress Monroe, Virginia, February 7, 1863. Address, McCutchenville, Ohio.

Morrison, Joseph F., June 6, 1861; died of chronic diarrhoea, at Pittsburg, Pa., November 5, 1862.

Morrison, John W. H., June 6, 1861; discharged at Falmouth, Va., January 26, 1863. Pastor M. E. Church, Central Ohio Conference.

Morrison, Thomas D., October 16, 1861; Corporal, July 1, 1863; transferred to 4th Ohio Battalion; lost in action soon after battle of Cold Harbor, June 3, 1864.

Morrow, William H., August 17, 1861; taken prisoner near Chickahominy; wounded in arm at Chancellorsville, May 3, 1863; arm amputated; discharged at Camp Dennison, Ohio; had six months experience on Belle Isle, at Richmond, where the sand was alive with fleas. Address, Dunkirk, Ohio.

Miller, Thomas I., September 14, 1861; left the regiment near Harper's Ferry, October 5, 1863, and enlisted in a Pennsylvania regiment.

Marquis, Samuel, August 17, 1801; discharged at Columbus, Ohio, January 8, 1862. Address, Dunkirk, Ohio.

Marquis, Hiram, June 6, 1861; died of chronic diarrhoea at Allegheny, Pa., November 13, 1862; buried at Dunkirk, Ohio.

McArthur, John, June 6, 1861; Corporal, July 1, 1863; not heard from since Wilderness, May 6, 1864.

Murphey, Allen, June 6, 1861. Address, Belle Center, Ohio.

McCoy, Thomas, June 6, 1861; killed at Chancellorsville, May 3, 1863.

Moore, Andrew M., June 6, 1861; taken prisoner at Port Republic, Va.; died of typhoid fever at Fort Delaware, October 25, 1862.

McTuttle, William, June 6, 1861.

Musgrave, Oscar E., June 12, 1861; transferred to Invalid Corps, July 1, 1863.

McCollum, James, October 16, 1861; transferred to 4th Ohio Battalion; Drummer. Address, Williamstown, Ohio.

Noel, William, June 6, 1861; wounded at Romney, September 25, 1861; discharged, October 22, 1862, to enlist in United States Artillery.

Nichols, John, M., June 6, 1861; discharged at Romney, November 30, 1863.

Newcomb, Arthur D., June 4, 1861; discharged at Romney, Nov. 30, 1861.

Nagle, Henry H., June 3, 1861; discharged at Harper's Ferry, October 26, 1862; Corporal; died soon after discharge.

Pfeiffer, Henry, June 6, 1861; wounded at Gettysburg, July 2, 1863. Deceased.

Philbrick, Jonathan S., June 6, 1861; wounded at Fredericksburg, December 13, 1862; transferred to Brigade Band, May 5, 1863. Address, Lincoln, Placer county, California.

Porterfield, William D., June 6, 1861; discharged January 9, 1862, to accept promotion in 82d Ohio Volunteer Infantry. Address, Omaha, Nebraska.

Ritzler, Joseph, June 6, 1861; died of typhoid fever, at Cumberland, Maryland, December 6, 1861; buried at Kenton, Ohio.

Ritzler, Nicholas D., Oct. 6, 1861; disch. at Newark, N. J., Oct. 23, 1862.

Rice, Asher, June 6, 1861; discharged at Williamsburg, Maryland, June 2, 1862. Died soon after.

Rice, John S., June 6, 1861; Sergeant, September 1, 1863; wounded at Wilderness, May 6, 1864; was prisoner at Andersonville and Salisbury until close of the war. (See his account.) Ad., Silver Creek, Hardin co., O.

Shuee, Edward F., June 6, 1861; Sergeant, August 3, 1863; wounded at Mine Run, November 28, 1863. Killed in arresting burglar, while acting as Marshal, in Dunkirk, Ohio, in 1881.

Sherman, Jacob, June 6, 1861; Corporal, July 1, 1863. Ad., Kenton, Ohio.

Sorgen, Edward, June 6, 1861; prisoner at Gettysburg, July 2, 1863; on Belle Isle seven months; Andersonville thirteen months; on steamer Sultana at time of her explosion. Address, Kenton, Ohio.

Schinderwoelf, William, June 6, 1861; wounded at Gettysburg, July 2, 1863. Address, Kenton, Ohio.

Shaffer, Richard, June 6, 1861; discharged at Harper's Ferry, October 22, 1862, to enlist in 4th United States Artillery. Lost his life at Chicago during the great fire.

Simons, Henry M., June 6, 1861; discharged at Washington, October 16, 1862; died October 12, 1862, at Fairfax Seminary, four days before his discharge papers were signed.

Stampfle, Jacob, June 6, 1861; transferred to Invalid Corps, November 20, 1863. Address, Grafton, West Virginia.

Skates, George, August 16, 1861; died near Kenton, Ohio, January 27, 1863.

Smith, Charles A., February 1, 1864; transferred to 4th Ohio Battalion.

Williams, William W., June 6, 1861; Sergeant; 2d Lieutenant, July 20, 1863.

Wren, Thomas, June 6, 1861; Corporal, October 1, 1862; wounded at Fredericksburg, December 13, 1862; transferred to Invalid Corps.

Wilcox, Bailey, June 6, 1861; discharged at Moore's Farm, Va., May 3, 1862.

Weis, Samuel, June 6, 1861; discharged at Washington, December 5, 1862. Buried at Kenton, Ohio.

Walker, James W., June 6, 1861; died at Romney, November 27, 1861.

Woods, John, June 6, 1861; discharged at Washington, December 24, 1862. Address, Dunkirk, Ohio.

Woods, Enos H., October 16, 1861; disch. Dec. 5, 1862. Ad., Dunkirk, O.

Winsett, Alfred, June 6, 1861; died at Philadelphia, October 4, 1862, of chronic diarrhoea.

Wilcox, George W., June 3, 1861; discharged, January 2, 1864, on account of wounds received at Gettysburg, July 2, 1863. Ad., Round Head, Ohio.

Wallis, William, Oct. 17, 1861; teamster; trans. to 4th Ohio Bat. Deceased.

Williams, John W. F., June 3, 1861; Sergeant, July 1, 1863; wounded in the hand at Spottsylvania, May 12, 1864. Address, Washington, D. C.

Zahner, Jesse, October 6, 1861; died at Georgetown, Md., Sept. 17, 1862.

―――:o:―――

## Company H.

Olmstead, Edwin B., Captain, April 27, 1861; June 5, 1861, in command of Pioneer Corps, in Shenandoah Valley; Chief Engineer in the construction of Fort Pendleton, Maryland; resigned October 17, 1862; Editor of Arcade *Leader*, and Pastor of Baptist Church, Arcade, N. Y.

Stroub, William S., Second Lieutenant, April 27, 1861; First Lieutenant, June 5, 1861; Captain, December 26, 1862. Deceased.

Pritchard, John R., Second Lieutenant, April 27, 1861; June 5, 1861; First Lieutenant, December 26, 1862; Captain, May 23, 1863; wounded at Fredericksburg, December 13, 1862. Address, Galion, Ohio.

Dickerson, Theodore H., May 24, 1861; First Sergeant; Second Lieutenant, September 12, 1862; First Lieutenant, December 26, 1862, and transferred to Company G. Address, Marion, Ohio.

Hill, George O., Second Lieutenant, February 18, 1863; First Lieutenant, and transferred to Company I, May 26, 1863.

Evans, John G., Second Lieutenant, April 28, 1863.

Anderson, Andrew M., 1st Lt., July 28, 1863; transf. to Co. C, Nov. 9, 1863.

Brophy, George, First Lieutenant, November 9, 1863.

Alexander, John, May 24, 1861.

Ankey, Joseph, October 7, 1861; died at Marion, Ohio, December 23, 1862.

Boyd, Harry L., May 24, 1861; 1st Sergeant, October 1, 1862. Address, Loveland, California.

Baker, Eben S., Corporal, May 16, 1863; taken prisoner at Front Royal and exchanged.

Bair, Levi, May 24, 1861; Sergeant, October 1, 1862; wounded at Chancellorsville, May 3, 1863. Deceased.

Baker, William R., May 24, 1861; transferred to Inv. Corps, Sept. 1, 1863.

Boyer, Elias, April 23, 1861; transferred to Co. K, June 1, 1861.

Brady, Jonathan S., May 24, 1861; Corporal, July 20, 1861; discharged at Newark, N. J., December 19, 1862. Deceased.
Barnett, Calvin J., May 24, 1861; discharged at Fort Gaines, October 30, 1862, and died soon after reaching home.
Blunden, Paul J., May 24, 1861.
Bruck, David T., June 3, 1861; Hospital Steward, June 17, 1861.
Byrns, William R., June 5, 1861; transferred to Invalid Corps.
Beckley, John, February 26, 1864; wounded in right shoulder, May 6, 1864, in Wilderness; transferred to 4th Ohio Battalion.
Bozman, James, February 26, 1864; transferred to 4th Ohio Battalion.
Bell, Thomas J., February 29, 1864; transferred to 4th Ohio Battalion. Address, Larue, Ohio.
Bell, John M., February 29, 1864; transferred to 4th Ohio Battalion.
Burris, Henry, February 26, 1864; transferred to 4th Ohio Battalion.
Bacon, George G., February 1864; transferred to 4th Ohio Battalion.
Clements, William R., May 24, 1861; taken prisoner at Harrison's Landing and exchanged.
Chambers, Solomon, May 24, 1861; discharged, January 24, 1863, to enlist in the United States Cavalry.
Corey, Harrison H., May 24, 1861.
Crow, Joseph E., May 24, 1861; discharged at Columbus, O., July 19, 1862. Address, Marion, Ohio.
Cline, William H., May 24, 1861; died of chronic diarrhœa, at Fort Gaines, October 17, 1862.
Culp, John V., May 24, 1861; Corporal, January 19, 1863.
Carpenter, Cyrus H , transferred from Company K, June 1, 1861.
Corbin, Joshua M. V., June 3, 1861; injured by a falling tree, January 28, 1864; died at Alexandria, Va., April 25, 1864.
Crusper, Lewis, June 3, 1861; transferred to Invalid Corps, Sept. 1, 1863.
Carlyle, Robert, June 12, 1861; wounded in the knees, at Po River, May 10, 1864. Address, Marseilles, Ohio.
Corbin, John B., June 3, 1861; discharged at Camp Pendleton, Maryland, October 26, 1861. Address, Augusta, Ohio.
Chapman, John F., Oct. 11, 1861; discharged at Fort Gaines, Nov. 20, 1862.
Cope, Christian, November 10, 1861; transferred to Fourth Ohio Battalion.
Curren, John, August 26, 1862; transferred to Fourth Ohio Battalion.
Crawford, John, Oct. 24, 1862; dis. at Alexandria, Oct. 3, 1863. Deceased.
Dickerson, Theodore, 1st Sergeant, May 24, 1861; 2d Lieut., Sept. 12, 1862.
Down, William B., May 24, 1861; Corporal; received the accidental discharge of a gun that a comrade was cleaning, and died, in a few days, at New Market, Virginia, May 7, 1862.
Dennison, John H., May 24, 1861; disch. at Romney, Va., Dec. 31, 1861.
Dewey, James, May 24, 1861; disch. Jan. 26, 1863, to enter U. S. Artillery.
Durfee, Nathan, May 24, 1861; wounded at Fredericksburg, Dec. 14, 1862.
Devore, Sanford W., June 3, 1861. Address, Lane, Franklin county, Kan.
Dutton, John W., Corporal, June 3, 1861; discharged at Newark, N. J., December 15, 1862. Address, Rantoo, Anderson county, Kansas.

DeWoolf, Joseph, February 26, 1864; transferred to 4th Ohio Battalion.

Dunson, James, February 29, 1864; transferred to 4th Ohio Battalion.

Elliott, James S., May 24, 1861; Corporal, September 1, 1862; wounded in the thigh at Po River, May 10, 1864.

Ehrheardt, August, May 24, 1861; discharged at Fort Gaines, Maryland, September 19, 1862.

Edgar, John, June 11, 1861; died in Licking county, Ohio, Nov. 13, 1862.

French, Henry C., May 24, 1861; Corporal, January 19, 1863; killed at Chancellorsville, May 3, 1863.

French, John, March 11, 1862; killed at Wilderness, May 6, 1864; had also been wounded at Mine Run, February 28, 1864.

Fields, Hiram, May 24, 1861; missing at Spottsylvania, May 12, 1864.

Godman, Charles C., May 24, 1861; promoted to Corporal, June 4, 1861; soon afterward to Sergeant; disch. at Beverly, Va., July 20, 1861.

Grimes, John, May 24, 1861; wounded as Po River, May 10, 1864.

Griswold, Alvin, May 24, 1861; wounded at Morton's Ford, February 6, 1864; at Po River, May 10, 1864.

Gurley, William M., May 24, 1861; Corporal January 19, 1863; killed at Chancellorsville, May 3, 1863.

Grimes, Levi, June 3, 1861; killed at Po River, May 10, 1864.

Gebhardt, John, June 11, 1861; died at Fort Gaines, October 14, 1862.

Giles, John M., June 18, 1861.

Halstead, Abraham, May 24, 1861; Corporal, January 19, 1863; wounded in left arm at Po River, May 10, 1864.

Hutchison, William S., May 28, 1861; discharged at Fort Gaines, November 3, 1862.

Hatch, William P., June 3, 1861; discharged at Fort Gaines, December 13, 1862. Deceased.

Harman, Jesse, February 29, 1864; transferred to 4th Ohio Battalion.

Hinton, William B., February 29, 1864; transferred to 4th Ohio Battalion.

Jones, Cornelius D., May 24, 1861; Corporal, January 25, 1862; discharged at Fort Wood, N. Y., October 19, 1862. Address, Waldo, Ohio.

Jones, Jasper L., May 24, 1861; disch. at New Market, Va., May 3, 1862.

Jones, John H., May 24, 1861; killed at Chancellorsville, May 3, 1863.

Johnson, William H., September 5, 1862; re-enlisted as Veteran, February 29, 1864; transferred to 4th Ohio Battalion.

Kelley, Josiah, June 3, 1861; discharged at Camp Kelley, Va., Jan. 25, 1862.

Kennedy, William, May 24, 1861; disch. at New Market, Va., May 10, 1862.

Kersey, James M., June 3, 1861; discharged at Harper's Ferry, October 9, 1862. Address, Green Camp, Ohio.

Knapp, John R., May 24, 1861; Sergeant, Sept. 4, 1861; Quartermaster-Sergeant, September 4, 1861.

Knapp, Charles S., May 24, 1861; Corporal; Sergeant, June 25, 1862.

Knapp, Matthew S., May 4, 11862. Address, La Rue, Ohio.

Kenyon, James, May 24, 1861; wounded at Po River, May 10, 1864. Deceased.

Kenyon, Harvey S., May 24, 1861; taken prisoner and exchanged; wounded at Spottsylvania, May 12, 1864. Address, Waldo, Ohio.

Kearfoot, John B., June 12, 1861; died at Washington, January 1, 1863, of wounds received at Fredericksburg, December 13, 1862.

Leatham, William, June 11, 1861; discharged at Camp Pendleton, October 21, 1861.

Lawrence, James H., June 12, 1861; disch. at Fort Gaines, Jan. 13, 1863.

Likens, Thomas C., May 24, 1861; Corporal, January 23, 1863; discharged December 31, 1863; re-enlisted and reappointed Corporal, January 1, 1864; wounded at Fredericksburg, December 13, 1862.

Likens, Robert, May 24, 1861.

Lee, James M., May 24, 1861; Corporal, July 20, 1861; Sergeant, September 1, 1861; discharged at Alexandria, April 29, 1863. Address Marion, O.

May, George H., May 24, 1861; Corporal, June 4, 1861; Sergeant, May 16, 1863. Address, Marion, Ohio.

Mount, Thompson, June 3, 1861; Corporal; discharged at Beverly, Virginia, July 20, 1861.

McGarey, Mathew S., September 4, 1861; discharged at Camp Keyes, December 31, 1861.

Martin, James H., June 4, 1861; dischgedar at Williamsport, Maryland, June 3, 1862.

McAbee, Newton S., transferred, June 3, 1861, from Co. F, and appointed Sergeant; commissioned 1st Lieut. in 11th O. V. I.

Miller, Samuel W., May 24, 1861; wounded at Po River, May 10, 1864.

Mouser, George A., May 24, 1861; Sergeant; died at Cumberland, Md., December, 1861, of typhoid fever. His last message was: "Tell mother I have not been as faithful as I ought to have been, but it is all right now; I can die happy trusting in Jesus."

Miller, Samuel F., June 3, 1861; died at Washington, November 21, 1862, of chronic diarrhoea.

Maunasmith, James, August 26, 1862; wounded in the knees, May 10, 1864, at Po River; transferred to 4th Ohio Battalion.

Manly, Columbus, February 26, 1864; wounded in the foot at Spottsylvania, May 12, 1864; transferred to 4th Ohio Battalion. Address, Larue, Ohio.

Manley, Samuel, February 27, 1864; transferred to 4th Ohio Battalion.

Osburn, William H., June 3, 1861; discharged at Camp Pendleton, Md., October 21, 1861.

Orth, George, October 7, 1861; re-enlisted as Veteran, February, 1864; transferred to 4th Ohio Battalion.

Patton, William, June 12, 1861; taken prisoner and exchanged.

Payne, Stephen, June 3, 1861; died at Cumberland, Md., Feb. 19, 1862.

Patterson, John, June 3, 1861; transferred to Invalid Corps, July 1, 1863. Address, Waldo, Ohio.

Patrick, John B., February 26, 1864; transferred to 4th Ohio Battalion.

Porter, George, May 24, 1861; re-enlisted February 26, 1864, and transferred to 4th Ohio Battalion.

Rauch, Frederick, May 28, 1861; discharged to enlist in Daum's 1st Virginia Battery, November 1, 1861.

Strawbridge, Robert I., May 24, 1861; Sergeant, May 24, 1861; 1st Sergeant, October 1, 1862. Address, Loveland, Cal., or Marion, Ohio.

Saiter, or Sester, Henry, May 24, 1861; Corporal, Sept. 1, 1861; wounded at Morton's Ford, February 6, 1864. Deceased.

Short, John, May 24, 1861, discharged at Fort Gaines, October 30, 1862. Address, Larue, Ohio.

Stone, Francis M., May 24, 1861; discharged at Fort Gaines, October 30, 1862. Deceased.

Snyder, George, June 4, 1861; discharged at Fortress Monroe, Sept. 25, 1862.

Selanders, Thaddeus, June 3, 1861; discharged at Fort Gaines, November 3, 1862. Address, Garrett, Anderson county, Kansas.

Sweetland, Abijah W., June 3, 1861; disch. at Washington, Dec. 17, 1863.

Shertzer, Silas, May 24, 1861; wounded in the neck at Spottsylvania, May 12, 1864. Address, Larue, Ohio.

Stull, Martin, May 24, 1861. Address, Brandon, Ohio.

Saylor, Henry G., May 24, 1861.

Selanders, William F., June 3, 1861. Died in 1885.

Shendoller, William, May 24, 1861; killed at Spottsylvania, May 12, 1864.

Smallwood, George H., Corporal, June 4, 1861; Sergeant, July 21, 1863; wounded at Chancellorsville, May 3, 1863; discharged December 31, 1863; re-enlisted and reappointed Sergeant, January 1, 1864.

Stockwell, Dexter, June 3, 1861.

Shoub, Marquis, June 12, 1861; transferred to 4th Ohio Battalion.

Stroub, Joel, August 2, 1861; transferred to 4th Ohio Battalion.

Seymour, John W., February 28, 1864; transferred to 4th Ohio Battalion.

Selanders, Valentine, August 27, 1861; transferred to 4th Ohio Battalion. Address, New London, Ohio.

Sagers, Elijah, February 22, 1864; transferred to 4th Ohio Battalion. Address, Larue, Ohio.

Shertzer, Jesse, February 22, 1864; transferred to 4th Ohio Battalion. Address, Larue, Ohio.

Towle, William H., October 7, 1862; transefrred to 4th Ohio Battalion.

Trickler, Samuel, March 24, 1864; transferred to 4th Ohio Battalion.

Van Buskirk, John, February 29, 1864; transferred to 4th Ohio Battalion.

Van Brimmer, William M., June 12, 1861; discharged at Columbus, Ohio, July 3, 1862.

Vestal, David, October 11, 1861; disch. at Bolivar Heights, Oct. 29, 1862.

Walker, James A., June 12, 1861; discharged at Columbus, Jan. 14, 1862.

Walker, James B., June 3, 1861; killed at Fredericksburg, Dec. 13, 1862.

Ward, Jonathan, February 29, 1864; transferred to 4th Ohio Battalion.

Wale, Jonathan, September 5, 1861; taken prisoner July 2, 1862; transferred to 4th Ohio Battalion. Address, Marshall, Ohio.

Ward, Andrew J., May 24, 1862; died at Martinsburg, Va., May 12, 1862, of consumption.

Warner, Charles, May 24, 1861.

Wartman, Joshua, May 24, 1861.

Weber, Jacob, May 24, 1861.
Wilson, Harvey, June 3, 1861; wounded at Mine Run, November 28, 1863. Address, Marion, Ohio.
Windsor, Chancey H., Oct. 11, 1861; died at Marion, Ohio, Dec. 10, 1862.

———:o:———

## Company I.

Powell, Eugene, Captain, June 4, 1861; resigned to become Major of the 66th O. V. I., October 22, 1861.
Constant, William F., First Lieutenant of Co. I, June 4, 1861; Captain, June 9, 1862; resigned November 23, 1862.
Ferguson, James, Second Lieutenant, June 5, 1861; First Lieutenant, June 9, 1862; Captain, November 22, 1862; died of wounds, February 15, 1863, received at Fredericksburg, December 13, 1862.
Lester, George, Second Lieutenant of Company, January 9, 1862.
Dickerson, T. H., Second Lieutenant of Company, September 30, 1862; First Lieutenant of Company E, October 17, 1862.
Spink, Reason B., First Lieut., December 19, 1862; resigned March 23, 1863.
Carr, Joseph H., 2d Lieut. of Co., Jan. 17, 1863; transf. to Co. C as 1st Lt.
Shoub, Samuel J., First Sergeant of Company, June 6, 1861, and Second Lieutenant, February 10, 1863; killed at Gettysburg, July 2, 1863.
Camp, William M., Captain, March 1, 1863, of Company I.
Hill, George O., First Lieut. of Co., May 26, 1863; resigned Nov. 28, 1863.
Watkins, Joseph W., Second Lieutenant of Company, July 28, 1863.
Alexander, Hosea W., June 5, 1861; wounded at Spottsylvania, May 18, 1864. Address, Delaware, Ohio.
Akum, Peter, June 5, 1861; received several mortal wounds at Fredericksburg, and died in a few hours, on December 13, 1862.
Bassinger, John R., June 5, 1861; transferred to Invalid Corps, July 1, 1863.
Baker, Orlando H., June 5, 1861; Corp., Aug. 8, 1861; Lt. in 174th O. V. I.
Bruner, Edwin J., June 5, 1861; Musician.
Barler, Barnabas, June 5, 1861.
Brooks, Andrew J., June 5, 1861.
Beddow, Garrett, June 5, 1861; wounded at Chancellorsville, May 3, 1863. Address, Berkshire, Ohio.
Black, Andrew J., June 5, 1861. Address, Berkshire, Ohio.
Brown, Henry C., June 5, 1861; Corporal, May 22, 1863; killed at Spottsylvania, May 18, 1864.
Brooks, Charles, October 10, 1861; killed at Chancellorsville, May 3, 1863.
Brownmiller, Reuben, June 5, 1861; died at Grafton, West Virginia, August 31, 1861, of typhoid fever.
Baker, Robert, June 5, 1861; died at Delaware, O., November 9, 1862.
Bell, Robert, June 5, 1861; died at Delaware, O., January 9, 1863.

Brooker, James, June 5, 1861; died at Finley Hospital, June 18, 1863, of wounds received at Chancellorsville, May 3, 1863.

Beacon, John, June 5, 1861; discharged at Washington, December 5, 1862.

Cruikshank, George, June 5, 1861; Corporal, June 10, 1861; Sergeant, July 1, 1863; transf. to Fourth Ohio Battalion, having re-enlisted as Veteran; Lieutenant; killed soon after in action near Petersburg.

Cutler, William, June 5, 1861; Sergeant, May 22, 1863. Deceased.

Carmichael, Albert, June 5, 1861.

Carpenter, George B., June 5, 1861.

Chase, Ebenezer, June 5, 1861.

Case, Harrington, June 5, 1861.

Cowles, George W., June 5, 1861; Corp.; dis. at Fort Gaines, Sept. 2, 1862.

Clark, Isaac, June 5, 1861; discharged at Camp Ohio, December 2, 1862.

Day, Charles, June 5, 1861; wounded in right side at Po River, May 10, 1864.

Dart, Jesse, Corporal; discharged at Falmouth, Va., May 16, 1863.

Dexter, Charles, June 5, 1861; discharged at Washington, October 30, 1862.

Dobbins, John W., June 5, 1861; discharged at Camp Keyes, Nov. 27, 1861.

Davy, William, June 5, 1861; discharged at Fort Gaines, Sept. 20, 1862.

Day, Ingham, June 5, 1861; discharged, at Fortress Monroe, October 22, 1862; died on his way home.

Evans, John G., Sergeant, June 5, 1861; Second Lieutenant.

Erwin, Anderson, June 5, 1861; dis. at Camp Pendleton, Md., Oct. 23, 1861.

Evans, David, June 5, 1861; discharged at Camp Ohio, December 31, 1862.

Farris, George W., June 5, 1861; disch. at Columbus, O., March 18, 1863.

Folk, Jonathan, June 5, 1861; transferred to Invalid Corps, Sept. 1, 1863.

Finch, Irwin M., June 5, 1861; Corporal, October 8, 1862; Sergeant, March 4, 1864; killed at Po River, May 10, 1864.

Gray, Alexander, June 5, 1861.

Grover, Sylvester A., June 5, 1861; discharged at Camp Pendleton, Maryland, October 23, 1861.

Gohl, John J., June 5, 1861; discharged at Camp Keyes, Va., Nov. 27, 1861.

Herman, John, June 5, 1861.

Hinkle, James W., June 5, 1861.

Howard, W. C., June 5, 1861; discharged at Camp Keyes, February 3, 1862, for wounds received at Romney, September 26, 1861.

Harrington, William, June 3, 1861; disch. at Columbus, O., June 30, 1862.

Irwin, William J., June 5, 1861.

Jennings, Reuben, June 5, 1861; missing since Spottsylvania, May 12, 1864.

Jones, John O., October 10, 1861; died at New York City, October 16, 1862, of chronic diarrhœa.

Johnson, Amos, June 5, 1861; discharged at Columbus, O., January 29, 1863.

Kyle, Hugh, June 5, 1861.

Kemp, William, June 5, 1861; died at Fortress Monroe, September 28, 1862, of chronic diarrhœa.

Keller, Thomas, June 5, 1861; died at Fortress Monroe, September 23, 1862, of chronic diarrhœa.

Kelley, Martin, June 5, 1861; discharged at Harper's Ferry, October 20, 1862, to enlist in the Fourth United States Artillery.
Lee, David S., June 5, 1861.
Liebenderfor, John, June 5, 1861; transferred to Brigade band June 24, 1863.
Lindsay, Joseph, June 5, 1861; discharged at Camp Keyes, Nov. 27, 1861.
Lyn, John W., June 5, 1861; disch. at Manassas Junction, June 24, 1863.
Lybrand, Archibald, June 5, 1861; discharged July 11, 1862, to accept commission in 73d O. V. I.
Lavelle, Lewis, June 5, 1861; re-enlisted and transferred to 4th O. Battalion.
McCulla, Wm. A., June 5, 1861; disch. Camp Pendleton, Md., Oct. 23, 1861.
Mathena, John L., June 5, 1861; discharged at Washington, Oct. 10, 1862.
Mathias, John L., June 5, 1861; discharged at Fort Gaines, Sept. 20, 1862.
Morgan, Lewis, June 5, 1861; re-enlisted and transferred to 4th O. Battalion.
Main, Martin, June 5, 1861; missing since battle of Chancellorsville, May 3, 1863.
Nettleton, Judson, June 5, 1861; discharged at Columbus, O., Feb. 28, 1863.
Powers, James, June 5, 1861.
Pettibone, Channing L., June 5, 1861; Sergeant; 2d Lieutenant; killed at Po River, May 10, 1864.
Potter, Gilbert M., June 5, 1861. Address, Jamaica, Ia.
Potter, Allen, June 5, 1861; killed at Spottsylvania, May 18, 1864.
Plant, Thomas, June 5, 1861; died at Washington, December 23, 1862, of wounds received at Fredericksburg, December 13, 1862.
Root, Emery J., June 5, 1861; Corporal, May 22, 1863; prisoner May 31, 1863; exchanged.
Rowland, Thomas W., June 5, 1861; Corporal, May 22, 1863.
Roloson, Benjamin, June 5, 1861.
Robinson, Coffman, June 5, 1861.
Roloson, Simon, June 5, 1861; killed at Gettysburg, July 2, 1863.
Reynolds, William, June 5, 1861; discharged at Camp Ohio, Jan. 8, 1863.
Slough, James S., June 5, 1861; discharged at Camp Keyes, Nov. 27, 1861.
Scott, Thomas W., June 5, 1861; disch. at New Market, Va., May 12, 1862.
Snell, Morgan, June 5, 1862; discharged at Fortress Monroe, Oct. 22, 1862.
Spaulding, John, June 5, 1861; discharged at Frederick Md., Dec. 13, 1863.
St. Clair, Earnest, June 5, 1861; Corp.; re-enlisted and trans. to 4th O. Bat.
Sheak, Jacob, June 5, 1861; killed at Gettysburg, July 2, 1863.
Sprague, Thomas, October 12, 1861; prisoner at hospital at Strasburg, Va.; died at Lynchburg, October 30, 1862.
Stickley, John E., June 5, 1861; died on his way home to Delaware, Ohio, October, 1862.
Stark, Henry C., June 5, 1761; died near Gettysburg, July 10, of wounds received July 2, 1863.
Strong, Daniel G., June 5, 1861; Corp., Jan 28, 1862; elected by vote of the regiment, and then commissioned as Chap. of the 4th O., May 1, 1863.
Shoub, Samuel J., June 5, 1861; 1st Sergeant; 2d Lieutenant, February 10, 1863; killed at Gettysburg, July 2, 1863.
Stevens, William C., June 5, 1861; was the "rousing drummer."

Stone, Horace W., June 5, 1861.
Shindeller, David, June 5, 1861.
Stark, Thomas E., June 5, 1861.   Address, Berkshire, Ohio.
Shearer, Barber, June 5, 1861.
Scott, James, June 5, 1861.
Shoub, Henry A., June 5, 1861; Sergeant, March 30, 1863; wounded at Chancellorsville, May 3, 1863.
Traxler, William, June 5, 1861.
Welch, Johnson, June 5, 1861.
Welch, Frederick, June 5, 1861; re-enlisted and transferred to 4th Ohio Bat.
Wickham, Israel I., June 5, 1861; transferred to Invalid Corps.
Wilson, John M., June 5, 1861; discharged at Harper's Ferry, October 22, 1862, to enlist in 4th U. S. Artillery.
Winstead, John, June 5, 1861; wounded at Gettysburg, July 2, 1863; died of wounds received in hand and legs, at Cold Harbor, June 3, 1864.
Wise, Demas, June 5, 1861; died at Frederick City, Maryland, December 12, 1862, of chronic diarrhœa.
Wigton, Charles H., June 5, 1861.

———:o:———

## Company K.

Brown, Albert H., Captain, June 4, 1861; resigned June 9, 1862; became Colonel. Address, Bloomfield, Ohio.
Durfee, Bradford R., 1st Lieut., June 4, 1861; Adj., June 5, 1861; resigned.
Garrett, William H., 2d Lieutenant, June 5, 1861; 1st Lieutenant, August 9, 1861; resigned December 1, 1862.
Camp, William M., 2d Lieut., Aug. 6, 1861; 1st Lieut., Co. G, Oct. 1, 1861.
Laird, George F., Captain of Company, June 29, 1862.
Thomas, Byron, 2d Lieutenant, June 21, 1862; 1st Lieutenant, December 26, 1862; resigned August 12, 1863.
Welsh, William, 1st Lieutenant of Company, January 5, 1863; transferred to Company A, February 23, 1863.
Dunlap, John, 2d Lieut. of Company, March 1, 1863; resigned Feb. 8, 1864.
Adler, George, October 28, 1863; transferred to 4th Ohio Battalion.
Apt, Sampson, June 4, 1861; Corporal, June 6, 1861.
Armstrong, Joshua, June 6, 1861; killed at paroled Camp, Annapolis, Md.
Ault, Joseph, June 4, 1861; discharged Jan. 29, 1862, at Camp Kelly, Va.
Bacon, Isaac, June 4, 1861; Corporal, June 6, 1861; disch. at Romney, Va.
Benevenuto, Ausano, June 4, 1861; Corporal, November 1, 1861; discharged October 18, 1862, to enlist in 4th U. S. Artillery. Address, Marion, O.
Beaver, John, June 4, 1861; wounded in the chest at Wilderness, May 6, 1864. Address, Marion, O.
Berry, William A., June 4, 1861; wounded at Morton's Ford, February 6, 1864. Address, Marion, O.

Booher, Daniel D., June 4, 1861; wounded at Cold Harbor, June 3, 1864. Address, Mount Gilead, O.

Boyer, Elias, June 4, 1861. Address, Cardington (or Merrito), O.

Boyer, Solomon, June 4, 1861; discharged March 9, 1863, at Washington. Address, Cardington, O.

Boyer, Samuel, June 4, 1861; discharged at Washington, March 6, 1863. Address, Cardington, O.

Boyer, Jacob, August 25, 1861; wounded at Gettysburg, July 2, 1863; transferred to 4th Ohio Battalion. Address, Marion, O.

Boyd, William I., June 4, 1861; detailed as hospital nurse, at Cumberland, Maryland.

Brenneke, Ferdinand, June 19, 1861; wounded in the hip, at Spottsylvania, May 12, 1864; transferred to 4th Ohio Battalton.

Bickle, Michael, June 4, 1861; died at Harper's Ferry, November 15, 1862.

Byers, Thomas, June 4, 1861; died at Cumberland, Md., March 17, 1862.

Brocket, Abel, June 4, 1861; discharged at Washington, January 1, 1863.

Bell, David, June 4, 1861; discharged at Washington, January 1, 1863.

Bacon, Thomas, June 12, 1861; discharged at Washington, January 19, 1863.

Camp, William M., June 4, 1861; 1st Sergeant, June 4 1861; 2d Lieutenant, August 9, 1861. Address, Bement, Ill.

Carter, John C., December 17, 1863; wounded at Po River, May 10, 1864; in the face at Cold Harbor, June 3, 1864; transferred to 4th Ohio Battalion. Address, Marion, Ohio.

Cayton, William, March 10, 1862; transferred to 4th Ohio Battalion.

Cunningham, Henry H., June 4, 1861; Corporal, March 10, 1862; wounded at Spottsylvania, May 12, 1864. Address, Marion, O.

Cooper, Sturgis W., June 4, 1861; transf. to Reg. Band; killed by a "bushwhacker," near Beverly, Va., July 14, 1861, being the first man of the regiment that had thus far met his death at the hand of the enemy.

Craig, Abel, June 4, 1861; killed at Chancellorsville, May 3, 1863.

Crowl, Peter, September 11, 1861; discharged December 3, 1862, at Harper's Ferry. Address, Lima. O.

Drake, Elam, Oct. 4, 1861; discharged Dec. 29, 1862, at Columbus, O.

Doren, John, June 4, 1861; discharged at Harper's Ferry, October 28, 1862.

Eply, Samuel H., June 4, 1861; member of Pioneer Corps. Address, Springfield, O.

Eply, Solomon D., June 4, 1861; Corporal June 24, 1863.

Erline, Christian, June 4, 1961; wounded at Harrison's Landing, July 3, 1862; discharged Oct. 18, 1862, at Harper's Ferry, to enlist in 4th U. S. Art.

Farnham, William H., June 4, 1861; musician.

Fell, Timothy, June 4, 1861; disch., Dec. 2, 1862, at Washington, D. C.

Filler, Frank M., June 4, 1861; discharged at Cleveland, Ohio, February 1, 1864. Address, Marysville, Ohio.

Free, Wesley, June 4, 1861; teamster.

Freeman, Asa P., June 4, 1861; Corporal, October 1, 1862; re-enlisted December 17, 1863; wounded in the side, at Spottsylvania, May 12, 1864; transferred to Fourth Ohio Battalion.

Fulmer, Lewis F., August 26, 1861; re-enlisted February 12, 1864; wounded at Wilderness, May 6, 1864; transferred to Fourth Ohio Battalion.

Fisher, James B., August 26, 1862; wounded at Mine Run, Virginia, November 28, 1863; transf. to Fourth Ohio Battalion. Address, Marion, O.

Fields, Richard I., June 4, 1861; taken prisoner while on a scout, May 4, 1862; exchanged and sent to Camp Chase, O. Address, Columbus, O.

Foss, Charles, June 4, 1861; died in New York City, November, 1862.

Goodenberger, Jacob, October 16, 1863; wounded at Po River, May 10, 1864; transferred to Fourth Ohio Battalion.

Gottshall, Charles A., September 27, 1863; transferred to 4th O. B.

Hardy, John, June 4, 1861; wounded at Harrison's Landing, July 3, 1862; taken prisoner on picket line at Cold Harbor, June 3, 1864. Address, Dayton, Ohio.

Hall, Dennis, June 4, 1861; wounded in side, at Spottsylvania, May 12, 1864.

Huggins, Simon, June 4, 1861; teamster Ambulance Corps. Ad., Marion, O.

Huggins, William I., June 4, 1861; teamster. Address, Marion, O.

Hornitt, Joseph M., June 4, 1861.

Hastings, Joseph, June 4, 1861. Address, Marseilles, Ohio.

Hiner, John G., June 4, 1861; discharged at Newark, New Jersey.

Haskins, Joel, June 4, 1861; discharged at Camp Dennison, June 21, 1861.

Harris, John, June 4, 1861; discharged at Camp Kelley, January 29, 1862.

Haine, Samuel E., June 4, 1861; Corporal, August 20, 1861; discharged at Washington, December 3, 1862.

Hale, Jonathan I., June 4, 1861; Corporal, June 6, 1861; discharged, March 12, 1862, at Columbus, Ohio.

Hoxter, Melvin C., May 24, 1861; re-en. as Veteran, Feb. 12, 1864; taken prisoner on picket line at Cold Harbor, June 3, 1864; transf. to 4th O. B.

Hutchinson, William I., October 4, 1861; transf. to Fourth Ohio Battalion.

Imbody, James W., June 4, 1861; died at Washington, December 7, 1863.

Irey, Thomas, August 1, 1861; transf. to Invalid Corps. Ad., Marion, O.

Joy, David, June 4, 1861; discharged at Harper's Ferry, October 28, 1862.

Johnson, John, June 4, 1861; discharged, January 29, 1862, at Columbus, O.

Jones, Isaac, February 5, 1862; died at Harper's Ferry, October 7, 1862.

Kade, John K., June 4, 1861; taken prisoner while on a scout, May 4, 1862; paroled and sent to Camp Chase, Ohio. Dropped from rolls.

Kessler, Edward, June 4, 1861; disch. from hospital at Newark, N. J., in 1863.

Kightlinger, John, June 4, 1861; died at Romney, Va., January 1, 1862.

Kightlinger, Ananias, June 11, 1861; wounded at Harrison's Landing, July 3, 1862; re-enlisted as Veteran, November 23, 1863; wounded, taken prisoner, then killed by our own guns, at Cold Harbor, June 3, 1864.

Kightlinger, Abram, June 4, 1861; re-enlisted as Veteran, December 13, 1863; missing at Spottsylvania, May 12, 1864.

Kirbey, Abner S., June 4, 1861; Corporal, March 1, 1862; transferred to Invalid Corps, November 18, 1863. Address, Fredericktown, O.

Kise, Samuel, June 4, 1861; discharged at Newark, N. J., Nov. 24, 1863.

Kise, Jacob, June 4, 1861; Corporal, September 25, 1861; discharged, November 24, 1862, at Washington.

Kopp, Frederick L., June 4, 1861; wounded at Mine Run, November 26, 1863. Address, Galion, Ohio.
Kohler, Henry, June 12, 1861; died October 23, 1862.
Knable, John, June 4, 1861; teamster; transf. to Invalid Corps, Oct. 1, 1863.
Koons, Franklin M., June 4, 1861; Corp., June 4, 1863; transf. to 4th O. B.
Lease, Robert, June 4, 1861; discharged at Columbus, O., August 24, 1862.
Likens, William W., Aug. 21, 1861; dis. from Cumberland Hospital in 1862.
Loyd, John L., June 4, 1861; Quartermaster Sergeant, June 27, 1861. Dropped from rolls.
Marquis, John P., June 4, 1861; disch. at Manassas Junction, June 27, 1862.
Meiley, Hiram, June 4, 1861; wounded at Romney, Virginia, October 26, 1861; discharged, August 4, 1862, at Columbus, Ohio.
Merchant, George B., June 4, 1861; Corporal, June 6, 1861; Sergeant, October 1, 1862; wounded, May 10, 1864, at Po River. Address, Mansfield, O.
Miller, William, June 4, 1861; discharged at Harper's Ferry, October 18, 1862, to enlist in the Fourth United States Artillery.
Moon, Thomas, June 4, 1861; discharged, October 18, 1862, to enlist in the Fourth United States Artillery, at Harper's Ferry.
Morris, Richard, June 4, 1861; Corporal, August 4, 1861; wounded at Morton's Ford, Virginia, February 6, 1864.
Mummea, John T., June 4, 1861; wounded at Harrison's Landing, July 3, 1862; re-enlisted December 23, 1863; taken prisoner on picket line at Cold Harbor, June 3, 1864; transferred to Fourth Ohio Battalion.
McBee, August 26, 1861; discharged, December 8, 1862, at Newark, N. J.
McCulloch, Thomas, June 4, 1861; wounded at Fredericksburg, December 13, 1862; transferred to Invalid Corps.
Oliver, Reuben, June 4, 1861; died at Cumberland, Md., April 7, 1862.
Rall, John, June 4, 1861; killed at Wilderness, Va., May 6, 1864.
Reed, Frederick, June 4, 1861; died at Washington, Nov. 4, 1863.
Robinson, William, June 4, 1861.
Robinson, William N., June 4, 1861.
Saiter, Franklin R., June 4, 1861; Sergeant, June 24, 1861; transferred to 4th Ohio Battalion. Address, Marion, Ohio.
Sprague, Charles, June 4, 1861; discharged October 18, 1862, at Harper's Ferry, October 18, 1862, to enlist in 4th U. S. Artillery.
Slack, George, June 4, 1861; discharged at Harper's Ferry, October 18, 1862, to enlist in 4th United States Artillery.
Strode, William, June 4, 1861; discharged at Harper's Ferry, October 18, 1862, to enlist in 4th United States Artillery.
Short, Joseph, June 4, 1861; wounded at Gettysburg, July 2, 1863; at Po River, May 10, 1864.
Shook, Henry J., September 29, 1863; wounded and taken prisoner at Spottsylvania, May 12, 1864. Address, Middle Branch, Ohio.
Schrantz, Alpheus, September 29, 1863; transferred to 4th Ohio Battery. Address, New Berlin, Ohio.
Smith, Silas E., June 4, 1861; shot in the bowels and killed at Wilderness, May 6, 1864.

ROSTER. 287

Smith, Alfred, October 4, 1861; disch. at Harper's Ferry, October 28, 1862.
Spring, Ralph, June 4, 1861; disch. Dec. 5, 1862, at Washington, D. C.
Studabaker, John. June 4, 1861; wounded July 3, 1862, at Harrison's Landing, Va.; taken prisoner at Chancellorsville, May 3, 1863.
Thomas, Byron, June 4, 1861; Sergeant, August 9, 1861; 2d Lieutenant, September 22, 1862, in Company K.
Ustick, Abner, June 4, 1861; Corporal, June 6, 1861; Sergeant, July 27, 1861; wounded at North Anna River, May 24, 1864. Address, Mount Gilead, Ohio.
Uhler, John F., June 4, 1861; Sergeant, June 6, 1861; 1st Sergeant, October 1, 1861. Address, Akron, Ohio—Cashier Second National Bank.
Wade, John, June 4, 1861; died at Bolivar Heights, December 19, 1862.
Warwick, William, Oct. 4, 1861; discharged Aug. 4, 1862, at Columbus, O.
Welchance, Isaac, June 4, 1861; wounded May 12, 1864, at Spottsylvania.
Welchance, Lafayette, January 24, 1862; died November 16, 1862, at Frederick, Maryland.
White, Albert, June 4, 1861; Corporal, June 6, 1861. Ad., Mt. Vernon, O.
Wilson, Wallace W., June 4, 1861; killed at Cold Harbor, June 3, 1864.
Yager, David T., re-en. as Vet. Feb. 12, 1864; trans. to 4th Ohio Battalion.
Yaugher, Jacob, June 4, 1861; trasferred to Brigade Band, June 24, 1863.
Yale, Philip, October 4, 1861; transferred to 4th Ohio Battalion.
Yox, Phillip, June 5, 1861; died August 15, 1861, at Oakland, Maryland.

———:o:———

## REGIMENTAL BAND.

Olenhausen, Frederick, Principal Musician, June 18, 1861.
Burgett, Amos, June 18, 1861.
Barr, Morgan, June 18, 1861.
Brueneger, Jacob, June 18, 1861.
Desvoigness, Julius, June 18, 1861.
Eichenberger, Godfrey, June 18, 1861.
Eichenber, John, June 18, 1861.
Rottman, Leonard, June 18, 1861.
Straub, Louis, June 18, 1861.
Tilton, Andrew J., June 18, 1861.
Young, Joseph, June 18, 1861.
Wittlinger, Augustus, killed at Harrison's Landing, July 3, 1862.